Admin911™:
Windows® 2000
DNS & WINS

Admin911™: Windows® 2000 DNS & WINS

DUSTIN **SAUTER**

Osborne/**McGraw-Hill**

New York Chicago San Francisco
Lisbon London Madrid Mexico City
Milan New Delhi San Juan
Seoul Singapore Sydney Toronto

Osborne/**McGraw-Hill**
2600 Tenth Street
Berkeley, California 94710
U.S.A.

To arrange bulk purchase discounts for sales promotions, premiums, or fund-raisers, please contact Osborne/**McGraw-Hill** at the above address. For information on translations or book distributors outside the U.S.A., please see the International Contact Information page immediately following the index of this book.

Admin911™: Windows® 2000 DNS & WINS

1234567890 FGR FGR 01987654321

ISBN 0-07-213154-3

Publisher
  Brandon A. Nordin
Vice President and Associate Publisher
  Scott Rogers
Editorial Director
  Wendy Rinaldi
Series Editor
  Kathy Ivens
Project Editor
  Lisa Wolters-Broder
Acquisitions Coordinator
  Timothy Madrid
Technical Editor
  Christian Branson

Copy Editor
  Chrisa Hotchkiss
Proofreader
  Brian Galloway
Indexer
  Valerie Perry
Computer Designers
  Gary Corrigan, Lucie Ericksen
Illustrators
  Michael Mueller, Lyssa Sieben-Wald,
  Beth E. Young
Series Design
  Gary Corrigan
Cover Design
  Greg Scott

This book was composed with Corel VENTURA™ Publisher.

To my wife, Ginger.
You are my inspiration.

Contents
at a Glance

Contents

Acknowledgments

I never thought writing a book would be so difficult. I have a newfound respect for all authors and the supporting cast of talent that is essential in making an average book a great book. Acquisitions Coordinator Timothy Madrid was great at keeping me on schedule and pointed in the right direction each step of the way. Without the help of Project Editor Lisa Wolters-Broder and Copy Editor Chrisa Hotchkiss, this book would have been a mess. Lisa and Chrisa were there every step of the way, keeping me honest while I attempted to butcher the English language and violate every grammar rule known to man. Thanks to Timothy, Lisa, and Chrisa for putting up with my shenanigans. I want to also thank Technical Editor Christian Branson, who did a bang-up job making sure I kept the B.S. at a respectable level. He is truly one of Microsoft's finest.

A very, very special thanks to Series Editor and Author Kathy Ivens. Without Kathy, I don't know what I would have done. She has been a wonderful mentor and an all-around good egg.

I want to thank my parents and all of my friends and family who were so understanding when I went from social butterfly to crusty hermit during the writing of this book.

I also want to thank Microsoft for making a fantastic operating system. I take a lot of pot shots at Microsoft throughout this book, but I really do think they have a great group of talented employees that produce superior products.

Finally, I want to thank my son Reid for making Appendix B so very special.

Part I

DNS

Chapter 1

DNS Architecture

Microsoft DNS, the Domain Naming System, has historically been portrayed as a complex and challenging technology that is essential for host-to-host communications. While it's true that DNS is the method of host-name-to-IP-address resolution and therefore essential, it isn't very complex or challenging at all.

Until recently, DNS was a peripheral service that many NT administrators either never had to deal with or did so very infrequently. That lack of exposure meant that they felt uncomfortable if they had to address the technology. (I know I was.)

Windows 2000 and Active Directory directory services change this paradigm. Rather than DNS being just a useful piece of Windows 2000 architecture, it has become a critical component that will make or break your Active Directory deployment.

It is also important for administrators to know and understand both the Microsoft and BIND implementations of DNS. It is commonplace to have both types of systems running in the same environment. I guess it is like the old saying, "You need to know where you came from to know where you're going."

This chapter addresses non-vendor-specific DNS concepts to present RFC facts about DNS. Sometimes I'll briefly comment or introduce a vendor's implementation, but I do this just for completeness. Have no fear, we'll be diving into some of the non-RFC features of Microsoft DNS soon enough.

The History of DNS at a Glance

DNS is a technology that evolved from necessity. Its historical parentage has roots in the Internet, and its evolution as a tool for today's corporate networks follows a logical path.

The Birth of the Internet

Believe it or not, Al Gore did not invent the Internet. The Internet was created in the late 1960s by the U.S. Department of Defense's Advanced Research Projects Agency (ARPA). At this time, local networking was extremely uncommon and wide area networking was just a pipe dream. Like many technology advances, change grew from necessity, and ARPANet was born.

ARPANet was designed to allow its employees to share data across multiple sites, which was unheard of at the time. ARPANet connected multiple systems using multiple proprietary protocols. This first iteration of ARPANet marked the birth of the Internet.

Although ARPANet was being used by many thousands of people in the 60s and 70s, its first boom came in the early 80s. In 1980, the Transmission Control Protocol/Internet

Protocol (TCP/IP) suite was introduced. Shortly after TCP/IP was introduced, BSD UNIX adopted the protocol for use in its operating system. This move became instrumental in the success of the protocol because BSD UNIX was widely used and was almost free.

Once TCP/IP became the adopted protocol, a method was needed to help resolve host names to TCP/IP addresses. Enter the Hosts.Txt file.

Early Name Resolution

Remembering the actual address of a device rather than its host name is something that is easy to do with a small number of devices, but infeasible with any significant number of devices. In fact, when dealing with more than a handful of systems, it's downright impossible. To address this problem, Hosts.Txt was created.

Hosts.Txt was a flat file that contained all host-name-to-address mappings. This prevented users from having to know every address of every machine that they needed to access. Instead, all they needed to know was the name of the device, and Hosts.Txt would do the rest.

Hosts.Txt was maintained on a central server by SRI's Network Information Center (NIC). A master file was kept on the NIC's servers that users downloaded at their convenience. This file was then placed on the user's machine, which enabled name resolution. If someone had a change that needed to be reflected in Hosts.Txt, such as a new device or address change, they would modify the file and send it to the NIC. The NIC would then collect changes and publish the updated file about every week.

Since Hosts.Txt was a flat file, all host names existed in the same namespace. This meant that no two devices could have the same name. While early on this was not a problem, once TCP/IP helped bring thousands and thousands of users on to ARPANet, name collisions became a problem. There were also problems in downloading what was becoming a large size file due to the increase in the number of hosts. This increased download traffic and file size also created a processing nightmare for the NIC. It became clear that another solution was needed to accommodate the new Internet. Additionally, as applications and services became TCP/IP aware, it became evident that something was needed to handle service-name-to-address mapping.

DNS was created from an effort of the NIC to create a name resolution database that was hierarchical and that could scale on a global basis. In 1984, RFCs 882 and 883 were submitted. Some time later, RFCs 1034 and 1035 were created to replace 882 and 883. RFCs 1034 and 1035 are the foundation documents for DNS as it is today.

DNS Architectural Fundamentals

DNS is the service that provides host-name-to-IP-address resolution for devices, services, objects, and entities. DNS leverages a hierarchical and distributed database in which each namespace is separated by a period (.). This permits naming and resolution of identical host names that exist in separate namespaces.

Many concepts and components are part of DNS. While this book introduces these items to you across many chapters, there are a few DNS fundamentals that you need to know in order to get the most out of the rest of this book. I want to focus on these major components and features:

+ Namespaces
+ Domains
+ Zones
+ Zone Transfers
+ Server Types
+ Delegation

Namespaces

A *namespace* is a logical grouping of devices or objects that exist in a common area. Within a namespace are sets of rules that govern the specifics of not only the namespace itself, but also devices and objects that are housed in that namespace. These rules are used to ensure uniqueness inside the namespace. The concept of a namespace allows devices that exist in different namespaces to have the same name, while at the same time preventing duplicate names within the same namespace.

The term *namespace*, although often used with respect to DNS, isn't exclusive to DNS. Namespaces occur in many different types of systems such as Windows Internet Naming Service (WINS), Distributed File System (DFS), and file systems.

In DNS, a domain namespace is used to separate groupings of devices. In a domain namespace, each domain is considered to be its own namespace and is separated from its parent- or child-level domain namespace by a period. Like all other namespaces, devices and objects within a domain namespace must be unique to that namespace but may be duplicated in other namespaces. This can be seen in the fact that almost every Web site in the world has a server with a CNAME (see the section on CNAME later in this chapter) of www. This is permitted because the CNAME www in the microsoft.com domain (www.microsoft.com) isn't in the same domain namespace as the CNAME www at sun.com (www.sun.com).

DNS resolves names for these domain namespaces by responding to name resolution queries from clients. A name server receives these queries and will either return the IP address of the name or service being queried or will forward the request to a name server that is authoritative for the domain namespace in which the resource or service lives. Don't worry if some of these concepts are new to you. I'll talk about these concepts in greater detail later in the chapter.

Domains

A domain is a logical grouping of devices, objects, and/or resources that, like namespaces, must conform to a common set of rules. Also like namespaces, domains aren't unique to DNS or the Internet. You're probably familiar with the concepts of domains within both NT and Windows 2000 Active Directory. A domain, as defined and used in the NT world, is in no way similar to an Internet domain, so in the context of this conversation, forget what you know about NT domains. The Windows 2000 Active Directory domain, on the other hand, is very close to the Internet definition of a domain in that it is dependent on DNS and a hierarchical structure.

Each domain has its own domain namespace. Each domain is joined or related to a parent-level domain, and potentially to a child-level domain. So, as shown in Figure 1-1, when you type www.microsoft.com, you're attempting to contact a device that exists in the Microsoft domain, which is a child-level domain of the com domain. In contrast, when you type ServerA.technet.microsoft.com, you're attempting to contact a device that's in the technet domain, which is a child-level domain to Microsoft that has a parent domain named com.

The above example is what it meant when I say that DNS uses a hierarchical database to resolve device and service names to IP addresses. Every domain must be represented in a domain namespace that is housed on a DNS server or servers. The DNS server or servers that host a DNS namespace are responsible for resolving all queries for devices in that domain.

Anyone can register and maintain a domain on the Internet, but there are certain domains that must be centrally owned and maintained for a number of reasons. These domains are referred to as root-level domains. The following are the existing root-level domains and their functions:

- ❖ .com – Reserved for commercial and business use
- ❖ .org – Reserved for nonprofit organizations
- ❖ .gov – Reserved for government agencies
- ❖ .edu – Reserved for educational entities
- ❖ .country-code (.usa, .eu, etc.) – Reserved for the respective country's use
- ❖ .net – Reserved for ISP use
- ❖ .mil – Reserved for military use
- ❖ .int – Reserved for international use

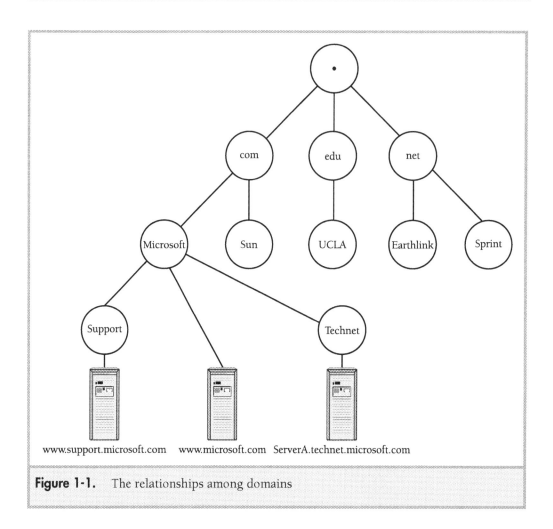

Figure 1-1. The relationships among domains

These root-level domains are authoritative for all subdomains within their extended namespace. In order to bring a new domain up on the Internet, you must have delegated control from one of the root-level domains.

Zones

Zones are the management boundary for the data responsible for name-to-IP-address resolution. You create a zone to partition a domain namespace into administrative chunks. This allows greater granularity for both administration and replication of data. A single zone can contain the data for a single domain namespace or for multiple domain namespaces.

Each zone, with the exception of an Active Directory Integrated zone, has a single zone file to house this data. This file, which is a database, can vary in naming format depending on each vendor's implementation. In all implementations, this file is loaded into memory at the time the DNS service starts and is written to during each change or transaction.

Zone Types

Traditionally, there are two zone types, primary and secondary. With the introduction of Windows 2000 and Active Directory, Microsoft implemented a new zone type called an AD-Integrated zone, which is primary in nature.

Like many other Microsoft implementations, although the new zone type brings extreme value to DNS, the concept of a directory-integrated zone is not defined in any RFC. More information about AD-Integrated zones is found throughout this book.

A primary zone is just what its name implies: the primary source of data for the zone in question. This zone is where all changes to DNS data are committed, and its associated file is loaded as the DNS service starts. Primary zones can be both forward and reverse in nature.

Secondary zones are read-only replica sets of primary zone data. Secondary zones transfer information from the primary zone at set intervals and can respond to queries from clients. However, secondary zones can't write information to the zone.

The main function of secondary zones is to distribute the processing load for DNS queries across many servers. In addition, they're sometimes used to house data on a server that is also primary for another zone in another namespace. In that case, the server houses its own primary zone, along with a secondary zone from another namespace, providing quicker and more frequent resolution for the other namespace. This prevents unnecessary queries from traversing the network. Secondary zones are also forward and reverse in nature.

A forward zone holds data that maps and resolves server name to IP addresses. (See Figure 1-2.) In other words, when a query is received to find an IP address of a given name, this is the zone that will satisfy the query. These zones are represented in the database by their Fully Qualified Domain Name (FQDN). Within a forward zone, there may be one or more domains. Within each domain there are records that map names to address.

A reverse lookup zone is the exact opposite of a forward zone. It's responsible for answering queries when the IP address is known but the host name is unknown. This feature is often used on systems as the primary security method or as a means to augment security. Many older applications and services implement reverse lookup to verify the identity of a device requesting data. This is useful when the application or service applies security based on a device name and/or IP address. Once a device contacts the application or service it will then perform a reverse lookup on the IP address of the client to ensure that the address matches the device's given name. This method of security in my opinion is not desirable and is being replaced by cross platform security standards such as Kerberos and Certificates.

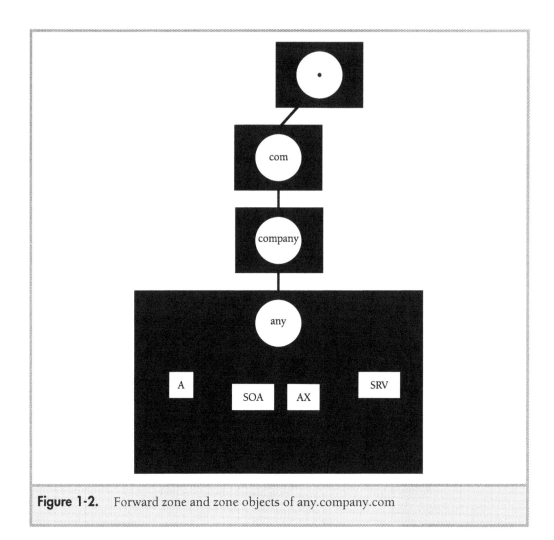

Figure 1-2.   Forward zone and zone objects of any.company.com

Reverse zones can appear in the database in multiple ways. The most common way is to create an in-addr.arpa zone to house the address-to-host name data. The makeup of these zones is a little different from that of forward zones, in that the network and part of the host IP address can actually be part of the zone name. A single reverse zone can either contain domains that reflect all IP segments and addresses from your organization, or each domain can be a delegated zone representing a single separate segment.

For example, if I have two IP segments, 10.27.51.x and 10.27.52.x, I could have two zones. One might contain 51.27.10.in-addr.arpa and all the pointer resource records (PTRs) for devices on the 10.27.51.x network. (See Figure 1-3.) The other might contain 52.27.10.in-addr.arpa and all the PTR records for devices on the 10.27.52.x network. Or I could choose to make one zone to include them both.

Zone Transfers

A zone transfer is the mechanism that replicates data from a primary zone to a server that is housing a secondary zone. The interval of replication is controlled by two events: a NOTIFY message and the SOA's Replication Interval.

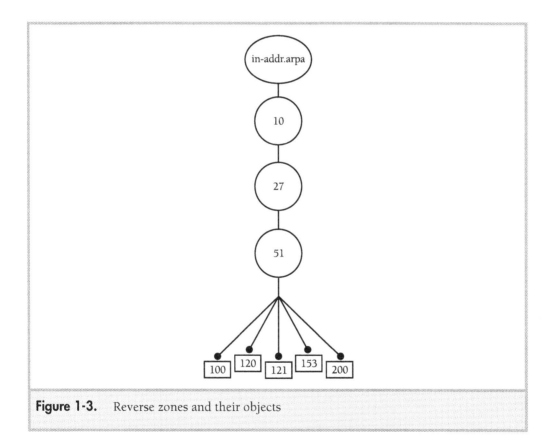

Figure 1-3.   Reverse zones and their objects

A primary zone can be configured to send NOTIFY messages to its secondary servers, which will trigger a replication request from the secondary to the primary. There is also a replication interval defined in the SOA that spawns an update process by letting the secondary servers "know" when to ask the primary for an update.

Once replication has been signaled, one of two types of replication events will occur: AXFR or IXFR. An AXFR transfer as defined in RFC 1035 is the original method for zone transfers and has been in use as part of the first DNS implementations. AXFR is a method for transferring all contents of a zone, not just the changes to the data. In other words, if you were to add a single host to the DNS database, the whole database must be replicated to the servers housing the secondary zones rather than just the change. This is accomplished by the secondary keeping an updated serial number for the master database or primary zone. Both primary and secondary know the current serial number. Once a change is made to the primary, the serial number is updated. When either the primary notifies the secondary, or the secondary asks the primary as a function of the update interval, the serial number on the secondary is compared to that of the primary. If the secondary doesn't have the most current database, replication of the whole database begins.

A more recent RFC, 1995, defines IXFR transfers, also known as incremental transfers. When IXFR is used, the serial number comparative process is used as detailed in the previous section on AXFR. The difference is in what data is replicated. Only the changes, or deltas, are replicated. IXFR has many advantages over AXFR, all of which are related to the value of being able to replicate only changes to the database instead of the whole database.

Name Servers and Resolvers

Okay, so now that you know what a zone is and what it does, it's time to learn where zones are hosted. Any server that hosts one or more DNS zones is called a name server. Name servers are responsible for answering queries from resolvers. There are three different types of name servers: primary master, secondary master and cache-only.

Primary Master Name Server

Primary master name servers are devices that host one or more primary zones. These devices are said to be authoritative for the zones that they own. In addition to primary zones, DNS servers in this role can also host secondary zone information, as well as a cache of resolved names. The cache collects all the names that have been resolved on behalf of a resolver. The cache is represented as a file in all DNS implementations, all of which use a different naming convention.

A primary master name server for any zone can be considered either its own, isolated root-level domain or a delegated zone from a valid root-level domain. In the case of a primary master name server that is hosting a zone that is configured as a root-level domain, it assumes that it's the ultimate authority for all name resolution data. As such, it won't forward any unresolved resolution request as servers using root hints will. This configuration is sometimes used in isolated testing environments or in any other environment that you want abstracted from the commercial DNS world.

In most cases, the primary name server is hosting a zone that is configured to be nothing more than a delegated domain from a valid root-level domain, which will be covered in the Delegation section of this chapter. When this scenario is in place, root hints are needed to foster accurate name resolution.

Root hints are entries for root-level domain server addresses in the DNS database. These entries are used to forward resolution requests when the name-to-address information isn't known locally by the DNS server. Root hints work by specifying which root-level servers are responsible for the appropriate root-level domains. In this way, a DNS server that receives a resolution request for a domain it doesn't own can send the request to the root-level domain that has delegated control of the request domain. After a series of recursive and iterative lookups, the answer is returned to the client.

Secondary Master Name Server

Secondary master name servers host secondary zone data. They are also sometimes referred to as slave servers. These devices can contain one or more secondary zones in addition to primary zones and cache information. As stated previously, these servers are used to answer queries for clients by searching their read-only copy of the DNS database. The behavior of transfers from the Primary Master name servers is defined in the SOA of the zone. This database entry lets the secondary servers know when they should inquire about potential updates, the current serial number, and the time to live (TTL) of the DNS database.

Cache-Only Servers

Cache-only servers are devices that host no zone information. Clients, or resolvers, are typically configured to query a cache-only server as their primary DNS source. The cache-only servers are configured to forward lookups to zones that are authoritative for the domain that houses the data being requested by the resolver. When the result set is returned to the cache-only server, the server stores the result in its cache before returning the answer to the resolver. This cache is parsed as each request for name resolution is received, so names that have been previously resolved can be retrieved out of cache rather than from another DNS server. This causes rapid name resolution to occur without causing network congestion for queries that have been satisfied.

Resolvers

A resolver is any client that has the ability to query a DNS database for name resolution. This means that all DNS servers, despite their DNS role, can also be considered resolvers since they can resolve names on behalf of the object actually requesting the data. I'll discuss in more depth how and why a DNS server would need to be a resolver later in this chapter.

Each resolver can have a Hosts.Txt file that serves as a local DNS database of sorts. The hosts file contains entries for the FQDN of devices as well as their IP addresses. When a resolver attempts to resolve a name, it checks its hosts file to see if there is an entry for the desired device locally. If no entry exists, a request is sent to the DNS servers that have been configured on the resolver.

Once a resolver gets a positive response back from either the hosts file or the DNS server, the information returned is stored in the DNS cache. This cache keeps records of recently

CODE BLUE

Because the resolver attempts to parse the hosts file before it contacts DNS, the system assumes that any information contained in the file is correct. An incorrect entry here results in the failure to contact the correct host or any host at all. In my experience, using hosts files causes most name resolution issues when you have a single resolver among many that can't resolve a name.

resolved device names to prevent redundant requests from being sent to a name server for data that the client already has knowledge about. The local cache is checked even before the hosts file is parsed.

Some resolvers also support a feature called negative caching. In negative caching, failed lookups are stored locally just as successful lookups are. This prevents a program or user from continually querying the DNS server for a device that has already been returned as "Not Found." Both cache types use an aging method with TTL to determine how long an entry remains in cache. The longer it remains in cache, the less network and DNS server traffic occurs, but at the cost of potentially stale data. The shorter an entry remains in the cache, the more dynamic the data, but this comes at a cost of higher processor and network utilization. Each resolver is configured independently when it comes to cache aging.

Each resolver also has some TCP/IP properties that affect the way the resolver interacts with DNS. The use of a DNS suffix allows a client to specify domain labels to tack on to a query for an unqualified name. An unqualified name is a host name that doesn't include any information about which domain it belongs in. An example of an unqualified name is www, while an example of a qualified name is www.microsoft.com. By placing microsoft.com into the list of domain suffixes, the unqualified name www is appended with microsoft.com and sent to the DNS server as a request for www.microsoft.com. A client can have an infinite number of DNS suffixes.

If more than one suffix is present, the resolver must use a suffix search order list to determine which suffixes get appended first. Let's assume that the resolver was configured to use both microsoft.com and compaq.com, but compaq.com is specified as the first suffix in the search order. In this configuration, an unqualified query for www would be appended with compaq.com and then sent to the DNS server. The unqualified name would be appended only with microsoft.com if there were no host record for www at compaq.com.

As you can see, placing domain suffixes in the correct order can greatly affect your name resolution experience. You should also limit the number of suffixes that are specified due to the potential performance hit. Once an unqualified query is sent to the resolver service, the service continues to append domain suffixes to the name until it either finds a host or runs out of suffixes to append. In the case of a user fat-fingering a name, it can take a great deal of time for the resolver service to append all suffixes to the incorrectly entered name.

NOTE: For those of you not familiar with the term "fat-finger(ing)" it means to hit the keyboard with your fingers in a fashion that is commonly seen when the human hand falls asleep. This results in the depressing of incorrect or undesired characters that you only notice *after* you press the Enter key. The fat-fingering is concluded once the fat-fingerer is finished cursing while waiting for the unavoidable error to display. I do this about 125 times a day.

Each resolver is also configured to use, at minimum, a primary and secondary DNS server. These primary and secondary DNS servers shouldn't be confused with the primary and secondary name servers. The primary and secondary DNS servers defined at the resolver dictate the order in which DNS servers are contacted when a query needs to be satisfied. This means that although a DNS server can be configured as the primary DNS server on a resolver, it may be a secondary name server.

Delegation

Delegation is the process of splitting or creating domain namespaces and giving administrative control of those namespaces to an owner who is different than the owner of the parent-level domain. Partitioning namespaces provides granular control and greater flexibility.

With delegation, a domain namespace within an existing zone is delegated to a separate set of DNS servers that host a separate set of zone files. This scenario makes it possible to implement multiple solutions and configurations without compromising any other namespaces.

You can see examples of delegation every time you use the Internet. As you know, the root-level domains are authoritative over all subdomains. Therefore, when you want to create a new domain on the Internet, you must have your desired domain name delegated to you from the proper root-level domain. For example, when Sun Microsystems wanted to make their domain available to the Internet community, they were delegated the domain name .sun from the owners of the .com domain. This created a domain name of sun.com, which allowed Sun to create a record for a device name of www and makes it possible for you to find their Web site when you type www.sun.com into your Web browser.

In this example, Sun is responsible for all aspects of management and implementation of its domain. This is done completely independent of the .com domain. In this respect, Sun can do anything that they please within their own domain, such as create new domains and delegate namespaces within the sun.com domain.

Names and Naming Rules

DNS, like any other directory service, has sets of rules that dictate what constitutes a valid name. Although each vendor's opinion about which name formats are acceptable in a DNS database varies, we'll focus on the BIND implementation because it conforms to all RFCs. We'll talk a little more about Microsoft's adoption of the Unicode character set, which is not an RFC, in Chapter 3.

Each name in a DNS namespace is composed of multiple labels, each separated by a period. A label isn't tied to a particular object type, so it can represent either a domain name, a device, or a service name. The location of the label indicates which type of object the label is. Keep in mind that the label to the far left of a FQDN is the host or service name. All the labels to the right of the farthest left label are domain names. There are some exceptions to this rule, but almost all exceptions have to do with the implementation of Dynamic DNS (DDNS).

Each device that is present in the DNS database has both a label and a FQDN. The label represents the device specifically, while the FDQN represents the complete path to the device. Think of it as the difference between a filename and a path.

Per RFC 1123, host names, which are also referred to as the label portion of a FQDN, should be able to be at least 64 characters in length. The RFC also goes on to state that DNS servers should be able to support up to 255 characters, although I don't know of any implementation as yet that exceeds 64 characters for the label. Host names can also contain only certain characters that have been deemed valid. Those characters are the following:

❖ A – Z

❖ a – z

❖ 0 – 9

❖ -

RFC 1123 also defines the formatting for the FQDN of any object. As alluded to earlier, the FQDN is a representation of the complete path to a given object within a domain and is created by combining multiple labels separating each with a comma. For example, in the FQDN www.microsoft.com

◈ www is the label of the host or server that is being requested.

◈ microsoft is the label of the domain in which www resides.

◈ com is the label of the root domain.

The complete FQDN has to conform to the same character rules as the label, and its total length, from end to end, cannot exceed 255 characters.

NOTE: Since the writing of this book, RFC 2181 has been adopted as an Internet standard. RFC 2181 updates valuable DNS information and rules, including naming standards. Per this RFC "any binary string whatever" can be used as a valid DNS character in a DNS label. This RFC is considered somewhat controversial and its adoption is sure to be slow. Because you won't likely see these changes anytime in the near future, the RFC 1123 naming rules will be used throughout this book.

Resource Record Types

Data in the DNS database can be represented in many different forms. These different forms, also called resource record types, serve different functions to aid in name resolution and service location. These records are placed into the database in one of three ways depending on the DNS implementation:

◈ Manually – Each record has to be created by hand in the database. All changes to the record also have to be updated by hand. This can become very time-consuming in a large environment.

◈ Dynamic Update from client – The client contacts and registers its DNS information directly with the DNS server per RFC 2136. All updates to previously registered data are also done by the client.

◈ Dynamic Update from Dynamic Host Configuration Protocol (DHCP) – The DHCP server that assigns an IP address to a client registers all records and updates on behalf of the client. All devices that don't use DHCP can either register with DNS dynamically or can have entries manually entered in the database.

For the purposes of this discussion, we'll assume that all records have been manually placed in the database (unless stated otherwise). Both dynamic registration methods are explained in Chapters 2 and 3.

Although there are many resource record types, I'm going to discuss only the most commonly used record types in detail. I'll cover other, less well known types with a brief summary.

SOA

Every DNS zone contains an SOA record. This record presents information to secondary name servers about the zone, its servers, and its records. The SOA record includes the following fields:

- ❖ Owner – Defines which host or domain this record belongs to
- ❖ TTL – Provides the time in seconds for which a resolver should cache this entry
- ❖ Class – Protocol family
- ❖ Type – Defines type (in this case, SOA)
- ❖ Authoritative Server – The authoritative server for the zone
- ❖ Responsible Person – Typically shows the e-mail address of the DNS administrator
- ❖ Serial Number – Used to keep data in secondary servers up-to-date by incrementing when changes are committed to the database
- ❖ Refresh – The amount of time that expires before a secondary checks for changes to the zone
- ❖ Retry – The amount of time that the secondary waits once a request has been sent to a primary
- ❖ Minimum TTL – Global TTL for any record that doesn't have an individual TTL defined

NS

This name server (NS) record contains servers that are authoritative for the zone. The record includes both primary and secondary servers.

A

This is the most commonly used record in DNS. This is the host record, which maps a device's host name or its FQDN to its IP address.

CNAME

This is an alias for a host that exists in DNS but is also known by another name. The best example of this is good old *www*. Each entity on the Internet doesn't have a device named www. Most organizations have a CNAME record for *www* that actually points to the real host name of the device. This is done for security and availability reasons.

MX

Short for mail exchange (MX), this record specifies a device that will route SMTP mail for an entity. This is a good example of a record that is defining a service rather than a host. You can define multiple MX records for a single domain to increase availability.

PTR

The pointer resource record (PTR) is a reverse lookup record. It maps the IP address to the host name and allows queries to be satisfied when the IP address is known but the host name is not.

SRV

The service location resource (SRV) record type is the backbone of DDNS. A SRV record defines all aspects of a service or application. This is done by defining many variables that haven't typically been found in DNS in the past, such as the following:

- ❖ Service – Defines the name of the service being provided
- ❖ Proto – Defines the protocol type to be used
- ❖ Name – A domain to which the record belongs
- ❖ TTL – The time to live for the record
- ❖ Priority – Used when multiple hosts are identified for a single service (The host with the lowest priority is used first.)
- ❖ Weight – Useful for load balancing because it indicates which servers should be accessed more frequently for a particular service
- ❖ Port – The protocol port to be used
- ❖ Target – Contains either the host name or the FQDN of the host that is housing the service

Less Famous but Important Resource Records

- ❖ AAAA – Maps host to IP address for IP version 6 addresses
- ❖ HINFO – Identifies the host's hardware type and operating system
- ❖ RP – The Responsible Person record used to identify who is responsible
- ❖ TXT – Can be used for any information for a host (Can sometimes include location, support, or general information.)

Resolution Methods

When DNS was conceived, it was expected that certain queries that were received by a name server could not be answered by the same server. This is a function of the distributed database that makes up the collective DNS environment. Although a server may not be authoritative for a record, or even know the location of the record, there must be a method to resolve the query. This is achieved through three resolution methods, recursive, iterative and forwarding.

Recursive Resolution

In a recursive lookup, the following events take place:

1. The resolver queries the DNS server for name resolution.

2. The DNS server receives the query and attempts to locate data.

3. The data is determined not to be found in any zone that the DNS server hosts.

4. The DNS server then acts as a resolver by contacting a DNS server that is authoritative for the domain.

5. The query is received by the correct server. The data is fetched and returned to the resolver.

6. The DNS server receives the data, caches it, and then provides the results to the resolver.

7. The resolver receives the query response and caches the results.

The recursive resolution method has advantages and disadvantages. The advantage is that processing and internal network load are reduced because the resolver has to ask only a single DNS server, which resolves the query on behalf of the client. This system keeps the resolver from having to make individual queries to multiple domains in an attempt to resolve a name. The performance of resolvers also increases when recursive lookups are used because all resolved names are handled by the organization's DNS servers and are therefore cached. Queries for the same data can be satisfied via the cache.

Now for the bad news. Although using recursion can reduce the load and increase the performance of name resolution from the client perspective, it increases the load and hinders performance of your DNS servers. This is a result of having the DNS servers act as resolvers that query on behalf of the clients. In my opinion, the benefits outweigh the cost. It's easier to upgrade your DNS servers or implement new DNS servers than to upgrade all the clients in your environment or increase bandwidth across the enterprise.

Iterative Resolution

Iterative resolution is the exact opposite of recursive resolution. With interative resolution, a DNS server returns a referral to the resolver, rather than asking on behalf of the resolver. This referral points the client to another set of DNS servers that are authoritative for the domain that hosts the data requested. This process is detailed below at a very high level:

1. The resolver queries the local DNS server.

2. The DNS server doesn't know where the data exists, but it knows the addresses of the DNS server that is authoritative for the domain. A referral is packaged and sent to the resolver.

3. The resolver receives the referral and then queries the referral server for the same information.

4. If the referral doesn't house the data, then it may send yet another referral to the resolver. This process will continue until the servers that are authoritative for the domain that houses the record are found.

5. The result set is sent back to the resolver, where it's stored in the local cache.

Iterative lookup provides a mechanism for facilitating resolution without incurring too much overhead in the process. Not many organizations use iterative lookups because of the cumulative effect the ensuing distribution of processing can have on an internal network. Iterative resolution is used by the root-level DNS servers for this exact reason. Can you imagine what would happen if the root-level DNS servers used recursive lookups? The Internet would be brought to its knees in a matter of moments.

Forwarding Resolution

Okay, right now, some DNS purists are pulling out their hair because I'm calling forwarding a resolution method. Typically, this term is reserved for recursive and iterative lookups, but like it or not, it also applies to forwarding. Forwarding isn't heavily implemented because it thumbs its nose in the face of the concept of root hints and typical DNS behavior. When a DNS server uses forwarding, rather than look for data from the root-level DNS server (or any other servers that have been defined as a root hint), it forwards all queries to one or more specified servers.

Forwarding tends to make tracing the path for resolution very difficult, in addition to increasing network traffic. The typical behavior of forwarding is to send all queries that can't be answered locally to the servers defined as forwarders, regardless of which domain the resources might live in. Recently, many ISVs have implemented smarter forwarding that allows you to assign a namespace to a server or sets of servers. This allows you to mix and match forwarding with root hints by forwarding only queries for certain domains while using normal resolution methods for all other queries.

Sample Scenarios

Is your head swimming with new concepts that have been presented in a seemingly illogical manner? Although I've read many books, white papers, and RFCs on DNS over the years, I've never before appreciated what it takes to write a book on DNS. DNS is very difficult to organize because so many different concepts intersect with one another. Many times, these concepts overlap with concepts that are out of the scope of DNS but must be explained for completeness. Enough belly-aching from the poor author and time for action. I've assembled a sample scenario as a method of detailing end-to-end DNS transactions. This should help you understand all of the concepts that have been explained in the previous pages.

The Environment

Company A has established a Web presence by registering a domain name of companya.com on the Internet. They've also implemented a separate namespace that is internal to the organization, which is used only for development. That second namespace is named companya.dev. Company A has implemented two zones for the companya.com namespace and one zone for the companya.dev namespace. Figure 1-4 illustrates the combined architecture, which is discussed in detail in the following sections.

Companya.com Architecture

The companya.com namespace, which is exposed to the Internet, is intended for the use of hosting Web services as well as internal resolution. This namespace uses two zones:

⬧ Companya.com, which houses only hosts that are exposed to the Internet

⬧ Internal.companya.com, which houses all host names for internal devices and services

The companya.com zone contains two DNS servers: one primary and the other secondary. The primary DNS server has a host name of com-dns1, a FQDN of com-dns1.companya.com, and an IP address of 10.100.1.10. The secondary server has a host name of com-dns2, a FQDN of com-dns2.companya.com, and an IP address of 10.100.1.11. Both servers are configured with the standard root hints, which reflect the Internet root-level name servers. Both servers are also configured to perform recursive lookups. This zone contains mostly A records for Web servers that enable Company A's customers to access vital services. The zone is supported by Company A's Web Support division.

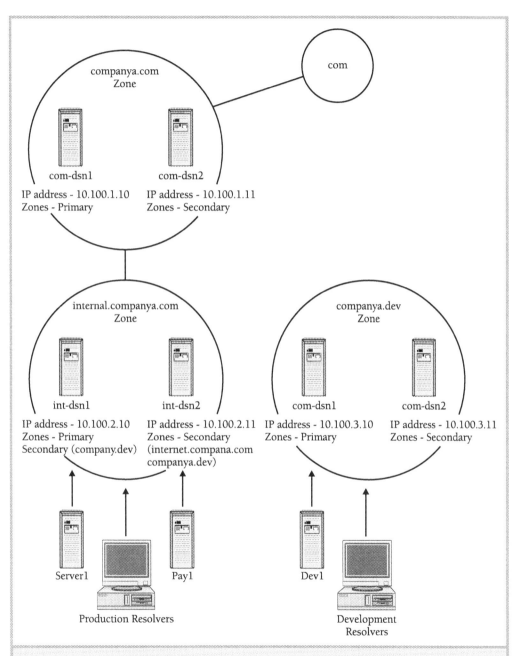

Figure 1-4.   The companya.com and companya.dev combined architecture

Internal.companya.com is a delegated zone from companya.com. This zone has two DNS servers; a primary and a secondary, both of which have been configured for recursive lookups. This zone contains records for all internal devices and services for Company A, and is supported by the Internal IT Support division. Both servers have also been configured to be secondary to the companya.dev domain, which enables production users to resolve names in the development namespace. The primary server has a host name of int-dns1, a FQDN of int-dns1.internal.companya.com, and an IP address of 10.100.2.10. The secondary server has a host name of int-dns2, a FQDN of int-dns2.internal.companya.com, and an IP address of 10.100.2.11.

Companya.dev Architecture

The companya.dev namespace is used to develop new software and service offerings. Devices that use the DNS servers that are authoritative for this domain need to resolve names in the companya.com domain. For this reason, forwarding to the companya.com DNS servers has been implemented. There is a single zone in companya.dev that is hosted on two servers, one primary and one secondary.

Client-Side Architecture

All clients are running Microsoft Windows 2000 Professional. All production desktops have been configured to use the primary and secondary DNS servers for companya.com for all host-name resolution including Internet name resolution.

* Desktops that are used for testing and development in the companya.dev domain use the companya.dev DNS servers for name resolution for development, production, and Internet names.

* All clients have a local host file that has a single entry for an intranet payroll and a personnel server named PAY1.internal.companya.com with an IP address of 10.100.2.20.

* All clients are configured to use DHCP and receive both DNS server addresses as well as the domain suffix of internal.companya.com from the DHCP servers.

Following the DNS Trails

This section presents a variety of scenarios and traces the way DNS works to resolve client requests.

A Client in Production Connecting to PAY1   An employee has a need to connect to PAY1 and change his exemption rate for federal income tax. After typing the URL pay1.internal.companya.com in the browser, the following occurs.

1. The browser sends a name resolution request to the resolver service for pay1.internal.companya.com.

2. The resolver service searches the client's local cache for a match. There are no matching resolved names.

3. The device searches for a Hosts.Txt file and finds one in the default NT location (*systemroot*\system32\drivers\etc).

4. The hosts file is parsed and an entry is found for PAY1 that has an IP address of 10.100.2.20.

5. The positive resolution is stored in the client's DNS cache for future use.

6. This information is passed back to the browser.

7. The browser establishes communication with the Web server at 10.100.2.20 and the client completes his business with PAY1.

8. Five minutes later, the user now realizes that he has entered some incorrect information that needs to be corrected immediately, so he opens a browser and types PAY1.internal.companya.com.

9. A request is sent from the browser to the resolver service.

10. The resolver service parses the cache for a match. A match is found.

11. The results are sent to the browser, which will initiate communications with the Web server at 10.100.2.20.

As you can see in this example, the local cache can increase the performance of name resolution.

A Client in Production Connecting to PAY1 after an IP Address Change on PAY1   A week later, another user needs to obtain some information from PAY1. Unbeknownst to her, the IT staff has recently changed the IP address of PAY1 to 10.100.2.21 due to an address conflict. Although the IT staff made the change in the DNS database, they forgot to inform those who are responsible for updating the client's hosts file about the change. So the hosts file still reflects an IP address of 10.100.2.20. Let's see what happens:

1. The browser sends a name resolution request to the resolver service for pay1.internal.companya.com.

2. The resolver service searches the client's local cache for a match. There are no matching resolved names.

3. The resolver service searches for a Hosts.Txt file and finds one in the default NT location (*systemroot*\system32\drivers\etc).

4. The hosts file is parsed and an entry is found for PAY1 that has an IP address of 10.100.2.20.

5. The positive resolution is stored in the client's DNS cache for future use.

6. This information is passed back to the application.

7. The browser attempts to open a HTTP session with the address of 10.100.2.20, but there is no answer from this address.

8. After several attempts the browser displays a "Server Not Found" error.

9. The client thinks that she has just mistyped the name of the server, so she enters the name into the browser again.

10. The browser hands the name request to the resolver service.

11. The resolver service parses the cache and finds an entry for PAY1 with an IP address of 10.100.2.20.

12. This address is passed back to the application.

13. Once again, the browser attempts to contact a host at the given address, and the attempt fails.

See, I wasn't lying when I cautioned against the use of hosts files earlier in the chapter. They did have their place several years ago, but now they tend to be the source of many hard-to-diagnose problems. Avoid the use of hosts files like the plague.

A Client in Production Connecting to Server1   Because the only entry in the client's hosts file is for PAY1, all other names are resolved through DNS. This is the case when attempting to contact a server named SERVER1.internal.companya.com:

1. A client attempts to ping SERVER1.internal.companya.com by opening a command window and typing ping SERVER1.

2. Because this request isn't qualified, the client's resolver service will locate its DNS suffix search order registry entries and then proceed to append the name given, SERVER1, with each entry until it can find a record with that name in one of the domains specified.

3. Because DHCP hands out internal.companya.com as the only DNS suffix, this is appended to the label given by the user and a query for SERVER1.internal.companya.com is sent.

4. Both the cache and the hosts file are parsed, but with no success.

5. The user has been configured to use the DNS server at 10.100.2.11 as the primary DNS server and 10.100.2.10 as the secondary DNS server, so the request is first sent to 10.100.2.11.

6. 10.100.2.11 receives the name query and checks its cache.

7. Because the cache didn't produce any results, the server searches its database. It finds the name and returns the IP address to the resolver after it stores the results in cache.

8. The resolver receives the results and stores these in cache before returning the response to the IP protocol stack.

9. Once the IP address is received, the ping executes using the IP address given.

As was the case with the previous examples, if the client attempts this process again minutes later, the resolver service parses the cache and returns the address from cache.

A Client in Production Connecting to www.technet.microsoft.com   In this example, you can see how recursive and iterative lookups work.

1. A user attempts to open www.technet.microsoft.com in a browser.

2. The browser sends the name resolution request to the resolver service.

3. The resolver service parses both the cache and hosts file before sending a resolution request to the 10.100.2.10 DNS server.

4. The DNS server receives the resolver's request, checks its cache, and parses its database for all known zones, but comes up empty.

5. Since 10.100.2.10 has been configured to use the companya.com DNS server as root server, it packages the name request and sends it to the 10.100.1.11 DNS server on behalf of the client. At this time, the 10.100.2.10 DNS server is acting as a resolver and as a result, the 10.100.1.11 server is oblivious to the fact that a device other than 10.100.2.10 is asking for the data. This is an example of a recursive lookup.

6. 10.100.1.11 receives the request, but it isn't authoritative for the domain in question. It examines the root of the FQDN of the requested device and then packages a request to the root-level domain responsible, in this case, .com. By sending this request to the .com servers, 10.100.1.11 is also acting as a resolver.

7. The .com server receives a request for *www.technet.microsoft.com* from a resolver at 10.100.1.11. The .com DNS server searches its database and finds a delegated domain name of microsoft.com. It packages the IP addresses of the DNS servers for microsoft.com that have been delegated, and sends this information in the form of a referral to the resolver at 10.100.1.11. This is an example of an iterative lookup.

8. The DNS server at 10.100.1.11 receives the referral, and a name resolution request is sent by its resolver service to the IP addresses given by the .com server.

9. The microsoft.com DNS servers receive the request from the resolver and sends the IP address of the host back.

10. The DNS server receives the IP-address-to-name data from the microsoft.com server, caches the data, and then sends the information to the resolver that requested it.

11. The internal.companya.com DNS server receives the information that it requested from 10.100.1.11. It caches the data and sends it back to the resolver that requested the data, in this case, the user's workstation.

12. The original resolver's resolver service (say that ten times fast!) receives the data and enters it in cache before handing it back to the browser.

13. The browser then establishes a session with the IP address returned by DNS for the host name ServerA and displays the contents of the page requested.

This example shows the most typical use of recursive and iterative resolution. In most cases, organizations use recursive resolution exclusively and rely on the iterative resolution provided by the root-level name servers.

A Client in Production Connecting to Server1 Using an Incorrect Name   Let's take one of the previous scenarios and add a twist. Let's assume that the client is attempting to ping the FQDN of SERVER1 but by mistake has typed SERVER1.*intrenal*.companya.com. Because that domain name doesn't exist, negative caching works in the following way:

1. The user opens a command window and types ping server1.intrenal.companya.com.

2. The resolution request is sent to the resolver service.

3. The resolver service parses the cache and hosts file but finds no matches.

4. The resolver service sends a name resolution request to the client's configured primary DNS server.

5. The DNS server receives the request but realizes that the data being requested has a domain label different from its own.

6. After parsing its cache, the DNS server sends the request to one of the companya.com DNS servers.

7. Server 10.100.1.10 receives the request, searches its cache for entries, and then searches its database for any delegated zones that host the *internal* domain.

8. Because none are found, a negative response is sent to the resolver, which is the internal.companya.com DNS server at 10.100.2.11.

9. The domain not found message is received by the DNS server and an entry is placed in its negative cache. This entry indicates that the host name is not found.

10. This domain not found message is sent to the original resolver.

11. The resolver service places an entry in its negative cache before retuning the results to the Ping program.

12. The Ping program then displays a "Host Not Found" error message.

13. The user is sure that the server does exist and, in disbelief, uses the down arrow to toggle through the list of stored commands that he has entered at the command line. When he gets to the "ping server1.intrenal.companya.com" command, he presses Enter.

14. The program then sends on a name request for server1.intrenal.companya.com to the resolver service.

15. The resolver service parses the cache and finds an entry in the negative cache.

16. The "Host Not Found" message is instantly sent back to the Ping program and an error is displayed again.

As you can see, the negative cache is useful at keeping redundant bogus queries off the wire. This is especially useful when you have a program that might be trying rapid successive entries of a bad name. Negative caching is a new feature in Windows 2000 and is configured with a default TTL for all entries of 300ms.

A Client in Production Connecting to 10.100.2.20   This section illustrates the concept and function of reverse lookup through the use of an example. Reverse lookup is sometimes hard to explain. I've read several books that attempt to explain it but most come up short, which is amazing because it's really quite simple. Let's see how I do, shall we?

1. A client in production is using NSLOOKUP (covered later in this chapter in the section "Troubleshooting and Monitoring Tools") to find the host name that is associated with the IP address 10.100.2.20 in an attempt to resolve an address conflict.

2. The resolution request is sent to the resolver service, which checks both the cache and hosts file for any PTR record that has the IP address in question. When this isn't found, the resolver sends the request to the DNS server at 10.100.2.10.

3. The DNS server receives the request, checks its cache for the data if the record isn't found, and then parses the database. Since the DNS server is hosting a reverse lookup zone, that is the location that is queried.

4. The DNS server takes the address 10.100.2.20 and breaks the record up into separate octets in an attempt to separate the host portion of the address from the network portion. The initial step at this is to take the first octet, 10, and find a domain of the same name in the in-addr.arpa zone (10.in-addr.arpa).

5. Once this domain is found, the next octet is taken and a query for a subdomain of the same name results. In this case, the DNS server looks for 100.10.in-addr.arpa.

6. The same is done for the third octet in an attempt to find 2.100.10.in-addr.arpa.

7. The DNS server has now stripped the entire network portion of the IP address off and has left the host portion, 20. The 2.100.10.in-addr.arpa domain is then queried for a PTR record with a value of 20. The data associated with this record includes either the FQDN of SERVER1 or just the host name.

8. This information is added to the server's cache and is then packaged and sent to the resolver.

9. The resolver receives this information, adds it to its cache, and then forwards it to NSLOOKUP.

As you can see, reverse lookup is handled much differently from forward lookup. I hope I illustrated the process well enough not to be clumped into my classing of other less-than-wonderful explanations of reverse lookup.

A Client in Production Tries to Connect to Dev1

We now have a client who works with the development staff but happens to be at her workstation, which is located on the production network.

1. The user attempts to map a network drive to an administrative share on DEV1 by typing \\dev1.companya.dev\c$ in the drive mapping GUI.

2. The Windows 2000 shell hands the name resolution request to the resolver service, which first checks the cache and hosts file.

3. The resolver service then sends a name resolution request to the client's primary configured DNS server, 10.100.2.10. As you may recall, 10.100.2.10 is a name server in the internal.companya.com namespace.

4. 10.100.2.10 receives the resolver's request. Because the DNS server has been configured to be a secondary name server to the companya.dev zone, it has a local copy of companya.dev's entries.

5. The server examines its cache before parsing its zone. The secondary zone is parsed and the data is returned to the resolver.

A Client in Development Connecting to Server 1   We just saw how resolution of an isolated domain can be achieved with the use of secondary zones hosted on a DNS server that are primary to other zones. Now let's look at the other solution, forwarding.

1. A client on the development network needs to access a file on a share located on SERVER1, so he attempts to map a network drive to \\server1.internal.companya. com\share1.

2. The resolver service checks the cache and the hosts file before sending a request to one of the companya.dev DNS servers.

3. The DNS server at 10.100.3.10 receives the request. It parses the cache and its database, but it can't find any zone information on the domain requested. Because the server has been configured to forward all locally unresolvable queries to 10.100.2.10, the request is forwarded. This DNS server is basically acting as a gateway to the production DNS environment.

4. 10.100.2.10 receives the query, examines the cache, parses the zone, finds the requested information, and returns it directly to the original resolver.

5. The client's resolver service receives the data, enters it in the cache, and then returns it to the application.

Troubleshooting and Monitoring Tools

This section covers those tools that are common or that can be used across multiple DNS implementations. Tools that are specific to Windows 2000 are discussed in the appropriate chapters of this book. The tools described here are in no way a complete listing of every DNS tool available. There are hundreds of tools, whose authors range from programmers for a DNS vendor to those who are just writing code as a hobby. Be careful about the tools you use with DNS. These tools are normally run in an administrative context, so any malicious code could be disastrous. Know your source.

NSLOOKUP

NSLOOKUP is the cornerstone of all DNS tools. Like it or hate it, it's been around for a long time and is *the tool* used for DNS troubleshooting. Many OS vendors bundle their own version of NSLOOKUP with their operating systems, or you can download a more recent version from the Internet.

NSLOOKUP is a command-line tool that's used to query DNS servers. It's useful for troubleshooting name resolution issues because it provides a painful level of detail about the query and the results.

NSLOOKUP has two modes: noninteractive and interactive. Noninteractive is used to return simple results of a query, while interactive provides verbose debugging output for the same query within a separate shell.

To use NSLOOKUP in noninteractive mode, use the following syntax:

nslookup (*name*) (*server*)

where

(*name*) = the owner of the record you're looking for

(*server*) = the name server that you want to query (If no name server is specified, the configured primary DNS server of the client is used.)

For example, if you want to find the IP address of SERVER1, enter the following:

nslookup server1.internal.companya.com 10.100.2.10

NSLOOKUP can be spawned in one of two ways. The simplest way is to type NSLOOKUP at the command prompt and press Enter. This opens the NSLOOKUP shell, where you can enter a number of commands. You can tell that you're in the NSLOOKUP shell when you see the following on your screen:

nslookup

Default Server: *Server Name*

Address: *IP Address*

>_

Your other option is to specify parameters when you launch the tool. This can save time, especially if you're looking for a specific piece of data. In that case, the syntax is the following:

nslookup (*-options*) (*owner*) (*server*)

where

(*options*) = optional switches (Each option must be separated by a space and proceeded by a hyphen.)

(*owner*) = the owner of the record that you're looking for

(*server*) = the name of the server that you want to query (If a server isn't specified, the configured primary DNS server of the client will be used.)

Options can be used either at launch time of NSLOOKUP, or specified in the NSLOOKUP shell. The choice is yours. The supported options for NSLOOKUP are enormous in number, and many of the options take additional switches for sub-options. Information on these switches are available in NSLOOKUP help by typing **help** in the NSLOOKUP Shell.

DIG

Domain Information Groper (DIG) queries name servers. It too has two modes: simple and interactive. Note that the switches and commands may vary from version to version and from implementation to implementation. You can grab a copy at ftp://ftp.is.co.za/networking/ip/dns/dig/.

DIG uses the following syntax:

dig @(*server*) (*domain*) (*query-type*) (*query-class*)–(*option*) +(*query*) where

(server) = the name of the server to be used (If no server name is specified, the current DNS server is used.)

(domain) = the domain in which the desired information resides

(query-type) = the type of resource records that should be retrieved

The supported values are the following:

+ A
+ ANY – all record types
+ MX
+ NS
+ SOA
+ HINFO
+ AXFR
+ TXT

(query-class) = the class requested in the query

The supported values are the following:

+ IN – Internet class
+ ANY – any and all class

(options) = the option parameters you want to use (The number of supported options for this program is enormous, and many of the options have sub-options available. The help files will guide you.)

DNS Expert

For those of you who just can't stomach the use of a command line tool, check out a utility called DNS Expert. This GUI tool encompasses all the functionality of every DNS tool that I have ever seen. It will front end any DNS server regardless of OS or DNS flavor. Its only downfall is its price. It really isn't too expensive considering what you get, but it sure isn't free. Check it out at http://www.menandmice.com/infobase/mennmys/vefsidur.nsf/index/2. (You can download a trial version).

Ping

Packet Internet Grope (Ping) is a great tool for checking basic name resolution in addition to connectivity. It uses the following syntax:

Ping devicename –(option)

where

devicename = the FQDN or unqualified host name to be resolved

–(option) = one of the values listed below.

The supported values are the following:

- ❖ –t – continues to ping until forced to stop by using Ctrl+Break
- ❖ –a – resolved addresses to host names
- ❖ –n *number* – specifies a number of echo requests to send
- ❖ –l *size* – specifies the buffer size to be used
- ❖ –f – prevents fragmentation of the packet
- ❖ –i *time* – specifies the TTL
- ❖ –v – specifies Type of Service
- ❖ –r *count* – record route for count hops
- ❖ –s *count* – record timestamp for current hop
- ❖ –j *host-list* – loose source route along host-list
- ❖ –k *host-list* – strict source route along host-list
- ❖ –w *timeout* – timeout in milliseconds to wait for a response

Chapter 2

Implementing a Microsoft DNS Architecture

Many Microsoft applications and services differ from the "typical" implementation or industry standard that governs the technology. Can anyone say NetBIOS name resolution?

In the case of Microsoft Windows DNS, Microsoft has made a few changes that affect the product's RFC compliancy. The good news is that almost all of these features are optional, which allows you to make a conscious decision to take a walk on the dark side instead of the decision being made for you. In most cases, these changes are actually useful and make a lot of sense, which is why I recommend the Windows 2000 DNS solution above all others that are currently available.

This chapter covers the specifics of implementing a basic Microsoft DNS architecture using the Windows 2000 DNS offering (not the same as the Windows NT 4 version, which was a joke). Along the way, I'll discuss new features that have been introduced, both those that conform to an RFC and those that don't. In addition, I'll illustrate in painful detail the tasks you must complete to install and/or configure each feature. (If you already know the installation routine or you've already installed DNS, you can skip the beginning sections of the chapter.)

I can't stress enough how paramount your DNS design is to your Active Directory. Your DNS design is the single entity that can make or break your directory.

Windows 2000 DNS/DDNS

DNS is packaged as a free service in all editions of Windows 2000 Server (Server, Advanced Server, and Data Center Server). This service conforms to the following RFCs:

- 1034 – Domain Names – Concepts and Facilities
- 1035 – Domain Names – Implementation and Specification
- 1123 – Requirements for Internet Hosts – Application and Support
- 1886 – DNS Extension to Support IP Version 6
- 1995 – Incremental Zone Transfers in DNS
- 1996 – A Mechanism for Prompt DNS Notification of Zone Changes
- 2136 – Dynamic Updates in the Domain Name System (DNS UPDATE)
- 2181 – Clarification to the DNS Specification
- 2308 – Negative Caching of DNS Queries

NOTE: Not all of these RFCs have a status of "Standard." Please consult Appendix B for definitions of RFC status and state, as well as the current status and state of a particular RFC.

Microsoft's claim of RFC compliancy brings up an interesting question whose answer depends on your perspective. When a service or application is named "RFC compliant" by the manufacturer, what does that mean? In my opinion, the status of "RFC compliant" means one of two things:

◆ The service or application only exposes the functionality that is found in RFCs—no more, no less.

◆ Some features in the product are RFC complaint while others are not.

The latter is the case with Windows 2000 DNS. Although it conforms to many RFCs, it also implements features that aren't defined in any RFC. This is typical of Microsoft.

Truth be told, most of the non-RFC aspects of DNS in Windows 2000 are useful and are provided as stop-gap measures to accommodate their customers' needs. As customers, we are constantly asking Microsoft to do really cool whiz-bang things with their product line, while at the same time we feel free to condemn them for doing what it takes to make our requests a reality. Damned if you do, damned if you don't. UNIX doesn't have this problem because the only thing UNIX administrators are afraid of more than fire is change.

Installing the DNS Service

Installing the DNS Server service is a rather painless proposition. Fortunately, one of the feature enhancements to Windows 2000 over Windows NT 4 was extended to the DNS Server service; you don't need to reboot the server after you've installed the service. You can install the service either before or after operating-system installation. If you choose to install the service after the server is built, you can spawn the service installation by using the Add/Remove Programs | Configure Your Server Wizard, or DCPROMO.

Installing DNS at Operating-System Setup

All versions of Windows 2000 Server have a consistent setup routine for installing DNS. The only variation you might need to consider in this type of installation is using an Unattended.txt file to automate your server build (instead of manually building the server).

Manual Installation

If you want to install the DNS Server service manually when you set up the operating system, installation begins in the GUI portion of setup. After you enter a password for the Administrator account, the Select Components screen appears. Then follow these steps to complete the process:

1. Double-click the Networking Components object.
2. Select the check box next to the Domain Name System component and click OK.
3. On the Select Components screen, click Next and continue with the rest of setup.

This installs the service without any configuration. Although the service will start at system boot, it won't be able to satisfy any DNS queries until you complete the configuration steps, which are discussed throughout this chapter.

Automated Installation

If you want to automate a server build by using the Unattended.txt file (or any other answer file), you must add the following sections and values to include the installation of the DNS service with the operating system installation:

[NetOptionalComponents]

dns=on

How you use the automation file doesn't change in any way with the addition of these items.

Installing the DNS Service after Operating-System Setup

Whether by mistake or by deliberate action, you might need to install DNS after the operating system has been installed. You can use the traditional Add/Remove Programs applet, the Configure Your Server Wizard, or the DCPROMO command to install the DNS service at any time.

Add/Remove Programs

We all know and love the Add/Remove Programs applet that is found in Control Panel. In addition to being the primary method for installing programs, you can also use it to install services after the operating system setup. To install DNS in this manner, complete the following procedure:

1. In the Add/Remove Programs applet, click Add/Remove Windows Components (in the left pane).

2. In the Windows Components Wizard window, scroll to locate and select the Networking Services object, and click the Details button.

3. On the Networking Services screen, select the check box for Domain Name System (DNS) and click OK.

4. Click Next on the Networking Components screen.

5. If prompted for the Windows 2000 Server bits, provide the correct path.

Configure Your Server Wizard

The Configure Your Server Wizard is that annoying screen that pops up every time you log on to a server as either Administrator or with an administrative equivalent account. This wonderfully useless screen won't stop displaying at every logon until you manually turn it off. Its purpose is to allow you to "easily" install and configure any service that is provided with Windows 2000.

Is it just me, or is the Configure Your Server Wizard a complete insult of your intelligence as an administrator? Are we too dumb to find the places to add and configure these components?

In my humble opinion, if you can't figure out how to install and configure a component on your own, chances are, you shouldn't even be touching a server in the first place. Despite my bitter feelings, here's how you can you add and configure DNS from the Configure Your Server Wizard:

1. From the left pane of the Configure Your Server screen, select Networking.

2. From the Networking drop down box, select DNS.

3. Click Set Up DNS to install the service.

4. If you're prompted to provide a path to the Windows 2000 bits, enter it here.

There is another, round-about way to install DNS from the Configure Your Server Wizard. By attempting to install Active Directory via Configure Your Server, you will launch the Active Directory Installation Wizard, also known as DCPROMO. The wizard prompts you to install DNS if a DDNS environment can't be detected.

DCPROMO

DCPROMO is the name of the executable that launches the Active Directory Installation Wizard. This application guides you through the process of promoting your lowly member or stand-alone server to the majestic status of domain controller. In the process of promotion, the wizard examines the existing DNS configuration of the server to determine if there is an RFC 2136–compliant DNS environment configured and available. RFC 2136 details dynamic updates to DNS (also called DDNS), which is mandatory for any Active Directory implementation. The wizard prompts you to install DNS if there is no existing environment or a non-DDNS environment is detected.

As the application examines the system, it comes to one of the following conclusions:

- The device is configured to use a DDNS environment.

- The device is configured to use a non-DDNS environment.

- The device is not configured for DNS at all.

Existing DDNS Environment If the device is configured to use an existing DDNS environment, nothing else will occur from a DNS perspective. After a check of the appropriate zone and its ability to accept dynamic updates, the wizard moves on.

Existing Non-DDNS Environment If the device is configured to use a non-DDNS environment, you're prompted with a message indicating that no DNS environment could be found that supports dynamic updates. You see this message after you provide the wizard with a domain name to assign to Active Directory.

Once you clear this message, a mini-DNS wizard is spawned. At this point, you can either let the wizard complete the configuration, or you can cancel out of the Active Directory Installation Wizard and configure DNS on your own before running DCPROMO again. Canceling out and completing the configuration on your own might be desirable if your configuration requires some specific parameters instead of the assumed values that the wizard implements. By installing DNS via DCPROMO, a standard forward zone—which accepts unsecured dynamic updates—is installed by default. This zone has a name that is the same as the name given to your AD domain.

What happens next is kind of interesting and annoyingly helpful at the same time. Because the wizard has detected a DNS environment, it attempts to configure your root hints for you. In this case, because the device is configured to use existing DNS servers, the wizard queries those servers to determine if they are root-level servers. If they are, then those servers' names and addresses are added to the root hints file. If the wizard can't find any root-level servers, it assumes that this domain is root and it creates a zone named ".", which signifies a root-level zone. This is called priming the root hints. This can be mildly annoying if you intend to change the device's root status once you place it into production. To resolve this, you must manually reconfigure your root hints. Wouldn't it be nice if it just asked you at runtime instead of assuming that you don't know what you're doing?

NOTE: Installing DNS by using the Active Directory Installation Wizard doesn't create reverse lookup zones.

No Existing DNS Configuration   If the device is configured to use no DNS at all, the process is similar to when a non-DDNS environment is being used. The only difference is the way that the root hints are handled and the addition of the DNS values to the TCP/IP configuration.

When the wizard examines the existing DNS information, determines that there is no existing DNS, and prompts to install and configure DNS on the device, it also checks to see if this device is capable of contacting root-level domains. It does this by querying the name servers listed in the Cache.dns file, which in a default installation contains the Internet root-level name servers. If these queries are unanswered, the wizard assumes that the device is a root-level domain. This results in the wizard creating a new zone with the name of ".", which signifies root. This is another example of priming the root hints.

No matter which of the previous three scenarios your deployment falls into, the screens and results are basically the same. Once you're finished, you have a DNS server that has a single forward zone that is AD-Integrated with a name that's the same as the name of your AD domain.

Root Hints and Forwarding on a Root-Level Domain

Considering what both root hints and forwarding are intended to do, it should come as no surprise that if your DNS server is configured as root, both features are unavailable. When you think about it for a moment, it makes perfect sense.

The concept of a root-level domain is that it knows about all. It is the single place in all space and time to which all other domains must be subordinate. Given that the root is supposed to know about all, why would you need to forward queries to any other servers?

The normal DNS lookup process should take care of that in a true root. As far as root hints go, why would you need root hints when you are the root?

While this seem to make sense here in print, you'd be surprised how many administrators can't figure out why their root hints and forwarding interfaces in the MMC are dimmed.

Changing the Root Status of Your Domain

If the Active Directory Installation Wizard has configured your DNS server as root when you didn't want this to happen, you can remove the root zone with the following steps:

1. Open the DNS MMC.

2. Double-click the server that is hosting the root zone.

3. Double-click the Forward Lookup Zone object in the left pane.

4. Right-click the zone named "." and select Delete from the shortcut menu.

Once the zone has been deleted, your server will fall back to the Internet root hints.

To add the root-level domain back to your DNS server, follow the instructions in later sections of this chapter that are appropriate for the zone type you want to use for root. When you create this new zone, you will signify that it is a root-level zone by naming it ".".

Configuring DNS

Now that you've installed DNS, it's time to configure the server and the service. This section discusses the different configuration options in DNS and introduces a few new features of Windows 2000 DNS.

The primary tool for configuring and maintaining your DNS server is the DNS MMC. There are a couple of ways to get this MMC on your list of available snap-ins. You can do either of the following:

❖ Run the MMC from the DNS server since it's installed as part of the service installation.

❖ Install Adminpak.msi on the device on which you want to run the DNS MMC, from the %SystemRoot%\System32 folder of any Windows 2000 server.

 NOTE: The Admin Pack installs every administrative-related snap-in for just about every service you can imagine. Because it is an MSI package, an installer wizard is launched to help you through setup. I make it a point to install this on every workstation that I might ever touch.

Sometimes you might not want an administrator to be poking around all the available MMCs that are installed with the Admin Pack. In this case, you can take the proper steps to make only the DNS MMC available. You can do this by registering the correct .dll with the system on which you want the DNS MMC to run, which causes the DNS MMC to appear in the list of available snap-ins. To accomplish this, complete the following steps:

1. Copy Dnsmgr.dll from %SystemRoot%\System32 of any Server product to %SystemRoot%\System32 of the device on which you want to run DNS MMC.

2. Open a command prompt and type **regsvr32 dnsmgr.dll**, and then press Enter. This registers the .dll and makes the snap-in available.

TIP: Use the /s switch to enable the registration to run silently.

3. Open a blank MMC and add the DNS snap-in.

You can compile these steps into a command file or a script and then send it to select administrators via Group Policy if you want. This is much easier than manually completing these steps everywhere.

Using the DNS MMC

As I said, the DNS MMC is the primary tool for administering the DNS database and servers that make up your environment. It's like all other MMCs: it has a tree pane on the left and a details pane on the right. Typically, the tree pane shows all DNS servers as well as their zones, both forward and reverse. The details pane shows the specifics of the selected object in the tree pane.

One of the common tasks in the DNS MMC is the creation of new resource records (RRs). To create an RR, right-click either the zone that appears in the tress pane or the empty space in the details pane and select New Record from the shortcut menu. The following are the Microsoft supported RRs:

❖ A – The host record. Defined in RFC 1035.

❖ AAAA – IPv6 host records that support new 128-bit IP addresses. Defined in RFC 1886.

❖ AFSDB – The Andrew File System Database server record. Described in RFC 1183.

❖ ATMA – The ATM address record used to map a domain name to an ATM address. Not defined in any RFC.

❖ CNAME – The CNAME (canonical name) record is an alias record that points to a device known by another host name. Described in RFC 1035.

❖ HINFO – The record that provides information on CPU, operating system, and other server-specific items related to the host. Defined in RFC 1035.

❖ ISDN – The record that maps domain names to ISDN telephone numbers. Defined in RFC 1183.

❖ MB – The record that defines mailboxes for entities in DNS. Defined in RFC 1035.

❖ MG – The record used to group MB records.

❖ MINFO – The record that specifies a domain MB to contact for administrative-related issues such as error receipt. Defined in RFC 1035.

❖ MR – A forwarder record from an old mailbox name to its new name. Defined in RFC 1035.

❖ MX – Mail Exchanger is the record that provides messaging routing to messaging hosts. Defined in RFC 1035.

❖ NS – Name Server is the record that defines servers that can answer queries for the zone. Defined in RFC 1035.

❖ PTR – The reverse address lookup record for hosts. Defined in RFC 1035.

❖ RP – The Responsible Person record specifies the MB of the admin or responsible person. Defined in RFC 1183.

❖ RT – The Route Through record provides mapping through a firewall for DNS access and Network Address Translation (NAT). Defined in RFC 1183.

❖ SOA – The Start of Authority record defines all information needed by secondary name servers for replication. Defined in RFC 1035.

❖ SRV – The Service locator record allows services to be published and resolved in DNS. Defined in RFC 2052.

❖ TXT – Holds text about an entity. Defined in RFC 1035.

❖ WINS – This record defines WINS servers to which resolution requests can be sent if they can't be satisfied in DNS. Not defined in any RFC.

❖ WINS-R – The WINS Reverse Lookup record allows reverse lookup of names through WINS when the name can't be found in DNS. Not defined in any RFC.

❖ WKS – The Well Known Services record defines service available for resolution. Described in RFC 1035.

❖ X25 – The record that maps a domain name to a public switched data network addresses. Defined in RFC 1183.

BUG ALERT Per RFC 1035, CNAME records in DNS should be used to allow a client to know only the alias of a device, but be returned the actual host name of the requested device. The client is then supposed to resolve that name and use the IP address to establish a TCP/IP virtual connection (VC) with the server. This is (and has been for years) the industry standard way of communicating with any device that has a CNAME in DNS in all implementations of DNS (including that found in NT 4). Microsoft has recently changed how CNAME works with Windows 2000. In my opinion, this change makes the DNS service not RFC 1035 compliant.

In Windows 2000, when a client resolves a CNAME, the device's actual host name is handed back to the client and resolved as specified in the RFC. The client establishes a VC with the server using its IP address. If the device to which the client is connecting is a Windows 2000 device, the client attempts to establish an SMB connection with the device, which is normal. What happens next is wacky.

When the client attempts to establish an SMB session with the server, it uses its CNAME in the Universal Naming Convention (UNC) or path to the server's share points instead of the device's actual name. Because the server has no idea about the CNAME record that has been placed in DNS, the session fails. The whole reason for CNAMES is to allow a device to be known by a name other than its own yet still be available to all clients.

Microsoft has claimed that this is a security measure to prevent spoofing. I don't understand this, but I may be a little thick. If the client is getting the IP address of the device and then establishes a VC, spoofing can still occur. The SMB session doesn't play into a spoofing scenario.

Microsoft's original response to this was to recommend a registry hack that allows the server to respond to specified alternate names. The result of this hack was that the CNAME was not really an alias record (because to work properly, the server has to be configured to use the name defined in the CNAME). I call that a device that has multiple host names. I'm not going to release the location and content of the registry hack because it's not supported at all in Windows 2000.

I've discussed the problem with Microsoft and hope that this will be fixed in the next version of Windows (and possibly fixed for Windows 2000).

Using the Configure the DNS Server Wizard

Like every other service that Microsoft provides, DNS has a wizard that is the preferred way to configure your DNS server. If you're like me, you've found wizards to be a thorn in your side, so you attempt to avoid them at all costs. This was the case for me with the prerelease Windows 2000 code, when I noticed that the DNS MMC would allow me to configure my server without running the wizard. I soon learned that this was a bad idea.

Although you can manually configure a new zone at any time, Microsoft recommends that the first zone be set up with the wizard. If you don't use the wizard to set up the first zone, two things will happen:

◈ You'll continue to see an error message in the MMC that indicates that the DNS server has not been configured, despite the fact that one or more zones might actually exist. This is more of an annoyance than anything else.

◈ More disturbingly, you'll find that although the DNS server is started and the zone will sometimes answer queries, the service is a little flaky.

Although I can find no official documentation of these problems, I've seen them firsthand. Sometimes queries fail, while other times zone transfers fail. Unfortunately, there's no consistency to this issue. So do the smart thing and use the wizard. If you've already created the first zone, make it "wizard-official" by following these steps.

NOTE: Any zone that is created by the Active Directory Installation Wizard is considered the first zone for a DNS server. In that situation, the following steps aren't required.

1. Launch the wizard by right-clicking the desired server's object and choosing Configure The Server from the shortcut menu (or by choosing Action | Configure The Server). Either action opens the inevitable Welcome screen, which lets you know that you've just chosen to run the wizard that you've chosen.

2. Click Next to move on to the next screen, which asks if you want to configure a forward zone now or later. Choose No, Do Not Create A Forward Lookup Zone, and click Next.

3. At the Confirmation screen, click Finish to complete the transaction.

You're now ready to rock and roll.

If you haven't already created the first zone, launch the wizard as described in the preceding instructions and step through the wizard screens as follows:

1. Move past the Welcome screen.

2. When the wizard asks if you want to configure a forward zone now or later, choose Yes, Create A Forward Lookup Zone.

3. Select the correct zone type; Standard Primary, Standard Secondary, or AD-Integrated (covered later in this chapter).

4. Enter the name of the zone.

5. If you've chosen a Standard zone, you're prompted to either create a new file or to import an existing zone file.

6. The wizard asks if you want to create a reverse lookup zone. If you choose the Yes option, move through the screens to select the zone type, enter the network ID, and name the zone. Then create a new file or use an existing file.

7. Click Finish on the Summary screen.

Zones and Zone Creation

Now that you've been forewarned about the Configure the DNS Server Wizard, let's talk about the more practical way to create a zone—manually. Before I detail the steps, I'd like to discuss some of the changes in the definition of traditional zone types, plus the addition of a new zone type in Windows 2000 DNS server.

The Microsoft-provided DNS Server supports both standard primary and secondary zone types. In addition, the service also supports a zone type that is unique to the Microsoft implementation called an Active Directory-Integrated zone, or AD-Integrated zone.

Standard Primary and Standard Secondary Zones

Although the name is slightly different, the concept—technology and use of Standard primary and secondary zones versus plain primary and secondary zones—is the same. As with all other implementations of DNS, a Microsoft Standard primary zone is the only zone that can accept changes to the database, while a Standard secondary zone is a read-only copy of the primary zone. Microsoft's naming and implementation of Standard primary and secondary zones is just a way of drawing a line between traditional zones and Active Directory-Integrated zones.

Standard Zone Data

The Standard zone's database is just a text file with a unique extension that houses its data and supporting files in the traditional Microsoft DNS location %SystemRoot%\System32\Dns. You might see any or all of the following files:

- *Name.domain*.dns – This is the zone file for the domain that has the same name as the file. The name of this file can be changed to a name different from the name of the zone, but I wouldn't recommend it.

- Cache.dns – This is the file that houses all root hints when the zone is not AD-Integrated.

- Dns.log – This is used to capture DNS logging information when configured via the DNS MMC.

- Boot (no extension) or Boot.dns – This is the BIND boot file that can be used to support certain configurations. The use of the boot file isn't defined in any RFC but is added for completeness.

Creating a Standard Zone

The creation of a Standard primary and secondary zone is straightforward:

1. Open the DNS MMC and right-click the server on which you want to create the zone.

2. Choose New Zone from the shortcut menu. This launches the New Zone Wizard.

NOTE: You can also launch the wizard by right-clicking the Forward or Reverse Lookup Zones folders in the MMC. You must select the appropriate zone folder before you right-click, or the New Zone command is dimmed.

3. Move past the Welcome screen and select Standard Primary from the Zone Type list. Select either a Forward or Reverse zone.

- If the zone is Forward, enter the name of the zone. Then specify a new or existing file.

- If the zone is Reverse, in the Network ID section of the screen, enter the network portion of the segment's address for which the zone is being created. For example, if you had a server with an IP address of 10.1.2.3 and a subnet mask of 255.255.255.0, the network ID is 10.1.2 and the host ID is 3.

    ◆ You can also create the zone by entering the correct in-addr.arpa zone name in the Reverse Zone Name dialog box. This is actually the purist's way to create a reverse lookup. (By specifying the network ID as detailed previously, the software is just taking the information and naming the zone for you.)

4. Specify a new or existing file, and click Finish on the Summary screen.

AD-Integrated Zones

Active Directory-Integrated (AD-Integrated) zones are a Microsoft-exclusive zone type. Rather than being housed as a single file, an AD-Integrated zone is housed in Active Directory on all of the domain controllers in the domain that AD-Integrated DNS was established. This enables all of the benefits of AD to be extended to the DNS database. AD-Integrating your zone is the best choice even if you're currently using another competing product. Switch!

Benefits of Active Directory Integration

There are many enhancements when using AD-Integrated zones over Standard zones, including security, replication, availability, and accessibility.

Security   One major benefit of implementing AD-Integrated zones over other solutions that provide dynamic updates is security above and beyond that defined in the DDNS RFC. The RFC detailing dynamic updates doesn't address registration collision or entry ownership. Entry ownership defines who or what can update the particular record and protects the entries in case of a registration collision, which occurs when two devices attempt to register the same name or sets of services in the same namespace. The problem which needs to be addressed is how to prevent an entity from modifying data in a DDNS zone that it doesn't own. How do you ensure that only a device that owns a record can update that record or that when a registration collision does occur it is handled correctly? These are critical questions that should be asked in any DDNS implementation.

    RFC 2137 is still just a proposed standard—which I guess doesn't matter given the fact that DDNS itself is described in a proposed standard RFC. Anyway, RFC 2137 details security for DDNS as it relates to the transaction between the client and server and the entries within the directory. The area of securing the dynamic transaction focuses on the encryption/validation/authorization methods used to secure communications between the client and server. RFC 2137, which has been partially inked by some of Microsoft's finest, recommends the use of digital signatures in conjunction with SIG RRs to secure entries. Unfortunately, Windows 2000 doesn't support RFC 2137 at this time. The lack of support might have to do with the amount of additional overhead that is incurred with the use of digital signatures, or it could be because it requires the addition of a PKI solution into any environment wanting to leverage it. Who knows? Clearly, Microsoft thought they had a better solution than that outlined in RFC 2137.

Microsoft has chosen to implement another solution that's available only in their DNS implementation. They make use of the globally unique identifier (GUID) associated with the device that is registering the entry to secure the same entry. The GUID is a unique number that's assigned to each object when it is created in the directory. Security by use of the GUID is achieved by giving the Creator Owner group Full Control permission over the objects. Once a device or entity registers resource records, its GUID becomes the Creator Owner for the objects that it has just registered. The result is that any objects registered by said device or entity will be updated only by the object with the same GUID. So if another device with the same name attempts to register the same records, the object won't be ACLed in a manner that would permit overwriting or modification of the record. This behavior is known as implementation of secure updates.

There is only one flaw with implementing an AD-Integrated zone caused by one if its strong points: Active Directory. Because the DNS records are replicated via AD, replication latency can create an interesting situation concerning security of entries. Be aware that updates to DNS can sometimes take a while to replicate throughout your enterprise, depending on its size.

For example, User A located in San Jose comes into work at 8:31 A.M., boots her machine, and registers the host name of Computer A with the AD-Integrated DNS server named DNS1. User B, who is located in Torrance, comes into work at 8:45 A.M., boots his machine, also named Computer A, and registers with his AD-Integrated DNS server, named DNS2, without error or issue. This duplication of unique host names is possible because both users are registering with different DNS servers that haven't had time to replicate their contents yet. Once the servers do get around to replicating data, a replication collision will occur as a result of the objects having the same Lightweight Directory Access Protocol (LDAP) name and path.

When replication collisions occur, AD handles them by assuming that the newest record or the one with the most recent timestamp is the correct record. Since User A's record is the oldest, AD will rename it with a random identifier known to administrators as a sign of collision, and then replicate what it thinks is the good record, User B's record, to the rest of the directory.

The good news is that this is no different from what it was in the Windows Internet Name Service (WINS). You were always at the mercy of name resolution data replication back then, whether you knew it or not. The chance of a naming collisons occurring in AD is greatly reduced because of its replication scheme.

CODE BLUE

An issue that I'd like to mention here (it's discussed in greater detail in Chapter 5) is how you address name registration when a device that dies is rebuilt using the same name but given a new GUID when placed into the directory when using secure updates in DDNS. At first, you would think there's no problem with this situation, but there is. Because the device's old records in DNS are secured by its old GUID, the directory won't be able to tell the difference between the same device that has been rebuilt or a new device trying to register the same data. The only way to resolve this problem is to hunt down and kill off the old registrations. Unfortunately, there's no built-in tool to do this. Check out Chapter 4 for details on how to use LDAP to do your dirty work!

Replication   Another neat feature that's enabled by implementing an AD-Integrated zone is the extremely granular replication of DNS entries. Because replication is handled by the directory replication engine, DNS replication occurs at the attribute level, not at the object level (as is the case with IXFR). Once your DNS entries are in the database, any changes to the object, such as an update to a timestamp or a change in the IP address of the record, are the only items replicated. For example, take a device that has registered an A record for Computer 1. Initially, the whole record is placed into DNS and is replicated between domain controllers. If the device were to get a new IP address the next day through DHCP, after it updated its IP address with its DNS server, only the new IP would be replicated to other DNS servers. This is a huge performance increase over even IXFR transfers, which replicate at the entry level. In the same scenario, if I were using IXFR, even though only my IP address changed, the whole record would be replicated to all DNS servers.

NOTE: Because this feature is available only between AD-Integrated zones, if you have implemented Standard secondary zones, they will need to continue to receive either AXFR or IXFR updates from the AD-Integrated zones.

There are also replication performance increases due to the compression algorithm used between domain controllers housing DDNS in AD. This compression scheme can reduce

WAN traffic by up to 85 percent when replicating domain contents, including DNS data. Now for those of you who come from an old-school DNS world, you may be thinking, "Big deal, the DNS database isn't that big, so there won't be that many replication events." Although this might have been true in the days when DNS housed only selective records that were placed manually in the database, the new initiative in Windows 2000 to move from WINS to DDNS will result in all of the devices and services that once registered in WINS to register in DNS. Within the next three years, DNS will be used more than any of us would've expected. In addition to the new and more widespread use of DNS, you'll see more frequent traffic as a result of dynamic updates caused by events like reboots or changes to the timestamp of an entry: more data with more dynamic properties.

Availability   Because all domain controllers in an AD domain that houses DNS will have a replica set of the database, availability is increased. Even if only one of your domain controllers is functioning as a DNS server, because all domain controllers already have the data, bringing a new DNS server online is a snap. All you need to do is install the service on one of the existing domain controllers and you are ready to resolve names. Also, because master copies of the database exist in multiple places, the level of impact due to corruption or failure is greatly reduced.

Accessibility   Because the database is housed in an LDAP directory, the number of tools available to access DNS data increases. You have the ability to script changes using any scripting language you're familiar with as long as they support LDAP. You can also write custom consoles and interfaces to massage DNS data. LDAP gives you endless possibilities when compared to DNS data access methods in the past.

Data Location

As stated before, the DNS database is housed in Active Directory. Active Directory itself is a single file named Ntds.dit that sits in the %SystemRoot%\System32\Ntds directory of all domain controllers by default. The DNS information exists in a Naming Context (NC) within the directory.

Naming Context

A *Naming Context* is a partition in the Active Directory that might or might not serve as a replication boundary. In theory, this allows data in the directory to have different security and administrative boundaries and configurations. DNS is one NC in Active Directory that isn't an independent replication boundary. This means that when you install an AD-Integrated zone on a domain controller of a domain, all domain controllers in that domain will receive a replica set of the DNS database. The only difference is that the other servers, although holding the data, haven't been configured for DNS and will therefore not answer DNS queries.

Because an AD-Integrated zone is an NC, not just a file, it can be manipulated either through the DNS MMC or through any tool that exposes LDAP objects that are contained within the directory. Two examples of such tools that are included with Windows 2000 Server are AD Users and Computers and LDP.

The ability to access the DNS data through any LDAP tool is a very nice feature indeed! It allows great flexibility in scripting and manipulation of DNS objects, because all objects are accessible via LDAP instead of some proprietary protocol or tool. By using any supported scripting language (VBScript, JavaScript, Perl), you can now make calls to AD and view or modify contents.

DNS objects in AD are just LDAP objects that are retrieved by the DNS service when a query is received. All objects are in the LDAP path:

ou=*domain.com*, cn=microsoftdns, cn=system, dc=*domain*, dc=*com*

where

* *domain.com* – The FQDN of the domain that houses the AD-Integrated zone

* *microsoftdns* – The DNS NC

* *system* – The System NC

* *domain* – The leftmost name of the domain that houses the AD-Integrated zone

* *com* – The rightmost name of the domain that houses the AD-Integrated zone

The dc= LDAP parameters are used to define a single domain level in an LDAP path. As a result, you might have more than two dc= parameters depending on the number of domains in your environment. For example, if you have two AD domains, one named dom1.domain.com and the other named domain.com, your LDAP path to the AD-Integrated zone in the dom1 domain is the following:

ou=dom1.domain.com, cn=microsoftdns, cn=system, dc=dom1, dc=domain, dc=com

The MicrosoftDNS Naming Context will always contain at least two objects within it. All objects that are direct child objects of MicrosoftDNS are not OUs, although their LDAP path and their display in AD Users and Computers appear as if they are. In reality, they are containers within the directory. In the MicrosoftDNS NC you'll see a dnsZone object for each AD-Integrated zone you've created.

In addition to finding a dnsZone object for each AD-Integrated zone you've created, you will also find a RootDNSServers object that also has a dnsZone object type. If you haven't guessed what's in this container, I'll tell you. It holds all of the root hints for a zone, whether they're customized hints or the Internet default hints.

Objects contained within any container that has a type of dnsZone are dnsNode objects. These dnsNode objects ate the entries that each client placed in DNS during the registration process. Each entry has a name that reflects the FQDN of the registration for any given object, both dynamically updated and manually created. Each AD object, including dnsZone and dnsNode, are defined in the AD schema.

Schema

A *schema* in any database is a template governing the data that can be contained in the database. It defines which type of data the database can contain, in addition to information on how that data should be configured. All objects in AD have a class associated with their object type in the schema. A *class* is a definition of an object type that contains information about the attributes that object must contain. For example, there is a User class in the AD schema, which allows user objects to be among those contained in its data.

Attribute Class

When a class dictates that a certain attribute will be part of an object, it references an attribute class. An attribute class defines a single attribute as well as the data that the attribute can store. For example, two attribute classes found in the default schema are userPassword and accountExpires. These attributes contain very specific information that is exposed by an object.

Each class contains two types of attribute classes: those that are mandatory and those that are optional. *Mandatory attributes* must be part of the object; otherwise, the object can't be created. *Optional attributes* are just as the name states—nice to have but not required. In yet another example, the user object has a class named User, a mandatory attribute of userPassword, and an optional attribute of accountExpires. This means that every user account created in AD must have a password (even if blank). It also means that while you can specify an expiration date for an account, you don't need to populate this attribute to create the object.

 NOTE: There's also a concept of relationships between classes that can define any class that is a parent or auxiliary class, which allows for inheritance or augmentation of attributes. Because none of the classes discussed here use these features, I'm not addressing that topic.

Each class has a default Access Control List (ACL) implemented. This ACL defines the default security that's established, despite any other configuration, when a new object that uses the class is created.

Now that we have some of the oversimplified explanations of schema, classes, and attribute classes out of the way, let's get back to the two object types that we're concerned with: dnsZone and dnsNode.

dnsZone

Each AD-Integrated zone created in the directory has an object in the Microsoft DNS container with a class of dnsZone. This is a structural class type and holds configuration information about the zone. dnsZone contains only one mandatory attribute, DC, which is used to specify classes that are domain components. dnsZone also has the following optional components:

❖ dnsAllowDynamic – Single value Boolean attribute that turns dynamic updates (DDNS) on and off

❖ dnsAllowXFR – Single value Boolean attribute that turns Incremental Zone transfers on and off. If IXFR is turned off, AXFR is used

❖ dnsNotifySecondaries – Multivalued Integer attribute that specifies which secondary servers should receive notification when there is an update to the zone

❖ dNSProperty – Multivalued octet string that holds multiple configuration parameters about a given zone

❖ dnsSecureSecondaries - Multivalued integer attribute that specifies which secondary servers should receive secure updates

❖ managedBy – Distinguished Name single value attribute that allows you to specify the owner and/or manager of a zone

NOTE: The contents of your optional attributes might be different due to modification of the default schema.

The default ACL for the dnsZone Class is as follows:

❖ Domain Administrators – Full Control

❖ Enterprise Domain Administrators – Full Control

❖ System – Full Control

❖ Authenticated Users – Create All Child Objects

❖ Everyone – Special (List Contents, Read All Properties, and Read Permissions)

NOTE: This is the default for a domain that hasn't implemented Pre-Windows 2000 Security. Therefore, the omission on the Pre-Windows 2000 group in addition to escalated privilege of the Everyone group is expected. Keep in mind that these security settings are applied to all new dnsZone objects created in AD.

You might run into certain situations where your idea of what the default ACL should be and Microsoft's idea of what the default ACL should be don't jibe. You have two options in this situation. You can either manually change the zone's ACL each time a new zone is created, or you can modify the security setting on the dnsZone class, which will change what the schema considers the default ACL for the class.

CAUTION: Before I go any further, I want to mention that the following steps involve modification to the schema, which is irreversible in Windows 2000. Also, any modification to the schema results in the complete replication of not only the schema, but also all contents of the Global Catalogs (GCs). In other words, if you do attempt this, do it after hours (preferably on a Friday) to ensure complete replication by the time users need to access the directory. One more word of caution: I can think of no reason to modify this default ACL, but you might, so I've added this for completeness. Enjoy.

1. Open the Active Directory Schema MMC in the security context of either the Enterprise Domain Administrator or the Domain Administrator of your root-level AD domain.

2. Under the Console Root object, double-click the Active Directory Schema object. This will cause the schema to be enumerated.

3. Once the Classes and Attributes object appear under the Active Directory Schema object in the left pane, right-click Active Directory Schema and select Operations Master from the shortcut menu.

4. Select the check box labeled The Schema May Be Modified On This Domain Controller. This unlocks the schema and allows the change.

5. Click OK.

6. Double-click the Class object in the left pane.

7. Scroll down and find the dnsZone object. Double-click it.

8. Click the Security tab.

9. Add the correct accounts and groups with permissions as needed.

10. Click OK when finished.

11. Right-click Active Directory Schema and select Operations Master from the shortcut menu.

12. Clear the check box The Schema May Be Modified On This Domain Controller to lock the Schema again. This step is very important. All objects that you create from this point forward will now implement your defined ACL by default.

The change should be available immediately, despite the fact that the GCs might not have replicated yet.

dnsNode

Each dnsZone object contains one or more dnsNode objects. dnsNode objects contain the data about resource records within a zone. Despite the type of resource record the entry is, (CNAME, A, SRV, etc.), the entry in the directory appears as an object with a class of dnsNode.

The dnsNode class is structural in nature, and it has only one mandatory attribute class, which is DC. It's optional attribute classes are as follows:

❖ dnsProperty – Multivalued octet string that contains configuration information about the zone that houses the resource record

❖ dnsRecord – Multivalued Octet String that contains all configuration information about the dnsNode, including resource record type, Unique Sequence Number (USN), last modification, etc.

❖ dNSTombstoned – Single value Boolean attribute that flags an entry as tombstoned, which means that it is as good as deleted. The valid values are True or False.

Just as with all other schema-defined classes, the security assigned in the ACL of the class in the schema dictates the default security of a newly created record. The default security is as follows:

❖ Domain Administrators – Full Control

❖ Enterprise Domain Administrators – Full Control

❖ System – Full Control

❖ Creator Owner – Full Control

❖ Everyone – Special (List Contents, Read All Properties, and Read Permissions)

NOTE: The default ACL of dnsNode is subject to change based on a particular implementation. The previously mentioned ACL is for a zone that accepts secure dynamic updates, so the addition of Creator Owner as an account that has full control of a new dnsNode object is needed.

As was the case with dnsZone, the default ACL given when a new object is created can be modified. All of the same warnings and declaimers mentioned in the "dnsZone" section should be noted here as well. I still don't know why you would want to do this, but….

1. Open the Active Directory Schema MMC in the security context of either the Enterprise Domain Administrator or the Domain Administrator of your root-level AD domain.

2. Under the Console Root object, double-click the Active Directory Schema object to enumerate the schema.

3. Once the Classes and Attributes object appear, under the Active Directory Schema object in the left pane, right-click Active Directory Schema and select Operations Master from the shortcut menu.

4. Select the check box The Schema May Be Modified On This Domain Controller to unlock the schema and allow the change.

5. Click OK.

6. Double-click the Class object in the left pane.

7. Scroll down to the dnsNode object and double-click it.

8. Click the Security tab.

9. Add accounts and groups with permissions as needed.

10. Click OK when finished.

11. Right-click Active Directory Schema and select Operations Master from the shortcut menu.

12. Clear the check box The Schema May Be Modified On This Domain Controller to lock the Schema again. This step is very important. All objects that you create from this point forward will now implement your defined ACL by default.

The Domain and Zone Relationship

Because an AD-Integrated zone is an NC within Active Directory, it makes sense that an AD-Integrated zone can be implemented only on a domain controller. When an

AD-Integrated zone is created on a domain controller, not only is the zone created in AD, but the domain controller that you used to create the zone becomes a source to answer queries for that namespace.

CODE BLUE

Once again, keep in mind that because Windows 2000 replicates all Naming Contexts within a domain to all domain controllers in the domain, creation of an AD-Integrated zone results in the creation of a MicrosoftDNS NC that's replicated to all domain controllers. This means that if you have 10 domain controllers in a domain, and only one of them has the DNS service installed, all 10 still have the DNS zone(s) in their replica set of the directory. That's a lot of additional replication traffic for the 90 percent of the servers that aren't DNS servers. The ability to selectively determine which NC gets replicated to which DC might be enabled in future releases of the product but is not supported in Windows 2000.

There is also a small problem with AD's inability to replicate certain NCs between domain controllers in multiple domains, as is the case with the MicrosoftDNS NC. Think of a scenario where you have both a root AD domain and a child domain, and you'd like to have all of your domain controllers act as DNS servers. Too bad. This isn't a possibility. Only the domain controllers that are in the domain where the zone was created can be authoritative for the zone. Actually, it isn't a problem with AD's technical inability to complete this task, because quite a few NCs are replicated between domains.

The real problem is a perceived security risk associated with allowing the NC to span multiple domains. The problem has to do with potential breaches of security when allowing a domain controller in one domain to update a NC that originated from another domain. This violates the security principles of a multiple-domain implementation. It would be nice to be able to use all of your available domain controllers to host DNS. Sure would cut down on costs.

One potential solution is to create multiple zones for a single namespace and leverage delegation. This scenario, which involves implementing a zone in one domain and then delegating another zone to a domain controller in another domain, is useful only if you not only have multiple levels of AD domains, but if you also have clients in those domains. Your only other option is to make your other domain controllers secondary servers, but because secondaries can't accept updates, they'll be of little overall value to Windows 2000 clients.

Creating an AD-Integrated Zone

After learning the differences between the zone types, it's time to configure an AD-Integrated zone. Theory is nice, but playing is fun too.

1. Open the DNS MMC and right-click the DNS server on which the zone will be created.

2. Select New Zone from the shortcut menu to launch the New Zone Wizard.

3. Go past the Welcome screen.

4. Select Active Directory-Integrated.

NOTE: If the Active Directory-Integrated option isn't displayed, the DNS server isn't a DC (so you can't perform this task).

5. Select Forward Lookup Zone or Reverse Zone.

At this point, your actions change depending on whether you're creating a forward lookup zone or reverse zone.

To create an AD-Integrated forward lookup zone, follow these steps:

1. Select Forward Lookup Zone.

2. Enter the name of the zone.

3. Click Finish.

TIP: You can complete the same task by first double-clicking and then right-clicking the Forward Lookup Zone object on the DNS MMC and selecting New Zone. The wizard will assume that you want a new zone with the same type of object you clicked, so don't click the Reverse Lookup Zone object unless you want to create a reverse lookup zone.

To create an AD-Integrated reverse zone, follow these steps:

1. Select Reverse Lookup Zone.

2. In the Network ID section of the screen, enter the network portion of the segment's address for which the zone is being created. For example, if your server has the IP address 10.1.2.3 and a subnet mask of 255.255.255.0, the network ID is 10.1.2 and the host ID is 3.

3. Alternatively, you can create the zone by entering the correct in-addr.arpa zone name in the Reverse Zone Name dialog box. This is actually the purist's way to create a reverse lookup zone. By specifying the network ID as detailed previously, the software is just taking the information and naming the zone for you.

4. On the Summary screen, click Finish.

Adding a New DNS Server to an Existing AD-Integrated Zone

If you have a DNS server that you would like to have house an existing AD-Integrated zone, you will have to configure it in a roundabout way. Follow the procedure in the previous section for creating an AD-Integrated zone, and when you get to the wizard screen that asks for the zone name, enter the name of the existing zone.

An error message appears, stating that a zone with the same name already exists and can't be created again. Click OK. Believe it or not, you've just added the zone to this server as an AD-Integrated zone. Funky way of doing it, huh?

BUG ALERT Keep in mind that when implementing multiple DNS servers that are hosting the same AD-Integrated zone, you must be aware of AD replication. Because DNS is replicated through Active Directory, it's possible that if you create a second DNS server soon after you create the first DNS server, you might cause a replication collision. If the DNS NC hasn't yet been replicated to the second DNS server and you attempt to add the AD-Integrated zone to the server, the DNS server won't find the existing zone and will therefore treat it as a new zone creation. As you might have guessed, once replication occurs there are now two zones with the same name and as a result a replication collision occurs. In a replication collision of zones only the newest zone will survive. To ensure that this does not happen to you, verify that the domain controller that you wish to house the AD-Integrated zone on has received the replica for the new zone before adding the existing zone to it.

Creating a Cache-Only Server

A cache-only DNS server's only task is to perform recursive lookups, return the results, and cache that data for use later. There really isn't any additional configuration besides the installation of the DNS service and DNS information in the TCP/IP protocol stack.

The server must have the DNS service installed, as detailed in the previous pages of this chapter, and it must also be configured to use any available DNS server.

Zone Parameters

Zone parameters are common across Windows 2000 zones. Unless specified otherwise, you can assume that any changes detailed here are made via the zone's Properties dialog box. To open a zone's Properties dialog box, double-click the zone to enumerate it, right-click the zone object, and select Properties from the shortcut menu.

Changing Zone Status

You can use the DNS MMC to pause a zone without stopping the whole DNS service. This is a nice touch when you need to change the configuration or contents of a zone without allowing users to view and/or modify the zone contents.

To accomplish this, click Pause on the General tab of the Properties dialog box. The button name then changes to Start, so you can use it to restart the zone.

Changing Zone Type

You can change the zone from its existing type (primary, secondary, AD-Integrated) to any other zone type. The only limitation is that you can't change an existing zone to AD-Integrated unless that zone is hosted on a domain controller.

You can change the zone type on the General tab of the zone's Properties dialog box. Click the Change button next to the current zone type to open the Select A Zone Type dialog box, and select a new zone type. You'll have to confirm the change.

NOTE: If you change a zone from an AD-Integrated zone to either a primary or secondary zone, a Zone File Name field appears on the General tab. The applet assumes that you want to use the generic naming scheme and location for your zone. To specify an alternate location or name, enter the new location in the GUI.

Configuring the Update Type

Standard primary zones can accept both manual and dynamic updates to the database. In a scenario where the update type is manual, each entry must be entered by an administrator. Dynamic updates provide a means for a device or object to register its own entries at certain intervals. By definition, secondary servers can only answer queries, so this discussion pertains only to AD-Integrated and primary zones. If you have a secondary zone that you want to have accept dynamic updates, you must first change its zone type to primary as outlined previously, and then complete the steps in this section.

By default, dynamic updates are turned off unless you created the zone through the Active Directory Installation Wizard. You can change the ability to accept dynamic updates at any time, but be aware that doing so might disrupt your user base.

A zone has three possible settings in the Allow Dynamic Updates? field on the General tab of the zone's Properties dialog box.

- No – A zone configured like this won't accept any dynamic updates. All entries must be configured manually, as in "old" DNS.

- Yes – This setting allows dynamic but unsecured updates to the zone. No GUID is associated with an entry, so anyone can overwrite any entry. Avoid using this setting at all costs.

- Only Secure Updates – This setting allows dynamic updates but enforces security of records and entries by using the GUID of a device, as explained earlier in this chapter.

Changing the status of dynamic updates is easy. Just select the correct choice from the drop-down menu.

Configuring Aging and Scavenging

Aging is a function that the Windows 2000 DNS service uses to handle stale records that can exist in a zone that accepts dynamic updates. Imagine that an employee has a computer named DeviceA, which is registering with DNS. After a technology update of all systems, the employee is given a new computer that now has the name ComputerA. In this case, both names are registered with DNS, but only one is valid. Without a way to purge the invalid records from the database, the zone can grow enormously and create greater administrative burden.

Just as is the case with security, the RFC that details dynamic updates doesn't address ways to remove invalid entries. To address this problem, Microsoft has implemented two features that are also found in WINS: aging and scavenging.

Aging is the process of placing a timestamp on each entry in the database to determine how old an entry is. Aging is also used by the client to determine when it's necessary to reregister a name or service with DNS. This ensures that the client name doesn't expire in the database. Aging is always enabled on DNS.

 NOTE: When using both dynamic updates and aging, manual entries receive a timestamp of 0, which prevents that record from timing out.

Scavenging provides a method for removing stale records. This ensures that invalid data is removed. Scavenging examines all records and identifies any that can be removed based on of the difference between the timestamp of the record and the current date. Scavenging isn't configured by default, but you can set it at the server, zone, or entry level. Scavenging is a manual process by default, but you can configure it to run at scheduled intervals.

Both aging and scavenging are configured independently at each server or instance of a zone. This means that if a zone is housed on three different servers, you can have three different sets of configuration options to establish your aging and scavenging policies. However, two settings remain constant: No-Refresh Interval and Refresh Interval. These are important settings; see the sidebar on the Refresh and No-Refresh Interval settings later in this section.

Configuring Aging and Scavenging for Servers   When you configure aging and scavenging at the server level, the configuration options specified are applied to all zones housed on that server. To configure aging and scavenging all zones on a server, follow these steps:

1. Right-click the server name in the left pane of the DNS MMC and select Set Aging/Scavenging For All Zones from the shortcut menu.

2. In the Server Aging/Scavenging Properties dialog box, select Scavenge Stale Records to enable scavenging.

3. Change the No-Refresh Interval value as desired.

4. Change the Refresh Interval value as desired.

5. Click OK.

NOTE: If you've specified different settings on any of the zones hosted on this server, you will be prompted to either keep the existing configuration of the zone or to apply the server settings over the zone setting.

Configuring Aging and Scavenging for Zones   Configuring aging and scavenging at the zone level overwrites the options defined at the server level. Settings that are specified for a zone at a particular server are independent of settings for the same zone hosted on another server. To set aging and scavenging for a zone, follow these steps:

1. Open the General Tab in the zone's Properties dialog box.

2. Click the Aging button.

3. In the Server Aging/Scavenging Properties dialog box, select the Scavenge Stale Records box to enable scavenging of records.

4. Change the No-Refresh Interval value as desired.

5. Change the Refresh Interval value as desired.

6. Click OK.

TIP: Any records that were already in the database when aging/scavenging were enabled won't be subject to timestamps or scavenging. This is why it's important to establish these settings early in your deployment.

Initiating Manual Scavenging

The events that kick off manual and automatic scavenging can be configured only at the server level. Here's how you initiate manual scavenging:

1. Right-click the server that you want to have scavenge its zones.

2. Choose Scavenge Stale Resource Records from the shortcut menu.

3. Click OK to confirm.

Configuring Automatic Scavenging

You can configure the server to periodically scavenge for stale records, and I recommend doing so:

1. Open the Properties dialog box for the server that you want to have scavenge its zones automatically.

2. Click the Advanced tab.

3. Select Enable Automatic Scavenging Of Stale Records.

4. Enter a value in the Scavenging Period box.

5. Click OK.

The No-Refresh and Refresh Interval Settings

No-Refresh Interval is a setting, in either days or hours, that specifies the minimum amount of time that needs to pass before an entity can refresh information in DNS. This not only decreases network and processing loads, but it also gives the data time to normalize in the database by preventing multiple registrations for the same object to be replicated at the same time. The default value is 7 days.

The Refresh Interval setting specifies how much time has to pass before a record can be scavenged. This value is kind of misleading because it alone doesn't specify the actual value. To determine the exact amount of time that must pass before a record is scavenged, you must add the No-Refresh Interval value to the Refresh Interval value. The result is the amount of time that can pass before a record is removed unless the client has updated it. Because the default value for the Refresh Interval value is also 7 days, the total time that must elapse without your device registering before it's removed from the database is 14 days.

Configuring Start of Authority (SOA)

The SOA settings on a zone define many parameters of the zone to secondary name servers, including the serial number of the zone, primary server, responsible person, and update parameters. All of this information is located on the SOA tab of the zone's Properties dialog box, and once configured, the data is placed in the SOA RR in the database.

Serial Number   A zone's serial number is used by the secondary servers to keep track of the last change they received from the primary server. Every time the contents of a zone change, the serial number in the SOA is incremented by a factor of 1. This is the number that the secondary server compares to its last known serial number for the zone. If the two don't match, the secondary server requests an update. You can change the serial number manually to force or "help along" replication.

Primary Server   For Standard zones, the primary server is consistent across all secondary servers and is used to point the secondary server at the primary server for administration and replication purposes. If the zone is AD-Integrated, the data that appears in this field is always the name of the server that's hosting this instance of the zone. For example, you might have two domain controllers, both of which host AD-Integrated zones named DC1 and DC2. If you examined the SOA for both devices you would notice that they each placed their own name in the Primary Server field by default.

If this isn't the behavior that you want, you can change the primary server field to point to one or more servers that you want to use as primary servers to the secondaries. You can do this by manually entering the FQDN of the server, entering its IP address, or using the Browse button to locate it.

NOTE: If you don't specify the FQDN and you don't have your domain suffix properly configured, your secondary servers might encounter problems related to resolution of the primary server's unqualified name. It's always best to use the FQDN rather than just the host name.

Responsible Person   You use the responsible person field to announce administrative responsibility for a zone to anyone who can get their hands on Nslookup. It's a little different in that the RP RR that can be placed directly into DNS because it's just a string in the SOA record. You do, however, need to point this entry at a valid RP or equivalent record in the database to enable messaging functionality for administrative purposes. This entry can be unique on each instance of an AD-Integrated zone that is hosted on multiple servers.

Secondary Aging   The following settings dictate the replication-specific events that concern the data found on the secondary server:

❖   Refresh Interval – The Refresh Interval value defined here dictates how long the secondary server will wait until it attempts to ask for updates to the zone from the primary server. By default, this value is 15 minutes.

❖   Retry Interval – This setting defines the amount of time between requests that a secondary server will wait after the Refresh Interval value has expired for a response from the primary server before requesting another update. The default is 10 minutes.

❖   Expires After – This setting is the amount of time that must elapse without an update from the primary server before all data from that zone is considered stale and removed. The default is one day.

❖   Minimum (default) TTL – This setting is the time to live (TTL) for individual records that have been received from the primary server as a result of replication. Removal via scavenging isn't a replicated event, so the secondary server must keep track of the records and remove them if necessary. The default value is one hour.

❖   TTL for this Record – Just as the name specifies, this setting ages the SOA record. The default is one hour.

Configuring Name Servers

The Name Servers tab of a zone's Properties dialog box allows you to add NS records to the database for any other DNS servers. Adding name servers is necessary only if you're using secondary servers, because the addition of NS records is automatic when you enable an AD-Integrated zone on a domain controller. You can use this list of valid name servers in conjunction with secure zone transfers to define which servers are authorized to receive zone transfers.

To add more name servers, click the Add button and either specify the name, enter the IP address, or click Browse to locate the name server you want. You can also set the TTL on this screen for the NS record.

Configuring WINS

The WINS tab allows you to forward all unresolvable name resolution requests to WINS. This makes it easier for an organization to move into DNS and use FQDNs from WINS and NetBIOS gradually. This feature, called WINS Lookup, is supported for both forward and reverse lookup zones. By enabling this feature and entering the IP addresses of the WINS servers, you place a WINS or a WINS-R RR in the database.

You can also modify the cache time-out and the lookup time-out for WINS. The cache time-out is used to specify how long results found in WINS are held in the DNS server's cache, and the lookup time-out specifies how long the DNS server will wait on WINS before assuming that it isn't going to respond.

WINS Lookup is supposed to work only after all other DNS-related methods of resolution have failed. Keep this in mind when considering the implementation of this feature. In addition to acting as a crutch/enabler to keep NetBIOS clients on the wire, it can slow down performance for all users of DNS because all unresolvable queries are subject to a WINS lookup. You can configure WINS Lookup for a forward zone or for a reverse zone. (Chapters 4 and 5 contain more information about interoperability issues related to DNS and WINS design considerations.)

To configure WINS lookup for a forward zone, perform these steps:

1. Click the WINS tab in the forward zone's Properties dialog box.

2. Select Use WINS Forward Lookup.

3. If you want this record to be maintained only on this server's zone, select Do Not Replicate This Record.

4. Enter the IP address of each WINS server to which you want to forward queries.

5. Click the Advanced button to open the Advanced dialog box, where you can adjust the Cache time-out and the Lookup time-out.

To configure WINS lookup in a reverse zone, perform these steps:

1. Open the reverse zone's Properties dialog box and click the WINS-R tab.

2. Select Use WINS-R Lookup.

3. If you don't want this record to replicate, select Do Not Replicate This Record.

4. In the Domain To Append To Returned Name section, enter the domain portion of the FQDN in which the device lives.

5. If you need to adjust the cache time-out and lookup time-out values, click the Advanced button.

Configuring Zone Transfers

Where would we be without good old-fashioned zone transfers? AXFR and IXFR are both supported in Windows 2000 DNS. You can use the Zone Transfers tab in the zone's Properties dialog box to configure the specifics of who gets the transfers, as well as how the notification of changes is handled:

1. Open the Zone Transfers tab of a zone's Properties dialog box.

2. Select Allow Zone Transfers.

3. Specify the servers to which the zone will be transferred, choosing from the following options:

   ❖ To Any Server – Not secure at all. Any device that asks for the zone gets it.

   ❖ Only To Servers Listed On The Name Servers Tab – Saves you the time of inputting the IP addresses of your name servers if they're the only ones allowed to replicate zone information.

   ❖ Only To The Following Servers – Transfers go only to those servers that have been explicitly stated on this screen.

If you select Only The Following Servers, specify the IP addresses of the servers you want to include.

You can also configure the zone to notify secondary servers when the data changes (this is the DNS Notify feature) by following these steps:

1. Click the Notify button to open the Notify dialog box.

2. Select Automatically Notify.

3. Select Server Listed on the Name Servers tab to notify that server.

4. Select The Following Servers to specify a different server (or multiple servers) by entering IP addresses.

NOTE: Microsoft has introduced a feature called *Fast Zone transfers* for servers hosting Standard zones. This feature makes it possible for the primary server to send more than one update to secondary servers in each packet. This is a big change over older implementations where only one change per packet was accepted. Be warned that non-Microsoft DNS servers don't know how to handle this feature and will fail to replicate zone contents if you enable it.

Configuring the DNS Server

Now that we've explored all of the options for configuring all supported zone types, let's talk about the server's DNS configuration. Settings that are configured here determine how the server interacts with clients and other DNS servers, rather than how the zone interacts with clients and other zones. The Properties dialog box for all DNS servers contains six configuration tabs that you can use to dictate the server's configuration. There is a seventh tab, but it's just the standard Security tab and adds nothing unique from a DNS perspective.

All changes made here result in registry changes on the DNS server. For a complete list of registry changes, please consult Appendix A.

Interfaces

This tab configures the IP addresses that listen for DNS queries from clients. This is useful if you have a device with more than one NIC and you want to channel all DNS-related traffic only to one card or address. This is an important feature if your device is acting as a firewall of an RRAS router because it allows you to be selective as to which segment's queries are answered.

Forwarders

Forwarding is asking another defined server (not a root-level server) to resolve a name query. This is useful if you have multiple dissimilar namespaces that must resolve names among themselves. In Windows 2000 DNS, forwarding isn't available for a root-level DNS server.

The Forwarders dialog box also allows you to configure how much time expires before a query is considered outstanding, and it is either sent to the next configured Forwarder or returns an error.

You can also turn off recursion in the context of forwarding. This forces the server to act as iterative, handing Forwarders back to the clients that are requesting data instead of finding the answer itself.

In this version of DNS, you have no way of associating a particular Forwarder with a domain name. This would be useful in situations where multiple namespaces are available for name resolution, but you only want certain queries for certain FQDNs to be sent to certain Forwarders.

Advanced

Use the Advanced tab to configure options that are important when Windows 2000 DNS is interoperating with another flavor of DNS. The following configuration choices are available in the Server Options section of the dialog box:

❖ Disable Recursion – This option forces iterative lookups to be performed only on this server.

❖ BIND Secondaries – This option is used to format data in a manner that won't break or corrupt any BIND-based secondary servers. This function prevents features such as fast zone transfers from being implemented.

❖ Fail On Load If Bad Zone Data – This option prevents the server from coming online if corruption is found in the DNS database.

❖ Enable Round Robin – If more than one IP address exists for a record, the IP addresses will be rotated when sent back to the client in an attempt to load balance across the multiple addresses.

❖ Enable Netmask Ordering – If more than one IP address exists for a record, DNS attempts to provide the clients with the addresses that are closest to them. This is how you enable subnet prioritization. (See the sidebar "Subnet Prioritization.")

❖ Secure Cache Against Pollution – This option tells the server to attempt to clean up results before placing them into cache.

In addition to the choices in the Server Options box, the following configuration choices are also available on the Advanced tab:

❖ Name Checking – This option specifies the supported naming format of entities that attempt to register. (See the sidebar "Supported Name Checking Values.")

❖ Load Zone Data On Startup – This option indicates the source of zone data for the server when the service starts. Your options are From Registry, From File, and From Active Directory And Registry.

❖ Enable Automatic Scavenging Of Stale Records – Selecting this option prevents you from having to manually run scavenges to clear up old records. If you configure scavenging here, it affects all zones hosted on the server. Specify an interval in either days or hours.

Subnet Prioritization

Subnet prioritization is a cool new feature available on all DNS servers no matter what type of zones they're hosting. This feature allows the DNS server to hand you an IP address for a record that's closest to you when more than one IP address has been specified for an RR. This is a potential replacement for round-robin, which rotates between the IP addresses when answering queries.

Supported Name Checking Values

If you're running a pure Windows 2000 DNS environment, you can take advantage of the fact that your system provides extended naming support. This feature is not RFC compliant, but it's nice to have. Each server can be configured to accept one of three types of names:

❖ RFC ANSI – Only supports names that use the character set defined in RFC 1123. This option is the only one to use if you require interoperability with non-Microsoft DNS servers.

❖ Non-RFC ANSI – Permits any character that you provide to it. Used to support characters that might have been supported in WINS but aren't RFC compliant. Don't use this setting if you plan to transfer zone information to a non-Microsoft DNS server.

❖ Multibyte (UTF8) – Allows a non-ANSI character set to be used, such as Unicode. Obviously not RFC complaint.

NOTE: Interoperability and design issues are covered in Chapters 4 and 5.

Root Hints

This tab displays the contents of either the root hints file or the RootDnsServers object, depending on the zone type that you have implemented. You can add or remove entries, or edit existing entries here.

Logging

This tab lets you set advanced logging for transactions. This can be useful for troubleshooting. Because it requires a lot of processing overhead, only enable these logs when necessary. Results are written to the %SystemRoot%\System32\Dns\Dns.log file, which you can view with any text editor.

Monitoring

This tab lets you run multiple tests against the DNS service hosted on the server to determine if it's functioning properly. The tests can be run a single time or looped. Unfortunately, the results aren't ported out anywhere and are available only in this GUI.

Configuring the DNS Services

Two services must be present on all DNS servers: DNS Client and DNS Server. You configure the DNS services the same way you work with any service provided in Windows 2000—

using the Services MMC that replaced the Control Panel Services applet in Windows NT 4. (See the guidelines for services configuration in the section, "Understanding Service Configuration.")

DNS Client Service

The DNS Client service enables requests and queries to be packaged and sent to DNS servers for resolution. The service must run on a DNS server to support recursive and iterative lookups.

   The DNS Client service is bundled in services.exe, found in %SystemRoot%\System32. The service starts automatically and has no default recovery options, does not depend on any service, nor does any other service depend on it. It logs on using the Local System account.

DNS Server Service

The DNS Server service runs on any device that is a DNS server or that just has the service installed but not configured. It's responsible for resolving FQDN for clients.

   The service is launched from Dns.exe, which is located in %SystemRoot%\System32. It loads automatically, has no default recovery options, and logs on as Local System. Although no services depend on it, the DNS Server service depends on the NT LM Security Support Provider and the RPC Service.

CODE BLUE

Did you notice what I stated when I explained the dependencies of the DNS Server service? The DNS service depends on NTLM! How dumb is this? When I first started working with Microsoft on Windows 2000 in the Joint Development Program, I wanted to create a brand new parallel environment for Active Directory that used only Kerberos. My utopian dream was quickly shot down when I learned that every time I stopped NTLM, my DNS service stopped. (This was in early Beta code when the Dependencies tab wasn't populated, so I had no way of knowing other than trying.) I tried to get this fixed but was unsuccessful because it would require a major overhaul of the system. Have no fear, I'm trying to get it fixed in the next version of Windows. In the meantime, live with it.

Understanding Service Configuration

Each Properties dialog box for a service in Windows 2000 is exactly the same, containing four tabs that hold configuration settings that you can use to modify or examine all items related to the selected service. The tabs are General, Log On, Recovery, and Dependencies.

Use these guidelines to understand the choices for configuring any service running under Windows 2000.

General Tab   This tab displays specifics of the service, including information about the location and name of the service, and its startup type. You can start, stop, pause, and resume the service here.

Log On Tab   Use this tab to specify whether the service logs on as a Local System Account or by using a standard user account. I recommend using the Local Service Account because it's not subject to any domain account and password policies. For example, if you're using password policies that include the need to change passwords periodically, assigning a user account to a service will probably cause the service to fail the day the old password expires. You can also use this tab to disable or enable the service for specific hardware profiles.

Recovery Tab   Use this tab to specify the computer's response if the DNS Server service fails. The options are designed to respond to repeated failure, and you can escalate the response as the failure problem grows. The following options are available:

* First Failure – Specify either Take No Action, Restart The Service, Run A File, or Reboot The Computer when the first failure of the service occurs.

* Second Failure – Specify either Take No Action, Restart the Service, Run A File, or Reboot The Computer when the second failure of the service occurs. This is handy if you want to first reboot the server in response to the first failure. But if it fails again, you might want to run a file that ports the error out to a log. (It's nice to have the granular options that didn't exist in Windows NT 4.)

* Subsequent Failures – Same options as those found for the first and second failures but applied to the third failure and beyond.

* Reset Fail Counter – Specifies the number of days that must elapse between failures before the fail count is reset. The fail count determines whether a failure is new, a second failure, or a subsequent failure. The default is 0 days, which means that it will never reset and any failure will be considered a subsequent failure. If your DNS Server service generally runs well, specify a larger number so that any failure is considered a first failure.

* Restart Service After – If you've chosen to restart the service as a result of the first, second, or subsequent failures, specify the amount of time the server waits before attempting to restart the service. The default is one minute.

◈ Run File – Specify the location and parameters to be used with the file you launch (if you chose the Run A File option for any failure).

◈ Restart Computer Options – Opens a dialog box that allows you to specify how long the server should wait to reboot after a failure. You can also specify a message that is sent to users. A message such as "Tuff luck, the server is going bye-bye and so is all of your data" is always nice to see pop up on your screen. Make sure to include your phone number for maximum enjoyment.

Dependencies Tab   This tab displays any dependencies this service has on other services, or any services that depend on this service. This is helpful for troubleshooting problems that might be created or compounded by other services. It's also a good way to make sure that you don't create bigger problems by stopping a service that another service depends on, thereby hosing both of them.

Uninstalling the DNS Server Service

I often ask myself why Microsoft implemented the Uninstall API feature, when half the time their own services don't use it. This is the case with DNS. When you uninstall DNS, your machine still has a ton of residual DNS junk sitting around. I think it can actually be considered more than residual because the Uninstall function leaves the database on the drive.

I'm not going to go over the use of the Add/Remove Programs applet for the purpose of removing the service. I already told you how to install it, and I know you're smart enough to figure it out. Instead, I'll go over the tasks that you need to complete to really uninstall the DNS service.

After you uninstall the DNS service, to the casual eye it looks as if the service has been completely removed. However, a number of places continue to hold on to DNS relics: the file system, the registry, and the event log.

Cleaning Up the File System

The Windows 2000 file system is probably the biggest offender when it comes to holding on to DNS information. When you remove a service from a Windows NT product, most if not all of the .dll and .exe files associated with the service are left behind. I guess the argument for this is that you can turn right around and reinstall the service by just pointing the install program at the destination location, and setup will find the old files and use them instead of requiring media.

Cleaning Up %SystemRoot%\System32

This location still contains all of the .dll and .exe files for DNS, even after the service has been removed. You need to manually remove the following files:

- Dns.exe
- Dnsmgmt.hlp
- Dnsmgmt.mcs
- Dnsmgr.dll
- Dnsperf.dll
- Dnsperf.ini

Cleaning Up %SystemRoot%\System32\Dns

This directory holds all of the DNS files for Standard zones, and all of its contents remain after you uninstall the DNS services. This might create a security issue because the server that DNS is being uninstalled from might be put into service for other functions. Who wants an accidental copy of their DNS database to be sitting on a server that might have been redeployed in a nonsecure fashion? The best fix is to delete the entire subdirectory.

Cleaning Up the Registry

Actually, the registry isn't too bad. The only items left behind are class registrations and some information about the DNS Server event log (discussed next). Although information is still in the registry, it isn't doing too much damage. If it's just bugging you to have it there, use Regedit.exe to search on all instances of DNS and remove them. Be careful not to remove any entries that have to do with DNSCACHE and/or DNSAPI because both are needed for DNS resolution.

Cleaning Up the Event Log

Annoyingly, after you remove the DNS service, you can still see the DNS Server event log, along with all of its entries. How did this get missed? To remove the log, you must remove its subkey in the registry. Open a registry editor and delete the subkey HKLM\System\CurrentControlSet\Services\EventLog\DNS Server.

Chapter 3

DNS Client Architecture

W indows 2000 is the first Microsoft operating system to use a service other than the Windows Internet Naming Service (WINS) as the primary method of registering and resolving names and services. The decision to move from WINS to DNS was long overdue. As the computing landscape evolved over the years, Microsoft became the only operating system developer that still used NetBIOS and WINS, which made interoperability difficult. It was also becoming clear to both Microsoft and IT administrators that in large distributed networks and environments of the modern-day corporation, NetBIOS and WINS didn't scale well. Faced with two grim truths—their operating system was becoming a roadblock for interoperability, and the stability of their family of network operating systems was being impeded due to scalability issues with WINS—Microsoft decided to make DNS their new primary name services technology.

Providing a DNS server to their customer was easy for Microsoft because DNS has been bundled with NT since 3.51. The more difficult task was modifying the operating system to use DNS over WINS, and to do so without breaking any applications or services that still depended on WINS.

Managing DNS Clients

Microsoft has provided a DNS client with all versions of their operating systems since Windows 3.1. These clients have always conformed to the RFC specifications for DNS. Until Windows 2000, all Microsoft DNS clients used DNS only as an auxiliary name resolution service. Pre-Windows 2000 DNS clients turned to WINS for dynamic registration of names and services, in addition to using WINS as the primary method to resolve all names. (See more detailed information about WINS in Chapters 6 and 7.)

The release of Windows 2000 marked the beginning of a seemingly NetBIOS-free era for Microsoft operating systems and services. For the first time, NetBIOS and WINS served as the auxiliary name resolution and registration service, taking a back seat to the new primary name registration and resolution technology: DNS.

DNS Usage

Before I talk about the components that make up a DNS client, you need to know how clients use DNS. How your client uses DNS depends on which operating system you're running. DNS clients are able to resolve (and possibly register) names in DNS.

Resolution

Resolution itself can be categorized into two types: resolution of names and resolution of services (also known as a service location).

Directory Service Client

Microsoft bundles the Directory Service Client (DSC) on the CD of all versions of Windows 2000 Server. Dsclient.Msi is an MS Installer package, located in **CDDrive:\Clients\Win9x**, that installs the Directory Service Client. DSC gives Windows 95, 98, and Me the ability to interact with Active Directory. Although the level of functionality is limited when compared to Windows 2000, DSC allows these clients to search and access objects published in AD, as well as query DNS for services hosted on AD. As I am writing this chapter Microsoft has just released DSC for NT 4, which is now available for download from Microsoft.

Name resolution in DNS is used to resolve either a host name to an IP address or an IP address to a host name, as was discussed in Chapter 1. All Microsoft operating systems since Windows 3.1 have supported using DNS to find device names and addresses.

Service location in DNS is the process of asking a DNS server to provide the client either single or multiple device names that are responsible for hosting a particular service. Service location was defined in a relatively new RFC and is supported out of the box only in Windows 2000. Windows 95, 98, and Millenium Edition (Me) support service location by installing the Directory Service Client (DSC).

Registration

Like resolution, registration can be grouped into two categories: name registration and service registration. *Name registration* allows a device to dynamically place A (host) and PTR (reverse lookup) records into the DNS database. *Service registration* is the dynamic process of service record (SRV) placement in DNS, which is used for service location. SRV records define a location, weight, and cost for a particular service hosted on a device.

The registration process can occur by having the client place records into DNS directly, or by using an intermediary service, such as Dynamic Host Configuration Protocol (DHCP), to place records into DNS on behalf of the client. Both methods of dynamic registration are supported in Windows 2000. See the section "DNS Registration" later in this chapter for more details.

Host Names

Each Widows 2000 device must be configured with a host name. A *host name* is an object name that is unique within its namespace. Although each Windows 2000 device should comply with all RFC naming rules, for purposes of backward compatibility with NetBIOS, you can choose to implement a non-RFC host name. If you want to comply with DNS RFC specifications for host names, your Windows 2000 host name can't be longer than 64 characters and can contain only the following characters:

❖ A – Z

❖ a – z

❖ 0 – 9

❖ -

If interoperability is more of a concern than RFC compliance, your host name can contain any character but cannot start with an asterisk character (*) per the NetBIOS RFC.

> **NOTE:** If you choose to implement non-RFC-compliant host names and you're dynamically registering your host data in DNS, your DNS environment must support non-RFC standard names and characters. If support isn't enabled for these types of names, your dynamic registration attempts will fail. To enable non-RFC host-name support on a Windows 2000 DNS server, set the Name Checking option to Non-RFC ANSI, as detailed in Chapter 2.

CODE BLUE

Unfortunately, you can't configure separate names for the host and NetBIOS names in Windows 2000 unless you modify the registry. Instead, in the graphical user interface (GUI), you're asked to provide only a "computer name," which is used as both the host and NetBIOS name. This can create some interesting scenarios because NetBIOS names support not only a 15-character length limitation, but also a completely different character set than host names. Although it's important to mention the connection between host names and NetBIOS names here, this topic and the potential pitfalls are discussed in Chapter 7.

Specifying a Host Name

You're asked to specify a device name when you install the operating system. Although you won't see the words "host name" anywhere in the installation process, this is what you're specifying when you give your device a name. You can specify a different host name after the operating system has been installed by completing the following steps:

1. Open the System Properties dialog box.

2. Click the Network Identification tab, which displays two important pieces of information.

   ❖ **Full Computer Name** – This is the Fully Qualified Domain Name (FQDN) of your device.

   ❖ **Domain** – This is the domain label used in the FQDN.

3. Click the Properties button.

4. In the Computer Name dialog box, type in the new host name for this computer, keeping in mind that it too will be used for the device's NetBIOS name.

5. After you enter the computer name, one of three things will occur:

   ❖ If you enter a name that's less than 15 characters and conforms to DNS RFCs, when you click OK, you'll be prompted to reboot your system in order for the change to take effect.

   ❖ If you enter a name that doesn't comply to DNS RFCs, you'll see an error message indicating that you're about to use a nonstandard name. Once you click Yes to continue to use the nonstandard name, you'll be prompted to restart your system.

   ❖ If you enter a name that's longer than 15 characters, you'll be informed that the name you're about to use is longer than a NetBIOS name is permitted to be, and, as a result, will be truncated. For more information on this error and its effects, please see the "Name Truncation" section in Chapter 7.

Domain Suffix

Your host name is only one of two components that make up your FQDN. The other component is the domain label, or the domain suffix. A *domain suffix* is the domain name portion of the FQDN that is used to qualify your device's host name.

Those of us who have been dealing with NT for years are familiar with the concept of domain membership as it relates to NT. However, the concept of domain membership as it relates to DNS domains and domain suffixes is quite different from what we're used to. In Windows 2000, your device can be a member of one AD domain, and at the same time be known by a FQDN that reflects a completely different domain name.

For example, a client with a host name of ComputerA is a member of an AD domain named ad.domain.com but has a domain suffix dns.domain.com. You might expect that in this scenario, the device's FQDN would be computera.ad.domain.com, but this isn't the case. Because the device has been configured to use a DNS suffix that is different from the AD domain name, its FQDN will reflect the DNS suffix, not the AD domain name. So even though the client is a member of the ad.domain.com domain, its FQDN is computera.dns.domain.com for DNS resolution and registration processes. You do have the ability to use your AD domain name as your DNS suffix by configuring the DNS client, as detailed in the next section.

Windows 2000 supports the use of three types of DNS suffixes: a primary DNS suffix, connection-specific DNS suffixes, and appended DNS suffixes.

Primary DNS Suffix

A primary DNS suffix is appended to the device's host name to establish its FQDN, which is then used to register the device in DNS. The primary DNS suffix is also appended to unqualified queries from the host to its DNS server. This permits an unqualified query for ServerA from hosta.domain.com to be sent to the DNS server as a query for servera.domain.com.

Only one primary DNS suffix can be configured on each device, and it may or may not be the same domain name as the AD domain in which the device has membership. Your device can either be configured to append only the primary DNS suffix to unqualified queries, or it can be configured to use the primary suffix in conjunction with domain devolution. *Domain devolution* enables the client to strip each domain label off the primary suffix, one at a time, to create a new FQDN used for unqualified queries. For example, domain devolution would change the name host1.domain1.domain.com to host1.domain.com if the name host1.domain1.domain.com couldn't be found. This new FQDN would then be sent to the DNS server for resolution. Domain devolution continues to strip off domain labels from the primary DNS suffix until either a name is found or the root domain is reached.

You can modify any device's primary DNS suffix by completing the following steps:

1. Open the System Properties dialog box.

2. On the Network Identification tab, click the Properties button.

3. On the Identification Changes screen, click the More button.

4. On the DNS Suffix And NetBIOS Computer Name screen, type in your desired DNS suffix in the Primary DNS Suffix Of This Computer box.

5. Select the Append Parent Suffixes Of The Primary DNS Suffix check box to enable domain devolution.

6. Close the dialog box. You will be prompted to reboot the system in order for the changes to take effect.

TIP: On the DNS Suffix And NetBIOS Computer Name screen, you'll find an option called Change Primary DNS Suffix When Domain Membership Changes. This option allows you to keep the primary DNS suffix and the name of your AD domain in sync at all times. This is useful if you're leveraging AD and you have devices that don't need to be known as hosts in another domain.

To enable domain devolution, follow these steps:

1. Open Network Connection in Control Panel and select TCP/IP Properties.

2. Click Advanced and go to the DNS tab.

3. Select the Append Parent Suffixes Of The Primary DNS Suffix option.

Connection-Specific Suffixes

Although a Windows 2000 device can have only one primary DNS suffix, you can specify alternate suffixes on each network interface card (NIC), which permits a different FQDN to be registered in DNS for each NIC. This feature is useful for devices that are multihomed and must be known by different names in different namespaces, as would be the case with a firewall or a Routing and Remote Access server.

To configure the connection-specific DNS suffix, complete the following steps:

1. Open the Advanced TCP/IP Settings for the NIC on which you want to configure the DNS suffix.

2. Click the DNS tab.

3. In the DNS Suffix For This Connection field, enter the alternate suffix you want this connection to use.

4. If you want this connection's suffix to be registered in DNS, select Use This Connection's DNS Suffix In DNS Registration.

NOTE: If you don't select Use This Connection's DNS Suffix In DNS Registration, the device will answer clients that directly reference this name, but it won't be resolved in DNS by this name.

Appended DNS Suffixes

Appended DNS suffixes are used for name resolution. When an appended DNS suffix is defined, it is used to change an unqualified query to a qualified query by tacking this suffix on to the host name attempting to be resolved. A device can have as many appended DNS suffixes as desired, but there can be some performance-related problems if too many are used. (See the section "Fine-Tuning Registration" later in this chapter.) Each DNS suffix is appended to an unqualified name in the order defined by the client until either the name is found or all suffixes have been exhausted.

You can add appended DNS suffixes by following these steps:

1. Open the Advanced TCP/IP Settings for the NIC on which you want to configure the DNS suffix.

2. Click the DNS tab.

3. Select the Append These DNS Suffixes (In Order) option to enable the addition of suffixes.

4. Click the Add button.

5. In the TCP/IP Domain Suffix box, type in the name of the appended DNS suffix that you want to use.

6. Click Add. The new suffix appears in the list of suffixes. This change doesn't require a reboot.

NOTE: The priority of a DNS suffix is defined by its location in the Append These DNS Suffixes (In Order) option. You can move the priority of any suffix higher or lower by selecting the suffix and then clicking on either the up or down arrow.

DNS Server Configuration

When using Windows 2000 you have the ability to configure your clients to send resolution requests and registration information to one or more DNS servers. In addition to being able to use multiple DNS servers, you can also set the priority of each DNS server, determining the order in which the client uses a particular DNS server.

You add a DNS server to the client by using the Advanced TCP/IP Properties dialog box. In the DNS Server Addresses section, click the Add button and specify the IP address of the additional DNS server. The server appears in the DNS Server Addresses, In Order Of Use list box. You can change the priority by selecting a DNS server in the list and using the arrow buttons to move the selected DNS server either higher or lower in the list.

CODE BLUE

You can balance DNS performance and availability by specifying multiple DNS servers on a DNS client. However, you can also cause yourself some longterm administrative headaches. Although there's no limit on the number of DNS servers you can specify, an administrative and performance cost is associated with specifying too many. If you specify too few DNS servers, you may be exposing yourself to an availability problem in respect to host name and service resolution. Also, the fewer DNS servers you define, the greater your chance of being affected by a DNS server outage.

What's the magic number? I recommend using no fewer than three DNS servers and no more than four. These numbers represent the right balance between availability and performance. Each server should be located in a different wide area network (WAN) location, if at all possible, to negate any chance of a single network failure causing complete DNS failure for all of your clients.

But here's the possible administrative nightmare: The more DNS servers that are defined on the client, the more likely each client is to have old servers in the client configuration. Administrators commonly configure too many DNS servers per client because many believe this ensures that DNS will function even if one or more DNS servers disappear. These same administrators sometimes feel that because the client keeps on working, due to the sheer volume of DNS servers defined, there's no need to clean up the configuration. As a result, some clients are using high-priority DNS servers that no longer exist. This can cause resolution and registration performance problems. A DNS client walks down the list of DNS servers in an attempt to resolve a name before issuing an error, so make sure that the servers with the highest priority are valid.

DNR, CRS, AND DCS = The Same Service

What do the Domain Name Resolver (DNR) service, the Cache Resolver service (CRS), and the DNS Client service (DCS) all have in common? They are all names that Microsoft has given to the same service, and the names are apparently interchangeable. All three terms are used in different documents to describe the same suite of resolution functions. From this point forward, to reduce confusion, I'll refer to the DNS Client service (DCS) as the single entity that encompasses all three names.

DCS is responsible for intercepting and satisfying all requests for host name and service resolution. When DCS receives a request for a host name, it takes the appropriate actions, using both information found locally on the client as well as information found remotely in DNS. The result is either a success or failure returned to the requesting entity.

Requests for name resolution are made by calling an application programming interface (API) named GetHostByName. When this API is called as a result of a name resolution request sent by an application, service, or user, DCS intercepts the request and resolves the name. I'll discuss the exact steps DCS takes to resolve a name in the "DNS Resolution" section of this chapter. But for now, just know that DCS resolves names on behalf of the client.

The DCS is configured through the Services MMC, which loads as part of Services.exe and doesn't depend on any other services (nor do any other services depend on it). By default, DCS logs on under the local system context, and it takes no corrective action if the service fails to load.

TAKE COMMAND

At the command line, the Domain Name Resolver service, the Cache Resolver service, and the DNS Client service are combined into one service, dnscache. You can stop and start the service (no matter what name you're personally using for it) with the following commands:

> **net stop dnscache**

> **net start dnscache**

DHCP Client Service

I bet you think that because your device is configured with a static TCP/IP address, you're not using the DHCP Client service. Wrong! The DHCP Client service is used on all versions of Windows 2000, no matter what the IP configuration is, to register host names in DNS.

Each time a Windows 2000 device starts, the DHCP Client service parses the system's registry for several registry data items and their values. Once these values have been read, the DHCP Client service determines if the device should register in DNS and, if so, which records should be registered. (For details, see the section "DNS Registration" later in this chapter.)

The DHCP Client service is spawned by the Services.exe suite of system services. It runs in the context of the local system and is not configured to take any corrective action if the service fails to load. You can manually start (or stop) the service in the Services MMC.

TAKE COMMAND

You can stop and start the DHCP Client service at the command line with the following commands:

    net stop dhcp

    net start dhcp

 BUG ALERT You can typically use the Services MMC to determine any dependencies related to a particular service. Although the Services MMC reports that the DHCP Client service doesn't depend on any other service, this isn't true. The DHCP Client service depends on the NetBT (NetBIOS) service. So, if you're planning to disable NetBIOS on your systems, think again. Check out the section "Reality Check: Can NetBIOS Really Be Disabled?" in Chapter 7 to learn the difference between what Microsoft says and what reality dictates.

Netlogon Service

The Netlogon service isn't used by all DNS clients for registration of data in DNS. Only domain controllers use the Netlogon service to place data into DNS. The Netlogon service on domain controllers is responsible for registering two types of records: SRV and A.

Netlogon registers all SRV records that are associated with AD domain controller functions. These functions include the role of Lightweight Directory Access Protocol (LDAP) servers, Global Catalogs (GCs), and the Kerberos Key Distribution Center (KDC), to name a few. Host (A) records for domain names are also registered by Netlogon for the AD domain that the domain controller hosts.

For each record that Netlogon places in DNS, a corresponding entry is placed in the Netlogon.dns file located in the **%*Systemroot*%\System32\Config** directory. This file is extremely useful for troubleshooting domain controller problems that are either related to the domain registering in DNS, or to the ability of clients to resolve services on the domain controller.

The Netlogon service is spawned by Lsass.exe, which is loaded at kernel boot and runs under the local system context. It's configured to take no recovery actions when the service fails. Netlogon depends on both the server and workstation services, but no services depend on it.

TAKE COMMAND

You can start and stop the Netlogon service at the command line by using the following commands:

net start netlogon

net stop netlogon

HOSTS File

For as long as I can remember, Microsoft has implemented its own flavor of a Host.Txt file in the operating system. This file, named HOSTS—which by default is located in **%Systemroot%\System32\Drivers\Etc**—is used as a local host-to-IP address-mapping table just as Hosts.txt was.

You can modify the HOSTS file with any text editor, but the file must always be located in the default directory location unless you specify an alternate location as follows:

Open a registry editor and go to the HKLM\System\CurrentControlSet\Services\ Tcpip\Parameters key. Change the value of the **DatabasePath** data item to reflect the new file location.

CAUTION: If you change the location of the HOSTS file, you must also move the following files to the same new location: LMHOSTS.sam, Services, Networks, and Protocol. The registry entry you modify is for all of those files, not just the HOSTS file.

Entries defined in the HOSTS file are parsed only during a name resolution request. If a match is found in Hosts, the name-to-address information is placed into the client's cache for later use. There's no way to turn the use of the Hosts file on and off; it's always there and always "on." The only way to avoid using it is to make sure the file is empty.

The HOSTS file can contain only host-name-to-IP address information. It holds no information about any other DNS record type, so there's no support for PTR or SVR entries.

CODE BLUE

Using a HOSTS file can significantly increase your administrative burden. As you'll see in the "DNS Resolution" section of this chapter, the HOSTS file is parsed before a request is sent to DNS. If, when the file is parsed, an entry is found that matches the record you're looking for, the DNS Cache Resolver service assumes that this data is correct. This means that bad, stale, or incorrect information in your HOSTS file is treated as if it were valid data. This could result in the name being resolved to the wrong IP address. Because HOSTS files can't be centralized, changing information is cumbersome, which leads to the information becoming stale.

There's no reason to use HOSTS files. If you need to resolve a name that's outside of your namespace, make your DNS servers secondary to the zone in which the other HOSTS are defined. Even enabling forwarding, which is kind of a sloppy way of resolving names, is a better solution than implementing HOSTS files.

HOSTS Syntax

The syntax used in a HOSTS file is very simple. There are no added features that extend the definition of what should be in a Hosts.txt file per the RFC. The syntax is as follows:

IP Address   FQDNofHost #Comment
Where:

- ◆ *IP Address* – The TCP/IP address of the host.

- ◆ *FQDNofHost* – The FQDN of the host that has the IP address defined in *IP Address*.

- ◆ *#Comment* – An optional field that can be used for a description or any comment about the host on the same line as the entry. Any entry that begins with the pound sign (#) is treated as a comment, no matter what its physical location in the file.

Client-Side DNS Cache

The client-side DNS cache provides a mechanism for holding on to host and service names that have been resolved. This means that the DNS client doesn't have to query DNS multiple times for a name that has already been resolved, and is therefore already known. Each time a name resolution request is sent to a DNS server by the DNS Cache Resolver service, the cache is parsed for a match first, even before parsing the HOSTS file. Any previously resolved names are resolved locally by the cache, without any additional network or DNS traffic.

The client-side DNS cache is enabled by default and can be disabled only by setting the **MaxCacheEntryTtlLimit** data item to 1, located in the HKLM\System\CurrentControlSet\ Services\DnsCache\Parameters key. (The default value is 86,400 seconds.) The lower setting prevents the cache from holding any cache results.

If DNS caching is enabled, there's no limit to the number of entries or the amount of memory that Windows 2000 allocates to the DNS cache. However, by default the client-side DNS cache can store only a maximum of 211 rows and 10 columns of data. You can adjust this limit by setting the **CacheHashTableSize** (rows) and the **CacheHashTableBucketSize** (columns) data items located in HKLM\System\CurrentControlSet\Services\Dnscache. Setting a cache limitation by using a maximum number of columns and rows instead of a maximum memory size is something unique to the client-side DNS cache.

Type **ipconfig /displaydns** at the command prompt to view the contents of the client-side DNS cache, as shown in Figure 3-1.

If your DNS cache becomes corrupt or polluted with data that's no longer valid, you can flush it. To purge the cache, enter **ipconfig/flushdns** at the command prompt.

NOTE: You can also clear the cache of a DNS server with the Windows 2000 Resource Kit tool, Dnscmd.exe, by entering **dnscmd <ServerName> /ClearCache**. For more information on other ways Dnscmd can help you administer your DNS servers, check out Chapter 5.

Two types of entries exist in the client's DNS cache: positive and negative. Both positive and negative cached entries are contained in the same cache but are represented differently.

Positive Caching

When any name has been resolved to an IP address successfully and is placed into cache, this is known as *positive caching*. Entries that are placed in the positive cache have a time to live (TTL) equivalent to either the TTL given in the answer to the query by the DNS servers, or by setting the **MaxCacheEntryTtlLimit** data item located in the HKLM\System\ CurrentControlSet\Services\DnsCache\Parameters key of the client.

The value assigned as the TTL is the greater of these two values. In any case, no matter how the registry is configured or which value the DNS server returns to the client, the TTL for positive cached entries can be no longer than one day.

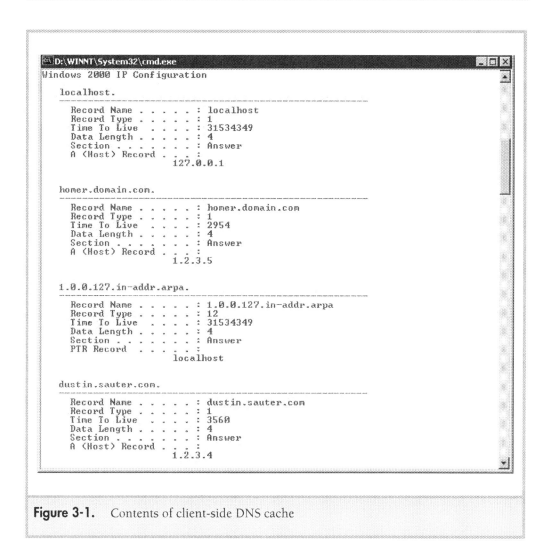

Figure 3-1. Contents of client-side DNS cache

All positive cached entries have the following attributes when stored in cache:

◈ **Record Name** – The FQDN of the device.

◈ **Record Type** – A numerical representation of the DNS resource record type of the resolved device. Although no documentation maps the record type value to a resource record type, the resource record type is stated in the cache. Here are the mappings for some of the more popular resource records:

+ 1 – A

+ 4 – NS

+ 12 – PTR

+ 33 – SRV

+ **Time to Live** – The TTL defined either by the **MaxCacheEntryTtlLimit** data item or the value returned to the client by DNS.

+ **Data Length** – The size of the name cached.

+ **Section** – The definition of how the client-side cache retrieved the mapping information.

Negative Caching

Negative entries in the cache represent an entity or device that couldn't be resolved by DNS. By storing all of the failed lookups locally, the client doesn't continue to ask a DNS server for a name that has already been returned as not found.

By default, each negative entry in the client-side cache has a TTL of 300 seconds. However, because the TTL is configurable, the reality is that negative entries placed into cache have a TTL that is equivalent to the greater value defined in either:

+ The value specified in the **NegativeCacheTime** data item that is found in the HKLM\System\CurrentControlSet\Services\Dnscache\Parameters registry key of the client

+ The value specified in the TTL in the zone's Start of Authority (SOA)

NOTE: Entries in the negative cache can't have a TTL of less than 1 minute or greater than 20 minutes.

Entries for negative responses from DNS store very little information in the cache. The only items that are housed in the cache are the FQDN of the failed lookup, a TTL, and an indicator that this entry is the result of negative caching.

DNS Registration

A Microsoft client can update DNS in two ways: direct registration and DHCP registration. In both cases, as specified in RFC 2136, Windows 2000 supports the dynamic registration only of A, PTR, and SRV records. For the purposes of registration, a distinction is made between domain controllers in this chapter and nondomain controllers (nondomain controllers include Windows 2000 Professional devices too) due to different behavior.

Direct Registration

Direct registration occurs when the client directly updates records in the DNS database. There is no middleware or helper service used between the client and the DNS server in a direct registration scenario. This method is supported only in Windows 2000. The following events cause registration to occur:

- Twenty-four hours passing since the last registration
- A TCP/IP configuration change
- A DHCP lease change
- A Plug and Play event that affects the Network Driver Interface Specification interface
- A Reboot/boot

All of these events cause the exact same chain of events to unfold. For the purposes of this discussion, in the following sections, I'll assume that the registration event is the result of a system boot or reboot.

TAKE COMMAND

You can force registration at any time on a Windows 2000 client by typing

ipconfig /registerdns

at the command prompt. This forces the system to reregister all DNS data, regardless of the existing state of the client. This command line also forces the reregistration of records registered by Netlogon.

How Nondomain Controllers Register Directly

A nondomain controller device, which is any device that isn't hosting AD, uses the DHCP Client service for all aspects of name registration. When names are registered, they're either unique in the zone or they are duplicated. Let's examine both scenarios.

Registration with No Name in Conflict

One of the first tasks that completes on the Windows 2000 client at boot time is the DNS discovery process. The system, using either the information that has been statically configured or that which has been sent through DHCP, attempts to locate the authoritative DNS server for the zone in which the host wants to register. The configured DNS servers are queried and return a response to the client, which includes the IP address of the authoritative name server.

The system also parses the registry at system boot and looks for the value of the **DisableDynamicUpdate** data item found in HKLM\System\CurrentControlSet\Services\Tcpip\ Parameters. If the value is set to 0 or the data item doesn't exist, then the system is configured to dynamically update DNS. If the value on the device is set to 1, then dynamic update is disabled and registration can't occur.

Once the system determines that dynamic updates can be performed, it parses the HKLM\ System\CurrentControlSet\Services\Tcpip\Parameters\Interfaces*InterfaceName* registry key, looking for the data item **DisableDynamicUpdate**. If this item doesn't exist or exists with a value of 0, then this interface supports dynamic updates. If the value of this item is set to 1, then dynamic updates aren't supported on this interface. All instances of HKLM\System\ CurrentControlSet\Services\Tcpip\Parameters\Interfaces*InterfaceName* are parsed to determine which NICs, if more than one is present, register information in DNS even if dynamic updates have been enabled on the system as a whole.

NOTE: If you want to change your client's behavior by either enabling or disabling dynamic updates on a particular NIC, you can either modify the registry item **DisableDynamicUpdate**, or you can clear the Register This Connections Addresses In DNS check box found on the DNS tab in the Advanced TCP/IP Settings dialog box.

After determining which NICs register data in DNS, the system must determine which type of data is registered. By default, the DHCP Client service registers only the A records of a device. To determine whether PTRs should be registered in DNS for this device, the system parses the HKLM\System\CurrentControlSet\Services\Tcpip\Parameters key and reads in the value of the **DisableReverseAddressRegistration** data item. If the value of this item is set to 0 or the data item isn't present, then PTR records are placed into DNS by the client. If the value is 1, then no PTRs for any NIC are placed into DNS.

Unsecured and Secured

Unsecured as it relates to DNS means that the client hasn't provided credentials to the DNS server that can be used, in conjunction with an access control list (ACL), to grant rights. Unsecured updates are still subject to encryption algorithms in use on the client and server.

Secured means the exact opposite. In a secured update, the client sends credentials that are used with an ACL to either grant or deny access. In the context of DNS, secured doesn't imply any additional protocol or transmission security.

Now that the system has established the type of records that have to be placed into DNS, it needs to determine the data contents of the records being registered. It does this by looking for the **EnableAdapterDomainNameRegistration** data item located in HKLM\System\CurrentControlSet\Services\Tcpip\Parameters\Interfaces*InterfaceName*. The value of **EnableAdapterDomainNameRegistration** specifies whether the system registers only its host name in DNS or registers the complete FQDN.

The system is now ready to send the registration request to the DNS server. The DHCP Client service takes the information that has been gathered about registration for the device and sends a registration request to the DNS server that is determined to be authoritative.

When the DNS server receives the update request, what occurs next depends on the configuration of the DNS server. A DNS server that accepts dynamic updates can either be configured to use unsecured updates or secured updates.

Direct Registration Using Secured Updates

If the DNS server is using secured updates, the following processes occur when the server receives a registration request from the client.

CODE BLUE

By default, all Windows 2000 clients initially attempt to send dynamic updates to DNS unsecured. If the unsecured update fails as a result of a secured configuration on the DNS server, the client attempts a secured update to DNS.

The default behavior of always trying unsecured updates first is unnecessary in an environment that strictly leverages secured updates, and may cause excessive and unneeded network traffic. I recommend changing this behavior by modifying the value

of the **UpdateSecurityLevel** data item in HKLM\System\CurrentControlSet\Services\
Tcpip\Parameters. Change the value to 256, which forces the client to use secured
updates, significantly reducing your network traffic.

Other supported values for **UpdateSecurityLevel** are the following:

❖ **0** – Sends secure dynamic updates only if DNS refuses nonsecure updates.
  This is the default behavior if the **UpdateSecurityLevel** data item isn't present.

❖ **16** – Sends only unsecured updates.

Although modifying this data item increases performance for your clients, keep in
mind that if you set either a value of 16 or 256, updates to an environment that doesn't
support your value will fail.

1. DNS uses the Globally Unique Identifier (GUID) of the device to verify that it has the
   ability to update the zone. If the machine has permission to write to the zone, the
   process continues. Permission levels can be determined only for a device which is
   defined directly in the ACL or which belongs to a group that has been defined in the
   ACL. If the DNS server can't find a match in the ACL, an access denied message is
   sent back to the client, and an event is recorded in the client's Event Log. Assuming
   the ability to write to the zone has been established, DNS then parses the database
   to find any duplicate names that are already registered in the zone. When none are
   found, the server writes the new records to the correct zone.

2. Once the records are written, they are secured by giving the Creator Owners group
   Full Control permission. In the case of this object, the Creator Owner is the device
   that created and registered the record.

3. The record is given a TTL, and the DNS server may also write some unique information
   about the record to the database for purposes of replication (depending on the DNS
   server implementation).

4. The DNS server packages a success message that includes the TTL for the records,
   which is 20 minutes by default. This message is sent to the client.

Direct Registration Using Unsecured Updates

If the DNS server is using secured updates, the following processes occur when the server
receives an update request from the client.

1. The DNS database is parsed to find any duplicate names that may exist in the zone. If no duplicate names exist, the records are written to the zone and given a TTL in addition to any other information written that is unique to the DNS implementation.

2. A success message is packaged with the TTL for the records and sent to the client.

3. The DHCP Client service receives the success message and adds this information to its cache. The system can now proceed with the rest of the boot process.

Registration with a Name in Conflict

The beginning of this section may seem familiar because the same processes occur as previously discussed in the section "Registration with No Names in Conflict." It's the end result that differs if a name is in conflict. I'm repeating the steps that lead to the discovery of the conflict for three reasons:

◆ I doubt you memorized all the procedures as you read them earlier when we examined registration without conflict.

◆ You may have used the index and jumped right to this section of the chapter (and didn't see the earlier discussion).

◆ It's easier to repeat the steps than to ask you to flip back and forth between pages.

DRC queries the device's configured DNS servers for a name server that is authoritative for the zone that houses the names attempting to be registered. This information is provided to DRC and is cached.

The system also parses the registry at system boot and looks for the value of the **DisableDynamicUpdate** data item found in HKLM\System\CurrentControlSet\Services\ Tcpip\Parameters. If the value is set to 0 or the data item doesn't exist, then the system is configured to dynamically update DNS. If the value is set to 1, then dynamic update is disabled and registration can't occur.

Once it's determined that dynamic updates are enabled, the system parses the HKLM\System\ CurrentControlSet\Services\Tcpip\Parameters\Interfaces*InterfaceName* registry key looking for the data item **DisableDynamicUpdate**. If this item doesn't exist or has a value of 0, then this interface supports dynamic updates. If the value of this item is set to 1, then this interface does not support dynamic updates.

All instances of HKLM\System\CurrentControlSet\Services\Tcpip\Parameters\Interfaces\ *InterfaceName* are parsed to determine if more than one NIC exists, and, if so, which NICs register with DNS.

The system must then determine which type of data will be registered. By default, the DHCP Client service registers only the A records of a device. To determine if PTRs should be registered in DNS for this device, the system parses the HKLM\System\CurrentControlSet\ Services\Tcpip\Parameters key and reads the value of the **DisableReverseAddressRegistration** data item. If the value of this item is set to 0 or the data item isn't present, PTR records are placed into DNS by the client. If the value is 1, then no PTRs for any NIC are placed into DNS.

Then, to determine the data contents of the records being registered, the system looks for the **EnableAdapterDomainNameRegistration** data item located in HKLM\System\ CurrentControlSet\ Services\Tcpip\Parameters\Interfaces*InterfaceName*. The value of **EnableAdapterDomainNameRegistration** configures the system to register either its host name in DNS or to register its FQDN.

The system is now ready to send the registration request to the DNS server. The DHCP Client service takes the information that has been gathered about registration for the client and sends a registration request to the DNS server that is authoritative.

The DNS server receives the registration request from the DHCP Client service. DNS parses the database and finds a duplicate record in the zone. One of the following events then occurs:

❖ If the record exists in an unsecured zone and has the same IP address as the device that is attempting to register it, DNS assumes it's the same device. The device is allowed to register the name, and the rest of the registration process proceeds.

❖ If the record exists in a zone that is secured and the existing record has the same IP address as the device that is attempting registration, DNS assumes that the two entries are for the same device. Because the zone is secured, even though DNS thinks that it's the same device, the existing record can't be updated unless the registering device is in the ACL of the existing record with the correct permissions. If access has been granted to the registering device, the process proceeds. If access hasn't been granted, then an access denied message is sent to the DHCP Client service on the Windows 2000 client.

❖ If the record exists in an unsecured zone and has a different IP address from the device that is attempting to register, there is a name collision. In the event of a name collision, a failure message is packaged and sent to the DHCP Client service indicating that the name is already in use.

❖ If the record exists in a zone that is secured and the existing record has a different IP address from the device that is attempting registration, a name collision occurs. Even if there is a name collision, it's possible that the registering client may be able to update the record (even though the record doesn't belong to it). The ACL of the record decides if the client is able to register the name. If the ACL grants the proper level of access to the device, it updates the record no matter which device owns the record. If the ACL doesn't permit the system to update the record, then an access denied message is sent to the DHCP Client service on the Windows 2000 client.

 NOTE: Because secured zones are updated by clients via ACLs, the behavior of **DisableReplaceAddressInConflict** is only implemented when using unsecured zones.

When the DHCP Client service receives the failure message as a result of a name collision, it is handed to the local system. The system then parses the registry to find the value of the **DisableReplaceAddressesInConflic**t data item found in HKLM\System\ CurrentControlSet\Services\Tcpip\Parameters. This item configures the device to either overwrite any entries in DNS that are in conflict, or to back out of the registration process. If the data item has a value of 0 or isn't present in the registry, the device is configured to overwrite any record that exists in DNS that has the same name. If the value is set to 1, the client doesn't overwrite the record; rather, it logs an event to the Event Log and backs out of the registration process.

CODE BLUE

The default behavior of all Windows 2000 devices is to overwrite any record that exists in DNS with the same name. If you're using unsecured zones, this can create some interesting scenarios and some support headaches. If two devices are configured to use the same name, in an unsecured zone the last device in registers its name and address information right over the existing record. Without a valid name registered in DNS, Windows 2000 can't completely participate in an AD environment and may have problems communicating with all other network devices that are not NetBIOS aware.

By allowing devices to overwrite existing entries, you add many unknown factors to your environment. Setting the **DisableReplaceAddressInConflict** item to 0 permits the last device that attempts to register a name to overwrite all existing data about the same name. This means that anyone can hijack another device's name at any time. You can expect many calls to your help desk relative to user's machine is working fine one minute and then broken the next. This configuration can also create some potentially interesting Human Resource issues because anyone can easily assume another well-known device name. You may also find that multiple users who want to use the same device name end up at odds with each another. They sometimes attempt to resolve the situation with multiple reboots per day, in an attempt to wrestle the name from another party.

Allowing a device to overwrite DNS information is just a bad idea. I highly recommend setting the value of **DisableReplaceAddressesInConflict** to 1, which changes the default Windows 2000 behavior. If you're using secured zones, you have nothing to worry about.

The DHCP Client service sends out another registration request, specifying that the DNS server overwrite the existing record. The DNS server then overwrites the data and sends a success message to the DHCP Client service on the Windows 2000 device.

Direct Registration of Domain Controllers

A *domain controller* is any device that has a Windows 2000 Server product installed and is hosting AD. Domain controllers behave differently from nondomain controllers due to their need to register SRV records in DNS. On a domain controller, the Netlogon service registers all SRV and A records for the domain, while the DHCP Client service registers A and PTR records for the host.

SRV records provide AD clients with the ability to query DNS for AD services hosted on a particular domain controller. Examples of SRV records include entries for LDAP servers, Global Catalog (GC) servers, and Kerberos Key Distribution Center (KDC) servers. Netlogon also registers an A record for the domain name of the AD domain that the domain controller is hosting. Don't confuse this with the A record that is registered for the host name.

Because you're unlikely to ever encounter duplicate SRV records or domain controller names (these names are normally very well calculated), I'm not going to discuss how domain controllers react to name collisions. Just for reference, though, the process is the same as detailed earlier in this chapter.

NOTE: During a normal system boot, some of the tasks related to registering host names and registering services occur simultaneously. For readability and to prevent confusion, in this section the host name registration process is presented first, followed by the service registration process.

Domain Controller Registration

DRC queries the device's configured DNS servers for a name server that is authoritative for the zone that houses the names attempting to be registered. This information is provided to DRC and is cached.

The system also parses the registry at system boot and looks for the value of the **DisableDynamicUpdate** data item found in HKLM\System\CurrentControlSet\Services\ Tcpip\Parameters. If the value is set to 0 or the data item doesn't exist, then the system is configured to dynamically update DNS with A records for the host name. If the value on the device is set to 1, then dynamic update is disabled and registration can't occur.

Once the system determines that dynamic updates can be performed, it parses the HKLM\ System\CurrentControlSet\Services\Tcpip\Parameters\Interfaces*InterfaceName* registry key looking for the data item **DisableDynamicUpdate**. If this item doesn't exist or has a value of 0, then this interface supports dynamic updates. If the value of this item is set to 1, then dynamic updates aren't supported on this interface. All instances of HKLM\ System\ CurrentControlSet\Services\Tcpip\Parameters\Interfaces*InterfaceName* are parsed to determine if more than one NIC exists, and which ones will register with DNS.

NOTE: Setting the **DisableDynamicUpdate** registry item enables or disables registration of records updated only by the DNS Client service, which includes A and PTR records. It's still possible to dynamically update records that Netlogon registers, such as SRV and A records for the domain, even if one or more adapters have dynamic updates disabled.

After determining which NICs will register data in DNS, the system must determine which type of data will be registered. By default, the DHCP Client service registers only the A records of a device. To determine if PTRs should be registered in DNS for this device, the system parses the HKLM\System\CurrentControlSet\Services\Tcpip\Parameters key and reads the value of the **DisableReverseAddressRegistration** data item. If the value of this item is set to 0 or the data item isn't present, then PTR records are placed into DNS by the client. If the value is 1, then no PTRs for any NIC are placed into DNS.

The system then needs to determine the data contents of the records being registered. It does this by looking for the **EnableAdapterDomainNameRegistration** data item located in HKLM\System\CurrentControlSet\Services\Tcpip\Parameters\Interfaces*InterfaceName*. The value of **EnableAdapterDomainNameRegistration** configures the system either to register just its host name in DNS or to register its FQDN.

The system is now ready to send the registration request to the DNS server. The DHCP Client service takes the information that has been gathered about registration for the device and sends a registration request to the DNS server that was determined to be authoritative. This request is only for host name registration.

The DNS server receives the registration request from the DHCP Client service, writes the record, and gives it a TTL before sending a success message to the domain controller.

So Your Domain Controller Is a DNS Server Too?

In many cases, especially when using AD-Integrated DNS, your DNS server is also playing the role of domain controller. This multirole configuration changes the way the system determines which IP addresses are registered in DNS via the DHCP Client service.

DNS servers that are also domain controllers support a registry item named **PublishAddress**, which is located in HKLM\System\CurrentControlSet\Services\Dns\ Parameters. This item allows you to configure which IP addresses are registered in DNS when multiple addresses exist on the server.

Domain Services Registration

When the Netlogon service starts on the domain controller, it parses the registry for the value of the **UseDynamicDns** item found in HKLM\System\CurrentControlSet\Services\ Netlogon\Parameters. **UseDynamicDns** configures the Netlogon service to either use or not use dynamic updates. If the value of **UseDynamicDns** is set to 0, Netlogon doesn't use dynamic updates. If the value is set to 1 or the data item isn't present, Netlogon uses dynamic updates.

Once it has been established that Netlogon supports dynamic updates, the system looks for the value of the **RegisterDnsARecords**, which is also located in HKLM\System\ CurrentControlSet\Services\Netlogon\Parameters. A value of 0 for **RegisterDnsARecords** prevents the A record for the domain that this domain controller hosts from registering in DNS. A value of 1, which is the default, allows the A record for the domain to register.

Netlogon then sends a registration request to the DNS server that is authoritative for the zone. The DNS server receives the request for registration, writes the data, and sends a success message to the Netlogon service on the domain controller, including a TTL for all records.

The Netlogon service receives the success message and caches the results. All names that have been written to DNS by the Netlogon service are recorded in the Netlogon.Dns file located in **%*Systemroot*%\System32\Config**.

Fine-Tuning Registration

Unfortunately, you don't have many options available for fine-tuning DNS registration. The only tuning that you can complete to increase client performance (besides the server-side performance optimization steps given in Chapters 2 and 3) is in the area of refreshing registered records in DNS.

No Refresh Interval

By changing the value for the no refresh interval, you alter the default amount of time that a DNS client must wait before it can update its information in DNS. You can adjust the default value of 7 days by setting the value of the No Refresh Interval field found on the Aging And Scavenging screen of a zone's Properties dialog box.

Setting a lower value for this item allows the data in DNS to be more dynamic, but this can come at the cost of normalized data. That's because an update occurring too close to the initial registration can cause the update to be overwritten by the original registration. Setting a value that is too high will reduce network and processing load for both the client and server but will cause data to be stale and potentially unreliable.

Refresh Interval

As you recall, the refresh interval sets the default interval at which the DNS client is to update its records in DNS. If records aren't updated in this interval, they become susceptible to any scavenging policy that has been established on the DNS server. A higher value reduces registration traffic but produces potentially stale data because the device updates less frequently. A lower value allows more dynamic data in DNS, but at the cost of network traffic and processing power.

You can modify the refresh interval value by specifying the desired time in days, hours, or minutes in a zone's Refresh Interval field. The Refresh Interval field is on the Aging And Scavenging screen of any zone's Properties dialog box.

Troubleshooting the Direct Registration Process

For the most part, direct registration is trouble free. Because your device is directly contacting the DNS server, there are less moving parts than other solutions that leverage middleware to register on behalf of the client (as is the case when using DHCP to register on behalf of your clients). If you're having problems registering your names and services with DNS, try the solutions described in the following sections.

Verify DNS Configuration

Check that you have been assigned a DNS server statically, by viewing the DNS properties of TCP/IP on the NIC, or check that you have been assigned a DNS server by DHCP, by typing **ipconfig /all** at the command prompt. If your device isn't configured to use a DNS server, this is your problem.

If you have configured DNS servers, verify that the client is configured to dynamically update DNS. Check that the Register This Connection's Addresses In DNS box is selected in the DNS properties of the NIC that isn't registering in DNS. If this box isn't selected, this is your problem.

Check the value of **DisableDynamicUpdate** in both the HKLM\System\CurrentControlSet\ Services\Tcpip\Parameters\Interface*InterfaceName* and HKLM\System\CurrentControlSet\ Services\Tcpip\Parameters locations. If either of these items has a value of 1, dynamic update has been disabled. This is your problem.

Check the DNS Cache for an Authoritative Name Server

Your client registers with the name server that is authoritative in the zone in which the update must occur. If your client is unable to determine the authoritative name server at boot time, you can't register in DNS. You can verify that an authoritative server exists by typing **ipconfig /displaydns** at the command prompt. Look for the NS record for the zone name in which you're attempting to register. If this isn't present, attempt to ping the authoritative DNS server.

Ping DNS Servers' Addresses

Ping the DNS server that is authoritative for the zone as well as any DNS servers that have been configured on the NIC. If you receive a reply from the server, move on to the next suggestion (checking the status of the DHCP Client service).

If you received a response that states *Pinging IPAddress with 32 bytes of data* followed by many request timeout errors, there's either a network problem or a configuration problem on the remote device.

Check the Status of the DHCP Client Service

The DHCP Client service is the entity that registers A and PTR records for the client. If this service is stopped or paused, registration fails. Use the Services MMC to verify that the service is up and running. If the service isn't started, enter **net start dhcp** at a command prompt. Once the service starts, enter **ipconfig /registerdns** at a command prompt to force registration of A and PTR records.

Verify Netlogon Service on the Domain Controllers

Domain controllers use both the DHCP Client service and the Netlogon service to update records in DNS. You may find that A and PTR records are registering in DNS, but SRV records are not. If this is the case, there might be a problem with Netlogon. Verify that the Netlogon service is started. If it isn't, enter **net start netlogon** at a command prompt, which will not only start the service but also force the registration of all records that Netlogon is responsible for updating.

View the contents of the Netlogon.Dns file located in **%Systemroot%\System32\Config**. This file lists all the names that have been registered by Netlogon. If this file is empty, you haven't registered any names.

Check Secured vs. Unsecured Updates on the DNS Server and Client

Both server and client must be configured to use the same security type. Verify that the **UpdateSecurityLevel** data item in the DNS client's HKLM\CurrentControlSet\Services\ Tcpip\Parameters registry key of the DNS client is set at a compatible level with the security that the DNS server implements.

Verify that DNS Servers Support RFC 2136

If your servers don't completely support RFC 2136, this is your problem. All DNS servers used by Windows 2000 clients must support RFC 2136 if you wish to dynamically update DNS.

Verify Security Permissions on AD-Integrated Zones

The security configuration of the zone may be the source of your problems. If you're using secured updates on an AD-Integrated zone, verify that the device attempting to register names in DNS has the appropriate privilege. If privileges aren't correct, you can't register names. Each entity that must update an AD-Integrated zone that is leveraging secured updates must have the Create All Child Objects permission on the zone that accepts the update.

DHCP Registration

Direct registration in DNS is available only to Windows 2000 clients, so what do you do for all of your non-Windows 2000 clients? You use DHCP to register records. Makes sense, right? It does if you've read RFC 2136.

DHCP and Option 81 Clients

RFC 2136 calls for the support of a Fully Qualified Domain Name option. This option, also commonly known as option 81, allows a DHCP client to send its FQDN to a DHCP server in the DHCPREQUEST packet. The DHCP server then uses this information to register host name data in DNS on behalf of the client.

The exact records updated in DNS by the DHCP server on behalf of the client can vary. In any situation, the DHCP server registers only A and PTR records for the client. Each client, as part of DHCPREQUEST, sends a flag in the FQDN option portion of the packet indicating what level of participation the DHCP server has in the registration process, if any. There are three possible values for the flag:

◈ 0 – The client registers the A record and the DHCP server registers the PTR record.

◈ 1 – The client requests that the DHCP server register both A and PTR records in DNS directly.

◈ 3 –The DHCP server registers both A and PTR records in DNS on behalf of the client.

NOTE: Because option 81 is currently supported by many different DHCP vendors, my discussions on DHCP are as vendor-agnostic as possible.

Understanding DHCP Communications

When a client attempts to obtain an IP address from DHCP, a consistent string of packets is sent back and forth. You should keep these communication strings in mind when you're using DHCP to register names in DNS on behalf of clients.

When a client boots, it broadcasts a DHCPDISCOVER message to the local segment. If your network is configured properly, this message is forwarded by the router to a preconfigured DHCP server by a process called Bootp Forwarding. Once the DHCP server receives the DHCPDISCOVER message, it broadcasts a DHCPOFFER message to the client. The DHCPOFFER message contains a temporary TCP/IP address for the client to use, along with any configured options, such as NetBIOS Name Server and Default Gateway. The client receives this packet and responds by sending a DHCPREQUEST packet, asking to use the address that DHCP has just sent. DHCPREQUEST is still a broadcast packet because the client hasn't been authorized to use the address sent in the DHCPOFFER packet.

Once the DHCP server receives the client's DHCPREQUEST packet, if the IP address hasn't been assigned to another client, a DHCPACK message is sent via broadcast to the client. The DHCPACK is an acknowledgement packet that lets the client use the IP address offered in the DHCPOFFER (along with the configured options). When the client receives a DHCPACK packet, it mounts TCP/IP using the provided address and options.

If, by the time the DHCP server receives the DHCPREQUEST packet, the IP address has already been handed out to another client, the server issues a NACK (short for No ACK)—a broadcast packet that lets the client know that it may not use the address sent to it in the DHCPOFFER. If the client receives a NACK, then the whole process must start over.

A DHCP server that supports option 81 registers names for two types of clients: those that support option 81 and those that don't.

Windows 2000 and Windows Me support option 81 by providing their FQDN in the DHCPREQUEST packet to DHCP. These clients also specify the level of registration involvement that they want DHCP to participate in on their behalf. They accomplish this by setting the flag in the DHCPREQUEST packet to 0 by default. This causes all Windows 2000 devices to request that DHCP register only the PTR on behalf of the client, provided that the DHCP server supports option 81. Windows 2000 and Windows Me support all FQDN option flags.

Changing Windows 2000's Default Option 81 Flag

By default, Windows 2000 clients set the flag found in the FQDN option portion of the DHCPREQUEST packet to 0. A flag setting of 0 indicates that the client wants to register its own A records in DNS but wants to use DHCP to register its PTR records. You can modify this behavior to allow the client to send a flag of 1 to the DHCP server. A flag of 1 indicates that the client wants DHCP to register both A and PTR records in DNS on behalf of the client.

To force a Windows 2000 client to send a flag of 1 in the FQDN option portion of the DHCPREQUEST packet, set the value to 1 of the **DisableDynamicUpdate** data item found in HKLM\System\CurrentControlSet\Services\Tcpip\Parameters. This change results in disabling dynamic update support on all interfaces found in the Windows 2000 client. Although dynamic updates are disabled, the client continues to place data in the FQDN option portion of the DHCPREQUEST packet. The difference is that with this registry modification, the flag that is sent in the packet has a value of 1.

You can also set this behavior by clearing the Register This Connection's Addresses In DNS option found in the DNS properties of each NIC in the device.

When a device that supports option 81 boots, the following processes occur:

1. The system attempts to obtain a DHCP lease by broadcasting for DHCP services via a DHCPDISCOVERY packet.

2. The DHCP server receives the DHCPDISCOVERY packet and returns a DHCPOFFER packet to the client, which includes the IP address to be used as well as any other DHCP-configured options.

3. The client receives the DHCPOFFER packet. It then sends a DHCPREQUEST packet back to the DHCP server. The DHCPREQUEST packet contains the completed fields for the FQDN option, including the device's FQDN and a flag level of 0.

4. Assuming that the DHCP server receives the DHCPREQUEST and sends back a DHCPACK, that DHCPACK contains another FQDN option that either mirrors or changes the data sent by the client.

5. The DHCP server uses its DHCP Client service to register any records on behalf of the client. This portion of registration behaves the same as if the DHCP server were registering A and PTR records for itself.

6. The client receives the DHCPACK and examines the FQDN option portion of the packet. If the flag defined here is different from that requested in the DHCPREQUEST packet, it is used. If there is no data in the FQDN option portion of the packet, or if it that portion doesn't exist, the client assumes that the DHCP server doesn't support option 81 and therefore registers all of its own records.

Understanding the Effects of Server Configuration

Occasionally, the DHCP server may not be configured to support some values that the client provides in the FQDN option portion of the DHCPREQUEST packet. In that case, the server changes values to match the server's configuration. This behavior is most often seen when a client has requested a level of support in the flag of the FQDN option that isn't supported on the server. For example, in the Microsoft implementation of DHCP, you can configure the server so that all, some, or none of the supported resource records (A and PTR) will be registered with DNS by the DHCP server. This setting overrides any service level the client requests. Therefore, if you configure your DHCP server so that it doesn't register either A or PTR for clients, even though the client may ask the DHCP server to register its A and PTR records in DNS, the client will be forced to directly register with DNS.

7. If the configuration of the client or server establishes that the client must register some records in DNS directly, the steps are the same as those outlined in the "Direct Registration" section of this chapter.

DHCP and Pre-Option 81 Clients

Certain devices are incapable of providing their FQDN to DHCP in the DHCPREQUEST packet. Windows 9x and NT clients are such devices. Instead, these clients provide only their host names in the DHCPREQUEST packet, which is appended with a preconfigured domain suffix on the DHCP server. Appending a domain suffix to the host name provided by the client generates an FQDN, which is then used in the registration process.

When a device doesn't support option 81, the following steps occur to register the device in DNS:

1. The system attempts to obtain a DHCP lease by broadcasting for DHCP services via a DHCPDISCOVERY packet.

2. The DHCP server receives the DHCPDISCOVERY packet and returns a DHCPOFFER packet to the client, which includes the IP address to be used as well as any other DHCP-configured options.

3. The client receives the DHCPOFFER packet. It then sends back to the DHCP server a DHCPREQUEST packet. The DHCPREQUEST packet contains the request for the offered IP address. There is no FQDN information in this packet, but the device's host name is given.

4. When the DHCPREQUEST is received by the DHCP server, the host name of the client is extracted from the packet before a DHCPACK is sent back to the client. The host name is then appended with a domain suffix that has been configured to be used for option 81 registrations, which produces the FQDN of the client. Both the A and PTR records are then registered on behalf of the client.

5. The client receives the DHCPACK and uses the IP address that has been assigned to start its network services. The device is completely unaware that it has a registration in DNS.

DHCP Security Considerations

When a DHCP server registers entries in the DNS database, it is subject to any and all rules that are enforced on every other device or entity that dynamically updates a zone. This means that in a DNS implementation that isn't leveraging secured updates, nothing else must be done. However, when using a zone that enforces the use of secure updates, you must consider other factors.

Secure updates depend on two sets of security principals. First, each zone that's configured to use secure updates must have a defined ACL, which either grants or denies entities access to add or remove DNS objects. Second, once an object is created, it must be secured in a fashion that allows only the owner of the record to update or modify the data. Consider for a moment how these requirements might affect DHCP when it's registering data on behalf of a host.

To affect DHCP registration of DNS data in a zone on behalf of another host, the zone must be secured to allow one or more DHCP servers to add dnsNode objects. You can do this in one of two ways:

◈ Create your own group, which contains one or more DHCP servers, and ACL the zone to allow this group to create new objects.

◈ Use a built-in group named DNSUpdateProxy. The DNSUpdateProxy group, which is located in the Users OU in a default installation of AD, is a precreated group that's already ACLed to allow its members to add objects to DNS.

Once records are placed into the zone, the group that created the records becomes the owner of the records and is the only group that can update the data.

CODE BLUE

If you're considering implementing the DHCP Server service on a domain controller that also houses a secured AD-Integrated zone, you may have a problem. Because a domain controller needs to be a member of multiple special groups in AD (to permit the Domain Controller to make changes to directory contents), it also has access to all entries placed into secured DNS. If you host a DHCP server on a domain controller, your DHCP server has full control over all objects in DNS. This is because the DHCP server is running in the same context as the DC. This completely circumvents any security you may have established and allows any device using DHCP registration to overwrite any record, including those that were manually implemented.

The bottom line is, don't implement DHCP on a domain controller.

CODE BLUE

Using DHCP to update records in DNS sounds like a win–win situation for everyone. However, in some circumstances, using DHCP to update records in DNS is a losing proposition. The ability to place devices into AD groups is a feature that is supported only in Windows 2000. If you're running any other operating system on your DHCP server, you're out of luck. Without the ability to grant selective access to a secured zone through the use of security groups, the zone may not be updated in a secured environment. You have a single choice: Upgrade to Windows 2000. Ouch.

Reality Check: Is Using DHCP for Dynamic Updates Practical?

While using DHCP to update records in DNS may seem like a slam dunk, it introduces quite a few interesting problems that can make its implementation a hard pill to swallow.

Consider the way that DHCP servers are ACLed to allow updates to the secured zone—they are all placed into the same security group. Also consider the way a record in DNS is ACLed once it's placed into the zone—only the owner of the record can update it.

Finally, consider the following three statements:

❖ DHCP uses the DHCPUpdateProxy or comparable group to create objects in a secured zone.

❖ All DHCP servers that have to update zones on behalf of clients must be members of DHCPUpdateProxy or a comparable group you created. If you use more than one DHCP server, they must all be in the DHCPUpdateProxy or comparable group to enable end-to-end registration for all clients. You never know which DHCP server your clients may get their addresses from.

❖ When a record is created, DHCPUpdateProxy or the comparable group you created is the owner; therefore, it's the only entity that can update the data.

After reading those three statements, the problem I'm introducing should be very clear. Because multiple servers are all owners of the same records via the use of a group, can't any of those servers update the data? Also, because these are all DHCP servers, doesn't that mean that there may be two different devices with the same name registering with two different

DHCP servers, both of which function as if they own this name? Because DHCP allows any device that plugs into the network to get an address and then register in DNS, doesn't this allow nonauthorized people, such as visitors and vendors, to modify data in DNS? What does this do to security?

When you enable option 81 in DHCP, you essentially unsecure a secured zone. How else would you describe a system that allows unknown users to enter data into a secured system and that fails to enforce any collision detection logic for even the most important records? So, while this feature may seem like a no-brainer to the casual observer, seasoned IT vets like yourselves would agree with me when I say you may be looking for another job if you use it.

Troubleshooting DHCP Registration

Troubleshooting problems related to updating DNS via option 81 requires very little effort focused on the client. Because the only participation that a client has is sending its host name, or FQDN, to DHCP, this registration type can break in only a few places. Most problems are caused by a breakdown of the processes between the DHCP server and DNS.

If you're struggling with option 81, use the following steps to identify the problem:

1. Verify the IP address obtained from DHCP.

   ❖ Type **ipconfig /all** at the command prompt. If you're seeing a valid IP address, subnet mask, and default gateway, you're getting an address from either DHCP or a static local configuration.

   ❖ Once you've verified that you have an address, view the properties of TCP/IP to verify that you haven't configured a static address. If you have configured a static address, you can't use DHCP to register your records in DNS; you must enter them directly or manually.

   ❖ If you're configured to use DHCP to get an address, but you aren't getting any IP information from DHCP, you have a network problem. You may also need to check the Bootp Forwarding configuration on your router and verify that the DHCP server is still on the wire.

   ❖ Check the properties of DNS in TCP/IP to ensure that the Register This Connections Address In DNS is not selected. If it is, the client uses DHCP only to register PTR records, unless DHCP is configured to override the client's request. Use this information to determine which records should actually be registered in DNS by DHCP.

2. Check the DHCP server's configuration.

   ❖ Ensure that the DHCP server that you're using has option 81 enabled.

   ❖ If you're having a problem with the DHCP server's ability to register names for pre-option-81-enabled clients, ensure that the server has been configured to append a domain suffix to any unqualified host names it receives. Use this information to check the DNS database for the host name that may have been placed into DNS with the wrong FQDN.

   ❖ Verify that this DHCP server, as well as any other DHCP servers, are members of the DNSUpdateProxy group or another comparable group.

   ❖ If you have any DHCP servers that are not Windows 2000, they can't be members of any security groups; therefore, they are unable to update a Windows 2000 DNS secured zone.

3. Check the DNS server's configuration.

   ❖ Verify that the DNS server is on the network and that its DNS server service or application is started.

   ❖ If you're using Windows 2000 secured zones, ensure that either the DNSUpdateProxy—or a comparable group that all DHCP servers are a member of—has been granted the Create All Child Objects permission on the zone. If you're using another DNS product, ensure that security is properly established.

   ❖ If you're using Windows 2000 secured zones, check the security applied to any existing dnsNode objects in the database. If there's an existing record that the client registered directly, it is ACLed with the client's GUID, and the DHCP server is unable to overwrite it. To resolve this issue, either reACL the object or remove it from the database.

DNS Resolution

DNS resolution is the process of using the information provided to DNS, either by dynamic update or manual creation, to find a host or service. This information is used to establish a session with the requested host. Registration is consistent across all versions of Windows 2000.

Except for the types of records that can be resolved, resolution in Dynamic DNS doesn't differ from traditional DNS. Instead of clients just resolving host names and information, they can ask DNS for services that reside on a particular host.

DNS Resolution Process

All resolution requests for records in DNS follow the same logical path.

The application, service, or user attempts to resolve a name or record by calling the GetHostByName API. The request is received by the API and is sent to the DNS Client service of the local machine.

The DCS receives the resolution request and parses the local cache. If a positive entry exists in the client-side cache, then the results are returned to the requesting entity. If a negative entry exists in cache, a name failure message is returned to the requesting entity.

If no entries are found in cache that match the query and the query is for an A record, the HOSTS file is parsed. If there is a match in the HOSTS file, the corresponding data is sent back to the requesting entity.

If there is no entry in HOSTS or the request is for a record type other than A, a name lookup request is created by DCS. The actual contents of the request varies from configuration to configuration. If the client has been configured with a primary DNS suffix, with alternate DNS suffixes, or to send an unqualified name to DNS, you may see different requests being packaged on different clients. Follow these guidelines to determine what will be sent in the resolution request:

❖ If the name being resolved is qualified, then it is sent as is.

❖ If the name being resolved isn't qualified, you haven't specified any alternate DNS suffixes, and you have a primary DNS suffix for the device, the primary DNS suffix is appended to the name that needs to be resolved. A request for the FQDN is packaged.

NOTE: If you specify the use of any alternate DNS suffixes, your primary DNS suffix is not appended to unqualified names unless it's explicitly defined as an alternate DNS suffix. Unfortunately, the logic isn't implemented that would allow you to try alternate suffixes only after the primary suffix yielded no results.

❖ If you have alternate DNS suffixes and the name being resolved isn't qualified, the first suffix is appended to the unresolved name. The new FQDN is packaged. If the name can't be found, then the next DNS suffix in the search order is appended. This creates a new FQDN that is sent to DNS. This continues until either a name is found or all suffixes are used.

DCS sends the lookup request to TCP/IP. TCP/IP creates a packet destined for the DNS server that has the highest priority in the DNS server list defined in the TCP/IP Properties dialog box.

In the case of success, failure, or a referral, the results are sent to the device's TCP/IP stack, which in turn hands the results to DCS. If the DNS server fails to respond, the device attempts to contact the DNS server five times at intervals defined in the registry item **DnsQueryTimeouts** located in HKLM\System\CurrentControlSet\Services\Tcpip\Parameters. When all five intervals have expired, the DNS server with the second highest priority is queried until either an answer is given or the values defined in **DnsQueryTimeouts** have expired. This behavior continues until all DNS servers configured on the client have been queried. Once all DNS servers have been queried without a response, an error is generated and sent to DCS.

DCS receives the data from the TCP/IP protocol stack and, depending on the results returned, takes one of the following actions:

◈ If the data being returned indicates that the host has been found, the results are placed into the client-side cache in the form of a positive entry.

◈ If the data being returned indicates that the host isn't found and the name is unqualified, then DCS attempts to append the next DNS suffix in the search list to the name to create a new FQDN. This new FQDN is then sent to TCP/IP for resolution. This behavior continues until the name is either found, and a positive entry is placed into cache, or until DCS runs out of suffixes to append. At that point, it puts a negative entry in the client-side cache.

◈ If the data being returned indicates that the host isn't found and the device has been configured to use domain devolution, then the leftmost label of the domain portion of FQDN is removed. This new FQDN is then sent to TCP/IP for resolution. This behavior continues until only two labels exist in the domain portion of the FQDN or an answer is found. If no answer is found and domain devolution is exhausted, a negative entry is placed in the client-side cache.

◈ If DCS receives a referral to another DNS server that may know the answer as a result of an iterative query, it packages another request that is sent to TCP/IP for resolution in DNS. This process continues until a name is found or a name-not-found error is received. In each case, a positive or negative entry is placed into cache (depending on the DNS server's response).

After the data has either been found or not found and a negative or positive entry has been placed in the cache, the application is notified. In the case of a name-not-found scenario, DCS hands the error to the GetHostByName API. If the name has been resolved, the data is sent to the GetHostByName API for eventual delivery to the requestor.

So How Are SRV Records Resolved?

SRV records are resolved basically the same way that all other records are resolved. So why am I taking the time to call your attention to SRV records? Because they are so heavily used in a Windows 2000 environment that you may be involved with SRV records more than any other record type.

When a client determines that it needs a particular service, a request is made of DNS to return to the client any relevant SRV records. When the DNS server receives the query for a service type, it parses the database and returns all hosts that are hosting the requested service to the client. Once the client receives a list of hosts that are hosting the service, the data is placed into the client-side cache. The client then attempts to resolve the host name with the highest priority that was specified in the SRV record. The DNS server receives the query and returns the IP address of the host to the client, which places the entry in cache. At this point, the client can establish communication with the device to gain access to the service.

Once the GetHostByName API receives the data from DCS, it hands it to the requesting application or service. The data is either a name not found error or the IP address of the host that needed resolving.

Optimizing DNS Resolution

Resolution of host data is the single DNS event that can make or break your DNS implementation from a user perspective. This is because resolution is the only event that has direct effects on clients and their immediate needs.

Take a gander at these hacks and recommendations to help keep DNS resolution running smoothly.

Client Configuration Considerations

You can make a number of GUI-based configuration changes to increase the performance of DNS clients.

Many people have a "the more the better" attitude about everything in life, including DNS server configuration. Just because you can specify an unlimited number of DNS servers on a client doesn't mean that it's a good idea. Too many DNS servers can do more harm than good. (See the code blue in this chapter about too many DNS servers.) Too few creates a reliability problem.

You should also limit the number of DNS suffixes that you specify on a client. Ideally, you should configure your clients to use the primary DNS suffix only with domain devolution enabled, which prevents excessive queries from being sent from DNS. Not only does this make administration easier, because you don't have to worry about updating both the client's DNS suffix and the alternate DNS suffix list, but it also increases performance. In general, the fewer suffixes you have, the quicker the results are returned to the client. This is because before a failure can be issued to a client, each suffix must be appended to the unqualified name and sent to DNS. As is the case with the number of DNS servers configured on a client, too few suffixes may result in premature failures being issued to the client.

The Importance of Qualified Names

Using unqualified names decreases performance to such a degree that it's criminal. When the client receives a request to resolve an unqualified name, it attempts to qualify it. This results in many name queries being sent to resolve a name that would have been resolved with a single query if it were qualified.

Although this may seem simple to you and me, it's a lofty concept to the average user and to our natural enemy, the developer. Users are familiar with NetBIOS names that don't require all of this domain business; as a result, most user lookups are unqualified. It's our job to educate the user on unqualified vs. qualified.

The developer, our natural enemy, will sometimes be inclined to place unqualified names into applications and scripts to save time. Why type out a 50-character string multiple times in a piece of code when you can just type out the host name? You must also educate the developers in your organization about the use of qualified vs. unqualified names.

Using qualified names instead of unqualified names is the single most performance-increasing change you can make on a DNS client. You can't buy this kind of upgrade. It's worth the training and communication effort involved to spread the word.

Changing the Default Number of A Records Returned

AddressAnswerLimit is a REG_DWORD registry item found on Windows 2000 DNS servers in the HKLM\System\CurrentControlSet\Services\Dns\Parameters subkey. This item configures the number of A records that are returned to a client in a single response when more than one A record exists for a host name. The default behavior is to send as many A records as are present in DNS to the client in a single response. This may not be desirable or wise in situations where an excessive number of A records are associated with a single host name. Using multiple responses allows the client to begin to process some of the A records before it has received any other records in subsequent responses. This can improve performance.

The supported values for the data item are 5 – 28, which represents the maximum number of records that are returned to the client.

Changing Forwarding Timeout

The registry data item **ForwardingTimeout**, in the HKLM\System\CurrentControlSet\Services\Dns\Parameters key of a Windows 2000 DNS server, is used to configure the maximum amount of time that DNS waits for a response to a forwarded query. By default, the DNS server waits 5 seconds on a single forwarder before sending another query to the next forwarder specified in the forwarding list. You can set this value to a lower number, which increases performance whenever a particular forwarder is down or the name isn't known by a forwarder (which responds slowly with that information). Setting this value too low, however, can cause the DNS server to prematurely move on to the next forwarder. You can also modify this value on the Forwarders tab in the DNS server's Properties dialog box by changing the number found in the Forwarders Time-Out (Seconds) box.

Adjusting the DNS Server's Cache

The registry data item **MaxCacheTtl**, in the HKLM\System\CurrentControlSet\Services\Dns\Parameters key of a Windows 2000 DNS server, configures the TTL for both negative and positive cached entries on the DNS server. The DNS's cache is used to satisfy requests from clients without having to parse the DNS database or send a request to another DNS server if the answer is already known. You can modify the default value of one day to a longer period of time to increase resolution performance for names that have already been resolved. A value that is too high comes at the cost of possibly resolving a name with stale or outdated data.

Tweaking Recursive Lookups

You can modify the behavior of recursive lookups to help the server return name-not-found errors more quickly. I know it sounds funny to think you want an error to come back to you in an expeditious manner, but you'd be amazed by how much time is wasted waiting on an answer that either never comes or comes back as a negative. Normally, if a name can be found in DNS, it should be found quickly. Otherwise, you should be notified quickly.

The data item **RecursionRetry**, in the HKLM\System\CurrentControlSet\Services\Dns\Parameters key of a DNS server, configures the maximum amount of time that a DNS server waits for a response from a recursive lookup before considering the query invalid. Expiration of this value causes the DNS server to issue another query. The default value is 3 seconds. Lowering this number gives the DNS server the ability to contact multiple DNS servers in the same amount of time it would take to contact one.

The data item **RecursionTimeout**, in the same registry key, configures the total amount of time the DNS server waits, no matter how many retries have been issued, before considering the name unresolvable. The default value is 15 seconds, but you can decrease that value to prevent excessive wait times for names that aren't found. Like many other settings, a value that's too low may cause bogus name not-found-messages.

NOTE: For a complete list of supported registry values for both the DNS client and server, please see Appendix A. For more DNS server optimization steps, please consult Chapter 4.

Troubleshooting DNS Resolution

Use the following procedures to troubleshoot DNS name resolution:

1. Verify TCP/IP configuration.

   ◈ Ensure that you have a valid IP address, subnet mask, and default gateway.

   ◈ Ensure that you have one or more DNS servers configured.

   ◈ Attempt to ping your DNS server. If you can't ping, you may either have a network problem or a network configuration problem on the DNS server.

   ◈ Enter **netdiag /test:dns** at the command prompt. The /test:dns switch outputs all information about the DNS configuration of the client, as well as information about which servers are authoritative and which records have been registered with DNS.

2. Attempt to ping another host name.

   ◈ Try to ping a well-know FQDN such as *www.microsoft.com*. If you're able to resolve another name, the problem is a result of bad data in DNS, your cache, or the HOSTS file.

   ◈ If you fail to get a response and your TCP/IP configuration is correct, you have a problem with your DNS server.

   ◈ Check your client-side cache.

   ◈ Enter **ipconfig /displaydns** at the command prompt. This outputs information about your client-side cache. If an entry is in the cache for the host that you're attempting to contact, verify that the address is correct. If the address is correct, there may be another cause of your failure to connect to the device. If the address is incorrect, there is either bad data in DNS or bad data in the HOSTS file.

3. Check your HOSTS file.

   ❖ Verify that there are no entries in the HOSTS file for the device you're looking for. If there is an entry, verify that the address is correct.

   ❖ If there is any bad data in your HOSTS file that has caused incorrect information to be held in the client-side cache, remove the entry or correct it. Then type **ipconfig /flushdns** at the command prompt to release all cached entries.

4. Check the domain suffix search order.

   ❖ If you're querying by using an unqualified name, ensure that you have the correct DNS suffixes added to the client configuration.

   ❖ If you're querying by using an unqualified name, ensure that none of the domains that you've specified as a DNS suffix have a device with the same name as the device you are looking for. This may cause DNS to return an answer from a domain that houses a host that isn't the host you want to connect to.

Chapter 4

Designing DNS

N
ow that you have all of the basic and advanced knowledge about DNS as a technology as well as Microsoft's Windows 2000 DNS offering, let's explore the most exciting part of any implementation: the design. In my opinion, the design phase is the best part of a technology's lifecycle. This is when you have an opportunity to start with a clean slate and craft something that you can be proud of.

Unfortunately, the line between a good design and a bad design is a thin one. A well-thought-out design in one environment can be a poor solution in another environment. As a result, I can't offer a single way to design your DNS environment, so in this chapter, I'll discuss the best practices.

Even though I want to cover all aspects of design, I'm not going to discuss some of the textbook recommendations found in typical "how to design" documents. I won't be addressing project plans, statements of work, business requirements, or training your help-desk staff. Those process-related tasks are important, but they have no place in a technical document.

If you haven't performed this type of work before and you're not familiar with the related processes, you should not attempt to design a DNS environment without expert help. DNS environment designs are large dollar items with extremely high visibility, so there is little room for failure or growing pains.

You must start by defining the scope of the work, which helps determine the tasks and goals involved with your implementation. Your scope-of-work definition may be the building block for documents that you will be asked to produce for management, both for an official statement of work, as well as a budget document.

You also need to consider the amount of interoperability between your new DNS architecture and any existing DNS implementation. Until you define how much and what type of interoperability you must achieve, you can't determine which features you can use. After you work out these basics, you can move on to the fun stuff—the design.

Determining the Scope of the Design

The first task is to scope it all out—frame your design. Putting parameters around what you are designing not only helps you determine what the end result of this endeavor should look like, but it also helps you determine what is important to your project and what is not. Too many times in IT, projects run awry because they lack scope and definition. You can avoid pitfalls such as being over budget or being late and not meeting expectations by starting with a solid scope of work: an easy task if you just answer a few questions.

Probably the single most important question you need to answer when you're designing a DNS architecture is "Does this DNS environment need to be available to internal users, external customers, or both?"

If you want to provide name resolution only to your internal users, your life is a bit less complicated than if you need a design that services both internal users and external customers. Answering this question allows you to determine how your namespace, security, and zones should be laid out and who should be able to access them.

The second most important question is "What level of interoperability do I require?" In many cases, even though you have an existing DNS environment, you don't need to plan for interoperability. However, if your environment does make interoperability a design goal, you're going to have to make some tough and politically charged decisions. Which namespace is authoritative for which data? Who owns the data? Why is the data given to that owner?

The following questions will further help you define your scope of work.

- **What is the business case for moving to WIN2K DNS?** – The answer identifies the value this technology brings from an end-user and business perspective. Make sure that both management and the user community have realistic expectations about the end result of your design. For example, you could probably show that the ability to update DNS names dynamically removes the need for time-consuming internal processes involved in creating records. This, of course, reduces IT costs and business losses for Dynamic DNS–aware clients.

- **What is the technology case for moving to WIN2K DNS?** – The answer helps you determine which features in the new technology you will implement to improve the state of IT. An example might be the increased reliability and availability provided by using AD-Integrated DNS.

- **What design flaws exist with the current architecture and how do you address them?** – Although this can be considered part of the technology case, it is important enough to be considered on its own. Use this information to learn from the mistakes of others. There is no such thing as a perfect design or implementation because as technologists, we are always at the mercy of the technology available at the time of implementation. Many times, what was impossible in the previously implemented system is easily completed on newer technology. Exposing problem areas in existing designs can be a risky proposition and may result in fortification of the existing environment instead of replacement. (Fixing is frequently cheaper than replacing.)

- **What is the feature set of the system that is either being replaced or that needs to interoperate with WIN2K DNS?** – Use this information to identify gaps in both of the products. This is a way to identify the need of third-party or middleware products and services. In many cases, the answer to this question can help you identify holes in your design or reveal some false assumptions about how technology is being used in your company.

✦ **What are the differences in supported features on each DNS solution?** – This information helps you determine which features are supported and usable in an interoperability scenario. If you have to make a decision about which technology will be the strategic direction, the answers to this question can help you determine how to get the most bang for your buck.

✦ **Which design details in the existing DNS environment are unique?** – Almost every environment contains some level of unique design or implementation. These features are usually implemented to support something that your company is doing in a nonstandard way. Identifying these features is paramount to designing an environment that meets the needs of all users, not just most users. More importantly, considering these design details in your plan means that the unique components will work just as they did before.

✦ **Will this design be complementing, competing with, or replacing an existing DNS environment?** – This essential question dictates your interoperability needs. As you will learn in the next section, the need for interoperability can alter your dream of designing the perfect environment.

Determining the Level of Interoperability

Once you have determined the scope of your project, it should be easy to complete the next step: determining the level of interoperability you'll need. You have only three interoperability options available to you: you need to interoperate, you don't need to interoperate, or you are building a new environment from the ground up, so interoperability is a short-term need.

Interoperability is only needed when DNS servers that must share zone data are of a different make or version. Therefore, DNS servers that participate in a delegated environments or those that send both recursive and iterative queries to other DNS server, have no need for interoperability. Don't confuse interoperability with RFC compliancy; they are two different issues.

Planning for Complete Interoperability

If you have determined that your existing DNS environment isn't going anywhere, you need complete interoperability. This means you need to determine what steps to take to ensure that multiple systems appear as only one system to clients.

A common interoperability scenario exists when an organization wants to leverage an existing BIND root and use Windows 2000 DNS somewhere else in the DNS architecture. In this case, AD is probably being implemented in a namespace that has been delegated to the Windows 2000 DNS servers from the BIND root.

For example, in one scenario, you may have an existing BIND root domain named domain.com that doesn't support dynamic updates. Because your AD implementation requires dynamic update support, you have chosen to implement a Windows 2000 based DNS solution. Since support for dynamic updates is established on a zone-by-zone basis, you are forced to implement a new zone that supports dynamic updates. The best solution in this scenario is to leverage your existing BIND root by having your dynamic namespace delegated to your from the root. This solution would allow you to build a zone that accepts dynamic updates named ad.domain.com (for instance) that has been delegated from your existing domain.com BIND zone.The advantage of this solution is that it allows the AD domain to reflect the existing root and namespace (domain.com) while still allowing dynamic updates to occur in the new zone (ad.domain.com).

Another scenario may require that you configure the DNS environment that is exposed to the Internet as the root of your namespace while configuring an internal DNS system to act as a delegated domain. For example, you can have an Internet domain named company.com, and delegate ad.company.com to the Windows 2000 DNS environment that is only accessible to your internal users or vice versa. Either way, interoperability is the key to success. Incidentally, both of these scenarios are plagued with security holes that are discussed later in this chapter, in the section "Establishing a Namespace."

The scenario that requires the highest level of interoperability is when your primary name server is either Windows 2000 DNS or BIND, and you are using one or more secondary name servers from a competing vendor. If your primary DNS server is Windows 2000 and your secondary server is BIND, you have to shut off many of the features found in the Windows 2000 DNS Server service to ensure data consistency. This is because some features that Windows 2000 implements are not RFC compliant or are RFC compliant but not supported in certain version of BIND.

Interoperability is only an internal design goal: it has nothing to do with DNS servers once a query has left your zones, and it has no effect on the client unless your Windows 2000 device is trying to dynamically update a server that does not support dynamic updates.

Planning for No Interoperability

If you determine that the existing architecture is not going to be retired but will run as a parallel service, you do not need to interoperate. If you are implementing a new parallel architecture using only Windows 2000 DNS servers, you can use all of the enhanced features found in Windows 2000 DNS without being concerned about support from a non-Microsoft DNS solution.

Although a legacy DNS environment will continue to exist, interoperability issues are not your concern. Consider yourself lucky. Unless you have the need to share zone data between dissimilar DNS servers, all other DNS communication and interaction is independent of any interoperability concerns. This includes all interaction as a result of recursive, iterative, and forwarded lookups because each is an RFC-defined transaction.

Planning a New Environment

If you have determined that the existing DNS architecture needs to be replaced with Windows 2000 DNS, or if you are building your organization's first DNS infrastructure, you are on easy street. In cases where your design does not need to consider any legacy DNS structures, you don't have to concern yourself with legacy support and interoperability issues. Those of you that have had to design anything around a legacy system are familiar with the added complexity that legacy systems bring to the table.

If you are replacing an existing environment, pay special attention to the section "Delegating to Bring Multiple Namespaces Together" later in this chapter. It covers issues related to transitioning an environment from one platform to another.

Component Design

You have to create a logical layout of your DNS implementation. If you are starting from scratch and have no legacy DNS environments to worry about, this task is simple. If you have to wrestle with an existing architecture, either to replace it or to interoperate with it, you have your work cut out for you.

The logic of a DNS environment is based on the components responsible for creating administrative and security groupings of resources. Your DNS architecture will encompass the following areas:

- Namespaces

❖ Zones

❖ The delegation model

❖ Security

Establishing a Namespace

A *namespace* is the entity that defines your environment to the internal and external world, so it is important to get it right. Designing the namespace is the most significant task in your design effort. The decision you make is more or less irreversible once you implement it. From a pure DNS-technology perspective, nothing is irreversible, but the truth is that factors such as customer familiarity with your name make it almost impossible to change your mind.

In addition to the customer limitations, AD naming is based on a DNS hierarchy. Because renaming an AD root is an illegal operation (and will not be supported anytime soon), the namespace that you have established when you built AD needs to be available for the life of AD.

Considering Internal and External Access

It can make a difference to your design if both internal and external clients use your DNS service. If external customers access your namespace, you need a name that is professional-sounding and reflects the function of your company. You should also consider a name that is creative and simple enough for your customers to remember easily. Because many namespaces are already owned by someone else, be prepared for the worst by composing several possible names to use. If your namespace is available only internally, however, you don't have to concern yourself with using a well-known or professional name. If your namespace is only available internally you can use any name that you wish, with a few exceptions (as detailed in the following Code Blue).

If you are not exposing your name to the Internet, then you don't even have to use a name that leverages one of the traditional root names (.com, .org, .mil, etc.). Using a root name that is illegal on the Internet ensures that a hacker will never gain access to your DNS data from outside of your organization because the namespace can't be resolved. This also lets you use a name internally, even if the same name is owned by someone else externally. For example, if your company's name is CompanyA and someone else has registered companya.com on the Internet, you could use the name companya.corp (which is RFC compliant but illegal on the Internet) as your internal namespace.

CODE BLUE

You might think that if your company name is already in use on the Internet, you can still implement the exact same name (with the same suffix) internally, without running into problems. Although this is possible, this is a bad idea. Even if your company is sitting behind a firewall and you think it's impossible that a request for your internal companya.com namespace (for example) could find its way to the companya.com namespace on the Internet, think again. There are many different ways—especially given the recursive and iterative nature of DNS—that a name request for an internal resource can find its way to the Internet (and in this case, ultimately to the wrong namespace). Try to avoid the practice of duplicating any namespace both internal and external.

Considering Namespace Delegation

The role that delegation plays in your namespace is an important consideration. If your namespace is delegated to you from another entity, that certainly reduces your options. In a delegation model, the delegated domain has a namespace that is an extension of the namespace being used by the domain that has delegated control. In that case, you need to concern yourself only with your own domain name.

For example, if your domain name domain1 is delegated authority from the company.com domain, the namespace that your DNS implementation is responsible for is domain1.company.com. You don't have the freedom to decide to use a completely different name such as domain1.ididitmyway.org. That is unless you convinced the DNS root owner to create a .org zone and delegate ididitmyway.org to you. Using either a zone that is pre-existing or implementing a new zone for the explicit purpose of delegation, is an acceptable solution.

Using the Company Name

Using your company name as your DNS namespace may not make sense. Mergers and acquisitions between businesses are common, and these actions can severely impact your namespace. Given the fact that renaming your namespace is extremely difficult at best and could even be impossible, ask yourself if it makes sense to use the business name as part of your namespace.

If there's any chance that your company may be involved with a merger or acquisition, you might be better off using a namespace that describes the type of business function that your organization fulfills instead of the company name. The only down side to using a function-based namespace is that the name might be confusing for customers. In that case, use the functional namespace internally and the company name externally.

Considering AD and Namespace Links

The Active Directory domain name and DNS namespace are linked. When you define an AD domain and a domain name, you must have a DNS server someplace that hosts a zone of the same name.

Once you build an AD root-level domain, it can never be renamed. If you need to rename your AD domain, your only option is to totally rebuild the AD with the new name (a nightmare). Given AD's dependency on the DNS namespace, you must establish the namespace right the first time.

Understanding the Naming Rules

A DNS label cannot be longer than 64 characters, and an FQDN cannot be longer than 255 characters. You may think that this provides plenty of room, but that's frequently not the case.

Design your namespace to be as flexible as possible, but don't push that flexibility to the point of untoward complexity. Implementing too many domains or using delegation excessively could bring you close to (or beyond) the 255-character limit sooner than you think.

You can also move outside of the supported character set by incorporating some non-RFC standard characters into your namespace. Although I don't recommend this, sometimes administrators have valid reasons for using non-RFC compliant characters (such as NetBIOS interoperability). If you plan on using non-RFC compliant names, consider that decision's impact on any interoperability needs.

 CAUTION: Using illegal characters makes your namespace unreachable by all non-Microsoft resolvers. For a list of legal characters, please consult Chapters 1 and 2.

Choosing a Zone Type

Choosing a zone type should be a fairly straightforward and painless process. You only need to look at which value each zone type brings to your design. Let's weigh the pros and cons of both Standard and AD-Integrated zone types.

Standard

- ◈ **Con** – DNS data is housed in a single jet database. This type of database is not very efficient.

- ◈ **Con** – Only one server can be the primary DNS server. This means that changes can be committed on only one server, which does not scale well in a large environment using DDNS.

❖ **Con** – Replication to secondary servers is in the form of IXFR. This causes more data to be replicated per object update than solutions using attribute-level replication.

❖ **Con** – Secure updates to zone data are not supported. This means that any and all records are subject to being overwritten at any time when using dynamic updates.

❖ **Pro** – Because the zone is housed in a separate database, DNS data will not be affected by AD corruption or failure. Housing DNS data in a separate database prevents situations where you are trying to fix AD but are unable to find directory servers and services by name, which makes troubleshooting and resolution a little difficult.

❖ **Pro** – Fewer TCP and UPD ports are used in zone transfers than in replication of DNS information when it is housed in AD. This means that using Standard zones makes transferring data through firewalls and filtered segments easier.

AD-Integrated

❖ **Con** – Data housed here is subject to all of the same outages that AD may encounter, which can make troubleshooting difficult. This problem can be designed around with the use of secondaries in conjunction with the AD-Integrated zone. (More on this in the sidebar "Ensuring Zone Availability in an AD-Integrated Solution" later in this chapter.)

❖ **Con** – All domain controllers in a domain in which the zone was established will receive replica sets of the DNS database even if the service is not installed.

❖ **Con** – This zone can't be housed in more than one domain at a time. Therefore, in implementations with multiple domain levels, only a subset of the total domain controllers can service DNS requests unless you use delegation, as detailed throughout this chapter.

❖ **Pro** – Replication of DNS changes are provided at the attribute level. This is even more efficient than IXFR.

❖ **Pro** – Because it uses AD replication to replicate DNS objects, content is compressed by 75 percent when sent to a domain controller that exists in another AD site.

❖ **Pro** – Using AD-Integrated zones is the only way to secure zone data to prevent unauthorized overwriting when using dynamic updates.

❖ **Pro** – Any domain controller in a domain with this zone type can accept a change to the database. This distributes processing load across multiple servers, eliminates the single point of failure associated with Standard zone solutions, and increases your return on investment.

Designing Forward and Reverse Zones

Once you have decided on the type of zone, you need not look any further than your namespace and delegation design to determine how to create both your forward and reverse lookup zones.

Forward Lookup Zones

Considering all of the information that you have gathered and the design decisions you have made so far enables you to determine the number of forward zones you must create. Create a forward zone for your namespace, and create additional forward zones for any delegated zones.

A forward lookup zone enables resolution of names for the devices and entities that call this zone's domain home. Forward zones are also the place that a DNS client using dynamic updates will place its A and SRV records. This is nothing new, and it isn't much work to design a forward lookup zone.

Reverse Lookup Zones

Creating reverse lookup zones can either be straightforward or a little hazy depending on your delegation model. Consider how a DNS client dynamically places PRT records into DNS; the DNS client searches for the appropriate and authoritative in-addr.arpa zone, and once it is found, places its PTR records into DNS.

From the client side, this process is pretty mindless. The client requests information for the in-addr.arpa zone from the DNS servers that it has been configured to use. Those DNS servers return the zone information that they are aware of, whether the information exists on a zone that this DNS server hosts or not. The DNS server returns the information for the first in-addr.arpa zone that it finds, whether it's right or wrong.

Because the client assumes that the data about in-addr.arpa that the DNS server is passing to it is correct, you must ensure that the DNS server finds the right zone. Although this may seem simple, consider scenarios in which multiple DNS environments have each implemented reverse lookup zones. In these situations, it is common to have two clients that are each configured to use DNS servers that host different reverse lookup zones. If you are not careful, both clients can end up querying and registering within two different in-addr.arpa zones.

The bottom line is that you can have only one in-addr.arpa zone in your entire DNS infrastructure. In-addr.arpa is like any other zone: only one authoritative zone can have that name, not multiple authoritative zones. Although having a single authoritative in-addr.arpa zone is an option if you will be implementing a brand new DNS infrastructure, those of you who have older technology to consider must be creative.

Sometimes, when another DNS infrastructure houses the in-addr.arpa, dynamic updates are not supported because of ownership. If you are implementing a new dynamic environment, you may be unable to change the environment that houses the reverse lookup zone. If you don't own it, you can't update it. Another group in your organization may own the data and be unwilling (or not ready) to implement a dynamic update solution. If so, adding records to the in-addr.arpa zone may be difficult. In all zone types except AD-Integrated, it is impossible to delegate administrative access to a zone without giving someone full control. This is true for both Windows 2000 DNS and non-Windows 2000 DNS implementations.

What are the chances that you will be granted administrative control over a zone that is owned by another group? If the chances are nil and you are unable to place records into the reverse lookup zone, you have four options available for adding records to in-addr.arpa:

◆ Build a process

◆ Leverage delegation

◆ Use aliases.

◆ Move the zone.

Building Processes to Add Records to a Reverse Lookup Zone You can build a process to address the problem of being unable to place records into the reverse lookup zone. Such a process might be as simple as formalizing a contact point in the group that owns in-addr.arpa, and using that point to focus requests for PTR creation, modification, or removal. On the other end of the spectrum, you might build a complete business process that includes opening either a trouble ticket or internal order to have the PTR created.

Having said that it's possible, I'm warning against it. Fixing a technology/political issue with processes is the worst thing that you can do. It wastes everyone's time and energy, and it tends to mask the underlying turmoil or organizational breakdown.

Using Delegation to Add Records to a Reverse Lookup Zone If you own blocks of IP addresses along subnet boundaries, then delegation is your best option. Because domains in in-addr.arpa are created at the subnet level, if you own one or more blocks of IP addresses in your organization, you can have your subnet's reverse lookup zone delegated to you.

For example, if you own all addresses in the 10.100.5/24 subnet, then the 100.10.in-addr.arpa zone could delegate 5.100.10.in-addr.arpa to you. Delegation of this space allows you to place records into the zone on your own. You can also allow clients that dynamically update DNS to register their PTR records in the delegated zone (provided that the delegated zone is housed on a DNS server that supports dynamic updates).

Using Alias Records for a Reverse Lookup Zone   The option to leverage alias records is most viable when you own a block of records on a subnet, but you don't own all of the records. In this scenario, CNAME records are placed in the appropriate in-addr.arpa zone. The data in the CNAME record points the resolver's request at a forward lookup zone that has been established in your DNS environment. That zone contains PTR records for the devices over which you have control. This forward zone must be created on your DNS servers, and it must be made known to the owners of the reverse lookup zone. Here is a detailed list of steps that must be completed to use aliases for reverse lookup:

❖ Create a forward zone hierarchy to house PTR records. It is typical to create a zone or domain named rev.*domain.com* that contains subdomains for each segment. For example,if you are housing some PTR records for the 10.100.5 segment, create a domain structure of 5.100.10.rev.*domain.com*. (This may be one or more zones depending on your implementation.) You need to communicate this location to the owners of the in-addr.arpa zone.

❖ Create a PTR record for each device that must be resolvable via reverse lookup. The PTR record is used and configured just as you would use and configure a PTR record in the actual in-addr.arpa zone.

❖ The owner of the 5.100.10.in-addr.arpa zone places CNAME records into this zone for each device that you own. For example, if you had devices in the IP range of 10.100.5.10 – 10.100.5.20, 10 CNAME records are created, one for each IP address. The CNAME record contains the name that the client is looking for, which is the alias. The record also contains the actual location of the record, which is the PTR in the forward lookup zone that you created. For example, in the case of a CNAME record for a device with an IP address 10.100.5.15, the actual name of the record is 15.5.100.10.in-addr.arpa because this is the location and data that someone requesting the PTR for the device 10.100.5.15 would query. The FQDN of the target or actual record is 15.5.100.10.rev.*domain.com*, because that is the record that contains the IP-to-host name mapping information.

If you use aliases as detailed, your reverse lookups will function a little differently. Once a client sends a reverse lookup request for the host name of 10.100.5.15 to the 5.100.10.in-addr.arpa zone, instead of DNS returning the PTR record, it returns a CNAME. This data, 15.5.100.10.rev.*domain.com*, is then used to query the new location for a PTR record. The query for the PTR record 15.1.100.10.rev.*domain.com* is received by the appropriate DNS server. The data is retrieved by the DNS server and is then sent to the client.

There are a few drawbacks to using aliases. First of all, this method requires some level of process to be in place because your records still depend on data that is housed in a zone over which you have no control. However, because the in-addr.arpa zone doesn't need to contain host name–specific data, you can modify all PTR data without requiring a change someplace else. As a result, even though this solution doesn't eliminate process totally, it reduces it significantly. The biggest problem that this solution presents is that all PTR records must be manually placed into DNS. DNS clients expect the in-addr.arpa zone and its subdomains to be the default location for dynamically placing and updating records. If this in-addr.arpa zone does not accept dynamic updates, automatic registration of PTR records will fail. This is a drag.

Moving the Reverse Lookup Zone   Moving the zone is the ideal option, but it's also the most unrealistic for administrators who find themselves in this in-addr.arpa pickle. You always have the option of moving the in-addr.arpa zone from the DNS environment that does not support dynamic updates to a DNS environment that does.

As wonderful as this solution is, you can expect a religious war about moving the reverse lookup zones out of the control of one group and into another. Once again, politics plays a role in technology.

Ensuring Zone Availability in an AD-Integrated Solution

Because all DNS data is housed in AD (when you're using an AD-Integrated zone solution), you face a certain increased level of risk and downtime from directory corruption or availability. Think about the difficulties of troubleshooting an AD problem if you cannot resolve the names of the domain controllers. Suppose the domain controllers themselves can't resolve names and services of other domain controllers because the directory that is housing this information is unavailable. If neither administrators nor domain controllers can resolve names, how can you find the services that need to be fixed? The solution is to use Standard secondary servers.

By establishing Standard secondary servers (secondary to the zone or zones you implemented in AD), a directory failure doesn't prevent you from resolving names and connecting to devices that need to be fixed. Because Standard zones house their data in a local database, a directory outage has no effect (unless there is directory corruption that is written to the secondary server from AD). When you use Standard secondary servers, if an AD failure does occur, just point all DCs at the Standard secondary servers. This enables name resolution while you are fixing the real cause of the AD outage.

To make this work properly, you must not only establish secondary DNS servers, but you must also kick up all of the timeout values in the Start of Authority (SOA). (See Chapter 2.) By increasing these SOA values, you prevent the Standard secondary server from asking the downed AD-Integrated zone for an update while it is down. If a query does occur, the values are high enough so that the data housed in the Standard secondary server should not time out and be removed from the database. If you feel that your Standard secondary DNS servers may be in danger of releasing records, you always have the option of changing the zone type to primary, which will force the secondary server to take over control and ownership of all records.

Deciding on Delegation

Delegation is a helpful tool that allows you to partition a single namespace into multiple administrative chunks. Partitioning DNS along administrative boundaries lets you give responsibility for that domain/namespace to another individual or group. This was extremely helpful back in the days when information needed to be placed into DNS statically. It allowed you to spread the administrative burden across multiple groups or areas of responsibility, without compromising the security of other namespaces or zones. Now that information can be placed into DNS dynamically, the need to delegate to is not quite as important.

Often, decisions about delegation arise to accommodate IT politics. In many corporations, administrators find themselves designing technology solutions around internal company politics, and designing DNS is no exception. You may want to design a namespace that is hosted on a single zone, but be forced to delegate subdomains to other IT groups because of uneasy political situations. Although politics can always spoil a good design, sometimes there are legitimate reasons to delegate.

Delegating to Bring Multiple Namespaces Together

Consider delegation if your corporation has multiple existing namespaces that are disjoined. Over time, many disjoined namespaces may be implemented across a single company. Sometimes these namespaces are themselves configured as root, and other times they are using the Internet root servers even if they have not been delegated a namespace from the Internet roots. Many problems arise from these scenarios, most of which have to do with name resolution outside of the native namespace, because resolution requests can't be sent to namespaces that a group of DNS servers don't know about.

If you have been charged with creating a new namespace or with upgrading an existing DNS implementation when more than one DNS root namespace exists, you can use delegation to collapse all of the independent namespaces into a single parent hierarchy. This allows you to have a single focal point for namespace administration, delegation, and resolution. This also helps clear any interoperability or resolution roadblocks associated with disjointed namespaces. Take the following steps to collapse multiple namespaces into a single hierarchy.

- ✦ Establish the namespace that will serve as the internal "root" of the hierarchy. This namespace serves as a parent-level domain to the other namespaces, and it is therefore considered a type of root. However, it may or may not be configured as a DNS root itself (which is why in this example root is in quotes).

- ✦ In the "root" namespace, place an A record in DNS for each of the name servers that are hosting a delegated zone. These are known as *glue records*, and they allow resolution of DNS servers to occur between the namespaces.

- ✦ Once you have established the "root" namespace and created your glue records, delegate namespaces for each separate namespace on your network.

- ✦ On each namespace that is acting as root, remove any existing root zones from the DNS database.

- ✦ On all namespaces, change the root hints to reflect the IP address of the name servers in the "root" domain.

CODE BLUE

You can use an FQDN to define a name server in the root hints, but this is not the recommended practice. If you choose to use the FQDN of a name server in the root hints, be sure that you have created glue records in the delegated zone. Otherwise, you will not be able to resolve the FQDN that you have specified.

After you take these steps, you will have a single parent namespace that resolves names for all of the namespaces that it has delegated, as well as any that are found as a result of its root hints.

Partitioning AD Replication

When you implement an AD-Integrated DNS zone, all zone data is placed into the directory partition of the domain where the zone is established. For example, suppose you have two AD domains that are related (domain.com and ad.domain.com). Implementing an AD-Integrated zone on one of them (e.g., ad.domain.com) means the zone data is present on domain controllers only in that domain. The zone data is not present on the other domain (domain.com). This behavior can be limiting because it forces all DNS-related traffic to a subset of the domain controllers you implemented in multiple domains.

You can use delegation to partition the zone data into separate AD-Integrated zones. Each zone exists in a separate AD domain. Breaking up a single zone that contains multiple DNS domains and placing each zone in a different AD-Integrated zone allows you to spread the DNS traffic load. Of course, this is of value only if you have significant DNS traffic associated with both zones.

For example, suppose you have a single AD-Integrated zone in the root-level AD domain named domain.com, which contains five domain controllers. This zone, which is also named domain.com, houses DNS data for a child-level AD domain named ad.domain.com, which also contains five domain controllers. When you set up the domain.com zone, all the domain controllers in the AD domain named domain.com will receive a copy of the DNS database, including records for devices in ad.domain.com. Because only the five domain.com domain controllers hold a replica copy of DNS, they are the only devices that register and resolve names for DNS clients requesting service for names in both ad.domain.com and domain.com.

Create a newly delegated AD-Integrated zone named ad.domain.com, housing it in the ad.domain.com AD domain. Then all 10 domain controllers can register and resolve DNS data. The domain.com DNS servers would be responsible for registering and resolving records within their namespace, and the five domain controllers in ad.domain.com would be responsible for registering and resolving records within their namespace. If you have multiple AD domains, but most or all devices exist in only one domain, there is little value to using delegation to increase performance.

Security Issues

Security should always be on your mind when you are designing your environment, but it shouldn't be your only concern. In this security-paranoid age, companies often sacrifice usability and availability for the sake of security. I always tell people that I can create the most secure system in the world by unplugging it from the network and encasing it in cement, which would prevent both network and console attacks. Although that statement is a joke, it does illustrate a valuable point: you need to balance security with usability and availability.

Namespace Security

If you intend to extend your namespace to the Internet, you must make security your number one concern. Extending a namespace to the Internet involves placing DNS servers in a location that is accessible to everyone who has an Internet connection, including hackers. These servers probably contain data about your organization's devices that should be kept confidential.

Although it may seem as if data that contains IP-address-to-name mappings is of little value, the exact opposite is true. If a hacker gains access to DNS data, he or she can actively search out devices that have interesting names (i.e., payroll1.domain.com) and find the IP address of the device. At that point, the hacker can attack the device. However, if you remove the ability to get to this data, you remove this problem. Think of it as security through abstraction. How can they hack a system if they don't even know its name or address?

Troubleshooting Namespace Security on the Internet

Some organizations implement Network Address Translation (NAT), which enables network administrators to use addresses that are illegal on the Internet but legal inside of their network. In most cases, NAT can also act as a firewall. If you are using NAT and/or a firewall, you reduce the chance of a direct hack. However, you don't eliminate the risk of hacking altogether.

When you make your DNS servers available to the Internet, you can either place them on the internal network and open ports in the firewall, or you can place them on the remote side of a firewall (also known as a demilitarized zone or DMZ).

If you allow your servers to reside on your internal network, consider the security involved in allowing traffic to flow into your network from the Internet. All port access is typically indifferent to the source and destination of the traffic, so all DNS servers in your network are subject to access from outside parties.

If you place your server on the remote side of a firewall or in a DMZ, you may have a requirement that zone transfers occur from the server in the DMZ to the servers in your internal network. This too requires opening ports, and also presents some additional security concerns related to the transfer of data. How do you ensure that the data being sent in a zone transfer is not being intercepted by another device or entity? How do you ensure that the device asking for the data is the actual device? How do you prevent a compromised DNS server in the DMZ from accessing and modifying data that sits on internal DNS servers?

If you need to provide both external and internal name resolution for the same namespace, you have to secure your internal DNS environment from hackers. Do not allow your DNS design to span—or be accessed by—both internal and external networks.

Instead, implement your external DNS namespace on servers that are accessible only by external resolvers. Those servers should contain only Internet-based devices and services. By placing only Internet-based name-to-address mappings in those DNS servers, the only information a hacker can extract is already publicly known: the addresses of your Internet devices.

Also, implement an internal namespace with the same name as the external DNS namespace that you exposed to the Internet (as long as you own the name externally). This other namespace is for your internal user base. It contains all devices and services present on the internal corporate network—even those that are Internet-related. All internal users are then pointed to the internal DNS servers for name resolution only of internal names.

You can then enable access to Internet devices that reside outside of your company by establishing a proxy server. A *proxy server* is a device that accepts all HTTP and FTP requests from clients and resolves all requests for HTTP and FTP documents or locations. Once you have established your proxy server, all clients' Web browsers are pointed to it, forcing the browser to send all HTTP and FTP requests to the proxy server instead of directly connecting to the device once its name has been resolved in DNS. By preventing Internet access to your internal DNS data and having internal users use a proxy service, you remove the security risk associated with making your namespace available to the Internet.

Implementing Zone Security

From a logical perspective, zone security is of real concern only to zones that are using dynamic updates, whether these are Standard or AD-Integrated zones. For zones that do not accept dynamic updates, you have additional security on top of the typical Windows 2000 security model. This security controls access and/or administrative control based on the credentials that you supply.

Standard Zone Security   When you configure a Standard zone to accept dynamic updates to DNS data, security is not your paramount concern. Standard zones do not maintain any security rights that govern what a user or object can do within the zone. This means that all transactions are completed, no matter who is requesting the change. I don't want to go into the painful details of the pitfalls of this type of implementation again because that information has already been provided in Chapter 3, but it is important to mention again.

When you implement a Standard zone that accepts dynamic updates, any name can be overwritten by anyone at any time, including names that have been placed into the database manually. Avoid Standard zones if you are using dynamic updates.

AD-Integrated Zone Security   The ability to secure registrations by using access control lists (ACLs) is one of the advantages of AD-Integrated zones. By default, when you establish a secured AD-Integrated zone, all users have the potential ability to write data in the zone. The data they can write depends on whether the record they are attempting to write is already present. The default ACL configuration of a secured AD-Integrated zone lets users place data into the zone only if the same data is not already present in the zone. A user can update an existing record or overwrite the record if he or she has been defined as the owner of the record. This ACL, which is detailed in Chapter 2, allows updates to the zone, while at the same time ensuring that an entity other than the owner can't overwrite any records.

This default security works very well. My only complaint is that it allows Authenticated Users, as well as Pre-Windows 2000 Compatible Access groups, to create objects in the zone.

Authenticated Users are users who have been validated by any domain within the AD forest. Pre-Windows 2000 Compatible Access is the Everyone group from any NT-trusted domain. This set of ACLs means that almost anyone who gets an IP address can write data to DNS. This may or may not be a concern to you.

You may decide that the default ACL isn't secure enough and choose to implement your own customized security. One way of customizing security is to create a group for all users that can update DNS data. Add that group to the ACL of any zone, and remove the Authenticated Users and Pre-Windows 2000 Compatible groups. However, this approach adds to administrative overhead especially if you are in a large environment. (See the sidebar "AD Group Limitations" for more information.)

On the other hand, this behavior is no different than the behavior found in WINS. WINS, as you will learn in Chapters 6 and 7, doesn't require you to be authenticated or authorized by any security system before it grants you the ability to write entries into the database.

If you want to modify the ACL of an AD-Integrated zone, you can do so on the Security tab of the zone's Properties dialog box. Remember that the new ACL you specify is valid only for new objects created in the zone. A new object also has a default ACL that is established by the object's schema configuration, so the ACL for an object is an aggregated set of permissions applied by the zone and object.

In all cases, with or without administrative modification, the same ACL is assigned to any records that are created in DNS (both static and dynamic records). All records have the same ACL, because from a schema security perspective, there is no difference between an object that is created by a dynamic update and an object that is created by Joe the Administrator. To the schema and the directory, objects are objects. Because administrators are creating these records in the database, there is no risk that anyone other than the administrative staff can update or remove those records.

For both static and dynamic records in DNS, you can modify the assigned ACL when you create the records. You accomplish this by changing the default ACL on the dnsNode object found in the AD schema. This process, as well as discussion of default ACLs, is detailed in Chapter 2.

CODE BLUE

Depending on how you modify the ACL, you may prevent the actual owner of an object from updating a record that was in place before the new ACL was applied. Always exercise caution when changing the default security of DNS objects. Changes affect not only data that is created from the point of the modification forward but also objects that have already been added to DNS under the previous security and ACL model.

AD Group Limitations

The well-documented limitation of groups in AD may affect your implementation if you choose to use special groups to grant access to write DNS data. In AD, some objects are not replicated at the attribute level the way DNS data is replicated. Unfortunately, one of those nonattribute-replicated objects is group membership. When a single change is made to a group in AD, the whole membership list is replicated to all domain controllers. While this is not a big deal for groups that have a small number of members, it is very inefficient for larger groups.

Therefore, Microsoft implemented logic that prevents you from adding more than 5000 users to a single group. In large environments, this can be a problem if you are planning to use specific groups to grant write access to DNS that may contain the majority of your users. At this time, the only way to overcome this limitation is to implement multiple groups and either nest them into other groups or add each group to the ACL.

I am happy to report that this limitation will be fixed in the version of AD that ships with the next version of Windows (the version we call by the code name Whistler).

Tweaking and Optimizing the DNS Design

The DNS design decisions you make are based on the DNS features you choose to implement. You must also consider configuration options that increase performance and aid in the resolution of host names and data.

Interoperability Options

If you need to intimately interoperate with another flavor of DNS, establish guidelines to make sure everything works optimally. There is a difference in the type of interoperability you need to facilitate recursive, iterative, and forwarded lookups (compared to interoperability of DNS servers that share zone data). If you don't adequately address your interoperability needs, you may find yourself trying to implement a solution that is not technically feasible.

RFC Compliancy

Consider using the RFC-compliant features found only in Windows 2000 DNS. Most of the time when Microsoft strays from RFC compliancy with a particular feature, you actually have the option to either implement the feature in the RFC way or the "other" way. This is a nice change from previous versions of DNS where you were stuck either dealing with a feature in its noncomplaint state or omitting it.

Just because a feature is RFC compliant doesn't mean that all of the functionality that was defined in the RFC is being implemented. In some cases, one DNS system may expect an RFC-complaint feature to act one way, but another DNS system expects it to act another way. You can see this in the way that CNAME records work on Windows 2000 clients, compared to the industry standard for CNAME resolution. (See Chapter 2 for details.)

Older DNS systems may be missing certain RFC-compliant features because those features were not available when that DNS server was implemented. One example is support for dynamic updates, which is available only on certain versions of Microsoft and BIND DNS servers.

Creating Options That Are Universally Supported

If you must interoperate with a variety of DNS servers, each of which uses different technology, you have to identify the lowest common denominator from a software and feature-set perspective. Determining the weakest link in the chain lets you know which features in Windows 2000 DNS are either in or out of scope. For successful interoperability, you can implement features that are supported only by all your DNS servers.

I have compiled a list of features, both positive and negative, that you can consider when determining what is in and out of scope. Each feature falls into one of two categories: those that you should implement and those that you should not implement.

Features You Must Have You shouldn't live without the following features:

   ❖ **Dynamic updates** – Not only is support of dynamic updates mandatory when implementing AD, but it is just a great feature that will someday allow us to get rid of NetBIOS and WINS. Dynamic updates can be used only on servers that support RFC 2136. While interoperability may seem to present a difficulty, you can work around the problem. Try creating a Windows 2000 DNS zone that supports dynamic updates, and convert any existing DNS server that does not support DDNS to either a secondary name server or a cache only server.

   ❖ **AD-Integrate** – I think that I have already beaten this point into the ground. Because this feature is supported only on Windows 2000 devices, you will not be able to provide any interoperability with non–Windows 2000 DNS servers unless they are configured as secondary name servers.

   ❖ **Secured updates** – If you don't use secured updates, your whole namespace is at risk. Using unsecured updates allows anyone to hijack anyone else's device and service name. Not only is this disruptive, but it also makes man-in-the-middle or imposter hacks easy to implement. Like AD-Integrated zones, this feature is supported only in Windows 2000 DNS because it is tied to AD-Integration. Any non–Windows 2000 DNS servers must be used as secondary name servers when using secured updates.

❖ **Fast zone transfers** – Although this feature greatly increases replication performance while reducing replication latency, you should use it only if all of your secondary name servers are either Windows 2000 DNS servers or BIND servers later than version 4.9.5. No other DNS servers support fast zone transfers.

Features to Avoid   You should avoid the following features in Windows 2000 DNS at all costs if you have interoperability issues:

❖ **DHCP registration (Option 81)** – This feature permits you to register your non–Windows 2000 or DDNS-aware clients in DDNS while circumventing security at the same time. Allowing DHCP to register on your behalf creates more problems than it solves. The alternative is to prevent non–DDNS-aware clients from registering in DDNS, which forces them to use WINS. This extends the life of your WINS environment.

❖ **Forwarding** – Forwarding allows you to circumvent the normal resolution behavior of DNS by querying namespaces other than those that would be queried through a normal recursive or iterative lookup. When you enable forwarding on your DNS servers, queries that cannot be resolved by namespaces hosted on the local DNS server are forwarded to all the DNS servers specified as forwarders. This occurs regardless of the domain suffix that has been appended to the host name that's being resolved. This means that even if you know that a resolution request for www.microsoft.com can be resolved only by a referral to the microsoft.com domain from the .com root-level domains, if you have a forwarder defined, it will be asked to resolve www.microsoft.com before the root-level domains are asked. This slows down all name resolution, especially if you have multiple forwarders defined.

TIP: A feature named *conditional forwarding,* which is available in the next version of Windows, allows forwarders to intercept and resolve names for certain namespaces instead of all namespaces.

❖ **Subnet prioritization** – Unfortunately, subnet prioritization doesn't use much logic to determine which device addresses are closest to the client when multiple addresses exist for the same host name. Instead, the DNS server examines the requesting device's address and compares that to the addresses that exist for the host name.

If the DNS server finds an entry that has the same network address as the client, that address is returned to the client. If the DNS server can't find a record that is on the same network as the client, the first address in the list is handed to the client. Because clients are rarely found on the same segment as servers, this feature is less attractive than using round robin. Using subnet prioritization may actually prevent true load balancing because unless the client is on the same network as the record being queried, DNS hands the client the first address in the list of multiple addresses for that record. Use round robin instead; it provides load balancing in all scenarios.

✦ **Non-RFC-compliant naming** – If you had been using non-RFC-compliant naming for your device names, you have two options. You can either rename your non-RFC-compliant devices, or you can alter your DNS configuration to accept names that are not RFC compliant. Enabling non-RFC-compliant names on a DNS server seems to be the less costly solution. In reality, enabling non-RFC-compliant names in DNS just extends the practice of using non-RFC-compliant host names and destroys any hope of interoperability with other DNS servers and systems. DNS servers that comply with RFC naming cannot host a zone, even a secondary zone, if the names contained in that zone are not RFC compliant.

✦ **WINS Lookup** – This feature, like forwarding, can result in excessively long name resolution response times. When WINS Lookup is enabled, all failed host-name resolution requests are sent to WINS for resolution. The system strips off the domain portion of the name and sends only the host name to predefined WINS servers. This causes a potential delay in resolution of names that do not exist. If you think about it for a moment, because most clients are still pointing at both WINS and DNS to register and resolve names, this feature does little but waste time in the current IT environment. A few years down the road when Microsoft has been producing clients that are truly not NetBIOS aware or dependent for several previous versions, most clients will be represented in DNS, and this feature will be useful only for backward compatibility. (For more information, check out the "Should I Use WINS Lookups?" section later in this chapter.)

Optimizing the Operating System for DNS

While installing the DNS service is pretty mindless, (setting up your first few zones isn't much more difficult), configuring your server's operating system can be a little tricky. If you don't take the time to configure your operating system properly, you may find yourself with a DNS server that is constantly overutilized and potentially unstable.

Configuring Preferred and Alternate DNS Servers

Windows 2000 has brought two more new pieces of terminology to its operating system environment: preferred DNS server and alternate DNS server. Simply put, a preferred DNS server is the same as a primary DNS server, and an alternate DNS server is the same as a secondary DNS server (in the context of the client DNS configuration).

From the client perspective, the behavior is still the same: preferred is asked first, and then each alternate is asked in order or priority. I believe the change was made to reduce the confusion about having DNS servers that were primary and secondary for zone data and also having DNS servers that were primary and secondary for name resolution.

Make sure that your DNS server is configured to use itself as the preferred DNS server. Because your DNS server needs to resolve names for hosts and services for its own internal processes, pointing your DNS client at the DNS Server service hosted on the local machine prevents DNS queries from being sent to another server. Instead, when the DNS server is properly configured to use its own DNS server service, all requests for DNS data are sent via a local procedure call (LPC) to the server's own service instead of being sent via RPC to another DNS server. Now for the tricky part. Unfortunately, while not difficult to complete, configuring your DNS server to use its own DNS Server service as a preferred DNS server isn't as easy as it seems. Microsoft fails to document the proper way to complete this task, which doesn't really help much.

If you complete what you may assume to be the logical configuration of inputting the IP address of your DNS server in the preferred DNS server field, you will find that you are still using RPC to resolve names.

Entering any valid IP address for the preferred DNS server, even if it is the address of the local device, causes a call to go out to the network protocol stack. Even though this request never makes it to the network, it is still formatted as an RPC call, sent down the network stack, and then sent back up the protocol stack to the DNS service. Eventually, the device recognizes that the request is destined for its own address. The process of internal routing a DNS packet to the network stack just to find the local DNS Server service is very inefficient.

The proper way to configure your DNS server's preferred DNS server address (say that 10 times fast) is to leave the preferred DNS server field blank in the TCP/IP Protocol Properties dialog box. When the primary DNS server field is blank and you click OK to close the Properties dialog box, an error message appears indicating that because the DNS server list is empty, the local address of the DNS server will be used.

After you close the TCP/IP Properties dialog box, opening it again displays the address of the preferred DNS server as 127.0.0.1, which is the loopback address of all TCP/IP devices. Using the loopback address configures the DNS Client service to send an LPC-based

DNS query instead of an RFC-based query. Although the system automatically places this address in this field, the GUI has logic built into it that prevents you from manually entering the loopback address into any field. In other words, you need the error to occur before your DNS server can be properly configured. This makes no sense to me.

Even though you can't add the loopback address as the primary DNS server through the GUI, you can add this value to the registry to achieve the same effect. Enter the value **127.0.0.1** into the **NameServer** data item found in HKLM\System\CurrentControlSet\Services\Tcpip\ Parameters\Interfaces\<*InterfaceName*>. Make sure the loopback address is the first address in the list, which forces the DNS server to use its local DNS service to satisfy DNS requests.

It is always smart to configure all devices to use multiple alternate DNS servers, and the DNS server itself is no exception. The server you use as the first alternate is not nearly as important as choosing which server is the preferred server. Your first alternate DNS server should be another DNS server that is hosting the same AD-Integrated zone that your DNS server is hosting. This ensures that if there is a problem with the local service, name resolution does not stop.

The next DNS server you configure as an alternative should be one of the Standard secondary DNS servers that you implemented (as I recommended in this chapter). Using a DNS server that is hosting a non-AD-Integrated zone for the second alternate DNS server is a good idea because AD corruption could render your preferred and first alternate DNS servers useless.

Configuring DNS Suffixes and Domain Devolution   The DNS suffix (or suffixes) you choose for your DNS server, along with its NIC (or NICs), determines how requests that the DNS server sends to other DNS servers are formatted. Both unqualified names sent to the DNS server in the form of a query and names that need to be resolved by a local administrator use the configured DNS suffixes to qualify names. Normally, you don't need to configure your DNS server to use any other DNS suffixes except those for the namespace that its database hosts. If you configure additional DNS suffixes to resolve unqualified names, you run the risk of slowing down name resolution for all unqualified queries.

Likewise, incorrect configuration of domain devolution can slow down resolution for unqualified names. Domain devolution specifies the way an unqualified name is resolved. You can either append all DNS suffixes configured on the DNS server, or append all of the domain names belonging to the domain to which the DNS server belongs. Normally, there is no reason to specify that domain devolution use DNS suffixes that are not associated with the domain hierarchy of the DNS server.

Configuring Application Response Settings

Application response settings determine how the processor, memory, and cache configuration of a server are tuned to accommodate the server's role. Two options are available in the Application

Response Setting dialog box, which you open by clicking the Performance Options button on the Advanced tab of the System Properties dialog box. The options are Optimize For Foreground Applications and Optimize For Background Services.

Setting the option to support foreground applications configures the server's resources to favor an application or service that is running in the shell or console of the Windows 2000 server. This means programs like Word, Access, or the DNS MMC have more processing time and memory allocated than services running in the background.

However, the DNS Server service that satisfies client requests runs in the background. Configuring your server to support background services gives services such as DNS and AD more processing time and memory. Therefore, you should configure application response to support background services.

Optimizing the Pagefile   Proper placement of a pagefile can greatly increase the performance of any device. The pagefile in Windows 2000 is always used, no matter how much RAM you have installed or how underused the memory subsystem may be. Windows 2000 loves its pagefile.

To determine the proper location for a pagefile, you must first look at the type of file that a pagefile is and the way that data is read from and written to it. When data is written to a file, it's either written sequentially or randomly.

Sequential writes start at the beginning of the file, and subsequent writes start at the point where the last write stopped. Sequential writes normally provide better read performance because data from the same process is more likely to be placed together. However, sequential writes have a lower performance level because the process always has to find the point in the file at which it can begin writing.

Random writes occur just as the name implies—randomly. Processes write to a random type file wherever they can find space. This sometimes causes data from the same process to be broken up across the disk, which is harder to read but much faster to write.

Because these two different types of files behave very differently with respect to disk usage, it's best to place each type on a drive that houses file types that behave the same way. The pagefile is a random write file. Data is committed in the form of pages wherever the memory subsystem can find space. Contention is another factor to consider when determining the location of not only the pagefile, but all files of substantial size. *Contention* results when two entities need access to the same third entity at the same time, forcing one of the requesting entities to wait its turn. Contention as it relates to files is the result of multiple requests to the disk subsystem and disk hardware for simultaneous file-system access.

If a disk has an excessive amount of contention, all processes suffer performance drags when reading and writing data. To prevent a contention situation that affects the system's pagefile, consider placing the pagefile on a SCSI or IDE bus that is not heavily accessed by another process. This means a disk other than the disk that holds the operating system, which is constantly performing reads and writes.

CODE BLUE

Now for the bad news about moving the pagefile. Unless the pagefile exists in its default location, which is the root of the drive that contains *%Systemroot%* and has the default pagefile name of Pagefile.Sys, the memory dump feature of Windows 2000 will not work. You can configure a memory dump for blue-screen events so that the contents of the system's memory are dumped to the pagefile. Upon rebooting, the data is written to a separate dump file, which you can examine to determine the source of the failure. For memory dumps to work, the pagefile must keep its default configuration.

This behavior is especially a problem for server configurations that require more than 4gb of pagefile. All versions of Windows 2000 support a maximum pagefile size of 4gb, so any additional pagefile needed will have to be maintained in a second pagefile.

Configuring Placement of AD DIT and Log Files

If you have wisely chosen to implement an AD-Integrated zone, you need to consider moving some of your AD-related processes off the disk that holds the operating system. This optimizes performance on your servers. If a server houses an AD partition and is also acting as a DNS server, you have to be concerned with the AD files (Ntds.Dit and the AD log files), as well as all the operating-system files.

 NOTE: Some Microsoft documentation recommends moving the AD Sysvol to a separate partition due to the potential risk of having it consume too much space. That risk can result in an operating-system failure. This is a manageability and security issue rather than a performance issue, so movement of Sysvol will not be addressed.

When you install AD, files are installed in many places, but I am concerned only with the placement of the actual directory, Ntds.Dit and the AD log files.

Ntds.Dit is the default file name for the copy of AD that the domain controller houses. This file houses all AD information, including any DNS information for AD-Integrated zones. By default, Ntds.Dit is located in *%Systemroot%***\Ntds**. You cannot rename the file, but you can move it. Ntds.Dit is a random-write file type.

The AD log files, named Edbxxx.Log, vary in size and name but are all placed by default in *%Systemroot%*\Ntds. The AD log files are used to track changes to the database for disaster recovery purposes. When a write needs to be committed to AD, it is first written to the log file named Edb.Log. Then it is written to the directory. The Edb.Log file continues to accept writes until it is 10 MB in size, at which time the current Edb.Log file is renamed to Edbxxx.Log (where *xxx* is a sequential number beginning with 1 and incremented as each new log file is created), and a new Edb.Log file is created. The Edb.Log files are sequential files, and they should remain on a disk that houses other sequential files.

Because the Ntds.Dit file is a random file type and the log files are sequential, they should not reside on the same disk. In addition to the difference in file types, there is also a great deal of potential contention for disk access, as some transactions are being written to the log files at the same time that the directory is being written to and read from. For the best performance possible, not only should Ntds.Dit and the log files reside on separate hard drives but they should also be isolated from the operating system. When you are considering disk configuration options for AD domain controllers, think about putting Ntds.Dit on a RAID 5 or mirrored RAID 0 partition that is housed on an isolated SCSI or IDE bus. Locate the log files on a RAID 1 partition that is housed on an isolated SCSI or IDE bus. Locate the operating system, along with its pagefile, on a RAID 5 partition that is housed on an isolated SCSI or IDE bus.

NOTE: Even though it is best to place the pagefile on a separate drive from the operating system when possible, given the high instance of contention if the pagefile is placed on the same bus as either Ntds.Dit or the log files, it is best to place it with the operating system.

Ntds.Dit and the log files can be located anywhere during the Dcpromo process that runs when you promote a member server to the status of domain controller. You can also move all of the AD-related files at any time after that.

Like many other processes in Windows 2000, there is a right way to do this and a wrong way to do this. It may seem easy to just dismount AD, move the files to the new location, and then modify the location values in the registry. However, this is not the right way to accomplish this task. Using any process other than Ntdsutil to move Ntds.Dit and the log files will result in an incomplete migration of data.

Using Ntdsutil to Reconfigure AD Files

Ntdsutil is a powerful command line–driven shell that allows you to complete a great many AD-related administrative tasks. This is the tool to use when you want to move Ntds.Dit and the AD log files to an alternate location after AD has been installed.

Although Ntdsutil can complete all of these tasks, it can successfully run only a few tasks when the domain controller is booted normally. Some tasks that involve manipulation of the AD files require that you run Ntdsutil in directory services restore mode.

Moving Ntds.Dit and the AD log files are tasks that cannot be done when a domain controller has booted normally. To move Ntds.Dit and the log files, complete the following steps:

1. Reboot the domain controller that will have its files moved.

2. When the boot selector displays, press F8 to open the Advanced Startup Option menu.

3. Select directory services restore mode and press ENTER to display the boot loader screen.

4. Select the installation of Windows 2000 that you want to boot into directory services restore mode.

5. When the domain controller has booted, open a command prompt and type **ntdsutil**. Press ENTER to launch the Ntdsutil shell.

6. Type **files** to enter the file management portion of the shell.

Use the following information to move a particular component or file:

❖ To view the current location configuration and other useful AD-file information, type **info** and press ENTER.

❖ To move Ntds.Dit, type **move db to %s** (where %s is the new location). You will see a few screens of information flying by that indicate the status of the operation. Just moving the file is not enough. You must also set the new path to Ntds.Dit for other processes that might need to access the file by typing **set path db %s** (where %s is the new location).

❖ To Move the AD log files, type **move logs to %s** (where %s is the new location). Once the files have been moved, you must set the log file path for any future process that may need to access them by typing **set path logs %s** (where %s is the new location).

❖ To exit the Ntdsutil program at any time, type **quit**. The first time you type quit and press ENTER, you move up to the root Ntdsutil shell, so you must type quit again to completely exit the shell.

NOTE: For a complete list of all supported commands for Ntdsutil, in the Windows 2000 Server Resource Kit, check out Appendix C: Active Directory Diagnostic Tool (Ntdsutil.exe).

Configuring Server Placement

Server placement isn't a task to take lightly. No matter how solid and optimized your DNS design may be, if you drop your servers into network locations that are poorly connected or are too far from clients that will be using its services, your architecture will suffer.

Unfortunately, there is no secret formula for determining where you should place DNS servers. The following general rules and guidelines are helpful.

General Guidelines for Server Placement

You need to document your network layout. In most cases, especially if you are using an AD-Integrated zone, you probably already defined your IP segments logically in AD. If you have not taken the time to document all of your IP networks and the links between them, you need to complete this task. This makes it easier to find logical places to deploy DNS servers.

Some administrators feel that it is most cost-effective to deploy network services in centralized locations, sometimes called network nodes. Using network nodes ensures that all infrastructure components are well connected to one another (because network nodes are normally well connected). This model lowers administrative and support costs because you don't have to support devices that may be deployed to other locations in your network. This centralized model is also more secure because controlling a grouping of servers in a central location is easier than trying to secure servers deployed in multiple locations.

If you are using AD-Integrated DNS, you must also consider the effect of replication traffic on noncentralized environments. In a domain that hosts an AD-Integrated zone, all DCs receive a replica of the DNS data and also a replica of all other domain contents. Placing DNS servers in noncentralized locations may significantly increase WAN traffic, which slows down network access for all users at that site. The network traffic generated from validation and name resolution is notably less than the traffic generated from replicating even an average sized AD domain. This means that having users validate and resolve over the WAN is more efficient than placing AD servers in non-node locations.

On the other hand, centralizing any service creates a situation in which the availability of your DNS service depends on a WAN connection being available to your clients. Unfortunately, the group or division that "owns" the network in IT departments is frequently not the same group that provides the small computing infrastructure. Therefore, a design that leverages centralized sites may not be as available as designs that involve deploying DNS servers to multiple locations. Locating DNS servers at the same location as your DNS clients greatly reduces the dependency on network availability.

In both a centralized and decentralized design, security should be one of your most pressing concerns, especially if you are using an AD-Integrated zone. The data in the DNS database should be considered confidential. If you are using AD-Integrated zones, you must remember that your DNS server is also a DC; therefore, it has a complete set of all AD objects in the domain on its hard drive. This makes physical security an important consideration. If someone can get to the console of your AD-Integrated DNS server, you are at risk for console hacks. Also, if it's not properly physically secured, your DNS server may grow legs and walk off. A missing DNS server is probably the worst security breach you can experience because the individual who has possession of the DC can take his or her time to hack in and compromise the directory.

Remember that each Windows 2000 DC has a directory services restore mode, which is secured through the use of administrative accounts in a Security Accounts Manager (SAM). (This allows you to bring the DC up without mounting AD, which is useful when you need to repair your DC.) The Windows 2000 SAMs can still be cracked very easily by tools like L0pthCrack, which can yield the ID and password of the Administrator account in the directory services restore mode. Administrative access to the directory services restore mode gives anyone complete access to the unmounted AD database. Physical security of DCs is extremely important!

> **TIP:** If you decide to implement a centralized model, consider placing cache-only DNS servers in decentralized locations. DNS servers that just cache lookups increase name resolution performance with a minimum of network traffic. For more information on how to configure your Windows 2000 DNS server to be a cache-only server, see Chapter 2.

Network Communication Considerations

DNS servers need to talk to other DNS servers, to clients, and to administrators. This means that your network must be able to route the traffic that is associated with all DNS functions via TCP and UDP ports. Luckily, in most corporate internal networks, TCP and UDP port access is not blocked or filtered. If your design will be implemented in a network that does leverage router filters, the following ports must be open on segments that need to access either other DNS servers or clients:

◈ **TCP/UDP 53** – Used by DNS clients and DNS servers to send and receive query requests. This port is the only one that you need to have open if you are just resolving names. However, other ports are needed for administrative purposes. You can change the port used to resolve DNS queries on DNS servers by modifying the **SendOnNonDnsPort** registry item found in HKLM\System\CurrentControlSet\Services\DNS\Parameters. Keep in mind that if you modify this value on the server, you must also configure all clients to use the new port number. If you don't, name resolution fails.

❖ **TCP/UDP 88** – Used to validate credentials supplied via a Kerberos ticket. Kerberos is an RFC-compliant authentication protocol that is supported in Windows 2000. Logon to a Windows 2000 DNS server for administration purposes occurs either over Kerberos or via Netlogon (using NTLM).

❖ **TCP 135** – Used to communicate with an RPC device until a dynamic port is assigned. Once two RFC endpoints (two devices talking via RPC) establish communication on this port, a dynamic port above 1024 is negotiated, and that port is used for all future communications.

❖ **TCP 389** – Used for managing only AD-Integrated DNS zones. It provides LDAP communication to Active Directory.

❖ **TCP 445** – Used for Netlogon authentication (which really occurs over NTLM) to a DNS server. If you are not validating on the DNS server by using Kerberos, you are using Netlogon. The authentication protocol you use depends on your specific implementation.

❖ **TCP 1024 and above** – Used in conjunction with the RPC endpoint mapper to move a session's communications off of a static port and onto a randomly assigned port that is negotiated between the RPC endpoints. The purpose of dynamic ports is to offload traffic from any given port, which allows communication with other devices on the same port. Because port communication is serial, if all RPC communication could use a single port, extreme performance degradation would occur.

❖ **TCP 3268 and 3269** – Used for LDAP communication to the Global Catalog service, which is an indexing service of sorts for the directory. Global Catalogs are used by DNS servers that are hosting an AD-Integrated zone to find objects in the directory. Although this port is never directly used by DNS, it is needed for Active Directory. Because you don't have an AD-Integrated zone without AD, this port must be opened.

CODE BLUE

As you may have noticed from the list of TCP and UDP ports that must be opened to facilitate complete DNS communication and management, almost every available port needs to be opened. If you were to configure your routers or firewalls to allow just DNS-related traffic to flow, you would require that several thousand ports be opened. If your filtering scheme must allow several thousand ports to be opened, is it really a filter? Isn't it more like a screen door on a submarine?

As I stated previously, port filtering doesn't tend to be a problem on internal networks for many corporations, but it does present an interesting problem when DNS servers and clients are separated by firewalls. This often occurs with interorganization partnerships or when placing devices in a DMZ. When it is necessary to secure one part of your internal network from another internal or external network, having several thousand ports opened just won't do. This is a problem for AD-Integrated zones because Standard zones require that only port 53 be opened.

The problem is best solved with IPSec because all IPSec traffic must flow through UDP port 500. It doesn't matter which port the data was originally destined for. All traffic destined for another network location is sent down the protocol stack, and it is intercepted by the IPSec driver, which uses an IPSec filter to determine if the destination device requires IPSec. If so, the configured encryption protocol is used to encrypt the data payload, which is encapsulated in a UDP packet destined for port 500.

This packet has a source address reflecting the address of the device sending the packet and a destination address reflecting the target device. The packet is routed through the network and arrives at the destination normally. The destination device recognizes that this is an IPSec packet and attempts to decrypt its payload with its key. If decryption is successful, the payload is sent up the protocol stack and arrives at the originally requested TCP or UDP port just the same as it would have been if the requesting device had sent the traffic over the network.

Configure your DCs to communicate with other DCs via IPSec, and don't include clients requesting DNS resolution in that configuration. If you do not configure your IPSec filter properly, clients may receive IPSec traffic when they are not supposed to. Because they lack the proper decryption key, clients won't be able to read the data. This is a nice solution that requires that the device separating your DCs allows only UDP port 500 and the support of IP forwarding of IP Protocol 50 and 51. This is much more secure than opening several thousand ports. However, there is a cost: IPSec must examine all inbound and outbound traffic to determine if it meets the criteria of the IPSec filter, which may degrade your server's performance.

Site and Replication Considerations

Whether you've implemented centralized or distributed server placement, if you have AD-Integrated zones, you also need to consider placement from an AD Site perspective. *Sites* in AD are collections of multiple TCP/IP segments that are bundled into a single logical object. Each Site serves not only as a replication boundary (providing scheduling and compression, but also as the mechanism responsible for pointing an AD user to the closest resource. This allows you, from a central location, to define the DCs that all users in segments X, Y, and Z should validate against. This sure beats the shotgun-request-and-use-the-first-server-to-answer-no-matter-where-it-is-located behavior of NT clients.

Even though Windows 2000 clients can use Sites to find most AD-published services, they don't use sites to find the closest DNS server. A DNS server in a site does not enable DNS clients to recognize it as being closer than another DNS server in another Site. You must configure clients to use DNS servers either through manual configuration or DHCP.

Placing DNS servers in each site is a good model. AD Sites provide replication compression. There are two types of AD replication: intersite and intrasite. When replication occurs intrasite, the replication changes are sent bit for bit across the network with the thought that if two DCs are in the same site, they should be well-connected and therefore, compression would not be of value. When replication occurs intersite, the DC compresses all replication traffic on the average of 75 percent before being sent to a replication partner. The use of compression allows DCs that are connected by slower links to replicate domain contents without bringing the network to its knees.

Keep this important information in mind when you determine where to place your DCs. If at all possible, place each of your DNS servers in different sites. If you allow all of your DNS servers to sit in one site (or DCs, for that matter), compression will not be used. And since by default, when you build an AD environment, all DCs are placed into the same site, you should design an adequate Site topology no matter how big or small your Windows 2000 deployment will be.

Using WINS Lookup

Windows 2000 DNS gives you the ability to forward any unresolved device names to WINS if an answer cannot be found as a result of normal DNS resolution. Microsoft has provided this functionality in an effort to help you move away from NetBIOS and into DNS. The idea is that as your clients and servers move to Windows 2000 and all future operating systems, they will become less dependent on WINS to the point that one day, NetBIOS will be disabled. This will leave only legacy clients existing in WINS who will be able to access the clients that are no longer using WINS through DNS. This situation creates the need for a mechanism that permits the clients that have NetBIOS disabled to resolve those legacy clients that still exist in WINS.

Should I Use WINS Lookups?

If you have read the rest of this chapter, you should know how I am going to answer this question. Configuring DNS to resolve names through WINS is one of the top 10 all-time bad ideas because it is a thief of processing power and network bandwidth. As the saying goes, "The road to hell is paved with good intentions."

First, let's look at how WINS lookups work. This will give you all of the information you need to make an informed decision about how you can use this feature. When a name resolution request is sent by a client to DNS, DNS still behaves as it should. DNS receives the client query for a name and determines in which domain that name lives. If the name exists in a domain for which the server houses a zone, then the local database is parsed. If the name exists in a domain that the DNS server has no intimate knowledge about, the request is forwarded through the typical recursive process. (Iterative configurations will not leverage WINS integration for reasons to be detailed shortly.)

If the name is not found by the normal recursive process, a name-not-found error is returned to the DNS server that received the original request, which is presumably also the DNS server that has been configured to look up host names in WINS. The DNS server examines the name that was attempting to be resolved by the client once the error is received. If the host portion of the FQDN is 15 characters or shorter, the domain portion of the name is stripped off and a query is sent to WINS for the device name. If the host portion of the name is longer than 15 characters, DNS has the logic implemented to realize that WINS can't support device names longer than 15 characters, so the name is not sent to WINS and an error is handed back to the client.

Once the device name is found to be 15 characters or under, DNS determines which WINS servers have been configured for WINS lookup. DNS treats these WINS servers the same way that a normal WINS client would treat WINS servers that it has been configured to use. So it is important to keep in mind that NetBIOS must still be enabled on any DNS server that hosts a zone, which used WINS lookups. If the name is found in WINS, DNS returns the name to the client. If the name is not found, then the client is sent an error.

When you enable WINS forward lookup in DNS, you are creating an entry in DNS called WINS. This record type holds the IP addresses of the WINS servers that the zone has been configured to use. As you may have guessed, this record type is not RFC compliant. You can also choose to enable WINS reverse lookup, which creates WINS-R records in DNS that hold information about which WINS servers should be used to reverse lookup names, as well as any domain suffix that should be appended to the results when they are returned to the client.

The WINS-R record type is also not RFC defined. The use of both WINS and WINS-R records in a zone that must be transferred to a non-Microsoft DNS server is prohibited and may cause a DNS server failure on the device that does not support the use of these records. Therefore, you can choose not to replicate the WINS and WINS-R records to any other servers besides the one on which the record was created. This solution requires that all DNS servers that need to use WINS and WINS-R records be independently configured with the same records, also configured not to replicate.

Now for the bad news: WINS forward lookups are configured on a zone-by-zone basis. Therefore, each zone that your query comes in contact with that has WINS lookup enabled will attempt to contact WINS if the name can't be found. For example, if you had a DNS environment that consisted of two zones, zone2.zone1.com, that were both configured to use WINS forward lookups, each zone would ask WINS to resolve a failed name. This adds quite a bit of overhead indeed.

In fact, overhead is the real problem with this feature. Not only does overhead extend how long a failed query response takes to be returned to the client; it also forces the DNS server to ask WINS for all failed resolution requests; this number tends to be equivalent to about a quarter of the successful lookups in DNS. All of these extra queries take processing power away not only from the DNS servers but also from the WINS servers, in addition to creating extra network traffic.

Designing WINS Forward Lookups

If I haven't convinced you yet that you don't want to use WINS lookups, at least I should point you in the right design direction. There are two schools of thought when it comes to figuring out the best design solution for your implementation. One methodology is to isolate a zone that just forwards requests to WINS, while the other involves using WINS forwarding in DNS zones just as you would recursive lookups. The solution that you choose should be the one that fits not only your administrative model but also your interoperability needs.

In a design that implements WINS and WINS-R records in the same zone with other DNS data, each zone that needs to resolve names in WINS is configured to use WINS forward lookups and optionally, WINS reverse lookups. This is the easiest but potentially most costly design choice of the two. First of all, unless you are running in a pure Microsoft DNS environment, you must configure each zone to use WINS resolution but not replicate the WINS and/WINS-R records to prevent a non-Microsoft DNS server from receiving the data in a zone transfer. Secondly, all failed lookups happen in the same zone and on the same hardware as all other DNS traffic, which is not ideal.

You have a second and more practical design choice if you want to resolve names through WINS: use a dedicated zone. Scenarios that use dedicated zones involve implementing a zone that has been delegated from your existing namespace that is used to house only WINS and WINS-R records. You must also then configure all of your clients that might potentially use WINS resolution to use this new domain name in their DNS suffix lists so that when a name cannot be resolved, the new zone will be asked to resolve the name. This solution is the best of the two (well, at least the lesser of two evils), but it is more costly from an administrative perspective because it involves configuration changes on all clients in addition to hardware to house a new zone.

Chapter 5

Managing DNS

D esigning a DNS environment is much easier than managing a DNS environment. The design portion of any implementation tends to generate a lot of work in a short amount of time. On the other hand, managing an environment involves completing a number of smaller tasks that span over the course of years. Managing DNS involves those daily tasks, both proactive and reactive, that result in 100 percent uptime and availability of your DNS service.

In this chapter, I'll discuss monitoring options for Windows 2000 DNS servers and the Windows 2000 operating system. Monitoring your DNS environment is the key to proactive DNS management. I will also focus on some key administrative tasks and ways to automate them. Finally, I will address disaster recovery in both AD-Integrated and Standard zone configurations.

Monitoring Tools

Monitoring is essential to any successful DNS deployment. Not only does it allow you to take more of a proactive role in your environment but it can also alert you to capacity issues and/or design flaws. By using the monitoring tools found in Windows 2000 and DNS, you can build statistical information about uptime and total capacity, and you can also identify potential problem areas. Without monitoring your DNS environment, you are really flying blind.

Your first step in making monitoring work is to build a baseline. It is difficult to determine how much growth or increased system utilization you're experiencing if you don't know what "normal" looks like on a particular DNS server. By building a baseline for each DNS server, you can determine what the normal conditions and events are for each device. This information should be compared to all successive monitoring efforts to determine if there has been any change in the system. These changes, good or bad, need to be analyzed and some corrective action might need to be taken. The corrective action will vary from a simple software configuration change to a major infrastructure overhaul. If you don't monitor your environment, how will you know the difference?

Several tools can help you provide monitoring and event notification. All of the tools mentioned in the following sections are useful not only in proactive monitoring but also for troubleshooting purposes.

Performance Monitor

Performance Monitor (commonly called PerfMon) is the performance monitoring tool included with all Windows 2000 operating systems. It provides basic capturing, reporting, and alerting capabilities for most major system components and services. When used properly, PerfMon can provide useful information that you can use to trend an existing environment and to call attention to bottlenecks on the local system.

PerfMon comes bundled with several DNS-specific counters to help you identify any DNS problems. Not all of them are useful to each deployment, but everyone should find enough counters to make using the tool worthwhile. I won't try to detail all of the DNS-related counters. That would be a waste of time because some of the counters border on useless. Instead, I will focus on some of the more important counters and will detail their usefulness.

NOTE: For this chapter, I am assuming that you are familiar with Performance Monitor and its use.

The following is a list of useful counters found in the DNS performance object. In some cases, I have defined two counters in the same bullet item. Multiple items in the same bullet represent counters that are related or that provide comparable functionality. When more than one counter is present per bullet, they are separated by a slash (/).

◈ **AXFR Requests Received** – This counter indicates how many full zone transfers were requested from secondary DNS servers.

◈ **Dynamic Update Queued** – This counter indicates how many dynamic update requests have been queued on the DNS server. These requests are waiting for processing time with the DNS Server service. This number should be as close to zero as possible. Anything above two is unacceptable and indicates a possible system bottleneck in the I/O system.

◈ **Dynamic Update Received/sec** – This counter provides good trending and usage numbers by displaying the total number of update requests received. This number is the sum of updates that are accepted and those that are denied.

◈ **Dynamic Update Received/Dynamic Update Rejected** – These two counters can be used together to determine the percentage of requests received in a given time that are either rejected or accepted. I don't think that I need to tell you which counter is which.

◈ **Dynamic Update TimeOuts** – This counter indicates the total number of times that a request could not be satisfied before the update packet expired. A high value indicates a performance problem on the DNS server or a network latency problem.

◈ **Dynamic Update Written to Database/sec** – This counter indicates the total number of dynamic updates written to the database in one second. It is useful in building trending information, in addition to indicating capacity and growth of your DNS environment.

❖ **IXFR Requests Received/IXFR Requests Sent** – These counters indicate the total number of incremental update requests received and sent by the DNS server. The receive counter is useful on primary DNS servers and the sent counter is useful on secondary DNS servers.

❖ **Recursive Queries/sec** – This counter indicates the total number of recursive lookup requests received by the DNS server. Another good trending counter.

❖ **Recursive Query Failure/sec** – This counter indicates the total number of recursive lookup requests that could not be satisfied in a given second. If this number rises suddenly, look for a new application or service that may have just been deployed, which may be using an incorrect name. This number will never be zero, but it should be fairly consistent.

❖ **Secure Update Received/Secure Update Failure** – Using these two counters together can help you identify widespread configuration problems. By default, each DNS client first attempts to update DNS in an unsecured manner. If the DNS server only accepts dynamic updates, then the initial update fails and the client then tries to send a secured update. If you took my advice in Chapter 3 with respect to changing the default client configuration, the receive number should be high and the failure number should be low. If most of your machines have the default configuration, these numbers will match almost one to one.

❖ **Total Query Received/sec** – Do I really need to explain what this is? All I can say is that it is another excellent counter for trending usage and capacity planning. In general, there is no high or low value. The high and low ends of this counter are hardware-specific, which is why building a baseline is so important.

❖ **Total Response Sent/sec** – This counter shows the total number of answers to queries received. This value should be almost equivalent to the Total Query Received/sec counter. Unless there is a problem, the DNS server should always send a client at least a failure or device-not-found message. Failure to respond to any query might indicate that a database problem or a timeout condition is being reached.

The following counters are found in the Process performance object. They detail the behavior of a particular process. For monitoring purposes, we are concerned with the DNS service.

❖ **% Privileged Time** – This counter indicates the percentage of time that DNS process threads executed code in privileged mode. When collected and trended over time, this number can help you identify misbehaving DNS code by calling attention to excessive spikes in usage.

❖ **% Processor Time –** This counter indicates the percentage of time that DNS threads were accessing the processor. If this number is high (over 60 percent), consider upgrading your hardware or increasing the number of DNS servers in your environment to help distribute load. Adding another processor is also helpful in lowering this number, which ideally should be no higher than 40 percent.

❖ **Handle Count –** This counter indicates the total number of handles currently in use by the DNS process. This number should grow and shrink but never continually grow. Continual growth can mean that you have misbehaving code installed and you should start looking for any DNS patches or fixes available from Microsoft.

❖ **IO Data Operations/sec –** This counter indicates the total number of I/O read and write operations issued by DNS to the file system, network subsystem, or any device. A high value can indicate that your DNS server is I/O-starved and might benefit from an I/O upgrade.

❖ **IO Read Operations/sec –** This counter indicates the total number of I/O reads issued to any I/O channel. When compared to the IO Write Operations/sec counter, this number can be helpful in indicating whether your DNS environment is more read- or write-intensive.

❖ **IO Write Operations/sec –** This counter indicates the total number of I/O writes issued to any I/O channel. When compared to the IO Read Operations/sec, this number can be helpful in indicating whether your DNS environment is more read- or write-intensive.

❖ **Page Faults/sec –** This is the number of times per second that the DNS process must fetch a page either from main memory or from disk if the requesting data is not found in the DNS working memory set. This number should not be excessively high unless your system is short on memory or the working set for DNS needs to be increased.

DNS MMC Logging

I wish every Microsoft service had the type of logging granularity that the DNS MMC provides. DNS allows you to select particular events and conditions that you would like captured to the DNS debugging log file (not to be confused with the DNS Event Log). You configure logging on the Logging tab found in a DNS server's Properties dialog box in the DNS MMC.

The Logging tab provides 11 different logging options: Query, Notify, Update, Questions, Answers, Send, Receive, UDP, TCP, Full Packets, and Write Through. Each logging option will either turn debugging on or off (depending on the state of the check box) in a particular area. Here is what is logged when each option is selected:

- **Query** – Logs all queries received from all DNS clients. Selecting this option will fill up your DNS log quickly.

- **Notify** – Logs NOTIFY messages sent to this DNS server from other servers.

- **Update** – Logs all dynamic update requests from DNS clients. This is another logging option that will fill the DNS log file quickly.

- **Questions** – Logs the question section of each DNS packet received on the DNS server. Useful in determining what each client was actually asking for.

- **Answers** – Logs the answer section of each DNS packet sent from the DNS server. Useful in identifying what was sent from DNS compared to what was received on the client.

- **Send** – Logs the number of DNS queries sent by the DNS server.

- **Receive** – Logs the number of DNS query messages received by the DNS server.

- **UDP** – Logs the number of DNS requests that were received over a UDP port.

- **TCP** – Logs the number of DNS requests that were received over a TCP port.

- **Full Packets** – Logs the number of full packets sent and received by the DNS server.

- **Write Through** – Logs the number of packets written through to the DNS database.

One word of warning: enabling debug logging will consume a significant amount of system resources. Therefore, enable debug logging only if you are attempting to troubleshoot a DNS problem. If you need trending and performance analysis, consider using PerfMon or a third-party tool. Logging is strictly a debugging/troubleshooting tool.

All transactions of a particular type are captured in the DNS debug log file, named Dns.Log. By default, Dns.Log is found in **%*Systemroot*\System32\Dns** and has a maximum file size of 4 MB. Both the location and the maximum size of this file are adjustable. You can adjust the log file size by altering the value of the **LogFileMaxSize** data item found in HKLM\System\CurrentControlSet\Services\Dns\Parameters. Once the log file reaches its maximum size, it will begin to overwrite events. You can also specify an alternate location for Dns.Log to reside by editing the **LogFilePath** data item found in HKLM\System\ CurrentControlSet\Services\Dns\Parameters.

BUG ALERT You have altered the **LogFilePath** registry data item and you have verified that the log file resides in the new location. Yet, when you click the Logging tab of your DNS server's Properties dialog box, you notice that the location specified in Log File Location On Server still reflects the default log location. Stop rubbing your eyes. Yes, the tool is incorrectly reporting the location of the log file.

This bug is well-known in the DNS code and still isn't fixed in SP1. Don't despair. Even though it may appear as if logging will not occur because DNS is still looking for a log file in the old location, this is not the case. DNS will log all data to the location that you have specified in the registry. It looks like the log location information is hard-coded into the GUI and not populated from the registry into the GUI as it should be.

DNS Event Log

When DNS is installed on a server, a new Event Log is added named DNS Server. The DNS Event Log, known as the DNS Server Event Log in some circles, records all informational, warning, and error conditions encountered by the DNS Server service. The amount of information that is placed into this log is not in any way configurable . What you see is what you get, and sometimes what you get with the DNS Event Log is pretty thin. Therefore, the DNS Event Log is useful at painting problems and error conditions only with a broad brush. It is a good tool that makes you aware of a problem, but if you need detailed information about what is actually occurring, you must enable DNS debug logging. Don't rely solely on the DNS Event Log for accurate problem identification.

DNS MMC Monitoring

Okay, so the DNS MMC Monitoring functionality is weak. That doesn't mean that it can't be useful (albeit extremely limited). The functionality on the DNS MMC Monitoring screen (found by clicking the Monitoring tab of any DNS server's Properties dialog box) allows you to test recursive and iterative lookups.

The only time this tool is even remotely useful is right after a DNS server has been set up. It allows you to send an iterative query (called a simple query on this screen) to the local database. You also can send a recursive query to your root servers to test offsite resolution. For some reason, you have the ability to schedule these tests to be run at set intervals. To establish scheduled tests, select the Perform Automatic Testing At The Scheduled Interval box and specify the interval at which the tests should occur.

That is all that this wonderful tool does. Almost a waste of a .dll, wouldn't you say?

CODE BLUE

Alright, I don't know if this is really a bug, but it certainly isn't a feature. If for some reason you have configured the DNS MMC Monitoring tests to run at an interval, you have probably noticed that the results of these tests don't seem to be recorded anywhere. When I first started playing with this "monitoring" tool, I expected to find the results of the tests in the Event Log or in the Dns.Log file. I found the test results in neither location. This tool records the success or failure of each test only on the Test Results screen of the Monitoring tab. How dumb is this? At least port the results out to a log or give us the ability to send an alert when one of the tests fails! Forcing administrators to open the DNS MMC just to view the results of a basic health test is ridiculous. If this tool weren't so worthless in the first place, I might be a little more upset about this "feature."

Common Administrative Tasks

In Chapter 2, I detailed how to use the DNS MMC to complete a number of configuration and administrative changes to the DNS database and its contents. Although using an MMC is ideal, in many cases, it is desirable to execute administrative tasks either from a command line or from a script.

Believe it or not, DNS does not have nearly as many Resource Kit or command line–based tools as WINS. There may be several reasons for this. One reason may be that WINS has been part of the Microsoft culture for longer and has had more opportunity for internal tool development. Another reason may be that because you can AD-Integrate DNS zones in Windows 2000, all data is made available through ADSI and LDAP. Allowing the DNS data to be accessed via ADSI and LDAP lets administrators write their own scripts using any Windows Scripting Host (WSH)–supported language. Who knows why there are fewer Microsoft-provided tools for this critical component? When it is all said and done, you have two choices for administering DNS with something other than the DNS MMC: dnscmd and scripting. I will discuss both dnscmd and scripting as they relate to a particular administrative function.

Dnscmd

The dnscmd tool is found in the Windows 2000 Support Tools. You launch dnscmd by running Dnscmd.Exe in the command prompt, followed by option switches. Unlike many other utilities, dnscmd does not launch a shell into which commands are entered interactively. Instead of using a shell interface, all options must be specified at run time.

The following is a generic dnscmd command string that displays some options that must always be defined. Descriptions of the command string's options follow.

dnscmd <ServerName> <Command> [<Command Parameters>]

where:

◈ **ServerName** – The name of the DNS server to be contacted. This option supports the use of the server's IP address, host name, and NetBIOS name. When using both the IP address and host name, RPC over TCP is used. When using the NetBIOS name of the DNS server, RPC over Named Pipe is used.

◈ **Command** – The supported commands that the dnscmd tool can complete. If a command is followed by a slash and a question mark (/?), the syntax of the command is displayed.

◈ **Command Parameters** – Any options that the specified command supports.

ADSI Scripting

The Active Directory Services Interface (ADSI) is a collection of COM objects that exposes the directory structure of AD to processes. ADSI is used as an API of sorts: it allows applications, services, scripts, or any other programming logic to gain access to objects housed inside AD. ADSI is not a new Windows 2000 feature. ADSI originated in the NT 4 space but was limited to accessing objects within NT's Security Accounts Manager (SAM) database. Now ADSI permits access to all of AD's contents and comes bundled with Windows 2000.

Once we were given the ability to AD-Integrate DNS data, ADSI became interesting from a DNS perspective. Because all AD data is accessible through ADSI, we can use ADSI to manipulate DNS data. This feature is nice because now we can write our own custom tools instead of waiting on Microsoft or a third-party developer to bring a management tool to market.

There are many different ways to access AD through ADSI. The easiest way to expose ADSI functionality is to use scripting. And wouldn't you know it, Windows 2000 comes with its own script interpreter shell named WSH. This preinstalled script interpreter gives you the ability to write Visual Basic, Java, and Perl scripts that can be used on any Windows 2000 device. Because all of the previously mentioned scripting languages provide access to AD via ADSI, you can choose the scripting language that is easiest for you to use.

Of the four supported script types mentioned, Visual Basic is the easiest scripting language to learn. Not only is it simpler than the others, but more support and documentation is available for Visual Basic Scripting (VBS) than for most other scripts. Once again, I want to reiterate that you can use any of the supported scripting languages to access DNS data when it is housed in AD, but for illustration purposes, I will use VBS.

Creating a New Zone

Although you could use scripting to create a new zone, it is not a good use of time. Creating new zones is not something that you will be doing frequently. Because creating scripts requires an investment in time and effort, they are most valuable when automating frequent tasks. Instead, try using dnscmd to create a new zone. Use the following syntax:

dnscmd (*ServerName*) **/ZoneAdd** <*ZoneName*> <*ZoneType*> [(*Options*)]

where:

* **ZoneName** – The FQDN of the zone to be created.
* **ZoneType** – The type of zone to be created. Supported values are the following:
    * **/Primary /file** <**FileName**> – Creates a primary zone using the filename specified.
    * **/Secondary /file** <**FileName**> – Creates a secondary zone using the filename specified.
    * **/DsPrimary** – Creates an AD-Integrated zone.
* **Options** – The supported options for the zone creation. Supported values are the following:
    * **/load** – Creates a new zone using an existing zone file.
    * **/a** <**AdminName**> – Establishes the zone administrator's e-mail address as an RP record.

Deleting a Zone

Deleting a zone is another task that is not fit for a script but is a perfect candidate for dnscmd. To delete an existing zone with dnscmd, use the following syntax:

dnscmd (*ServerName*) **/ZoneDelete** <*ZoneName*> **/DsDell /f**

where:

* **DsDel** – The zone specified should be deleted from AD.
* **F** – Execute without confirmation.

Changing a Zone Type

Use dnscmd to change an existing zone type to another zone type with the following syntax:

dnscmd (*ServerName*) **/ZoneResetType** <*ZoneName*> <*Property*> [(*Options*)] where:

❖ **Property** – The zone type to which the existing zone will be changed. Supported values are as follows:

  ❖ **/Primary /file <FileName>** – Changes the zone type to Standard primary by using the filename specified.

  ❖ **/Secondary <MaseterIPAddress> /file <FileName>** – Changes the zone type to Standard secondary that is a slave to the master DNS server specified. This zone is created by using the filename specified.

Creating New Entries

It isn't always feasible to use the MMC to create new entries in DNS, especially if you have a substantial list of entries that need to be created at once. For this task, it makes sense to use a script when possible. By using a script, you can write in the logic, if needed, to pull entries from a spreadsheet or database and create new dnsNode objects in an AD-Integrated zone. Unfortunately, creating entries in an AD-Integrated zone also involves placing the IP address of the object you are creating into the dnsRecord attribute of the dnsNode object. This is unfortunate because the data field that is used to populate the IP address or host-name information (depending on if the record is an A record or a CNAME record) uses hex. This complicates the task of creating a script that imports a list of devices that need to be created in DNS, to say the least. Converging the multiple decimal values that make up a device's IP address into a hex value cannot be easily achieved in a script.

When creating new entries in DNS, stick with dnscmd. Hopefully, most of your clients who must have a host name in DNS will dynamically update so that the need to create static records is infrequent. Here is the syntax to add a record to DNS with dnscmd:

dnscmd (*ServerName***) /RecordAdd <***Zone***> <***NodeName***> [/Aging] [<***TTL***>] <***RRTyple***> <***RRData***>**

where:

❖ **Zone** – The name of the zone to which this record will be added.

❖ **NodeName** – The name given to the record when it is added.

❖ **/Aging** – The switch that determines that this record should be subject to aging and scavenging. By default, records placed into DNS statically are not subject to aging or scavenging.

❖ **TTL** – The syntax used to specify the TTL for this record if **/Aging** has been used.

❖ **RRType** – The type of record to be created. Supported values are A, NS, CNAME, MB, MD, PTR, MF, MG, MR, MX, RT, AFSDB, SRV, SOA, AAAA, TXT, X24, HINFO, ISDN, MINFO, RP, WKS, WINS, and WINS-R.

❖ **RRData** – The data placed into the record. The exact information placed into this field needs to match the data that will be expected from **RRType** (i.e., an IP address should not be in the **RRData** field of a CNAME record). For a complete listing of which data is supported in each **RRType**, please type **dnscmd /recordadd /?**.

Renaming Existing Entries

You can use the following sample script to rename an existing DNS entry. With a little modification, you can use this script to import names of devices that need to be renamed from an external database or spreadsheet.

Set Container = GetObject ("LDAP://dc=*DnsZoneName*, cn=MicrosoftDns, cn=System, dc=*domain*, dc=*com*")

Set NewObjectName = Container.MoveHere("LDAP://dc=*OldDnsEntryName*, dc=*DnsZoneName*, cn=MicrosoftDns, cn=System, dc=*domain*, dc=*com*" , "dc=*NewDnsEntryName*")

where:

❖ **DnsZoneName** – The AD container name that is housing the AD zone. This will be the same as the AD dnsZone object name. Depending on your zone delegation model, there may be multiple "dc=" entries that lead to the location of your DNS object.

❖ **dc=domain, dc=com** – The FQDN of the domain that houses the DNS object. There may be more than two "dc=" entries depending on your domain and DNS design.

❖ **OldDnsEntryName** – The current host name of the object that will be renamed. This should be equivalent to the name of the dnsNode object.

❖ **NewDnsEntryName** – The name that the dnsNode object will be given.

Deleting Existing Entries

You can remove existing DNS entries by using both dnscmd and a script. Consider using dnscmd for those one-off or infrequent deletions and scripts to automate the removal of several entries. Automating the removal of DNS records should be of special interest to you if you have implemented zones leveraging secured dynamic updates. As you recall, when using secured updates, each entry in DNS is secured using the globally unique identifier (GUID) of the device that placed the record into the database. While this is a great way to ensure that only the device that originally placed the record into DNS can update that same record, it can be problematic if your device suddenly dies or has a directory identity change. Because the

GUID owns the DNS record, not necessarily the machine, if a new GUID is generated for the device, the device will not be able to update its own name in DNS. Events that can change a GUID include rebuilding a device and removing/rejoining the AD domain.

If your device can't update its own name because of a GUID change, the easiest way to resolve the issue is to remove the device's old entries. Once the old entries are removed, the device will not be prevented from registering its records in DNS.

You can use the following sample script to "seek and destroy" entries with the name specified.

ON ERROR RESUME NEXT

Set ou = GetObject("LDAP://dc=*DnsZoneName*, cn=MicrosoftDns, cn=System, dc=*domain*, dc=*com*")

Call ou.delete("dnsnode", "dc=*EntryName*")

where:

◈ **DnsZoneName** – The name of the AD-Integrated zone name. Your environment may have multiple entries representing each delegated zone.

◈ **dc=domain, dc=com** – The FQDN of the domain that houses the DNS object. There may be more than two "dc=" entries depending on your domain and DNS design.

◈ **dnsnode** – The class of object to be deleted. This should never change unless this script is modified to delete another object class.

◈ **EntryName** – The host name as it appears in the entry. Keep in mind that entries for records in subdomains contained within a zone will have a host name that reflects not only the host name but also the domain label preceding the name of the zone. For example, if you had a zone named domain.com that had a subdomain named sub, a host with the name homer would have a dc of homer.sub. Depending on your environment, you may need to implement multiple "Call ou.delete" lines of code, each representing a different domain level. Using the same scenario, if you didn't know where in the DNS environment homer registered its records, one "Call ou.delete" line would delete any object found with a name homer (dc=homer) and the other would delete any object with the name homer.sub (dc=homer.sub). This is why it is important to place the error-handling statement at the beginning of the script. Without error handling defined, a single error will halt the whole script.

Now let's remove an entry with dnscmd by entering the following syntax:

dnscmd (*ServerName*) /RecordDelete<*Zone*> <*OwnerName*> <*RRTyple*> [/f]

where:

- ❖ **Zone** – The name of the zone from which this record will be removed.

- ❖ **OwnerName** – The name of the device where the deletion should occur.

- ❖ **RRType** – The type of record to be deleted. Supported values are A, NS, CNAME, MB, MD, PTR, MF, MG, MR, MX, RT, AFSDB, SRV, SOA, AAAA, TXT, X24, HINFO, ISDN, MINFO, RP, WKS, WINS, and WINS-R.

- ❖ **/f** – The state of dnscmd's conformation mode. Specifying this switch will cause the command to execute without confirmation.

What About SRV Records?

If I have done a good job of explaining what can occur when a device is given a new GUID in respect to secured zones, you should be asking yourself the following question: What happens to the SRV records that a domain controller has registered when it is given a new GUID?

You may find that, by no choice of your own, domain controllers need to be rebuilt often. When these "new" devices are brought back onto the network with the same name, they receive a new GUID from AD. This new GUID is not the same GUID used to create all of the records that now exist in DNS for the domain controller. The old GUID owns not only the standard DNS entries but also all of the SRV records that the domain controller registered before its untimely demise.

At first, this may seem like an administrative headache because domain controllers register SRV records in many different places, and each one needs to be found and removed. Luckily, the ACL on SRV records gives Enterprise Domain Controllers Full Control by default. This means that even if another device registered SRV records with its GUID, any other domain controller can overwrite its records at any time. So, in the case of a domain controller that has been rebuilt and given a new GUID, you need to ensure only that the A and PTR records are removed. All of the other records will be dynamically updated, thanks to the rights given to the Enterprise Domain Controllers.

Disaster Recovery

When DNS works, it works well. When DNS breaks, it breaks well, too. Having a sensible disaster-recovery process in place can help you quickly recover from any DNS-related problems. Remember, without name resolution, it doesn't matter how available all of your other servers and services are. If they aren't resolvable, then they are as good as down for most users.

Disaster recovery needs to be addressed in different ways depending on your chosen implementation. A disaster-recovery plan will look one way for Standard zones, but it will look completely different for AD-Integrated zones.

General Disaster-Recovery Guidelines

Here are some general guidelines to follow when crafting a disaster-recovery plan. They may seem like common sense, but . . .

❖ **Dry run** – Never assume that your backups are successful. If you do, you will probably find out that you are wrong at the most inopportune time. On a quarterly basis, create an OU containing useless data. Let that OU and its contents replicate around the directory, and then delete it. Now test your restore process and procedures by trying to restore that OU. Make it a habit to complete this type of testing. It is harmless, and it is a good way to test not only your software, but also your process.

❖ **Offsite storage** – Consider storing backup media not only in the same physical location as the domain controller that you are backing up but also at an alternate physical location. In many cases, having an offsite backup could save the day. Such cases would include fire, flood, or an earthquake. Don't assume that because you backed up directory contents from one domain controller, they won't be restored to another.

❖ **Secure your backups** – Keep in mind what other information is held in a backup of AD besides the DNS information. All sorts of potentially sensitive data exists, including IDs, passwords, and in some cases, Social Security Numbers. Treat these backups as confidential.

❖ **Use Standard secondary servers** – I know I already said this, but it is worth mentioning again. Consider using Standard secondary servers that transfer zone data from your AD-Integrated zones. These administrative-only DNS servers can be used in case of global DNS failure (check out Chapter 4 for details).

AD-Integrated Zones

If you have implemented AD-Integrated zones, your biggest disaster-recovery concern should be AD. Because all DNS data is held in AD, you are bound by the same restrictions as any AD disaster-recovery plan. This is both a blessing and a curse.

While there are some disaster-recovery advantages to AD-Integrating your DNS zones, there are more disadvantages. When compared to the flat file that Standard zones implement, dealing with data loss is a multi-master, change-anywhere, corrupt-anywhere environment, AD-Integrated DNS is much more complex than Standard DNS. Be that as it may, AD-Integrated DNS is still a great solution.

Replication-Based Disaster Recovery

Because DNS is housed in the directory, replication-based disaster recovery is extended to the DNS database. Because all domain controllers in the domain in which an AD-Integrated zone has been implemented will have a copy of the DNS database, your chances of being affected by a single server outage are greatly reduced. By replicating all domain contents to all domain controllers, all but one of your domain controllers could suffer from a catastrophic failure and your data would still remain intact.

Replication-based disaster recovery mitigates most concerns and issues surrounding one or more devices failing, but it doesn't address all disaster-recovery scenarios. Replication-based disaster recovery is a viable solution only in situations where DNS data is not corrupt or has not been deleted from the database.

When data corrupts in a partition of AD, that corruption can be replicated to all domain controllers. If corruption is replicated to all domain controllers, even though all domain controllers are available, they may all have bad data. Likewise, if data has been removed from DNS as a result of an accidental or deliberate deletion event, all domain controllers will also eventually receive the deletion notice. Once the deletion notice is received on a particular domain controller, the data is immediately removed. As you can see, in the case of a deletion event or data corruption, replication-based disaster recovery is of little value.

CODE BLUE

In both the case of corruption and removal of data, a slight chance exists that you can save your data before it is too late. Because replicating DNS data is not an urgent and immediate event in the AD replication scheme, it may be possible to find a domain controller that has not yet received the change. If you can find a domain controller that hasn't replicated the corrupt or deleted data into its local database, you can instantly break replication between that device and all other domain controllers.

By breaking replication, you are essentially firewalling off that domain controller from the other domain controllers that have the undesired data. You can then perform an authoritative restore of the DNS data. Once this restore is complete (as explained in the next section), the data that the quarantined domain controller holds will be viewed by AD as the most recent data. Because it is the most recent, it will overwrite any other corrupt data or deleted data once replication is reestablished.

Backup/Restore-Based Disaster Recovery

If the good old replication-based disaster recovery failed, your only hope is to restore from media—that is, if you have backed up your data. Backing up DNS data when it resides in AD means you must have knowledge about backing up the directory itself. The same is true of the restore process. Unfortunately, I can't discuss DNS disaster recovery unless I discuss AD disaster recovery. I am going to keep the discussion focused on DNS, but sometimes, to completely explain a feature or component, I must drift into the AD disaster-recovery process.

When backing up AD and its contents, two classifications of data are important: system state and AD. When you back up system state, you are backing up all of the state information that identifies a particular domain controller as an individual device. System state is restored in cases where a domain controller has been rebuilt but needs to maintain its original identity. It is entirely possible to bring a new domain controller up to replace a failed domain controller without restoring the system state onto it. Even though it is possible to do this, being able to reproduce a domain controller exactly as it was before failure is beneficial.

When the AD gets backed up, not only does the directory file (Ntds.Dit) get backed up, but so do all of the log files, SYSVOL contents, and AD-specific registry information. This data is the core of the domain controller. Because AD is so heavily tied to a domain controller, certain bits of the backed up AD data may not properly restore to any domain controller besides the domain controller from which the backup was taken. This is one of the reasons you want to back up system state.

When it's time to restore the AD data (including the DNS data in AD), you can either restore the data in nonauthoritative or authoritative fashion. When data is restored in a nonauthoritative fashion, data written to the domain controller from the backup media has the same Update Sequence Number (USN) assigned to it that was present at backup. Domain controllers use the USN of an object to determine if changes being sent to it are newer than the version of the object that resides in its database. When data is restored in a nonauthoritative fashion, it will be overwritten by any replica copy of the restored object that has a higher USN.

This little problem is resolved by performing an authoritative restore. In an authoritative restore, the USN of the restored object is increased either by a default value or by a user-defined value. Once the object has been resorted with a higher USN than any of its replicas in the domain, it becomes the most recent record. Once replication occurs, a record that has been restored by means of an authoritative restore will overwrite any other replica copies of the same data.

If you need to perform an authoritative restore, you can do so with Ntdsutil. As you may recall from the last chapter, Ntdstul is a powerful command-line shell that lets you manipulate the directory directly. It is also the tool that you use to perform authoritative restores. To authoritatively restore your DNS data, complete the following steps:

1. Boot the domain controller where the DNS data will be restored to, into Directory Services Recovery Mode. Enter Directory Services Recovery Mode by selecting the Directory Services Recovery Mode option in the Advanced Startup Options.

2. Once in recovery mode, restore the backed up Ntds.Dit and log files to the domain controller using your native Windows 2000 or third party backup utility of choice.

3. Once the restore process has finished, run Ntdsutil.Exe.

4. Once in the Ntdsutil shell, type **authoritative restore** and press ENTER.

5. Once in the Authoritative Restore shell, you have a few options:

   ❖ If you wish to mark the whole local directory as authoritative, type **restore database**, keeping in mind that all data in the local database will overwrite all data on all other domain controllers at the next replication interval.

   ❖ If you want to restore only the DNS data, which I recommend, go to the next step.

6. Type **restore subtree LDAP://LDAP Path to the dnsZone object to be restored**. Press ENTER. Now all USNs for all objects in the specified location will be updated. All other data in the database that you have restored will still contain its original USN and will be subject to overwriting when replication occurs.

7. Once the authoritative restore is complete, reboot your domain controller into normal mode.

You are done. Just give AD enough time to replicate contents to and from this domain controller. Depending on the size of your AD, this could take a while.

Standard Zones

When compared to an AD-Integrated zone, disaster recovery for Standard DNS servers is a breeze. All data in a Standard zone is held in a single file *ZoneName*.Dns. Because primary DNS servers are the only devices that can update a Standard zone, all other DNS servers are read-only. Therefore, if one of the Standard secondary DNS servers fails or corrupts its local copy of the database, just delete the database. Once the database on a secondary server has been removed, if the proper relationship has been established between it and the primary server, all contents of the zone will be replicated back to it.

If the failure or corruption occurs on the primary DNS server, simply stop the DNS Server service. Then copy the backed up database file over the old database file and restart the DNS Server service. You also have the option of restoring the database to another location; then you can change the database location from which the particular zone loads in the DNS MMC to reflect the new location. If the corruption has not replicated to the secondary servers yet, you also have the option of changing one of the secondary servers to a primary server. Its uncorrupted database will then be replicated to all of the secondary DNS servers.

Part II

WINS

Chapter 6

WINS Server Architecture

T he Windows Internet Name Service (WINS) is Microsoft's implementation of a Network Basic Input/Output System (NetBIOS) name server. WINS, like DNS, is used to resolve device names to TCP/IP addresses for clients and servers.

Unlike DNS, WINS resolves NetBIOS names to IP addresses rather than host names to IP addresses. Both NetBIOS names and host names serve the same goal, which is to identify a device or entity within a namespace.

Why WINS in Windows 2000?

Until Windows 2000, the primary method of name registration and resolution for Microsoft clients was WINS. In Windows NT 4 and earlier, NetBIOS is so essential that it has its own Network Device Interface Specification (NDIS) interface called NetBIOS over TCP (NetBT). Programmers were encouraged to use NetBT to gain network access for their applications. Windows 2000 now uses DNS as the operating system's primary name registration and resolution service, and programmers are now encouraged to use either the Winsock interface or the Transport Driver Interface (TDI) to gain network access.

Despite the philosophical change in name resolution preference, several factors still make the complete eradication of WINS impossible, even in a pure Windows 2000 environment.

As Microsoft released information about Windows 2000, before and during its beta test period, the company proclaimed that the new operating system would allow you to trash your WINS environment and move to a 100-percent DNS environment.

Not so. Microsoft has realized that WINS is here to stay for a while. As a result, the WINS service is available in all versions of Windows 2000 server, many applications such as the Terminal Services Client won't work without it, and the DNS Server service depends on it (explained in Chapter 7). Don't believe the hype. NetBIOS is still a very important component in Windows 2000.

Understanding NetBIOS

To completely understand the need for WINS, you need to learn about the evolution of NetBIOS. NetBIOS is defined in RFCs 1001 and 1002, which detail all aspects of the technology, including the NetBIOS name resolution and registration processes, as well as the need for a NetBIOS name server.

Both RFC 1001 and 1002 were authored in early 1987 (known to some as the dark ages of computing). At that time, many proprietary solutions were used to interconnect computer systems to share data. The major problem with these early LANs was that because each interconnection solution was proprietary, it was exclusive to a single hardware vendor. This made connecting devices from multiple vendors impossible. Consequently, organizations had to live without networking or buy solutions from a single vendor. Either option is quite limiting.

NetBIOS was one of many purposed initiatives with the goal of resolving connectivity issues by linking dissimilar systems together through the use of a standard network interface. IBM was a major proponent of NetBIOS and championed its use by implementing it on their systems even before the RFCs were drafted. Although a popular myth is in circulation that IBM inked the NetBIOS RFCs, this isn't true. Both RFCs clearly state that they are vendor-independent documents that detail the NetBIOS specification. They also go on to state that for purposes of illustration, examples given in the RFC deal with the IBM implementation. There was some obvious link between IBM and the author of the RFC, but to me, that link isn't crystal clear.

Combined, RFCs 1001 and 1002 illustrate the NetBIOS interface that is used to provide services and data to applications and users across a network, between dissimilar machines. TCP/IP is defined in the RFCs as the protocol that's used to deliver all NetBIOS-related traffic. Each NetBIOS-enabled device is configured to expose a NetBIOS interface to both the operating system and to applications. This interface is responsible for abstracting the specifics of the network from the requesting entity. The interface does this by handling all transportation (via TCP or UDP), communication, name registration, and name resolution tasks on behalf of the application or service.

Name Registration and Name Resolution

Name registration is the process a device or entity performs to register all of its NetBIOS names with the NetBIOS name server, which enables the device to be resolved by other devices. This process, which is spawned by the client, is detailed in Chapter 7.

Name resolution is the process of finding the address of a device when only its name is known. In NetBIOS, a client can resolve a name from three possible locations: a broadcast, an LMHOSTS file, and a NetBIOS name server.

◈ Broadcast – In a scenario in which NetBIOS uses broadcasts, the source device attempting to locate the target device sends a broadcast packet to the local segment requesting that the device that belongs to the name return its address. All devices on the local segment examine this packet, and those that aren't the intended recipient discard the message. Because broadcasting causes extra processing on all devices on the segment, and also because broadcast requests are unable to transverse routers, its implementation was and is limited.

❖ LMHOSTS – LMHOSTS files are flat files that contain name-to-address mappings, and are found either on a central server or on the hard drive of each client. When a name must be resolved, this file is parsed. If a match is found, communication is established. The administrative overhead of this solution makes it practical only in small organizations.

❖ NetBIOS name server – The NetBIOS name server is loosely defined in both RFCs and is expanded on by Microsoft in their WINS offering. It provides a means for devices to dynamically register and house their names in a central database. All devices are also configured to query that database when name resolution is needed.

Despite the method you implement, once an IP address has been resolved to the name, the NetBIOS interface can establish communication with the other device using TCP/IP.

NOTE: Microsoft provides additional functionality and other potentially authoritative resources for resolving NetBIOS names in certain implementations by using Microsoft Enhanced Node Types. Check out Chapter 7 for complete details.

NetBIOS Names

To use NetBIOS, a device must have a NetBIOS name. The exact definition of a NetBIOS name varies slightly from vendor to vendor because the RFC states only that the NetBIOS name must be no longer than 16 characters and that all available characters are valid. The only real limitation in the RFC is that no NetBIOS name can start with an asterisk. These are broad definitions when compared to the DNS naming standards, wouldn't you say?

The Microsoft implementation of NetBIOS names allows a maximum of 15 characters. This limit permits Microsoft to reserve the sixteenth character for system, service, and application registration. True to the RFC naming rules, any Microsoft device can have a NetBIOS name that contains any combination of alpha and numeric characters but can't begin with an asterisk. In line with the RFCs, each Microsoft client registers its name with its NetBIOS name server, which can be WINS or any other comparable solution.

NetBIOS 16th Character

Microsoft NetBIOS clients use the available 16th character to register any service or application that they host, which enables WINS to also act as a service locator to NetBIOS clients. These services and applications can include those present in the operating system such as the workstation service, or as a result of installed applications such as SQL Server.

When a requesting device attempts to resolve a service name, it queries the NetBIOS name server to see if the correct 16th character is appended to the device's name. For example, if you were to open SQL Server Enterprise Manager and attempt to add a server to manage named BAILEY, the device hosting SQL Server Enterprise Manager would contact WINS and request the IP address of the SQL entry for BAILEY. If BAILEY didn't register its SQL service with the SQL 16th character in WINS, the effort fails. If BAILEY has registered the SQL 16th character, the IP address is returned to the resolver and SQL Server Enterprise Manager establishes a SQL session with the address returned by WINS.

Microsoft clients support many types of 16th characters, including the following:

❖ *computer_name*[00h] – Registered by the Workstation service, which facilitates connectivity to other systems and their shares.

❖ *computer_name/user_name*[03h] – Registered by the Messenger service and used to send messages to the object in the form of net send or winpopup. Both the computer and the locally logged on user register this type, which allows a message to be sent to either one.

TIP: Using the 03h record is a great way to find an owner of a device, which is a difficult task in an NT environment. Just look for the 03h record with the same IP address as the computer you're seeking. You'll find the logon name of the last user, and you can use the logon ID to search an HR database or even the Security Accounts Manager (SAM) of a Master User Domain (MUD), for the full name.

❖ *computer_name*[06h] – Registered by Routing and Remote Access Service (RRAS or RAS).

❖ *domain_name*[1Bh] – Registered by each Windows DC operating as a domain master browser.

❖ *computer_name*[1Fh] – Registered by Network Dynamic Data Exchange (NetDDE), which is used for cut-and-paste functions.

❖ *computer_name*[20h] – Registered by the Server Service. This allows clients to connect to hosted shares.

❖ *computer_name*[21h] – Registered by the RAS client.

❖ *computer_name*[BEh] – Registered by the Network Monitoring Agent service.

❖ *computer_name*[BFh] – Registered by the Network Monitor utility.

❖ *domain_name*[1Ch] – Registration containing all IP addresses of all domain controllers in a domain. This entry can hold up to 25 IP addresses.

❖ *domain_name*[1Eh] – Registered by the master browsers, sometimes referred to as the segment master browsers. Represents a group of Master Browsers.

❖ *domain_name*[1Eh] – Registered by all devices that are capable of becoming any browser role.

❖ *group_name*[20h] – Registered for an *Internet Group,* which is a logical administrative grouping of resources.

❖ _MSBROWSE_ [01h] – Registered by the Master Browser of a segment.

WINS Architecture

When Microsoft released Microsoft Network Client (MNC) 3.0, the company made a decision that would affect its operating-system line for years to come: MNC 3.0, which ran on MS-DOS, supported NetBIOS as a network interface.

WINS, Microsoft's implementation of a NetBIOS name server, was first offered in Microsoft's LAN Manager product. WINS is loosely based on the RFC specifications for a NetBIOS name server. As was the case with DNS, deviations from the RFC were implemented to make the service more stable and scalable. Because WINS leverages both RFC- and non-RFC–compliant features, Microsoft now refers to it affectionately as an Enhanced NetBIOS name server.

Microsoft provides the WINS service on all versions of Windows 2000 server and supports WINS client functionality in all versions of Windows 2000, including Professional.

The WINS Server Service

The WINS service is the responsible for launching the WINS server and its database. This service, configurable through the Services MMC, is housed in an executable named Wins.exe that is located in the %SystemRoot%\System32 directory.

This service starts automatically when the Windows 2000 server boots and logs on under the Local System context. If the service fails, the default configuration is to restart the service on the first, second, and subsequent failures.

No services depend on WINS, but WINS depends on the following services:

❖ NTLM Security Provider – Provides NT LAN Manager (NTLM) authentication services.

❖ Remote Procedure Call – Provides intersystem communications, such as replication requests.

❖ Security Accounts Manager (SAM) – Found on any Windows 2000 device that isn't functioning as a domain controller. I've been unable to determine from Microsoft why the dependency exists.

WINS Components

WINS uses a flat namespace instead of the hierarchical namespace that DNS uses. A flat namespace provides no way to partition the data into separate logical units. This means that all NetBIOS names in WINS exist in a common space, requiring unique names for every device and entity. This limitation means that WINS doesn't scale well in large environments and increases your amount of administration to ensure uniqueness.

The WINS architectural components cover three categories:

* WINS server – The WINS server provides name registration and resolution services to clients. It also serves as an application/service locator. It houses and maintains the WINS database in addition to serving as a potential replication point to and from other WINS servers.

* WINS clients – WINS clients register their NetBIOS name information with WINS servers and also act as resolvers. All Microsoft operating systems can be configured as WINS clients. Starting with Windows 2000, you can turn off WINS in favor of DNS for registration and resolution services. Chapter 7 discusses WINS clients and the ability to turn off WINS.

* WINS proxies – A WINS proxy is a WINS device configured to act on behalf of other devices that can't directly use WINS. WINS proxies are also discussed in Chapter 7.

WINS Server

The WINS server is the heart and soul of the WINS architecture. It's the device that is responsible for either accepting or denying name registration requests from WINS clients. It's also the focal point of name queries for Windows 2000 clients if either DNS hasn't been configured on the client, or the requested name can't be found in DNS.

You can install WINS at the same time you install the operating system (using either a manual or automated process), or afterwards.

Installing WINS During Setup

To install the WINS service during an interactive operating system setup, select WINS from the Networking Components screen during the GUI portion of setup.

To include WINS in an unattended server setup, add the following to the answer file:

* Add a section named [NetOptionalComponents].

* Add a value of **wins=on**.

Installing WINS After Setup

To add the WINS service to a running server, use the Add/Remove Programs applet in Control Panel. Click the Windows Components icon in the left pane to open the Windows Components Wizard and select WINS on the Networking Services screen.

NOTE: You can also use the Configure Your Server Wizard if you've opted to let that screen continue to appear when you boot the server, or you can use the Advanced menu in the window that appears when you open the Network and Dial-up Connections applet. (Choose Optional Networking Components from the Advanced menu.)

Configuring the WINS Service

As soon as you install WINS, the service can begin to accept queries and registrations. Technically, nothing else needs to be done; the service runs without any further configuration. Although this is a nice feature, helpful for administrators who want to get the service up and running quickly, it's dangerous. A rushed implementation of WINS can be a huge mistake—one that might adversely affect your network for many years.

Although the service works immediately, take the time to examine configuration options and identify those that should be tweaked and optimized for your enterprise. The primary tool used to tweak and optimize your WINS servers is the WINS MMC.

Installing the WINS MMC

You can add the WINS MMC to a device in any of three ways: install the service, which adds the preconfigured MMC; run the Admin Pack as described in Chapter 2; or register the WINS MMC snap-in on any device (which lets you administer WINS from that box).

To register the WINS MMC snap-in on any device, complete the following steps:

1. Copy the Winssnap.dll from %SystemRoot%\System32 of any Server product to the same folder on the target device.

2. Open a command prompt, type **regsvr32 winssnap.dll**, and then press Enter. This registers the .dll and makes the snap-in available. (Use the /s switch to run silently.)

3. Open a blank MMC and add the WINS snap-in.

NOTE: If you've opened a blank MMC before you register the Winssnap.dll, the WINS snap-in won't display as an available snap-in until the MMC is closed and opened again.

Using the WINS MMC

The default WINS MMC (Winsmgmt.msc in Programs | Administrative Tools) has at least three objects in the tree pane: WINS, Server Status, and the current WINS server.

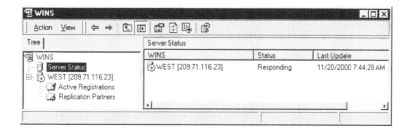

WINS Object

The shortcut menu that displays when you right-click the WINS object offers the same commands available from the MMC window menu options. However, you can use the WINS object's Properties dialog box to gain additional control over the display and behavior of WINS servers.

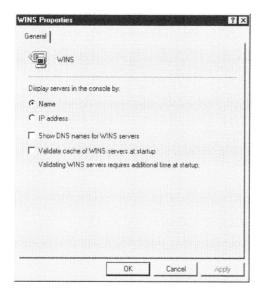

The options Display by Name and Display by IP Address may be confusing because both the name and IP address are always displayed anyway. The choice is really the sort order—

whether to display the servers in alphabetical order by name or by ascending IP addresses. You can opt to display the DNS name (FQDN) in addition to the server name and IP address.

You can choose to validate the cache of WINS servers during startup. This is actually a validation of connectivity for the servers you added the last time you used the MMC. You don't need to use this feature if you use the default WINS MMC because the MMC runs in user mode, and any servers you add are automatically saved when you close the console. However, if you used a blank MMC and added the WINS Management snap-in (author mode), you must remember to save the console before you exit. The option to validate the cache is a safety net in case you didn't explicitly save your console after adding servers.

Server Status Object

Select this object to manually refresh the status of each server in the MMC. (Right-click and choose Refresh from the shortcut menu; or select the object and choose Action | Refresh.) You can use the Properties dialog box to change the Refresh Interval. (The default is five minutes.)

Server Object

Each server you add to the WINS MMC has two child-level objects in the tree pane: Active Registrations and Replication Partners.

 ❖ Active Registrations – The name of this object is somewhat misleading because it's capable of viewing active, released, expired, and tombstoned registrations. This is the place to directly manipulate the WINS data.

> **NOTE:** For the purposes of this book as well as in conjunction with industry lingo and mumbo-jumbo, the terms *record* and *entry* are interchangeable.

 ❖ Replication Partners – This is the place where you establish new replication endpoints with other WINS servers.

Working with Active Registrations

The Active Registrations object appears under each WINS server that's displayed in the MMC. This object contains the entries in the WINS database.

Database Entries

Each computer registers its name and services with the WINS server. Each registration that a WINS server receives is placed into the database as an entry. Depending on the amount of services hosted on a given computer, several entries can be entered into the database for a single device. Entries are considered either dynamic or static in nature. Dynamic entries are automatically placed into WINS by the device, while static entries are placed into the database manually.

Avoid Static Records

Try to steer clear of static records. The primary use of static records is to track non-Microsoft clients that use NetBIOS to become resolvable to NetBIOS clients. This is really the only reason to consider static entries, and even then, think twice. Instead, if it's at all feasible, use host records in DNS. Static records add a huge administrative overhead, and they're frequently the source of hard-to-diagnose problems.

Static records are replicated to each WINS server in a replication topology. Each WINS server that receives a copy of a static record takes ownership of the record and will continually update its version ID to ensure that the record isn't removed. Placing updated version IDs on all static records also ensures that all WINS servers receive a replica copy. This can cause static records that were removed from one WINS server to be replicated back to your WINS server from a replication partner. For details on how to remove static entries, please see Chapter 9.

Entry Types   Entries in the database are categorized into four types: Unique, Group, Internet Group, and Multihomed.

* Unique – The entry that's used to associate a name with an IP address. A unique name can have only one IP address. An example of a unique name is a computer named Server1.

* Group – A grouping of objects that are assumed to be valid on any subnet in the network. The grouping either doesn't have any IP address information, or it has multiple IP addresses.

* Internet Group – A logical administrative grouping of any object type. Internet Groups, or *special groups*, as they're sometimes called, are used for special user-defined administrative groups. These Internet Groups are sometimes used to group resources such as file servers and printers.

* Multihomed – The entry that's used to register a unique name that has more than one IP address. This is typically a device with multiple network interface cards.

Entry Attributes   Every entry in the database has a specific set of attributes. Some attributes are provided by the client as part of the registration and renewal process, while others are provided by the WINS server. Here are the available attributes of any entry in the WINS database:

⬥ Record Name – The NetBIOS name associated with the record.

⬥ Type – A representation of the sixteenth character that the client registers.

⬥ IP Address 1–25 –A WINS entry can house up to 25 IP addresses depending on its type. Each one of these attributes houses a single address.

⬥ State – The lifecycle state. This attribute can have a value of either active, released, extinct, or tombstoned (covered later in this chapter).

⬥ Static – The attribute that indicates whether the record is static or dynamic.

⬥ Owner – The IP address of the WINS server that last registered or renewed the record. This defined WINS server is known as the owner of the entry.

⬥ Version – The version ID of the record, which is incremented like a DNS serial number when a change occurs. Used to determine if replication needs to occur between WINS partners and is also used in case of a replication collision.

⬥ Expiration – The day and time that the record's TTL expires. At expiration time, the state changes from active to released. This is normally equal to the date of registration or renewal plus the number of days indicated in the Renew Interval.

Understanding Version IDs

WINS servers use version IDs to track changes to the WINS database. An ID is given to each new entry in the database and to each record that's updated. The WINS server keeps track of the current highest version ID in order to know which ID needs to be assigned for the next record, and also to identify updates that haven't been sent to replication partners yet. A random version ID scheme using hexadecimal characters is generated when a WINS server is built, which ensures uniqueness among WINS servers. You can manually change this number, but Microsoft doesn't recommended it (nor do I) because it can cause existing records to be overwritten or not replicated.

Working with Entries

You can locate and remove entries with the Active Registrations object in the WINS MMC.

Finding an Entry   To find an entry, right-click the Active Registrations object under the appropriate server and choose one of these search methods from the shortcut menu:

Find By Name – This method allows you to specify all or part of the name of the entry you're looking for. In the Find By Name dialog box search field, enter a partial or full name. You can select the Match Case check box if you want the search to be case sensitive.

Find By Owner – Use this method to show all the records for all owners, or for the current owner (the server that holds the MMC you're using).

Filtering Records   When you use the Find By Owner method, you can filter out certain record types. Click the Record Types tab and select only those types that you want to display.

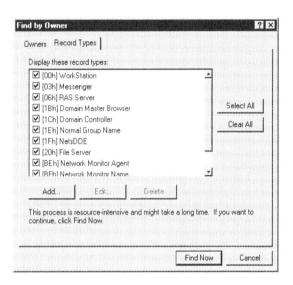

CODE BLUE

Windows 2000 WINS is missing a feature that was available in Windows NT 4, and the fact that this has been stripped from the Windows 2000 MMC limits your options for finding records. The missing feature allowed you to search the WINS database for an IP address in addition to searching by the owner and NetBIOS names. This was useful when you needed to track down a device, owner, or registration when only an address was known. Think of it as a quasi reverse lookup record.

Without this feature, you have only two ways to search by IP address when using Windows 2000 WINS. The first way is to keep an NT 4 WINS server on the wire that is replicating with your Windows 2000 servers. You can then use the search feature in the NT 4 WINS Manager utility. The second way is to export the database to a text file (see the section "Exporting Data" later in this chapter), and import that file into SQL Server, where you can query the SQL database for a particular IP address. Neither of these options is efficient or desirable. We will discuss the role SQL can play in WINS management in Chapter 9.

Deleting an Entry   To delete an entry, find its record using one of the previously mentioned processes. Right-click the record and choose Delete from the shortcut menu. The Delete Record screen offers two options:

❖ Delete This Record Only From This Server – This record will be removed only from this WINS server. It will remain on all other WINS servers until the other WINS servers' verification interval has expired, in which case, the other WINS servers will attempt to validate the record with the record's owner.

❖ Replicate The Deletion Of This Record To Other Servers (Tombstone) – This has the same effect as a record for which the extinction timeout has expired. As a result, the record is given a status of tombstone and is replicated to all servers. The record will be removed at the next scavenge interval. This way is preferred over deleting the record from only a single server because it will result in timely removal of the record from all WINS servers.

Creating a Static Entry   To create a new static entry, right-click the Active Registrations object under the server to which you're adding the static entry, and choose New Static Mapping from the shortcut menu. In the New Static Mapping dialog box, enter the following information:

❖ Computer Name – Allows you to define the NetBIOS name to which the device will respond.

❖ NetBIOS Scope – Allows you to associate this record with any predefined NetBIOS Scope. I won't even go into this because I've never known anyone to use NetBIOS Scopes, and its support in future versions of WINS is doubtful.

❖ Type – Allows you to select a predefined entry type. Supported types for static entries include the following: Unique, Group, Multihomed, Domain Name, and Internet Group.

❖ IP Address – Allows you to add one or more IP addresses to the record depending on what type you've chosen and that type's support of more than one IP address.

CODE BLUE

Another handy feature found in previous versions of WINS was the ability to view a list of all static entries housed in the WINS database. This was useful in situations where you needed to quickly get an inventory of all of your static entries. For some reason, this feature has been stripped out of Windows 2000 WINS, so static records are now bunched together with all other entries in the MMC. To get the same information, you're forced to be a little creative.

Your first option is to search the database through the GUI for the device name that you know has a static entry. This isn't helpful if you're trying to ascertain a complete list of previously unknown static entries.

Your second option is to export the database to a comma-separated file. (See the section "Exporting Data" later in this chapter.) This file can then be used with Access, SQL, or any other database to query for the occurrence of a static flag. The query produces a list of all entries that are statically defined in the WINS database. It's too bad you have to go to such great lengths just to take a look at your own data.

Migrate On/Off

Once a static record is created in WINS, the default behavior is for WINS to treat it like any other dynamic record. This means that unlike previous versions of WINS, static records can and will be overwritten by a dynamic entry with the same name. The behavior is changed via the Migrate On/Off setting found on the General tab of the Properties dialog box for the Replication Partners object. By clearing the Overwrite Unique Static Mappings At This Server (Migrate On) check box, you prevent the WINS server from registering a dynamic entry when a static entry with the same name is found in the database.

NOTE: Unless this setting is consistent on all WINS servers participating in a replication topology, you might witness erratic behavior relative to static records overwriting dynamic records, and vice versa.

Importing Data

WINS supports importing WINS records from LMHOSTS files into its database. This is useful if your organization has invested a lot of resources in maintaining LMHOSTS files but is now moving to WINS. Because all devices dynamically register, the real value of importing occurs when the LMHOSTS file you're using contains entries for machines that don't have the ability to dynamically register in WINS.

To import an LMHOSTS file, right-click the Active Registrations object under the server into which you want to import data, and select Import LMHOSTS File. In the Open dialog box, locate and select the LMHOSTS file, and then click OK.

Exporting Data

The Export Data feature allows you to port the contents of your WINS database to a .csv or .txt file. You can then import the file into a database or spreadsheet program.

NOTE: This feature was also available in previous versions of WINS by using an NT 4 Resource Kit tool called Winsdmp.

Each row in the dump represents a single record and a comma separates each value. The following values are supported:

❖ Record Name – The NetBIOS name of the entry

❖ Type – The sixteenth character of the NetBIOS name as well as the actual sixteenth character name (i.e., workstation, server, etc.)

❖ IP Address – The IP address of the record

❖ State – The value that defines active, released, expired, or tombstoned

❖ Static – The value is empty if the record is dynamic; otherwise, displays the word *Static*

❖ Owner – The IP address of the WINS server that owns the record

❖ Version – The current version ID of the entry

❖ Expiration – The day and time that the record will change its current state to the next state in the progression if the record isn't updated

BUG ALERT The Export utility in Windows 2000 that replaces the NT 4 Winsdmp utility lacks one major feature that renders it almost useless. It's unable to report on more than one IP address per entry in the text dump of the data. This becomes a problem with certain records, namely the domain record (1ch), which can have up to 25 IP addresses defined. Although Winsdmp exports all IP addresses to the text file, the Windows 2000 Export utility reports only the first address in the list. This is unacceptable, especially if you're using the text dumps to complete some advanced reporting or administration via another database product.

   The only resolution to this problem is to manually record or identify the IP addresses for records that support more than one IP address. Yikes! This is one of the reasons that importing data into a directory that can be accessed via many scripting tools using LDAP (as is the case with AD-Integrated DNS) is of such great value. If the WINS data were LDAP integrated, then all data could be accessed by any tool using LDAP, not just the tools that Microsoft provides.

 BUG ALERT Winsdmp is a great utility and is the only way you can get a text dump of the WINS database in NT 4. The Export function is a great utility and is the only way you can get a text dump of the WINS database in Windows 2000. Unlike Reese's Peanut Butter Cups, the results from each of these utilities aren't two great tastes that taste great together.

   The utilities differ in how they place data: the data that Winsdmp places in many fields of the .csv file isn't the same data value type coming from a Windows 2000 export file. In a couple of cases, even when the fields are the same between the two utilities, the data that they each place into the fields is not compatible. On the surface, this might not seem like a big deal, but if you're required to compare two separate WINS databases from two different versions of WINS to find duplicates, as is often done in merger and acquisitions activities, this can be very painful. Chapter 9 provides a full discussion of merging WINS environments and ways to work around this problem, but I just wanted to make you aware of this "feature" at this time.

   To export the database, right-click the appropriate server and select Export List. In the Save As dialog box, select a location, specify a format, and name the file. Then click Save.

Configuring Replication Partners

Replication is the mechanism that synchronizes contents among multiple WINS servers so that all WINS servers have a copy of all the WINS entries that have been registered with all other WINS servers. The ability to have all records on all WINS servers offers many advantages over implementations that don't leverage replication.

In addition to providing a holistic view of your network, replication increases the availability and fault tolerance of your WINS servers. Because each WINS server has a complete set of all entries that every other WINS server has, your impact is much less if a WINS server fails. Upgrades of both hardware and software on the WINS servers are less invasive when you have multiple WINS servers configured for replication. You can take a server offline for maintenance and still register and resolve the names that the downed WINS server owns, since all other WINS servers have its records. Each replication endpoint is defined on a WINS server as a replication partner. A WINS server can be configured as a pull partner, a push partner, or a push/pull partner.

Pull and Push Replication

A *pull partner* is a WINS server that pulls (requests) replication of updated WINS database entries from other WINS servers at a configured time interval. Pull partners ask the other WINS server for the highest version ID that it has assigned to a record. If this ID is higher than the ID that the pull partner knows about, the pull partner will initiate replication. In this process, the pull partner asks the other WINS server to send it only the entries that have a version ID that's higher than its last known highest value. This causes only the changes in the database to be replicated, not the whole database.

A *push partner* is a WINS server that pushes or notifies other WINS servers of the need to replicate their database entries. Push replication occurs after a specified number of changes to the version ID, and you can determine how many changes should occur before the push partner sends an update notification to the other WINS servers.

As you might have guessed, devices that are set up as push/pull partners will not only push their changes to the other WINS server, but they will also ask that server for any changes. This is the default (and recommended) replication partnership for all WINS servers in an enterprise. (Design considerations that pertain to replication are discussed in Chapter 8.)

NOTE: There's a common misconception that the replication roles of push and pull are linked together. Although a push on one WINS server must be complimented by a pull on the target WINS server, this doesn't mean that all WINS servers must replicate content in both directions. For example, if WINS1 had a pull relationship with WINS2, WINS2 would need to have only a push relationship with WINS1, which would enable records to replicate from WINS2 to WINS1 but not from WINS1 to WINS2. In certain situations, you might want to replicate data only to a WINS server instead of to and from a WINS server.

Creating and Configuring a New Replication Partnership

To establish a new replication partnership, right-click the Replication Partnerships object under the appropriate server and choose New Replication Partner from the shortcut menu.

In the New Replication Partner dialog box, enter either the NetBIOS name or the IP address of the WINS server with which you want to establish a replication relationship. Click OK to create a push/pull partnership with the defined server.

To configure a replication partner, right-click the WINS server in the details pane, and choose Properties from the shortcut menu. Click the Advanced tab and, in the Replication Partner Type text box, configure this server's relationship to Push, Pull, or Push/Pull.

Establishing Replication Partnerships Using Multicast

WINS can now use multicast to find and configure replication partnerships between WINS servers. Although this idea might sound great, it can create potential security issues. When Enable Automatic Partner Configuration is enabled on the Advanced tab of the Replication Partner's Properties dialog box, any WINS server supporting multicast will find all other WINS servers supporting multicast and will automatically add itself to the replication topology. This behavior occurs no matter who implements the server, authorized or not.

Although I don't recommend using this feature, if you do enable Automatic Partner Configuration, the following options appear:

- Multicast Interval – The frequency of a multicast request for new WINS servers

- Multicast TTL – The amount of time that expires before the WINS server considers the multicast packet outstanding

Establish the Default Push and Pull Configuration Parameters

Instead of configuring each replication partner after you've added it to the Replication Partners object, you can specify some global parameters that all partners will automatically use. The ability to configure the dynamics of a replication partnership in one place is helpful if you have a large environment that requires all servers to have the same push or pull configuration.

Default Pull Events   Settings established on the Pull Replication tab found in the properties of the Replication Partners object set the default pull configuration for all replication partners created. You can set the following:

- Start Time – Configures the time that pull replication will start. This setting is used only after the service is started. After that, the Replication Interval setting is used.

- Replication Interval – Specifies how often after the initial pull (defined in the Start Time setting) this WINS server will ask the pull partner for any version ID updates.

- Number Of Retries – Specifies the number of times that the WINS server should retry a pull from a partner before the partner is considered down.

- Start Pull Replication at Service Startup – Forces a pull to occur at service startup despite the defined start time.

- Use Persistent Connection For Replication – Enables a continuous virtual connection (VC) for the partner.

The Advantages of Persistent Connections

Persistent connections is a handy feature that lets you maintain a constant TCP/IP virtual connection between two WINS servers for the purpose of replication. If you've dealt with a large number of WINS servers placed throughout a heavily congested WAN, you know that this constant connection is a big deal. Most problems with replication in a large environment are caused by failures to establish a VC each time replication must occur, as is the case with pre-Windows 2000 WINS. Microsoft claims that this feature may increase processing load and slightly decrease performance. I haven't found this to be true, but even if I did, the performance decrease would have to be substantial to negate the increase of replication stability that persistent connections provides. Use it. It rules.

Default Push Events   Settings established on the Push Replication tab found in the properties of the Replication Partners object set the default push configuration for all replication partners created in the Replication Partners object. You can set the following:

- At Service Startup – Indicates that a push event should be triggered at service startup no matter how many changes to the version ID have occurred.

- When Address Changes – Gives you the ability to push records as soon as the IP address of a record changes. Use this setting with caution, as it can significantly increase replication traffic.

- Number Of Changes In Version ID Before Replication – Represents how many increments to the version ID must occur before a push is spawned.

- Use Persistent Connections For Push Replication Partners – Enables a continuous VC for the partner.

NOTE: The default settings established in the properties of the Replication Partners object affect only new replication partnerships, not those already established.

Establishing Pull Configuration Parameters

If you need to configure each replication partner separately, you can do so by opening the Properties dialog box of any server appearing in the Replication Partners object and clicking on the Advanced tab.

Modifying Pull Events If you need to modify the properties of a pull event, the following settings are available:

- ❖ Use Persistent Connection For Replication – Enables a continuous VC for this partner.

- ❖ Start Time – Configures the time that pull replication will start. This setting is used only right after the service is started. After that, the Replication Interval setting is used.

- ❖ Replication Interval – Specifies how often after the initial pull—defined in the Start Time setting—this WINS server will ask the pull partner for any version ID updates.

Modifying Push Events If you need to modify the properties of a push event, the following settings are available:

- ❖ Use Persistent Connection For Replication – Establishes a constant VC between this server and the push partner.

- ❖ Number Of Changes In Version ID Before Replication – Represents the number of updates to the last known version ID that must occur before changes are pushed to the replication partner.

Preventing Promiscuous Replication

In some environments, the contents of WINS are considered confidential, so the default setting to replicate only with configured WINS partners is desirable. In certain instances, you might want to enable replication with any server that requests replication of WINS contents. To enable a WINS server to either push or pull to or from your server, even if that WINS server is not a configured replication partner, you must clear the Replicate Only With Partners option found on the General tab of the Replication Partner object's Properties dialog box. Keep in mind that this will allow any unauthorized server to replicate to and from your WINS server.

Forcing Replication of All Partners

In addition to the scheduled replication, you can manually force replication of all partners. To accomplish this, right-click the Replication Partners object in the tree pane and choose Replicate Now from the shortcut menu. On the confirmation screen, click Yes.

Forcing Replication of a Single Partner

To force replication of a single partner, select the Replication Partners object in the tree pane. In the details pane, right-click the server you want to replicate with and select either Start Pull Replication or Start Push Replication. When the dialog box opens, choose Start For This Partner Only and click OK.

Deleting a Replication Partner

To delete a replication partner, right-click the server in the details pane and choose Delete from the shortcut menu. Click Yes on the confirmation screen, and when you're asked if you wish to purge all references to the deleted server from the WINS server, you should select Yes.

If you do remove all references to the deleted server at the time you remove a replication partner, all entries that the deleted partner owns remain in the WINS database of the existing server or servers. If you accidentally choose to keep the entries in the existing WINS database, you have two methods of resolving your dilemma. You can either wait for the verification interval to expire, which will cause the existing WINS servers to eventually "learn" that entries from that owner are stale and need to be removed, or you can manually remove the owner's records. Removal of the owner's records is the preferred method and can be accomplished with the following steps:

1. Right-click the Active Registrations object of the WINS server from which you want to remove the owner.

2. Select Delete Owner from the shortcut menu.

3. In the Delete Owner dialog box, highlight the owner you want to remove and choose one of the following options:

    ❖ Delete From This Server Only – This option causes the records to be deleted from only this server, leaving the records on the other servers. If you choose this option, you should know that at the next replication interval, another WINS server will replicate this owner's data back to your database. Use this option only if the data from an owner is corrupt in the local database but is good on another data source.

    ❖ Replicate Deletion To Other Servers (Tombstone) – This method is preferred because it causes all servers to be notified that the records are expired. Each server will then remove the records at the next scavenge interval.

If you've chosen to remove the records from all servers, when you click OK, you'll see a dialog box indicating that to complete this task, the current WINS server must take ownership of the records from the deleted owner. Click Yes.

Blocking Owners

Deleting an owner is a pretty drastic step. You might want to merely block any and all records that an owner owns from replicating. You can do this on the Advanced tab of the Replication Partner's Properties dialog box. This feature was available in pre-Windows 2000 WINS but only by adding a registry data item named PersonaNonGrata.

WINS Server Configuration

Each WINS server is configured via its Properties dialog box in the WINS MMC. Some of the configuration settings help you optimize the performance of your WINS servers; other settings are designed to help you view, tweak, and troubleshoot the server and the database.

Updating Statistics

Each WINS server keeps statistical information about the WINS service, including vital statistics such as the number of registered names, number of successful and failed queries, and last scavenge time. By default, statistics are updated every 10 minutes, but you configure a new interval on the General tab of the Properties dialog box.

To view the statistics, right-click the server's object in the tree console and choose Display Server Statistics from the shortcut menu.

Database Backup and Restore

In addition to any server backup procedures you might have implemented, WINS gives you the ability to back up its database separately. By default, no database backup is configured, but you can change this on the General tab of the server's Properties dialog box in the WINS MMC.

Configuring Automatic Backups   To configure backup of the WINS database, enter a location for the backup file in the Default Backup Path text box. The folder you select must be present on the local machine (no network drives permitted).

After you manually back up the database for the first time (discussed next), WINS automatically backs up the database every three hours.

BUG ALERT The Help files say that as soon as you enter a location for the backup, automatic backups begin. That's not correct: you must perform a manual backup to initiate the automatic backup procedure.

You can also specify a backup whenever the WINS server is stopped or the server is shut down by selecting the Back Up Database During Server Shutdown option.

CAUTION: Selecting the option to back up every time the server is shut down can substantially increase the time it takes to restart the server.

During the first backup, WINS creates a \Wins_bak\New folder under the target folder you named in the dialog box.

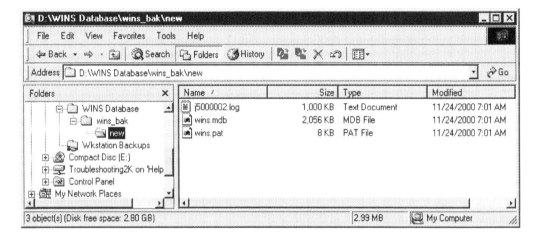

CAUTION: Each backup overwrites the previous backup, which is not terrific, so make sure you're also performing regular server backups.

Performing Manual Backups   You can force a backup by right-clicking the server in the tree console of the WINS MMC and choosing Back Up Database from the shortcut menu. The Browse For Folder dialog box opens with a preselected location:

◆ If you entered a backup location on the General tab of the server's Properties dialog box, that location is selected.

◆ If you didn't configure a backup location, the root of your system partition (usually C:\) is selected.

CAUTION: If your database is large, backing up takes quite a while and also consumes a lot of system resources.

Restoring a Database Backup   To restore a database you backed up as described in the previous section, follow these steps:

1. Stop the WINS service by typing **net stop wins** at the command prompt. Wait for the confirmation message. (It might take a while.)

2. Right-click the server and choose Restore Database from the shortcut menu.

NOTE: If you've failed to stop the WINS service, the Restore Database command is dimmed on the shortcut menu.

3. In the Browse For Folder dialog box, navigate to the location of the WINS backup (the folder you specified, not the subfolder created by WINS) and click OK.

After restoring the database, Windows 2000 automatically restarts the WINS service.

Restoring a Database from Other Backup Media   If you didn't configure a backup location and you didn't manually back up the database, you can restore the database from the server's regular backup if you believe the server's database is corrupt. However, you can't restore directly from the backup media. Instead, restore the WINS database files from the backup media to a folder on the server. Then follow the steps in the previous section to restore the database.

Aging and Scavenging

Aging and scavenging of entries is basically the same in WINS as it is in DDNS. *Aging* is the process of specifying a TTL for an entry, and *scavenging* is the process of finding and removing entries that have exceeded their TTL.

Configuring Aging   Aging is configured on a server-by-server basis, using the Intervals tab of the server's Properties dialog box in the WINS MMC. The aging settings determine many factors that affect the way WINS clients interact with the WINS server. You can configure the following values:

❖ Renew Interval – The frequency for client registration renewals, after which the record is released. Clients begin attempting to renew their name registrations when an eighth of the specified time has elapsed. The default value is six days.

❖ Extinction Interval – The amount of time that expires before a record changes from a released state to an extinct state. The default is four days. This value must be smaller than the Renew Interval value.

❖ Extinction Timeout – The amount of time that must expire between the time a record is marked for extinction and the time it is actually scavenged. The default is six days.

❖ Verification Interval – The value that defines when a WINS server should verify that a record that it doesn't own is still valid in the database. This occurs only if said record hasn't been updated as a result of replication. If the verifying server finds the record to be valid, then its new information is updated. If it finds that the record is no longer valid, it's removed from the database of the verifying WINS server. The default is 24 days (which is also the minimum time allowed).

It's important to understand what occurs as a result of the previously stated values. Once an entry is received, it is given a TTL as defined in the Renew Interval value. If this record isn't updated in the specified timeframe, the WINS server changes the entry's status from active to released. Putting a record in a released state allows any other device or entity to register the same name without causing a challenge response.

After the Extinction Interval value expires, the record's status is changed from released to extinct. This is done to permit the WINS server to replicate this updated record status to all other WINS servers. Keep in mind that this event will occur at the time equal to the sum of the Renew and Extinction Interval, which by default would be 10 days from the time the device or entity registered the name.

Once the Extinction Timeout value expires, the record's state is changed from extinct to tombstoned. A tombstone state, which is replicated to all WINS servers, indicates that this record can be deleted from the database at the next scavenge interval. Once again, this event depends on the execution of the events caused by the Renew and Extinction Intervals, so it won't occur until the sum of the Renew Interval, Extinction Interval, and the Extinction Timeout is exceeded (by default, 16 days after the device or entity registers the name). This is not to say that on day 16, the record will be removed from the database. Actual removal is a result of a scavenge.

The previously mentioned process is fine and dandy for records that the WINS server owns, but what about records that have been replicated from other owners? This is where the Verify Interval comes into play. Sometimes updates aren't replicated for one reason or another, in which case, the WINS server uses the value in the Verification Interval to check on the status of any record that it doesn't own and which hasn't been updated. In a default configuration, a WINS server asks the owner of any records that haven't been updated in 24 days what the status of the entry is. If an updated status is found, then the record is also updated on the verifying WINS server. If no record is found on the owner, then the record is immediately marked as tombstoned.

Managing Scavenging   *Scavenging* is the process of finding any records that have been configured as tombstoned and removing them from the database. This is done to reclaim disk space, but if you've worked with Jet, you know that this really happens only when you compact the database. Scavenging automatically occurs at an interval that is equivalent to half the value defined in the Renew Interval, so in a default configuration, every two days.

CODE BLUE

> The scavenging process uses the system clock in association with the uptime of the WINS service to determine when scavenging should be initiated. This means that scavenging will make its first run of the database when half the renew interval has expired (after the WINS service has started). If WINS is restarted, the counter resets. This factoid is important to keep in mind if you're using any automated scripting to complete tasks like offline compaction, which require stopping the service. If you need frequent restarts of the service, ensure that the Renew Interval is set low enough so that half of its value isn't longer than the interval between restarts of the WINS service, otherwise scavenging will never initiate.

To manually configure scavenging, right-click the server that you want to scavenge records from and choose Scavenge Database from the shortcut menu. Click OK on the dialog box that indicates that the scavenge has been queued on the server.

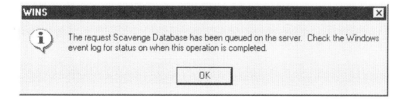

To verify success, either check for event ID 4328 in the System Log of Events Viewer, or open the Server Statistics dialog box in the WINS MMC to see the time of the last manual scavenge.

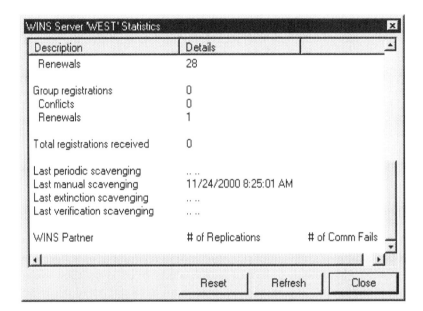

CODE BLUE

Although you can check for either event ID 4328 or the value of the last manual scavenge in the WINS Server Statistics dialog box, both of these events signify only the beginning of the scavenge process. No event or record allows you to ascertain when scavenging has completed unless you turn on Detailed Event Logging (discussed later in this chapter).

Database Verification

Microsoft claims that the verification feature is new to WINS in Windows 2000. Truth be told, this feature has been included since NT 3.51. The only difference found in Windows 2000 implementation is that you can configure it via the GIU, while NT 3.51 and 4 required a registry hack. In any case, this feature allows the WINS server to check the validity and consistency of records in its database that are owned by other WINS servers.

Configuring Automatic Verification   You can configure automatic verification to run at a set interval, but it should be used sparingly. It consumes a huge amount of resources for both the WINS server that is verifying the record as well as the owner. This feature can also consume a lot of network bandwidth. I recommend using this only when you absolutely need to, for example, just before you merge two WINS environments (discussed in Chapter 9).

To enable database verification, go to the Database Verification tab in the server's Properties dialog box and follow these steps:

1. Select the Verify Database Consistency Every check box and specify an interval for running the verification.

2. In the Begin Verifying At section, enter the start time in military format.

3. Enter a value in Maximum Number Of Records To Verify In Each Period. The default is 3000 records, and I wouldn't recommend exceeding this unless you have good reason.

4. In the Verify Against section, select either of the following:

    ❖ Owner Server – The server verifies the particular record against the record's owner.

    ❖ Randomly Selected Partner – The server asks other servers, selected randomly, to provide verification for a record even if that server isn't the owner of the record.

Performing a Manual Verification   You can also perform a manual verification by right-clicking the server and choosing Verify Database Consistency from the shortcut menu. The system displays a warning message about the performance levels that might be affected. Click Yes to proceed anyway.

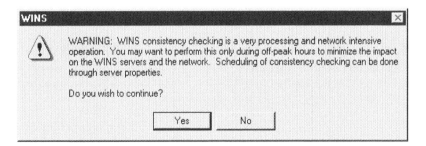

Detailed Event Logging

Just as with WINS in NT 4, you can selectively enable detailed WINS logging to the Event Log. Even though with today's hardware, this won't create too much of a performance problem, you should still use it sparingly. Be warned that this option will record so many WINS-related events that you might be unable to find any useful data due to the sheer size and number of events recorded. Even the use of filtering sometimes can't help you find an event in a full Event Log. When you have an excessive number of logs being generated, finding the right event can be difficult.

To enable detailed logging, go to the Advanced tab of the server's Properties dialog box and select the option Log Detailed Events To Windows Event Log.

CAUTION: If you enable Detailed Event Logging, be sure to also increase the size of your System Log. By default, this log is very small and is configured to overwrite when it runs out of space. As a result, if you don't increase the size, the data you're looking for might be overwritten.

Burst Handling

WINS servers can now support high-volume or "burst" server loads. This feature is called *burst handling*. When burst handling is implemented, the server hands back temporary successful registration to clients during times of high load. The names that are registered when burst handling is active aren't committed to the database, saving the overhead associated with checking the database for duplicate names. This is extremely useful during periods of high registration, such as at 9:00 A.M. when all your users start their computers.

When the WINS server sends the successful registration response to the client, it contains a very low TTL (five minutes by default) for the registration. (TTLs are normally equivalent to the Renew Interval defined on the server.) Because the client's registered names have low TTLs and the default behavior of the client is to attempt to renew its names at an eighth of the length of the TTL, the client will attempt to renew its names after approximately one minute. If the server is still too busy, the name is renewed through burst handling again, and the process repeats itself until the server can process the registration normally.

NOTE: Burst handling is a wonderful feature, but it can potentially cause problems. Because it doesn't check the database to ensure uniqueness, two devices on the same network with the same name could both think they have valid and unique names, which isn't good. However, despite its potential pitfalls, I recommend using this feature.

To enable burst handling, go to the Advanced tab of the server's Properties dialog box and configure the Enable Burst Handling option with one of the following settings:

- ❖ Low – Allows 300 registration requests in queue before beginning burst mode
- ❖ Medium – Allows 500 registration requests in queue before beginning burst mode
- ❖ High – Allows 1000 registration requests in queue before beginning burst mode
- ❖ Custom – Allows you to specify your own number of requests to be held in the queue before bursting starts

WINS Database and Log Files

The WINS database is built on Microsoft's Jet database technology. Although the Jet engine is capable of supporting complex hierarchical databases, as is the case with Active Directory, its implementation in WINS provides only a flat database to the service. The default location for WINS database files is %SystemRoot%\System32\Wins and includes the following files:

- ❖ Wins.mdb – The default name for the WINS database.

- ❖ Winstmp.mdb – The temporary WINS database used as an index during maintenance procedures such as compaction.

- ❖ J50.log and J50XXXXX.log – The files that are used to recover the database if the WINS service suddenly stops. The log file J50XXXXX is incremented by a hexadecimal number from 0 to F. New files are created when a log reaches capacity. Information that needs to be committed to the WINS database is first written to one of these logs. Once the information is written to these logs, it is then written to the WINS database. These files are deleted after a successful shutdown of the service or after a successful backup.

CAUTION: Don't delete the J50XXXXX.log files. They are your lifesavers if you need to recover the database. By keeping a good maintenance schedule of backups, you can keep the number of log files low.

- ❖ J50.chk – The key file for recovery. It keeps track of which transactions have been successfully written from logs to the database itself. Each time a successful write is performed to the database, this file is updated with a checkpoint of transactions committed to the database. As a result, the system knows which records have been committed and which are outstanding.

- ❖ Res#.log – The reservation logs, res1.log and res2.log, are created at the time you install the WINS service. They hold space for the WINS database by taking up 10 MB of space each. Should your server run out of disk space, these log files prevent the service from abruptly terminating. Rather, the service is gracefully stopped and an event is written to the Event Log.

You can change the location of the WINS database files by specifying a new location in the Database Path text box on the Advanced tab of the server's Properties dialog box. Making this change causes the WINS service to stop automatically. The files are moved to the new location, and the service is automatically restarted. Therefore, don't perform this action during a period of high registration.

Uninstalling the WINS Service

You might want to uninstall the WINS service from one or more servers (depending on changes in your enterprise configuration). Uninstalling the WINS service is much cleaner than uninstalling the DNS Server service. It isn't perfect, just better. After you uninstall WINS, the file system and the registry continue to hold data.

CODE BLUE

Remember, uninstalling the WINS service from a server doesn't automatically remove that server from the replication topology of your WINS environment, nor will it remove entries that the removed server owned. You must manually remove the replication partnership as well as remove the entries from the database, as detailed in the "Configuring Replication Partners" section earlier in this chapter.

Cleaning Up the File System

The WINS uninstall goes the extra mile by removing the files associated with the WINS database. This is nice because you don't have to worry about an old copy of the database just sitting around on an old WINS server. However, the WINS directory is left intact. Because this directory is empty, it's really only an annoyance, but it can be removed with no adverse effects.

The executables and .dll files for the service are left on the server (as is the case with DNS). If you want to completely clean your server of any trace of WINS, remove the following files in the %SystemRoot%\System32 directory:

❖ Wins.exe – The WINS service

❖ Wins.mib – The management module for SNMP monitoring of WINS

❖ Winsctrs.dll – The Performance Monitor counters

❖ Winsevnt.dll – The library of WINS events used to report errors in the Event Log

❖ Winsmib.dll – The SNMP support for WINS

❖ Winsrpc.dll – The WINS RPC service

❖ Winssnap.dll – The WINS MMC snap-in

Cleaning Up the Registry

WINS leaves a few minor registry entries behind. All of these entries are related to the registration of the MMC and .dll files related to the service. These are just annoyances that take up little space in the registry. If you feel compelled to remove them, do so at your own risk. There are too many to mention given their trivial nature, but you can find them by searching the registry for all occurrences of the word *WINS*. Be careful that you don't delete any supporting entries for either the WINS client or the Winsock interface, both of which will be returned in your search results.

Okay. That's a wrap . . .

Chapter 7

WINS Client Architecture

s I stated in Chapter 6, when Microsoft introduced NetBIOS into the Microsoft Network Client 3.0 in the early 1990s, a strategic decision was made that would be the source of much pain and controversy for over a decade. Although the Microsoft Network Client 3.0 was the first client to support the NetBIOS standard, a true WINS client didn't appear until Windows 3.1, which boasted enhanced functionality in the area of NetBIOS name registration and resolution. Windows 3.1 was also the first operating system to be offered immediately after WINS became a permanent fixture in the LAN Manager Server product. At this point, what was once referred to as a NetBIOS client was now referred to as a WINS client, and NetBIOS RFC compliancy was forever a relic of the past for Microsoft operating systems.

Managing the WINS Client

A *WINS client* is any computer configured to use a WINS server to register and resolve NetBIOS names. A server or workstation of any type can be configured as WINS client, even a server that is configured as a WINS server. Every operating system that Microsoft has produced within the last 10 years has the ability to be a WINS client. The following Microsoft clients support WINS:

◈ Windows 2000 Server (Server, Advanced Server, Data Center)

◈ Windows 2000 Professional

◈ Windows NT Server (3.5–4)

◈ Windows NT Workstation (3.5–4)

◈ Windows 95/98/ Millennium Edition (Me)/CE (all versions)

◈ Windows for Workgroups

◈ Windows 3.*x*

◈ Microsoft LAN Manager

◈ MS-DOS 3.0–6.22 (via Microsoft Network Client 3.0)

NOTE: In addition to Microsoft-provided WINS clients, some operating systems from other software vendors leverage NetBIOS and are capable of interacting with WINS. The method for establishing interaction varies. Some operating systems, such as OS/2, support WINS out of the box. Others require the use of a third-party application or service. Linux and UNIX, for example, can use products like Samba to interoperate.

A few components are found on every WINS client: Network Interface, NetBIOS Name, Node Type, WINS server configuration, Resolver Service, Cache, and the LMHOSTS file. In this chapter, I'll focus on the Windows 2000 implementation of these components.

Network Interface

Windows 2000, like many previous Microsoft operating systems, exposes two programming interfaces for network access: NetBIOS over TCP (NetBT) and Winsock. They both serve the same purpose: to abstract the details of the network from an application or service.

NOTE: Winsock is outside the scope of this chapter because it handles direct TCP/IP socket-to-socket communication requests, not NetBIOS.

NetBT

The NetBT interface is an application programming interface (API) that programs use to gain network access. NetBT acts as an abstraction layer by hiding the detailed inner workings of the network from the application or service. This enables developers to concern themselves only with how and when the application interacts with the NetBT interface, instead of having to be concerned about which type of network their programs are accessing. Programmers write to NetBT, and NetBT handles all network communication on behalf of the requestor.

NetBT can be accessed directly or indirectly. When NetBT is used directly, the requesting service or application directly calls functions in the NetBT interface. Using NetBT directly is an easy programming solution for developers who need to access the network without having extensive programming knowledge or familiarity with the NDIS stack. While it is easiest to program applications and services to use NetBT directly, accessing NetBT directly provides lower performance than other solutions.

When using NetBT indirectly, applications and services call functions in the Transport Driver Interface (TDI). TDI is another abstraction layer that is located in NDIS and is used to provide TCP/IP direct connections between systems. When a call to TDI is received that needs to be satisfied by NetBT, TDI forwards the request to NetBT. Indirectly communicating with NetBT provides better overall performance. However, this approach can be more difficult to implement from a programming perspective because it requires greater programming skills. The Windows 2000 Workstation, Server, Browser, Messenger, and Netlogon services all use NetBT indirectly.

TAKE COMMAND

Nbstat, the NetBT status utility, provides some useful information about local and remote devices' current state of NetBIOS.

One of the more useful functions that you can't find anywhere but in Nbtstat is the ability to view all currently established NetBIOS connections. To view the NetBIOS connection table for a device, enter the following at a command prompt:

Nbtstat –S*<IPAddress>*

where

IPAddress = The address of the device whose connection table you want to examine. If no name is specified, the local machine is used.

NOTE: NBTSTAT also supports *–s<HostName>*, which can be used to specify the host name of a device rather than its IP address.

NetBT is another one of those services in Windows 2000 that you can't touch or see unless you take some extreme measures. The NetBT interface driver, Netbt.Sys, loads at system startup as a kernel mode driver but can't be controlled via the Services MMC. All configuration information about the NetBT interface is found in the HKEY_LOCAL_MACHINE\ System\CurrentControlSet\Services\NetBT registry key.

Tuning NetBT

NetBIOS is installed (and runs) by default on all installations of Windows 2000. It comes preconfigured and tuned to what Microsoft believes to be the best performance settings for all implementations. As the old saying goes, "the road to hell is paved with good intentions." Microsoft's guess at what will be best for your environment isn't always actually the best solution for you. The following sections outline some of the more useful registry settings that can modify NetBT's default behavior.

Datagram Buffering   By default, NetBT allocates 128 KB of memory to a buffer that's used to house outstanding NetBIOS datagrams sent to other clients to establish communications. As each datagram is received on the remote system, an acknowledgement is sent back to the sender. When the original sender receives an acknowledgement, the datagram is removed from the buffer to create space for other outstanding datagrams. If this buffer becomes full, NetBT won't send any more datagrams until space is freed.

This default buffer size can be modified by adding a REG_DWORD data item named MaxDgramBuffering to the HKEY_LOCAL_MACHINE\System\CurrentControlSet\Services\NetBT\Parameters registry key. Valid values for this data item are 0–0xFFFFFFFF, which is the hex representation of the total KB of memory that you want to commit. Although this item doesn't exist in the registry until you create it, the default buffer size is 128 KB.

You might find it useful to modify the buffer size if your device is in a remote network location that has particularly slow network links, which could result in longer times between datagram sends and acknowledgements.

Refresh Timeout   The refresh timeout value is used by a WINS client to establish the refresh interval when a device attempts to register a NetBIOS name with WINS. This value is only valid until the WINS server's Renew Interval is sent to the WINS client as a result of a successful registration. This value can be modified by adding a data item named InitialRefreshT.O. with a type of REG_DWORD to the HKEY_LOCAL_MACHINE\CurrentControlSet\Services\NetBT\Parameters subkey. Supported values are 960,000–0xFFFFFFFF, which represents in hex the number of minutes before the first renew attempt of the device. The default system value is 16 minutes.

KeepAlive   *KeepAlives* are used to maintain a heartbeat between two systems that have established a TCP session. This allows both machines to sit idle but still keep the session alive. Session KeepAlive settings are used to determine the amount of time, in milliseconds, between KeepAlive transmissions to another device. If a KeepAlive isn't received in a specified amount of time, the session is terminated. You can adjust the default value of one hour between KeepAlive messages by modifying the SessionKeepAlive data item found in the HKEY_LOCAL_MACHINE\CurrentControlSet\Services\NetBT\Parameters key. Supported values are 60,000–0xFFFFFFFF, which is a hex representation of the number of seconds that will expire before another KeepAlive is sent.

NOTE: For a complete listing of supported NetBT registry settings, please see Appendix A.

Disabling NetBT

An alternative to performance tuning NetBT is to remove it from your systems. One of the advertised features in Windows 2000 is the ability to remove NetBIOS from any device by disabling NetBIOS over TCP/IP, which is actually a rather deceptive claim on Microsoft's part.

Although eradication of NetBIOS is a nice ideal, it's not something that will happen soon. Here are the steps that you must take to "disable" NetBT:

1. Open the Properties dialog box of your network interface card (NIC).
2. On the General tab, click the Internet Protocol (TCP/IP) object in the Available Components list.
3. Click Properties.
4. On the TCP/IP Properties screen, click the Advanced button.
5. Click the WINS tab.
6. Select Disable NetBIOS Over TCP/IP.
7. Click OK.
8. Click OK again to close the NIC's Properties dialog box.

These tasks must be completed on each NIC that you wish to disable NetBIOS on. There is no global setting to disabled setting to disabled NetBIOS on all NICs. Although these steps won't truly disable NetBIOS, executing this procedure can still result in application and service problems. The issues that arise when disabling NetBIOS are discussed in Chapter 10.

Reality Check: Can NetBIOS Really Be Disabled?

If you buy into the Microsoft theory that once DDNS has been deployed and is being used as the primary name service in your environment, you don't really need NetBIOS, NetBT, WINS, and other services, it's tempting to perform the steps described in the previous section to enhance system performance.

However, it doesn't work as logically as it appears to. Although direct access to NetBT is prevented, indirect access is still permitted. This means that although you've disabled NetBT on each NIC in your system, all services and applications still have the ability to access NetBT via TDI. Although Microsoft isn't admitting this, I can point to several events that confirm this statement. You can prove this to yourself: disable NetBT on all of your NICs, and then use the information provided in the following sections to see for yourself whether NetBIOS is really disabled or just directly inaccessible.

Registry Information Still Loading   After you've disabled NetBT on each NIC and rebooted, check the HKEY_LOCAL_MACHINE\System\CurrentControlSet\Services\NetBT key. Just the existence of a key doesn't mean anything, but if you look at the data items in this key (see Figure 7-1), you see something that might surprise you.

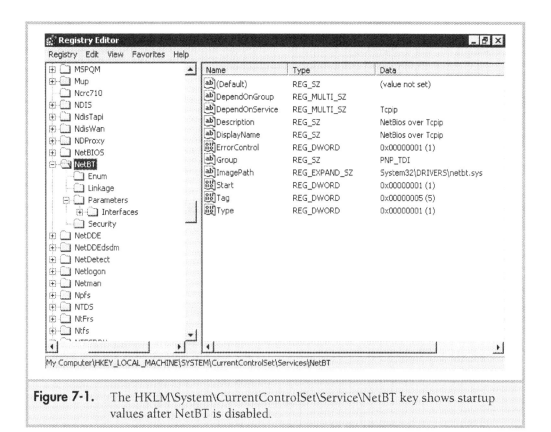

Figure 7-1. The HKLM\System\CurrentControlSet\Service\NetBT key shows startup values after NetBT is disabled.

This is the registry for a machine that had NetBT disabled. Notice that NetBT is still configured to load at system startup. Two data items make this apparent: ImagePath and Start. ImagePath defines the location of the driver that loads, which in this case is Netbt.Sys. Although ImagePath by itself doesn't cause the driver to load, the Start data item does. The Start data item in each key located in HKEY_LOCAL_MACHINE\System\CurrentControlSet\ ServiceName contains a value that is read in by the kernel at system startup. The value of Start dictates at which state of the boot process the driver should be loaded into memory. NetBT has a Start value of 1, which indicates to the kernel that it should load as a critical system component as soon as the kernel initializes. Other drivers that have a Start value of 1 are the keyboard, mouse, and video driver.

CAUTION: Don't attempt to remove or modify any registry information with respect to the NetBT driver. Doing so will render your system unbootable.

Driver Remains in Memory   You might be thinking "So what? Registry information is left behind all the time. This doesn't mean anything." In most cases, I would agree with this statement. Fortunately, it's easy to visually verify whether the NetBT driver is actually loading into memory or whether the registry information is being ignored.

A new tool to Windows 2000 is the System Information MMC. This neat utility (also available in Windows 98 and Windows Me) lets you see many configuration and environmental settings that affect your operating system, such as drivers and modules loaded into memory. Figure 7-2 shows the drivers that are currently loaded into memory on a server that has had NetBT disabled. Notice that not only is NetBT loaded into memory, but as a result of its initialization, the NetBIOS driver has also been loaded. The whole NetBIOS crew is here!

NOTE: You can also verify which drivers are loaded into memory by booting your system into debug mode and then using the Debug.Exe tool. Accessing the contents of memory in this fashion can be a little tricky, so I recommend sticking to the MMC.

Also notice that the driver is reporting to the MMC that it can be stopped, as indicated by the true value of the Accept Stop column. Let's try to stop, it shall we? After typing **net stop netbt** at a command prompt, the system issues a warning message.

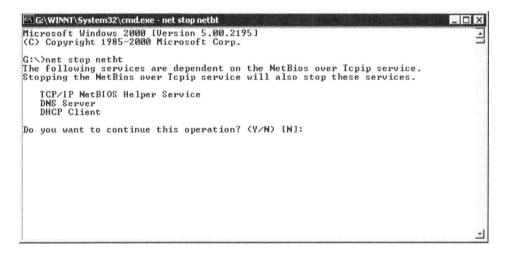

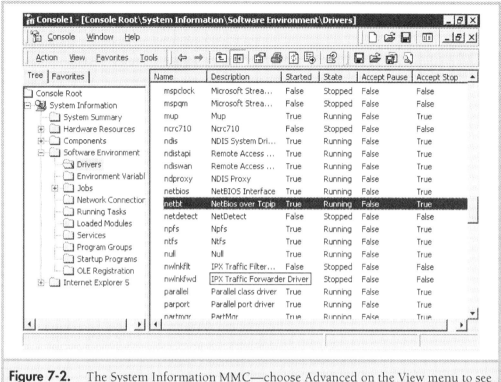

Figure 7-2. The System Information MMC—choose Advanced on the View menu to see these columns.

Is it just me, or are you also amazed that DNS, the technology Microsoft is using to replace NetBIOS, is itself dependent on NetBIOS? This blew my mind. As you can see, manually stopping NetBT will also stop the DNS Server, DHCP Client, and TCP/IP NetBIOS Helper services.

NOTE: Even though you might not be using DHCP to provide your device with an IP address, the DHCP client is still responsible for registering all host names in DNS on all Windows 2000 systems. Therefore, stopping NetBT not only prevents a DNS server from answering queries, but it also prevents clients from participating in DNS dynamic updates.

If you tell the system to continue the operation, the system reports its progress as the services are stopped.

```
G:\WINNT\System32\cmd.exe                                        _ □ ×

G:\>net stop netbt
The following services are dependent on the NetBios over Tcpip service.
Stopping the NetBios over Tcpip service will also stop these services.

   TCP/IP NetBIOS Helper Service
   DNS Server
   DHCP Client

Do you want to continue this operation? <Y/N> [N]: y
The TCP/IP NetBIOS Helper Service service is stopping.
The TCP/IP NetBIOS Helper Service service was stopped successfully.

The DNS Server service is stopping.
The DNS Server service was stopped successfully.

The DHCP Client service is stopping..
The DHCP Client service was stopped successfully.

The NetBios over Tcpip service is stopping........
The NetBios over Tcpip service could not be stopped.

G:\>
```

You can see that all dependant services successfully stopped except NetBT—the command you entered failed. In addition, the operating system, apparently not realizing that the command failed, attempts to restart NetBT. (Even though you and I know it didn't stop, Windows 2000 is apparently unaware of that fact.) If you attempt to straighten out this mess by trying to stop the NetBT service again, entering **net stop netbt** produces the error message "The service could not be controlled in its current state." I have no idea what the system means by this (controlled?), but I can guess that the operating system can't tell whether the NetBT service is currently stopped or running.

A normal, logical assumption is that you might need to start the service again. Enter **net start netbt** at a command prompt to accomplish this. Oops, the operating system can't start the service because the service is already running.

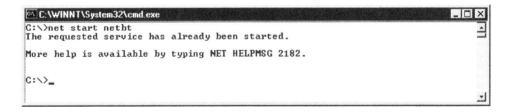

```
C:\WINNT\System32\cmd.exe                                        _ □ ×
C:\>net start netbt
The requested service has already been started.

More help is available by typing NET HELPMSG 2182.

C:\>_
```

Congratulations! You've just completely hosed Windows 2000. Nicely done! You'll now experience inconsistent network access and overall odd behavior, which can only be resolved by rebooting.

Sniffing the Network   I think that I've established the fact that NetBT is still enabled, despite the fact that you've disabled it by Microsoft standards. To prove that NetBT is still being used, place a protocol analyzer on a segment with a NetBIOS-disabled device access. Capture packets as you attempt to establish a Sever Message Block (SMB) session with another device that has NetBIOS disabled. You'll notice, upon close examination, that many session requests are sent through the NetBT interface. This is proof that NetBT is still an active interface even after you've disabled it; the system is allowing indirect NetBT access via TDI in critical Windows 2000 components.

All of this conflicts with direct statements made by Microsoft and could be bad news for Microsoft's efforts to distance itself from NetBIOS as much as possible in Windows 2000.

NetBIOS and TCP/IP Direct Connect

Not only is NetBIOS difficult to support from an application and interoperability perspective, but it can also be a resource hog when enabled on Windows 2000 devices. By default, all Windows 2000 clients have the ability to establish sessions with other devices by using NetBIOS or TCP/IP direct hosting. TC/IP direct hosting is a feature that supports the use of host names to establish direct TCP/IP virtual connections between systems. TCP/IP direct hosting has been positioned by Microsoft as the only way a Windows 2000 device will communicate with another device once NetBIOS has been disabled. As we've just seen, Microsoft's statements are not accurate.

Until Microsoft really removes NetBIOS, every time you attempt to connect to another device, your system will attempt to establish the connection using both NetBIOS and TCP/IP direct hosting at the same time. The first service to get an answer is the winner. This default behavior can be the source of network and processor performance problems due to the increased workload associated with trying to connect to a device two times for a single session.

NetBIOS Name

Every WINS client needs to be configured with a NetBIOS name. As detailed in Chapter 6, this name is used in conjunction with the sixteenth character of a service or application and is registered with WINS.

NetBIOS Naming Rules

A NetBIOS name can be configured only by an administrator or the equivalent and can be no longer than 15 characters long. The NetBIOS name of a device can't contain any spaces, and its first character can't be an asterisk. Although these rules are broad, I encourage you to adhere to the DNS naming standards as detailed in Chapters 1 and 2. This ensures that when you do make the commitment to DNS, your machines don't have to be renamed to comply with DNS naming rules.

TAKE COMMAND

Nbtstat allows you to view all NetBIOS names that are configured for your device along with their sixteenth character by typing

nbtstat –n

Changing the NetBIOS Name

The NetBIOS name that was assigned to a device at setup can be changed at any time on all Windows 2000 Professional devices and on any Windows 2000 Server product that isn't configured as a domain controller. Renaming domain controllers isn't currently supported due to the object renaming process that would need to occur from a LDAP perspective in Active Directory that would result in substantial changes in the directory architecture.

To change the NetBIOS name, right-click My Computer and choose Properties from the shortcut menu. On the Network Identification tab, click Properties and enter the new name in the Computer Name field. Follow the prompts, including a reboot, to complete the process.

Name Truncation

The maximum number of characters supported in a NetBIOS name is 15. The maximum number of characters supported in a DNS host name is 64. So what happens when you want to use all of the characters available to the host name, but you must still use NetBIOS? The answer is name truncation.

If you attempt to configure a device to use a computer name that's longer than 15 characters, Windows 2000 will crop any characters after 15 to generate your NetBIOS name, while leaving your host name alone. For example, if you attempted to use a device name of thisisareallylongname, which is 22 characters, the NetBIOS name of the device would be thisisareallylo but the host name would still be thisisareallylongname.

You can view both the host name and the NetBIOS name on the Network Identification tab of the System Properties dialog box by clicking the Properties button. The host name appears in the Computer Name field. Click the More button to see the NetBIOS name.

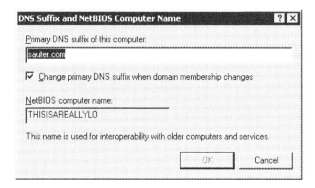

This information can't be changed here. It is automatically generated by using the information provided for the host name.

Node Types

All WINS clients have a defined NetBIOS node type, which dictates how the host will process NetBIOS name resolution. The NetBIOS RFCs define four NetBIOS node types: B, P, M, and H.

Broadcast Node (B-Node)

When a Windows 2000 device is configured as B-Node, it attempts to resolve NetBIOS names through the exclusive use of broadcasts. A B-Node device broadcasts name resolution requests that are examined by all machines on the same segment. If a match is found, the matching device replies by means of a direct IP reply to the B-Node device. If no match is found, then the name is considered unresolvable. This node is limiting due to its dependency on broadcasts, which aren't routable. Using B-Node is recommended only in networks where there is a single segment, but it's the configured default node for Windows 2000 devices if no WINS servers have been configured.

Point-to-Point Node (P-Node)

P-Node devices query only their configured WINS servers for name resolution. If the name isn't found on the WINS server, no other course of action is taken. This node type, although once considered one of the least sexy options, is the only way to fly, in my opinion.

When using P-Node, you assume that your WINS servers know about all NetBIOS names throughout your environment. If you design and implement your WINS environment properly, this assumption is correct. The only "drawback" to using P-Node is that it won't broadcast for the name if the WINS server is unable to resolve the name. I put the word *drawback* in quotes because I don't believe that P-Node's advertised shortcoming is a shortcoming at all, but rather gives this node type an advantage over other node types.

How many servers or workstations that you connect to are located on the same segment as your device? Of those that are on the same segment as your device, how many aren't registered with WINS? Most networks have an extremely low number of devices in the network that are located on the same segments as clients accessing them, yet are not registering or resolvable through WINS. This small number represents the number of devices that will be affected if you chose to configure your devices as P-Nodes due to its lack of broadcast resolution support.

 NOTE: Keep in mind that the Microsoft implementation of P-Nodes allows the WINS client to ask its LMHOSTS file, HOSTS file, and DNS server to resolve the name if all NetBIOS avenues have been unsuccessful, as will be discussed when we talk about Microsoft Enhanced Node types.

The advantages of avoiding a broadcasting-based node type are significant. In a normal network, up to 20 percent of network bandwidth on a segment can be consumed by broadcast traffic, most of which is useless in today's distributed networks. By reducing broadcast traffic, you can reclaim a substantial amount of network bandwidth. There is also a small performance increase realized on each workstation by reducing broadcast traffic because of the reduced number of broadcast packets that each device must examine.

Mixed Node (M-Node)

M-Node, or Mixed Node, combines the functionality of B-Node and P-Node by first broadcasting for name resolution and then querying WINS. The problem with using M-Node is that it will always cause broadcast traffic even if the device is registered in WINS. I can think of no situations in which this node type would be beneficial at all.

If you're that dependant on broadcast, chances are that you haven't gotten around to implementing WINS yet.

Hybrid Node (H-Node)

H-Node is a hybrid of P-Node and B-Node configurations. This node type queries WINS for a name, and if it isn't resolved, a broadcast is issued. This is the default node type on all Windows 2000 WINS clients.

H-Node has a disadvantage when compared to P-Node, in that it attempts to locate a client via broadcast if the name can't be found in WINS. As I stated before, you're unlikely to need to resolve a name via broadcasts if it isn't resolvable in WINS.

Microsoft Enhanced Nodes

Windows 2000 supports the use of all RFC-defined node types in what Microsoft calls "an enhanced fashion." Because the RFCs haven't been updated since their creation, Microsoft had to take some liberties when implementing node types to augment functionality. Each basic node type defined in the RFCs is referred to as a Microsoft Enhanced node type when implemented in Windows 2000.

Microsoft Enhanced Nodes define extra measures taken by the resolver service, above and beyond those defined in that particular node type. All nodes, when enhanced, attempt to resolve a name by using the LMHOSTS file, the HOSTS file, and DNS, after the normal processes defined in the RFC-compliant node type have failed.

For example, if your machine is configured for H-Node and you attempt to resolve the name ComputerA, the following occurs:

1. ComputerA's NetBIOS cache is parsed.

2. If the name wasn't found in cache, a request is sent to the configured WINS server.

3. If the name isn't resolved, a broadcast request is sent.

4. If enabled, the local LMHOSTS file is parsed (as a result of the Microsoft Enhanced Node).

5. If this name still isn't resolved, the HOSTS file is parsed (also a result of the Microsoft Enhanced Node).

6. Finally, DNS is queried by appending the device's configured domain suffix to the name being resolved (once again, a result of the Microsoft Enhanced Node).

Here's a breakdown of how each node type resolves names when it's enhanced:

- B-Node – Cache, Broadcast, LMHOSTS, HOSTS, DNS
- P-Node – Cache, WINS, LMHOSTS, HOSTS, DNS
- M-Node – Cache, Broadcast, WINS, LMHOSTS, HOSTS, DNS
- H-Node – Cache, WINS, Broadcast, LMHOSTS, HOSTS, DNS

NOTE: The automatic use of the LMHOSTS file, HOSTS file, and DNS server aren't defined in any RFC as being a by-product and/or resolution path available to any RFC-defined node type. So, although Microsoft is implementing RFC-compliant features into their modified node types, the node types themselves aren't RFC compliant due to the use of these "extra" features.

Configuring the Node Type

There are only two situations in which the operating system will modify your node type automatically:

- If you remove all WINS configuration information on a client, the node type is changed from H to B.
- If you configure a device to use WINS, the node type is changed from B to H.

NOTE: You can also configure any DHCP server to provide a node type to clients that request IP addresses.

Other than the previously mentioned exceptions, if you want to use a node type other than what's provided by default, you'll have to modify the registry.

To change your node type, create a new REG_DWORD data item named NodeType in HKEY_LOCAL_MACHINE\System\CurrentControlSet\Service\NetBT\Parameters. The supported values for the NodeType data item are

- 1 – B-Node
- 2 – P-Node
- 4 – M-Node
- 8 – H-Node

NOTE: This data item will override any occurrence of the data item DHCPNodeType, which is used to house the node type given during an IP lease by a DHCP server.

TAKE COMMAND

You're probably familiar with the Ipconfig utility. You can use it to display a device's node type by examining the node type value reported when you enter **ipconfig /all** at a command prompt.

You can get the same information from a tool that comes with Windows 2000 called Netdiag. This extremely useful tool can be found in the Support\Tools directory of the CD of any version of Window 2000 Server. Netdiag is installed by running the support tools setup program (or 2000rkst.Msi). To display the node type, enter **netdiag /test:ipconfig /v** at a command prompt.

This command, in addition to providing the node type, gives you a comprehensive view of your IP configuration, including information on domain membership of the device, the domain GUID, and the device SID.

WINS Server Configuration

WINS server usage is configured on a NIC-by-NIC basis, which permits a great amount of flexibility for mobile and multihomed clients. In addition to specifying which WINS servers to send name resolution requests to, you're also able to define their priority, which defines the order in which WINS servers are queried.

A new feature in Windows 2000 is the ability to support up to 12 WINS servers per NIC. Although that might look like a great enhancement to the casual observer (the type of person those "New features in Windows 2000" bullet lists are targeted to), this feature really buys you very little. WINS clients use their configured WINS servers a little differently from what you might expect.

Priority vs. Primary and Secondary WINS Servers

Now that up to 12 WINS servers can be configured per NIC, the concept of primary and secondary WINS servers is no longer valid. Although Microsoft sometimes still mentions "Primary WINS" and "Secondary WINS" devices in various technical documents, these terms no longer make sense. Instead, what was known as a primary WINS server is the server with the highest priority, and the secondary WINS server is known as the server with the second highest priority. Don't blame me folks, I don't make the rules—I just break them.

Throughout this book, I'll avoid using the terms primary and secondary WINS servers despite their continued and incorrect use in many technical documents.

When a resolution request needs to be satisfied by a WINS server, the client sends the request to the WINS server that has the highest priority. If the WINS server returns any response, including "Name Not Found," the client assumes that this WINS server is completely authoritative, and if it doesn't know the answer, none of the other configured WINS servers will either. The only time that another WINS server is queried is if the first WINS server never responds to the WINS client's requests.

The ability to specify 12 WINS servers is of value only from a disaster-recovery perspective. Even in a disaster-recovery scenario, it's highly unlikely that you would ever have more that two WINS servers fail at the same time. What specifying 12 WINS servers does allow you to do is specify a large number of WINS servers in a list that most likely won't be maintained, resulting in old WINS server addresses being left on devices for many years to come.

All WINS server information is configured on the WINS tab of the TCP/IP Properties dialog box, which is where you specify the IP addresses of the WINS severs as well as their priority.

Optimizing WINS Client-to-Server Processes

Little can be tuned via the GIU when it comes to WINS; however, the registry is chock-full of values you can manipulate to increase performance.

NameSrvQueryCount By default, a WINS client allows three queries to a WINS server to be unanswered before the WINS server is considered unavailable, which causes the next WINS server in the list to be used. To modify this behavior, edit the value of the

NameSrvQueryCount data item, located in HKEY_LOCAL_MACHINE\System\ CurrentControlSet\Services\NetBT\Parameters. NameSrvQueryCount supports values of 0–0xFFFF, which represents the number of retries.

Changing the value to a lower number can be useful if your clients are configured to use a large number of WINS servers. In effect, you're creating a quasi load-balancing solution. Please keep in mind that if all configured WINS servers are considered unavailable as a result of a value that's too low, the WINS client doesn't query any WINS server that it has already queried, and the query will fail. Modify this setting with care.

NameSrvQueryTimeout   This setting is kin to the NameSrvQueryCount data item. NameSrvQueryTimeout, located in HKEY_LOCAL_MACHINE\System\CurrentControlSet\ Services\NetBT\Parameters, specifies how long the client should wait after a query response has been sent to a WINS server before it issues another query to the same WINS server. The NameSrvQueryTimeout data item is REG_DWORD in format and supports a value range of 100–0xFFFFFFFF, which represents the number of milliseconds that must expire before another query is sent. The default value is 1500 milliseconds, or 1.5 seconds.

Increasing this value can be useful in situations where the WINS clients and servers are separated either by great WAN distances or by slow links. However, if you set the value too high, it can significantly increase how long it takes to resolve a name if a WINS server is down.

WINSDownTimeout   When a device configured to use WINS boots, NetBT waits for a predetermined amount of time before it allows the system boot to proceed if a WINS server can't be contacted. WINSDownTimeout is a REG_DWORD data item that needs to be created in HKEY_LOCAL_MACHINE\System\CurrentControlSet\Services\NetBT\Parameters. The default value when no data item exists for this boot event is 15 seconds. Supported values are 1000–0xFFFFFFFF, which defines in hex the number of milliseconds that NetBT will wait on the WINS servers upon boot.

This value can be lowered for users who are frequently roaming to locations that aren't connected to their home network. It can also be increased to compensate for a particularly slow network link, which might cause premature WINS failure detection. In either case, excessive modification of this value might cause system boot latency problems.

NOTE: For a complete listing of supported WINS registry settings, please consult Appendix A.

Resolver Service

Every WINS-enabled device needs to be able to send name queries to its configured WINS servers. Just as in the process of resolving a FQDN through DNS, NetBIOS queries WINS by using a resolver service called the NetBIOS Name service. The NetBIOS Name service is initiated by NetBT when an application or service requests name resolution.

Resolution requests are intercepted by NetBT and sent out by the NetBIOS Name service to the configured WINS servers. When the data is found, the WINS server returns the values back to the NetBIOS Name service, which then hands the answer back to the NetBT, and ultimately back to the requesting entity.

The NetBIOS Name service is another one of those services that is intangible from an administrator's perspective. Think of it as a subfunction of NetBT that's called when NetBT sees fit. So in this respect, the service can't be started or stopped by a human, but rather, is started and stopped as a result of NetBT, which itself is a phantom service.

TAKE COMMAND

You can view all of the names that have been registered and resolved via NetBIOS as well as which method was used to resolve them (i.e., broadcast, WINS, etc.) by entering **nbtstat –r** at a command prompt.

Troubleshooting Name Resolution

Name resolution is a simple process, and troubleshooting problems is a rather straightforward process. Following are the steps to take if you're having problems accessing a network device.

1. Attempt to ping the device name.

   ❖ If you get a response back from the device, then the problem might be related to the application or service that you're running. A successful ping of a NetBIOS name rules out NetBIOS resolution problems.

   ❖ If you received a response that states *Pinging IPAddress with 32 bytes of data* followed by many Request Timeout errors, there's either a network problem, a configuration problem on the remote device, or bad data in WINS. However, name resolution is working. Go to step 3.

   ❖ If your ping fails with either an Unknown host or Unknown device error, the problem is name-resolution related. Go to step 2.

2. Verify your WINS configuration.

    ❖ If you don't have a WINS server configured, this is the source of your problem.

    ❖ If you have one or more WINS servers configured, attempt to ping each of them paying special attention to the WINS server with the highest priority.

    ❖ If any of the WINS servers fail to respond to a ping, there's a network problem, a problem with the WINS server, or you have the wrong IP address configured. Verify that you have the correct IP addresses and try this step again.

    ❖ If all of the WINS servers respond to a ping, ensure that you haven't set the *NameSrvQueryTimeout* value too low. If this isn't your problem, go to step 3.

3. Verify WINS data.

    ❖ Use the WINS MMC to search for the device name you're attempting to resolve. If the data is found and appears valid, but it has a different IP address than the IP address reported when attempting to ping the device, you might be loading bad data from LMHOSTS, HOSTS, or DNS. Got to step 4.

    ❖ If the data isn't found in the WINS MMC, the device hasn't registered in WINS. See the "Troubleshooting Registration" section of this chapter for help in determining why the device you are trying to access is not registering in WINS. .

4. Verify LMHOSTS, HOSTS, and DNS.

    ❖ View the LMHOSTS file to ensure that there are no invalid or old entries. If you find any, they might be the cause of your problem. Remove them and then enter **nbtstat – R** at the command line to flush the NetBIOS cache.

    ❖ View the Hosts file to ensure that there are no invalid host names. If you find any, they might be causing your problem. Remove them from the HOSTS file and then flush the DNS cache by entering **ipconfig /flushdns** at the command line.

    ❖ View the DNS database using either the DNS MMC or NSLOOKUP, depending on your configuration, and verify that host data in DNS is correct. If bad data is found, replace it. You must then flush your client's DNS cache by entering **ipconfig /flushdns** at the command line.

The NetBIOS Cache

The NetBIOS cache is responsible for caching all name resolution responses received on the local machine. This cache is found on all Microsoft operating systems and contains two types of entries: those that are dynamically learned, and those that are preloaded. In all cases of NetBIOS name resolution, the NetBIOS cache is checked first and is always assumed to have the most correct information.

Dynamically Learned Cache Entries

Dynamically learned entries are placed into cache as a result of a query or broadcast to resolve a NetBIOS name. Successful query results are stored in the NetBIOS cache, which is parsed in subsequent queries. This enables queries to be satisfied without increasing network traffic if the results are already known locally.

As entries are dynamically placed into cache, each is given a time to live (TTL). The default TTL for NetBIOS cache entries is 420 seconds. The entry remains in cache until the TTL expires or the cache is flushed. If the cache becomes full, a first in, first out (FIFO) algorithm is implemented to purge the entries that have been in cache the longest. The space freed by this process is used to house new results.

Preloaded Cache Entries

Some entries are placed into the cache as a result of an event called preloading. Preloading is implemented in LMHOSTS by specifying a #PRE tag before an entry in the file. When the NetBIOS cache is loaded, either as a result of system boot or by manual reload, the LMHOSTS file is parsed and any entries that have a #PRE tag are loaded into the cache. (LMOSTS entries are described in the "LMHOSTS" section of this chapter.) Preloaded entries, also commonly referred to as static entries, don't have a TTL and remain in cache indefinitely.

TAKE COMMAND

To view the contents of your NetBIOS cache, open a command prompt and enter **nbtstat –c**. The system returns the cache table, which details the name, IP address, type, and TTL of all dynamic and static entries.

Although data in the NetBIOS cache is always assumed to be correct, you might find instances where the response that has been cached is incorrect, causing connection and session problems. Because there is no way to remove a single entry from the cache, you must flush the NetBIOS cache to correct any problems resulting from bad data in the cache by entering **nbtstat –R** at a command prompt.

To check the status of a remote machine's cache, enter **nbtstat – a** *<HostName>* or
Nbtstat –A *<IPAddress>*

If no data is given after the –a or –A switch, the tool assumes you want to view the local
machine's cache.

> **NOTE:** Flushing the cache will cause a complete cache reload. In a cache reload, all
> preloaded records in the LMHOSTS file will be placed back into cache, so if your problem
> stems from a bad entry in LMHOSTS, running nbtstat –R won't resolve your issue. If your problem
> stems from an incorrect entry in the LMHOSTS file, you must edit it and remove the bad entry.
> After the bad entry has been removed, the cache can then be flushed to purge any bogus
> cached data about the name-to-address mapping.

Optimizing the Cache

Under normal circumstances, the NetBIOS cache doesn't need any modification.
Unfortunately, most of us work in places where there is no such thing as a normal
circumstance. Following are some registry settings that can help you optimize your
system's caching mechanism.

CacheTimeout   This registry setting establishes the default TTL for dynamic cache
entries. By default, cached entries remain in cache for 10 minutes. You can modify
the TTL by changing the value of the CacheTimeout REG_DWORD data item found in
HKEY_LOCAL_MACHINE\System\CurrentControlSet\Services\NetBT\Parameters, to a
hex value between 60000–0xFFFFFFFF. The hex value translates to the number of minutes
that's assigned to the TTL for an entry.

Increasing the timeout for cached entries can reduce network and WINS processing
loads. This reduction of load comes at the cost of fresh data. The longer you leave an entry
in cache, the more likely the information will change, making the cache stale.

Size/Small/Medium/Large   This setting establishes the default size of the NetBIOS cache.
The default setting for this value depends on whether the WINS client is also acting as a
WINS Proxy. (See the section "WINS Proxy" later in this chapter.)

If the WINS client isn't a WINS Proxy, the default size of the cache is 16 KB. If the device
is a WINS Proxy, the default size is 256 KB. You can adjust the default value by modifying

the Size/Small/Medium/Large data item located in the HKEY_LOCAL_MACHINE\System\ CurrentControlSet\Services\NetBT\Parameters registry key to a value of 1, 2, or 3. Here's an explanation of each value:

- ❖ 1 – Defines a small cache size, which is 16 KB in size
- ❖ 2 – Defines a medium cache size, which is 128 KB in size
- ❖ 3 – Defines a large cache size, which is 256 KB in size.

NOTE: For a complete listing of supported cache-related registry settings, please consult Appendix A.

LMHOSTS

The LMHOSTS file serves the same function for NetBIOS as the HOSTS file serves for DNS, which is that of a local mapping of names to IP addresses. This flat file, typically located in %Systemroot%\System32\Drivers\Etc, isn't defined in any RFC and is exclusive to the Microsoft implementation of NetBIOS.

If you're using LMHOSTS, you must always have an LMHOSTS file located in the default directory, even if it's just to redirect the parser to a central LMHOSTS file. A central LMHOSTS file is located on a server and can be parsed by all clients that have been properly configured.

Entries are placed into LMHOSTS manually, using any text editor. Each time NetBIOS starts on a device that's configured to use LMHOSTS, the file is parsed for any entries that are to be preloaded. Each entry defined as needing to be preloaded is placed into the NetBIOS cache with no TTL, as explained before. Entries that aren't defined as preloading aren't loaded into the cache until NetBT parses the file in an effort to find a name.

LMHOSTS Syntax

The LMHOSTS file supports many different extensions, also known as tags, using some very particular syntax. The supported form for LMHOSTS is the following:

IP Address   NetBIOSName   Extensions   Comments

For example, an entry for a device named ServerA, which is the HR database server, has an IP address of 10.200.6.2, and should be loaded into cache at system boot, has the following entry in LMHOSTS:

10.22.6.2   ServerA   #PRE   #HR Database Server

LMHOSTS supports the following extensions:

◆ #PRE – Flags the record with the #PRE tag indicating that the record needs to be loaded any time NetBT starts or when the NetBT cache is reloaded.

◆ #DOM:<*domain*> – Associates the record configured with #DOM as being a member of the domain name specified. Used for browser-based functions.

◆ #BEGIN_ALTERNATE – Lets the parser know that what follows should be parsed only if the name can't be found in the main body of the LMHOSTS file. It is a header for entries that contain locations for alternate or centralized LMHOSTS files that can be parsed if needed. If you use this extension, you must also specify the #END_ALTERNATE extension in addition to an #INCLUDE entry for each alternate file location.

◆ #INCLUDE<*filename*> – Specifies an alternate location for an LMHOSTS file. This is used when implementing a centralized LMHOSTS file. The Universal Naming Convention (UNC) format for specifying a filename is supported in this tag.

◆ #END_ALTERNATE – Lets the parser know that all alternate locations for LMHOSTS files have been exhausted. Must be used in conjunction with the BEGIN_ALTERNATE extension.

NOTE: If any verbiage that's proceeded by the pound sign (#) doesn't conform to one of the supported extensions, the parser assumes it to be a comment, which is ignored by the parser.

As was the case with HOSTS files, I discourage the use of LMHOSTS. As you can see from the examples given in the "Node Types" section of this chapter, information in LMHOSTS takes precedence over other naming sources such as DNS. Using LMHOSTS can cause name resolution problems that can be difficult to troubleshoot and ultimately create unnecessary administrative overhead.

Configuring LMHOSTS

A sample LMHOST file exists in all installations of Windows 2000, and it contains examples of the tags used for each entry. Configuring your device to use LMHOSTS files requires that an LMHOSTS file is in the default location, %Systemroot%\System32\Drivers\Etc, and that you've configured the device to use the LMHOSTS file via the GUI.

After you've added valid entries to the LMHOSTS file, ensure that the Enable LMHOSTS Lookup option is set. The Enable LMHOSTS Lookup option is set by default and is located on the WINS tab of the TCP/IP properties dialog box for any NIC. The device is now ready to use LMHOSTS.

Optimizing LMHOSTS

Because LMHOSTS isn't in use much any more, the number of registry settings that directly affect its use are limited. A complete list of LMHOSTS registry settings can be found in Appendix A.

LmhostsTimeout   This value defines how long the WINS client will wait for the parser to return results from the LMHOSTS file. This REG_DWORD data item is found in HKEY_LOCAL_MACHINE\System\CurrentControlSet\Services\NetBT\Parameters. LmhostsTimeout supports a range of hex values from 1000–0xFFFFFFFF, which defines the timeout in milliseconds (6000 milliseconds or 6 seconds by default).

Manipulating this value can be useful if you've configured multiple #INCLUDE tags in the LMHOSTS file, which can cause latency as the parser contacts multiple LMHOSTS files. Setting the value too high may cause excessive latency if you have a large number of #INCLUDE statements in your LMHOSTS file.

WINS Proxy

Back in the days of NT 3.5, many operating systems were leveraging NetBIOS. Because networks were so small, the implementation of NetBIOS on those operating systems was normally limited to the use of B-Node functionality.

For Microsoft, having customers who had some devices that supported Microsoft's implementation of NetBIOS that leverage WINS and other devices that only supported broadcast was disastrous. How would these two types of devices find one another across a router? More importantly, how was Microsoft to sell its server product as a one-stop solution for both Microsoft and non-Microsoft clients if its interoperability could not be achieved? Enter WINS Proxies.

How WINS Proxy Works

A WINS Proxy is a device that listens on a network segment for NetBIOS broadcast traffic and forwards it to a preconfigured set of WINS servers. When a name is found in WINS, the answer is returned to the WINS Proxy, which then sends it to the requestor. This functionality allows clients that would normally be limited to resolving names only on their own network segment to resolve names found in WINS.

Take the following scenario. You have a B-Node client on a segment that is attempting to resolve a device name of ServerA, which is located on another segment. Let's examine how this transaction would occur both without and with a WINS Proxy.

Without a WINS Proxy

◈ The B-Node client broadcasts a request for the IP address of a device named ServerA.

◈ Each device on the segment accepts the broadcast packet and then examines the data. Because there's no match on the network, all devices discard the request.

◈ The B-Node waits for a response until the broadcast query timeout value has expired, at which time it will return a "name not found" error to the requesting application or service.

With a WINS Proxy

◈ The B-Node client broadcasts a request for the IP address of a device named ServerA.

◈ Each device on the segment, including the WINS Proxy, accepts the broadcast packet and then examines the data. The WINS Proxy realizes that this, like all broadcasts' name resolution requests, needs to be resolved on behalf of the client.

◈ The WINS Proxy searches its NetBIOS cache for a match. If the name is found, it's returned to the requestor. If the name isn't found, the WINS Proxy packages a resolution request that's sent to its configured WINS server.

◈ The WINS server receives the query for ServerA, searches its database, and returns the IP address to the WINS Proxy.

◈ The WINS Proxy receives the query response from the WINS server. The results are placed into the NetBIOS cache for future use.

◈ The IP address of ServerA is returned to the requesting B-Node device.

NOTE: It is important to remember that the WINS Proxy doesn't participate in the registration of NetBIOS names; therefore, interoperability between a B-Node client using a WINS Proxy and an H-Node Microsoft client can't be ensured unless the H-Node client can resolve the name of the B-Node client.

Enabling a WINS Proxy

Although WINS Proxies were a useful feature when they were first introduced, they are rarely used today. Evidence of the lessening importance of the WINS Proxy can be seen in the fact that in NT 4, you could configure a device to be a WINS Proxy in the GUI, but in Windows 2000, the only way to enable this role is through a registry modification. It, like many other features whose configuration has been limited to registry hacks only, is on its way out the door.

Any Microsoft client dating back to Windows 3.11 can be a WINS Proxy. Its functionality hasn't changed between its first implementation and the current implementation found in Windows 2000, which is kind of odd for a Microsoft product. After all, we are talking about a company that has "upgraded" their screen savers for every operating system release.

To make your existing WINS client a WINS Proxy, first ensure that WINS is configured and working. Then change the EnableProxy data item's value from 0 to 1. This entry is located in HKEY_LOCAL_MACHINE\SYSTEM\CurrentControlSet\Services\ Netbt\Parameters.

WINS Proxy Implementation Considerations

Consider the information in the following sections if you plan to implement WINS Proxies on your network.

Physical Placement

WINS Proxies should be installed on each subnet that contains B-Node clients that need to resolve NetBIOS names for devices on other network segments.

Each segment should have no more than two WINS Proxies due to potential overloading of the WINS server. Because WINS Proxies intercept all name-resolution requests, each WINS Proxy on a segment will query the WINS server for the same data.

Client Behavior

The behavior of a B-node client doesn't change when a WINS Proxy is added to the local subnet. If the first name resolution query times out while the WINS Proxy is still searching for the name, the client broadcasts again. If the WINS Proxy has the answer cached by the time it intercepts the subsequent query, the WINS Proxy answers the client. If the answer isn't in cache, the WINS Proxy again attempts to resolve the name on behalf of the client. Because of this behavior, keep in mind that depending on how many times the client is configured to broadcast for a name, the WINS Proxy might receive a rapid secession of resolution request from the same client for the same name.

Name Registration, Renewal, and Release

All WINS clients must be able to register, renew, and release their names with a WINS server. While the specifics of the communications between the WINS client and WINS server varies for each different transaction, the responses that the WINS server sends to the WINS client is constant for registration, renewal, and release.

A WINS client can receive three possible responses from a WINS server when registering, renewing, or releasing a NetBIOS name: no response, positive, or negative.

- No response – Just as the name implies, the WINS server doesn't respond to the request from the client. The action of the client in the case of no response depends on what type of request is being ignored, as well as how many times the client has received no response from the server.

- Positive – The WINS server has accepted a registration or renewal request from the client. A positive response includes the TTL for the registration, which is equal to the Renew Interval on the WINS server.

- Negative – The WINS server finds a conflict or another reason to reject the WINS client's request. When this message is received, the process on the WINS client that spawned the request will either fail or attempt to use another resolution method.

NOTE: A WINS client sometimes receives a Wait for Acknowledgement (WACK) response from a WINS server. This response occurs only when a name attempting to be registered is in conflict with another entry in the database. See the section on duplicate names later in this chapter.

Name Registration

Registration is the process of placing new NetBIOS information into the WINS database. A WINS client attempts to register all NetBIOS name-to-IP-address information in WINS at system boot. If the WINS client receives no response from the WINS server, the client will attempt to register again every 10 minutes until a positive response is sent from the WINS server. There is no limit to the number of times that the registration attempt will be retried. This behavior can't be modified.

When a device attempts to register names, the actions of both the WINS client and server depend on the uniqueness of the information being registered. NetBIOS information can either be unique to the database, or be in conflict with another entry in the database.

Registering a Unique Name

When a WINS client attempts to register names that are unique to the WINS database, the process is easy and straightforward. The WINS client, at boot, attempts to register all NetBIOS names with the WINS server that's configured with the highest priority in the client's list of WINS servers.

When the WINS server receives the registration request, it checks its copy of the database for duplicate entries. If no duplicate records exist in the copy of the database that the WINS server houses, the server sends a positive response to the client after creating the record in the database and updating the record's timestamp and version ID. In this response, all registrations are given a TTL that is equivalent to the Renew Interval that's configured on the WINS server.

Registering a Duplicate Name

Sometimes the WINS server finds an entry in its database that has the same NetBIOS name as the device attempting to register its names. When the WINS server finds a duplicate name, the steps that occur depend on several factors, including the state of the existing record, the type of record (unique name or groups name), and ownership.

From a WINS client perspective, registration of a duplicate name always looks the same. The WINS client sends a registration request to the WINS server. The WINS server examines its database and finds a duplicate. Once the duplicate is found, a WACK is sent to the client. The WACK lets the client know that the WINS server is "thinking" about issuing either a positive or negative response, which prevents the registration request from timing out. Eventually, either a positive or negative response is issued to, and accepted by, the client.

From a WINS server perspective, the measures taken to determine if the device attempting to register a duplicate name is sent a positive or negative response differs depending on the existing record. The WINS server must consider the following factors relative to the existing record:

◆ Data in the entries – In some cases, a device might be attempting to register a name that it has already registered but failed to release. In this case, there's no duplication.

◆ State – The state of the record may be active, released, or tombstoned. The only time a registration request is denied is when the state is active. Existing records with a state of released and tombstoned are considered expendable because they have either been released by the original client, or they are ready for removal via scavenging.

◆ Type – Many types, such a groups and domains, support multiple devices registering the same information. If the type is unique, the registration request may be denied depending on other factors.

◆ Static – If the record is static, the action of the WINS server depends on the state of "Migrate On/Off," which either allows or prevents dynamic entries to overwrite static entries.

◆ Ownership – The WINS server that owns the existing record can be important because the WINS server must take ownership of the record if it is to modify or remove it from the database.

Using these criteria, if the WINS server determines that there is duplication, it may send a name query request to the device that owns the registered record in the database. Name query requests are sent to the owner of the record three times with an interval of 500 milliseconds between each request. If the WINS server receives an answer, the record is assumed to be valid and a negative response is sent to the client attempting to register the name. If no response is received, the owner of the original record is assumed to be no longer valid and a positive response is sent to the WINS client attempting to register the names. All of the steps that cover the previously mentioned process and the potential variables are detailed in the following sections.

Registration When Duplicates Have the Same IP Address   Sometimes the WINS server receives a registration request whose NetBIOS names and IP addresses both appear to be in conflict with an existing record. In these situations, it's assumed that the machine requesting registration is the same device that registered the existing record. The following actions take place:

1. The WINS client sends a name registration request to the WINS server.

2. The WINS server receives the request and examines the database.

3. When a duplicate record is found, a WACK is issued to the WINS client.

4. After the WACK is issued, the WINS server examines the entry and finds that the IP address that the existing entry has and the IP address of the requestor are the same.

5. Ownership of the record is determined and modified:

   ✦ If the owner of the existing record is the same WINS server that received the request, the TTL of the record is updated, its state is changed to active, and the version ID is incremented.

   ✦ If the owner of the existing record isn't the same as the WINS server that has received the request, ownership is transferred. Because a WINS server can't update a record it doesn't own, the nonowner WINS server takes ownership of the existing record. Once ownership has been transferred, the TTL, state of the record, and its version ID are updated.

6. After ownership has been established, the WINS server sends back a positive response to the WINS client that includes the new TTL.

Registrations When Duplicates Have Different IP Addresses   If both the requesting device and the existing entry don't have the same IP address, the record is considered a valid duplicate and measures are taken to resolve the issue.

1. The WINS client sends a name registration request to the WINS server.

2. The WINS server receives the request and examines the database.

3. If a duplicate record is found, a WACK is issued to the WINS client.

4. After sending the WACK, the WINS server examines the existing record for several conditions before sending a name query request.

   ❖ If the state of the existing record is released or tombstoned, the WINS server attempts to establish ownership. Go to step 6.

   ❖ If the entry is active, go to step 5.

   ❖ If the existing record is determined to be static then, by default, it is subject to being overwritten. Go to step 7.

5. Once the record has been determined to be active, the WINS server sends out a name query request to the device that registered the record. This is done in an attempt to determine if the device is still valid. If no response is received, the WINS server takes ownership of the record. If the name query request yields a response, then a negative message is sent to the WINS client.

6. If the record has been determined to be stale, the WINS server takes ownership of the entry.

7. The WINS server then updates the record with the IP address of the device attempting to register the name. The record is also given a state of active and its TTL and version ID is updated before the positive response is sent to the WINS client.

8. The WINS client receives the WINS server response and takes the following action:

   ❖ If the response is negative, the client logs an error to the Event Log indicating that a duplicate device is on the network. All NetBIOS functionality is disabled until a valid name is registered.

   ❖ If the response is positive, the client updates its naming information with the TTL and all NetBIOS network services are started.

Registering a Name When a Collision Occurs

Two devices can sometimes legally register the same name in two different WINS servers' databases. Because a WINS server checks its replica of the database for duplicates only when a client attempts to register names, a duplicate name might exist on another WINS server but might not have been replicated yet. Once replication does start, a collision occurs.

A collision is the result of an entry or record with the same name being owned by two different WINS servers. Because WINS is a flat namespace, and all names must be unique, there needs to be a mechanism to resolve naming collisions. WINS handles naming collisions by examining both records and tombstoning the record with the oldest timestamp. Last one in wins—no pun intended.

Troubleshooting Registration

Most registration issues are the result of connectivity problems, protocol problems, or duplicate name errors. If you suspect a name registration problem, try the following steps.

1. Verify IP configuration.

   ❖ Ping the WINS servers. If this works, your TCP/IP configuration is correct. Go to step 2.

   ❖ Ping your default gateway. If this works but you're unable to access your WINS server(s), there is either a network problem or a configuration problem with the WINS server.

2. Verify WINS configuration.

   ❖ Examine the priority of your WINS servers. If any are not responding to pings, remove them from the list or change their priority.

   ❖ Use **nbtstat –n** to view a list of names that have attempted to register with WINS as well as their status.

      a. If some entries have a status of conflict, then one or more names are duplicated in WINS. Go to step 3.

      b. If some entries have a status of registered, there's no problem with the registration process. Your problem probably lies elsewhere.

◆ Use **netdiag /test:wins** to produce a connectivity test of WINS and NetBT.

    a. If one or more of your NICs reports that NetBIOS has been disabled, this is the cause of your problem.

3. Verify WINS data.

◆ Search your WINS database for the name of the device that you're attempting to register.

    a. If you find a duplicate device, this is the cause of your problem. Resolve the duplicate name.

    b. If you don't find any data matching your device name, go to step 4.

4. Verify NetBT and NetBIOS services.

◆ Open the System Information MMC and navigate to the Software Environment – Drivers object and view the status of both the NetBIOS and NetBT services.

    a. If either service is stopped, verify that all registry settings in HKLM\System\CurrentControlSet\Services\Netbt are correct.

Renewal

Renewal is the process of updating existing entries in the WINS database with new information to ensure data freshness. By default, a WINS client attempts to renew its NetBIOS information with the WINS server at set intervals.

The first attempt to renew a name occurs at one-eighth the TTL defined on the WINS server. If this first attempt at renewal is unsuccessful, the client will attempt to renew its name every 10 minutes with the WINS server that has the highest priority until one hour has expired. If the WINS server with the highest priority doesn't respond, the WINS client will then attempt to renew its name with the WINS server that has the second highest priority, every 10 minutes until one hour has passed.

The process of trying the WINS server with the highest priority for one hour and then trying the WINS server with the second highest priority for another hour will continue until the TTL has expired. At TTL expiration, all NetBIOS network services will cease to function.

CODE BLUE

The registration, renewal, and release processes only use the WINS servers configured with the highest and second highest priorities. If you've configured 12 available WINS servers, as permitted in Windows 2000, only two of the 12 are used for resolution. So tell me, how is it useful to resolve names with WINS server number three if you can't register with WINS server one or two? Seems to me that a failure of only two WINS servers can prevent any name resolution from occurring no matter how many WINS servers have been configured. Once again, there is not much value to configuring more than two WINS servers in Windows 2000.

Once a name is renewed, the TTL is refreshed on the entry in the WINS server's database as well as on the WINS client. Its version ID is also incremented to ensure replication of the updated record to other WINS servers.

TAKE COMMAND

Name refresh can also be forced by using Nbtstat. A new switch in Nbtstat forces all NetBIOS names to send a release notification to the WINS servers and then immediately refresh all the names. This is useful if you've changed IP addresses without rebooting and you want the WINS server to be made aware of the changes instantly. To use this feature, enter **nbtstat –RR** at a command prompt.

Releasing a Name

When a WINS client shuts down, it sends a release notification to its WINS server with the highest priority. When the WINS server receives this notification, the state of the record is changed from active to released and its timestamp is changed to reflect the current system time plus the extinction interval (to permit eventual scavenging). This change in the state allows any other device to register the names that were just released by the client.

Unfortunately, the whole release concept doesn't always work correctly. In fact, in my experience, a textbook release of a NetBIOS name is the exception, not the rule. Many factors can cause a device not to release its name, such as an abrupt shutdown or failure to contact a WINS server in a timely fashion during shutdown. If a device has been shut down and the WINS server was never made aware that it could change its state to release, a "silent release" has just occurred. *Silent release* is just a nice way of saying failure to release.

In a silent release, the entries registered by the client that is shut down still appear as active. As a result, the next time the same client boots, a duplicate entry will be found and ultimately resolved, as detailed previously.

Chapter 8

Designing and Managing a WINS Environment

D esigning a WINS environment is a relatively simple process. Make no mistake about it, WINS design is not totally mindless work. Although designing a WINS environment is easier than designing a DNS environment (which isn't that difficult either), you are still capable of making some bad design decisions that will plague you for years. It can also be said that WINS maintenance is simple—until something goes wrong. When something substantial goes wrong with WINS, the problem tends to be difficult to resolve.

In this chapter, I discuss some general WINS design principles. You may already have a WINS infrastructure in place, but it never hurts to review good design principles. You never know when you might discover a problem with your design that forces you to reevaluate your implementation.

I will also cover management of WINS servers and their databases. Normally, WINS runs great and appears to be a touchless solution. Therefore, administrators often think that just because WINS appears to be touchless, it should be touched less. However, ninety-nine percent of all WINS problems are the result of not maintaining the WINS servers—and more importantly, the Jet database. (This statistic was produced using undiscovered evidence.)

Designing Your WINS Environment

Designing a WINS environment is less complex than designing DNS because the product itself is less complex. At the heart of its simplicity is the fact that WINS servers never have to interoperate with other WINS servers produced by other software vendors. Let's face it, DNS is simple until you start introducing interoperability scenarios that deal with issues such as support of multiple namespaces, replication, and security. Because WINS is not completely RFC compliant and no other software vendors in the world produce another NetBIOS Name Server product, any interoperability issues are limited to those concerning different version of WINS in the same environment.

Although it is less complex, designing a robust and available WINS environment is not easy. WINS servers are accessed more than most people realize. A WINS environment that consists of approximately 100,000 devices must be able to service 12–18 million queries and well over 1 million registration requests a day. These numbers are very impressive, especially when you consider that some DNS servers on the Internet aren't even seeing this kind of traffic. Its high utilization, combined with the fact that most network access depends on WINS, make WINS a mission-critical component.

Capacity Planning

Even if you have already implemented a WINS environment, you must constantly assess and reassess its ability to support increased capacity. If you have read any Microsoft documentation on WINS server capacity and recommended load numbers, you have been misled. Microsoft first published capacity numbers indicating that you should implement a primary and backup WINS server for every 10,000 WINS clients. These numbers were published back in the heyday of NT 3.51, when the first generation Pentium chip was the new kid on the block and no one knew what a Pokemon was. While these numbers may have been valid many years ago, they are ludicrous and outdated today.

There were two reasons for these low-capacity numbers: hardware and the Jet database. When hardware was a limiting factor, many software vendors commonly released software that could be run only on the fastest processors available. Today, most software will run on the lowest class of processor available and in some cases, even those that are not being produced anymore. We are currently in an age where the hardware has far outpaced the needs of the software. In terms of updating the WINS capacity numbers, hardware is no longer a bottleneck.

The Jet database, and to some extent, the operating system, have been the most limiting factor in permitting higher capacity WINS servers—even in the NT 4 space. As you have read in previous chapters, Microsoft has implemented a brand new Jet database in the Windows 2000 release of WINS. This database, while far from perfect (or even nearly perfect, for that matter) is much better than those found in previous versions of NT. It can accept many more transactions in a given time than the last version of Jet, and it corrupts far less.

Unfortunately, it is just as bad as its predecessor at reclaiming whitespace. So while it performs better, if you don't keep on top of the whitespace issue, you may experience performance equivalent to or worse than NT 4 WINS. The operating system is much, much faster than NT 4. More importantly, its support for multiprocessing is greatly enhanced to the point where justifying multiple CPUs is not difficult, as was the case in NT. In both single- and multiple-processor scenarios, Windows 2000 outperforms NT 4, which obviously benefits WINS.

Back to the capacity numbers in question. They are so out of date that it's comical. Unfortunately, no formula can be used to determine the maximum number of WINS clients that a single WINS server can support. This formula doesn't exist because each server's capabilities can and will vary slightly from another server's capabilities. The only way to determine how many WINS servers to deploy is by trending your environment before (if applicable) and after your WINS deployment. The performance counters that you want to pay special attention to are discussed in the "Performance Monitoring" section found later in this chapter.

In general, two WINS servers that have a single PIII 700MHz processor (which is the low end of the currently available servers) with 256 MB of RAM and SCSI drives can service anywhere from 30,000 to 40,000 WINS clients. You may need to deploy more WINS servers to compensate for slow network links or excessive routing, but all network issues aside, this number is realistic and achievable. If you decide to implement multiprocessing, each server can service even more clients. Every environment is unique, though, which is why trending and analysis are so critical to properly sizing your environment.

NOTE: When talking about WINS planning, servers are normally referred to in pairs. You should never deploy a WINS server that doesn't have a partner, even if that partner is also a partner to another WINS server. Redundancy in WINS servers is key.

Server Hardware

I don't want to spend a whole lot of time on hardware. Although it is important, I'm assuming that you are already familiar with which particular hardware components are better than others after reading the hardware discussion in Chapter 3. However, it is important to profile the hardware use of a WINS server.

The hardware needs of a WINS server aren't that different from servers hosting other databases, including AD and DNS servers. The only major difference is the amount of changes that occur in WINS as compared to other database-based services. Arguably, WINS handles more read and write transactions than AD due to each WINS client's constant need to register and resolve names. (The validity of this statement depends on your environment, of course.) Each client registers all of its NetBIOS information, which is at minimum three entries, every time the client is rebooted or the time to live (TTL) of the device's record expires.

In addition to each client registering multiple services, each client also uses WINS to resolve NetBIOS names. Because of these constant updates and queries, not only does WINS have the potential to work harder than AD, but WINS also handles more transactions than even a completely populated DNS environment that supports dynamic updates. Most DNS clients register only a single record in DNS (A record), which is a third of the average registration that WINS sees. Because even Windows 2000 clients still heavily depend on NetBIOS, until we move either to a NetBIOS-free operating system or to one that depends far less on NetBIOS than Windows 2000 does, WINS will continue to resolve considerably more names than DNS, while being updated more frequently than AD.

If you had to rate the importance of components in a server as they relate to WINS, I/O would still be the most heavily used component. Your I/O subsystem needs to be up to the task of constantly parsing a sometimes-bloated database that may contain hundreds of thousands of entries—in a timely fashion. The server's processor will be the second most used component, followed by memory.

Unlike AD-Integrated DNS, where memory was more heavily used than processor, WINS tends to be more processor starved than memory starved. Processor is used in WINS more because the WINS databases typically don't grow too large. An average sized company that properly maintains its database should have a WINS database in the area of 30–60 MB. This small database doesn't use nearly as much memory as an AD-based DNS solution, where the database housing DNS and all other AD data could be several gigabytes. The network subsystem is the next most heavily used subsystem due to the light but constant network chatter with WINS clients.

Software Considerations

Choosing the software is easy; who else produces a NetBIOS Name Server? Your choices are extremely limited. Configuring the operating system and the WINS Server service to run optimally is essential to a robust WINS environment. Take a look at the following sections for tips on how to keep your WINS servers running like the hot rods they are.

Server Roles

For some reason, many administrators feel compelled to install multiple services on a single server. I don't know if they do this in an attempt to get the most bang for their buck, or if some other reason motivates them that I am unaware of. No matter what the reason, installing WINS on a server that is serving another role is not wise. Installing WINS on the same devices hosting another service or role causes problems in contention and stability.

It goes without saying that if there are fewer services on a server, it will be accessed by fewer users. If there are fewer users accessing the server, then there will be less contention for system resources. Contention robs our servers of precious resources every chance it gets. The WINS service can easily consume most of the available resources of a server all by itself. Keeping WINS on its own member servers will positively affect performance.

Loading a server up with multiple services or roles can also cause stability issues. The more services that a server hosts, the more likely that a failed or misbehaving service can cause a crash to occur. There is something to be said for simplicity when assigning roles to your servers. You must also consider the service pack and hotfix issues that may arise when placing multiple services on a single server. Microsoft releases fixes constantly not only for the base operating system but also for each service and product that they produce.

Because service packs and hotfixes rarely, if ever, touch only one component on a device, the more services you host on a single server, the greater the chance that an update to one component will break another component. The simple solution is to separate the WINS service from other services. By separating the WINS service from other services, the list of service packs and hotfixes that need to be installed is reduced. You also eliminate the possibility that updating another component will cause WINS to fail.

Under no circumstances should your WINS server ever be a domain controller. These two roles are so similar that there would be constant contention for the same system resources.

Optimizing Disk Access

I will assume that you have chosen to implement WINS as the only service on a server that is a member of a domain instead of a domain controller. While this is the optimum role configuration, there is still work to be done to optimize the operating system and WINS files. There are several areas of concern when optimizing the local configuration of your WINS server. There is the ever-present operating system and pagefile concern, which is found on any server. Additionally, WINS brings with it a database and several log files, as you read about in Chapter 6.

From a trend and usage perspective, the WINS database is a random read/write file. Random files have data placed into them at the first location found. When a single read transaction occurs in a random write file, it will occur from different locations in the file. Random files are quick to write and slow to read for these reasons. The WINS log files, on the other hand, are sequential in nature, meaning that there is a known point where writing to the file will begin. This point always comes after the point at which the last write stopped.

In a truly ideal scenario, you should attempt to keep all of the random files on the same disk and/or controller as other random files while placing the sequential files on the same disk and/or controller as other sequential files. As always, the operating system should be placed on its own hard drive. If at all possible, the operating system should even reside on its own hard drive controller, isolated from the WINS database. Placing the pagefile on the same drive as the operating system is considered acceptable but never optimal, even on a WINS server. The WINS database should be on its own hard drive and/or controller using RAID 5, which will eliminate most I/O contention while increasing fault tolerance. The WINS logs should be placed on their own drive and/or controller using RAID 1, which will reduce contention as well as increase the write performance that is critical to log files.

Unfortunately, given the size of most WINS databases and their lack of appeal, it is difficult to justify the cost associated with optimizing the file system. (Ask any manager what AD is and he or she will know; ask what WINS is, and you'll get that deer-in-the-headlights look. That look seriously impacts funding.) The reality is that you are more likely to place the operating system, pagefile, WINS database, and WINS log files on the same disk.

If you do choose to move the WINS files to separate partitions, you will have to do so after the WINS service is installed. The WINS setup process does not allow you to specify alternate locations for the WINS database and logs at run time. Instead, all files are installed in the *%Systemroot%\System32\Wins* folder without question or input. The only way to relocate the WINS files is to edit the registry to reflect the new location.

To change the location that the WINS database resides in, complete the following steps:

1. At the command prompt, type **net stop wins**.

2. Perform a backup of the WINS database as detailed in the "Disaster Recovery" section of this chapter.

3. Copy the Wins.Mdb and all .log files, except for the .chk files, to their new location.

CAUTION: The .chk file is used to determine which changes have been committed from the log files to the database. The .chk file contains file system path information to the current location of the database. If it is moved with the rest of the WINS files, it will reflect the old path to the log file. This location mismatch can cause problems in the WINS database and may potentially interrupt the WINS service. If the .chk file is not moved, a new file is created when WINS starts. WINS then reads in all log files and makes any changes to its database that are contained within the logs but not in the database. Once all of the changes that a log file contains are written to the database, the log file is deleted.

4. Once the files are done copying, open the 32-bit registry editor (Regedt32.Exe).

5. Open HKLM\System\CurrentControlSet\Services\Wins\Parameters.

6. Edit the **DbFileNm** REG_EXPAND_SZ data item to reflect the new path to the WINS database.

7. Edit the **LogFilePath** REG_EXPAND_SZ data item to reflect the new path to the WINS log files.

8. At the command prompt, type **net start wins**.

Configuration Guidelines

When you configure your WINS server, you must address a few key areas to achieve the best performance and availability possible. While there are not nearly as many configuration options that can directly affect WINS performance and availability as there are for DNS, consider addressing the potential problem areas described in the following sections.

WINS Configuration   Each WINS server, like any other network device, must be configured with the correct TCP/IP options. Besides the normal statements about your WINS server needing to have a static IP address, proper subnet mask, default gateway, etc., you need to pay special attention to your WINS server's WINS configuration. Don't forget that a WINS server is also a WINS client, and as such, it must be configured to use one or more WINS servers for the purposes of resolution and registration.

There are two schools of thought to consider when deciding on the WINS configuration for your WINS server. The Microsoft-recommended method is to configure your WINS server's TCP/IP protocol to use its own address as both the primary and secondary WINS server addresses. By using your own IP address, all WINS calls will be redirected to the local WINS service instead of sent to another WINS server.

The other method is to configure the WINS server to use other WINS servers as its primary and secondary WINS servers. Using other WINS servers' addresses provides for more fault tolerance than the Microsoft-recommended method. Which method is the best choice? Depends on whom you talk to. To make the correct decision, you need to understand why Microsoft recommends one method over the other.

There is a little phenomenon that may occur on WINS servers called *split registration*. Like any other WINS client, a WINS server will attempt to register its names with the server that has been configured as the primary WINS server. In this case, the primary WINS server is the local machine. In many cases when this initial registration attempt is sent, the WINS service has not yet been stated on the local WINS server. Because the WINS service is not available on the local machine, the device will then attempt to register its records with the device configured as the secondary WINS server. If the secondary WINS server is any server other than the local machine, the WINS server will begin to register its names with it.

As the WINS server is in the process of registering its records with the secondary WINS server, if the WINS service starts on the local machine, all names that have not yet been accepted by the secondary WINS server will be immediately registered with the primary WINS server. This creates a situation where all the records that the WINS device owns are registered across multiple WINS servers. The term "split registration" means just that: the splitting of a single device's NetBIOS registrations between two WINS servers.

Split registration is the reason that Microsoft recommends not to configure your WINS server to use any other WINS server's address besides its own. If split registration does occur, there may be temporary name resolution issues when resolving the name of the WINS server. In some cases, the WINS server has registered the same name in both locations and an eventual replication collision will occur. This replication collision will be resolved through the normal WINS collision process.

Consider for a moment the problem at hand. It isn't the fact that the WINS server is pointed completely away from its local WINS database that's causing the problem. Instead, the problem occurs as a result of the WINS server being configured to use its own WINS service and the WINS service of another device. Microsoft skirts around the real problem by stating in a single Knowledge Base (KB) article that the WINS server can sometimes register records in its local database even if no address has been entered in for primary and secondary WINS. In this article, Microsoft causally mentions the behavior of WINS placing records in its own database independently of the normal NetBIOS process; they do not mention this in any other document. From everything that I have read and seen, the WINS server never registers its addresses in its own database unless it has been configured to do so.

If you don't believe me, try an experiment. Configure primary and secondary WINS servers that are not on the local WINS service. Reboot the device and place a sniffer on the WINS server's local segment. By viewing the local database, the remote database, and the sniffer trace after boot, you will see that all of your WINS servers' records are registered in the other databases, not in the local database. I also find it interesting that in every KB article that Microsoft has published about split registration, all examples of failure involve a WINS server pointed to itself and another WINS server in every scenario. Blaming an undocumented behavior that causes a WINS server to register with itself no matter what its local configuration dictates is a red herring.

Instead of resolving the problem correctly by indicating that your WINS servers should be pointed at other WINS servers for registration, Microsoft just has you point all of your WINS servers at their local services. There is a major logic flaw with this solution. If a WINS server is pointed only at itself and there is a database corruption problem, how will you log on to the device to resolve the issue?

If the WINS server's database that is answering any console request for name resolution can't resolve the domain name that you are attempting to log on to, how can you access the server to fix it? If you can't find a domain for logon, then your only course of action is to use the local Administrator ID and password to gain access to the device. Using or even obtaining the local Administrator ID and password is not feasible in most companies because of the cost of changing the account information once it is known. Unless you have completely moved to AD and done your best job to disable NetBIOS, you won't be able to log on to these boxes at all. Then again, if you have removed NetBIOS from your network and you totally depend on DNS, why do you need to worry about a WINS server in the first place?

Using another set of WINS servers as the primary and secondary WINS servers solves all of these problems. This type of configuration prevents split registration and ensures that if there is a local database problem, you can log on to the device and resolve the problem as soon as possible.

So what can happen even if split registration does occur? What's the worst-case scenario? It depends on your configuration. The worst-case scenario can occur in implementations where WINS is hosted on a server that is also an NT or Windows 2000 DC. (I told you not to do that!) In these cases, if split registration does occur, it can have much more of an adverse impact on your environment than when it occurs on a normal member server. Because the WINS server is also a DC, it registers domain records that should never be subjected to split registration. All of the domain records (1CH, 1BH, and 1EH) are group-type entries in WINS; therefore, in some cases of split registration, it is possible for some of the addresses in the domain records to be registered in one WINS database and some on the other.

This a problem because WINS does not replicate at the attribute level; instead, each record is replicated as a whole. For example, imagine that two different WINS servers have 1CH records for the same domain. One server has the first five addresses of the domain controllers, while the other has the other five domain controllers' addresses. When a replication collision occurs, only one record or the other will survive, not the aggregate. But even in this scenario, the WINS server will eventually reconcile these entries and register all of the correct data in the database. And because split registration occurs only when the device is rebooted, your chance of failure is very limited, especially if you are in the habit of rebooting only after hours (which would give the WINS boxes time to reconcile the database before these records were accessed).

Other than the previously detailed scenario, split registration has no impact because all WINS transactions between WINS servers do not depend on names. Also, all client communication with the WINS servers is IP-based, so not being able to resolve your WINS server's name for a short time is of little consequence to WINS servers and clients. I think that the decision is pretty clear. Using Microsoft's recommendation for a WINS server's WINS configuration will prevent your WINS server from becoming inaccessible by name for a short time but at the cost of supportability. If your WINS server is down and you can't fix it because you are unable to log on, telling management that you are unable to fix your device because of Microsoft's configuration recommendations is of little comfort. If you have configured your DCs to be WINS servers too, split registration is a valid problem, but as long as you follow my configuration guidelines, you will be fine.

Beware of Microsoft Support's View of Split Registration

I do want to caution you against a disturbing habit that a few employees of Microsoft's support channels have. If you place a support call that has anything even remotely to do with name resolution, Microsoft will instinctively ask you about your WINS configuration. From conversations that I have had with certain individuals in Microsoft's Premier Support organization, I have learned that Microsoft has trained their support staff to keep a close eye out for potential problems caused by split registration.

This sometimes causes Microsoft support to ignore the facts of your problem in favor of blaming your problems on split registration. I have even been involved with problems where a sniffer trace clearly shows all names being handed back to an ailing client by WINS. Even though the problem was not believed to be a name resolution issue, Microsoft insisted that split registration was to blame. Even in the face of a sniffer trace showing that the WINS servers were responding, they still told me that my problem was due to my WINS configuration.

Why am I telling you this? I don't want you to waste valuable troubleshooting time fixing problems that don't really exist. Not all individuals at Microsoft fall victim to this way of thinking, but it does occur frequently (either that, or I have just been lucky enough to work with the few people who believe that split registration is at the bottom of every problem).

Tuning the Server Service Optimization   Establishing the correct Server service optimization setting critically affects how your device will manage its memory needs. Server service optimization settings determine how much memory is dedicated for local and network processes and how buffers are managed. You can configure your server optimization by displaying the Properties dialog box of the File and Print Sharing For Microsoft Networks service that is bound to your network card. Once in the File and Print Sharing For Microsoft Networks properties screen, the following options are available:

- ❖ **Minimize Memory Use** – This option allocates the minimum amount of memory and buffering to the Server service, which frees those resources for use in other processes and services.

- ❖ **Balance** – This setting attempts to balance the amount of memory allocated to local processes and network process, but it does a poor job at both. I have never seen this used or even recommended.

- ❖ **Maximize Data Throughput For File Sharing** – This setting allocates a substantial amount of memory for file-caching purposes. It should be used only on file and print servers.

- ❖ **Maximize Data Throughput For Network Applications** – This option configures the server to allocate as much memory to the network processes as possible. It is the recommended setting for all network services such as DNS, WINS, domain controllers, and Exchange servers.

Like most other configuration options, determining which setting is best for your server depends on which other roles or services your servers are performing. In general, registration and resolution in WINS benefit most from this Server service optimization setting: Maximize Data Throughput For Network Applications.

However, this configuration can cause a lot of thrashing if you are running any other processes at the console. *Thrashing* occurs when data is excessively paged to and from the pagefile on the hard drive, and it is symptomatic of low memory availability. If you set your

Server service optimization to Maximize Data Throughput For Network Applications and you experience thrashing, change the configuration to Minimum Memory Use, which will still favor a network application, just not so heavily.

TIP: Using the WINS MMC on the WINS server is considered a local process and therefore may cause thrashing if your device is configured to use Maximize Data Throughput For Network Application. To receive the benefits of this optimization setting on your WINS servers without compromising your ability to administer your server, consider running the WINS MMC from another machine.

Scheduling Priorities   Windows 2000 allows you to configure an entity called application response. You configure this setting by clicking the Performance Options button found on the Advanced tab of the System Properties dialog box. Application response supports two configuration options: Applications and Background Services.

When you define any setting on the application response screen, you are bumping up the scheduling priority of a service or application in a roundabout way. Setting this option one way or the other provides more processing time to the configured option. Configuring the application response setting to Applications provides a higher priority for applications that are running in the local shell or console, which means that these types of tasks will be favored over all other tasks when scheduling processor time. Likewise, setting this option to Background Services provides more processor time for services that are servicing users over the network, such as WINS. For maximum performance, set this option to Background Services on your WINS servers.

Network Configuration   WINS needs a significant number of TCP and UDP ports opened to support administration as well as normal NetBIOS operations. If theses ports are not opened, WINS will be unable to answer client requests, replicate, or be managed. The following is a list of essential WINS ports:

- ❖ **TCP 42** – Used to replicate WINS data.
- ❖ **TCP 135** – Used for WINS management via the WINS MMC or comparable tool. This port is used until a dynamic RPC endpoint is mapped to a port above 1024, which frees the port to service other requests.
- ❖ **TCP/UDP 137** – Used to "publish" the NetBIOS Name Service, communicate to a WINS proxy, WINS registrations, and for WINS lookup.
- ❖ **UDP 138** – Used for all aspects of NetBIOS communication. NetBT datagrams.
- ❖ **TCP 139** – Used for NetBT service session negotiation.

❖ **TCP/UDP 1024 and above** – Used for RPC communications between the WINS servers and clients. Once the communication begins at a static port (one that has been previously defined), a dynamic port is negotiated. Using a dynamic port frees the static port so it can listen and communicate with other clients.

Server Placement

Placement of WINS servers is probably the biggest contributor to the creation of overly complex WINS designs. For some reason, administrators think that all users need to have a WINS server sitting right next to them. Sometimes, the argument for deploying WINS servers in multiple locations is centered on network performance; other times, it is done to ensure that WINS is available in case of a network outage. Either argument is flawed.

You are best served by placing your WINS servers in central locations. WINS uses a replication engine that, even in Windows 2000, is pretty flaky. It is much more reliable than NT 4 WINS replication, especially when you use persistent connections, but it still is touchy about the network latency. Network latency is such a problem for WINS that although a server is up and accessible, replication may fail because the partner's packets weren't being received in a timely manner.

You are less likely to experience replication problems if you deploy your WINS server only to locations that are considered network nodes or locations that are well connected to other locations, such as data centers. By placing your servers in well-connected sites, you help ensure that convergence time remains low. Your WINS environment will do no one any good if it is close to the users but unable to replicate its contents. Sure it will be up, but the data will be stale.

As I stated before, administrators just love to place WINS servers at every network location to make sure that users can access them quickly and constantly. There are a few problems with this logic. First of all, WINS-related traffic is chatty but light. WINS packets are very small, and in most cases, they require only that a packet is sent and another packet is received. So while your devices might be talking to WINS a lot, not much is being said. Even when users are communicating with a WINS server that is in poor health and/or is slow, the communication process happens so rapidly that delay times occur in the range of 150 milliseconds. If you can tell the difference between one process that runs 150 milliseconds quicker than another, you are an amazing individual indeed.

Furthermore, placing WINS servers close to the users to ensure availability doesn't always work as planned even in the case of a network outage. While implementing a WINS server at every location or most locations may seem like a good way to circumvent network outages, it is a viable option only if most or all of the servers that the users of that site need to access are local to the site. Being able to resolve a server's name is of little use if you can't communicate with that device because it is on the other side of a downed network link.

By deploying too many WINS servers in locations that are not well connected, you do have a lot to lose. Deploying a large number of WINS servers not only creates more of an administrative burden but also causes an overly complex replication topology. Overly complex replication models often suffer from extreme latency, which, in some cases, can cause a record to take over a day before being replicated to all partners. As you see in the next section, the more replica partners you have established, the more bloated your database will become.

Replication Design

Replication topologies can fit into one of three categories: hub and spoke, daisy chain, and hybrid. Each topology has advantages and shortcomings, so it is up to you to weigh the cost of each to determine which topology model will drive your replication design. Even if you already have a replication topology in place, you should always be reevaluating your environment to assess the need for modification.

Hub and Spoke

I know I just said you need to decide for yourself which replication topology works best for your environment. That doesn't mean I can't share my opinion with you, does it? I think the hub-and-spoke topology is hands down the best model that provides the greatest mix of availability and low replication latency.

In a *hub-and-spoke design*, WINS servers are bunched into clusters of devices. These clusters are configured with one server in the middle of the topology (the hub) and all of the other servers having a direct replication relationship with the hub (the spoke). As shown in Figure 8-1, the server named WINS1 is the hub server, while servers WINS2, WINS3, and WINS4 are spokes. As you can see, a change in any location can be replicated to any partner in two hops by way of the hub. In addition, when a change is replicated from a spoke to a hub, that change is made available to all other WINS servers at the exact moment that the hub receives the update to the database. This allows multiple WINS servers to replicate the change from the hub to their database at the same time, which cuts down on replication latency significantly.

Let's use an example to look at the advantages and disadvantages of a hub-and-spoke topology. A new user starts work on Monday morning. She has been given a new computer and booted it up while she is connected to the network for the first time. Her PC is configured to use WINS4 as the primary WINS server and WINS3 as the secondary WINS server. As the PC boots, it registers its NetBIOS names in the database located on WINS4. Assume that replication is scheduled to occur at a 30-minute interval. (I don't want to talk too much about replication configuration specifics until the "General Replication Considerations" section, so just accept this at face value for now and discount any push update triggers that

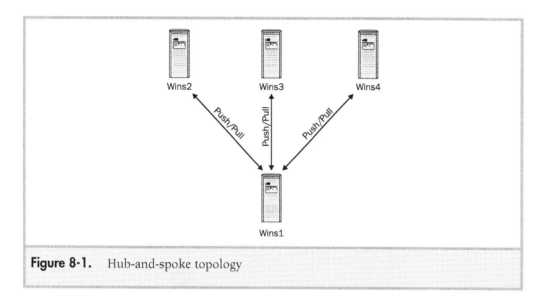

Figure 8-1. Hub-and-spoke topology

would cause replication to occur more quickly.) The record for the new user's PC will be replicated to WINS1 in no more than 30 minutes after boot.

In the worst-case scenario, the record is then replicated to all other WINS partners at the next replication interval, which is 30 minutes. This means that there is a 60-minute or less convergence time for data in this WINS environment. The next morning, the same user boots her machine and receives a new IP address from DHCP. This new IP address is entered into the database of WINS4. When WINS4 attempts to replicate with WINS1, it determines that WINS1 is down and aborts all replication attempts. Until WINS1 is repaired, WINS2 and WINS3 have stale data, which reflects the old IP address of the user's computer. As you can see, the hub-and-spoke topology provides very rapid replication, but there is a single point of failure in the hub.

In large environments, clusters of hub-and-spoke topologies are commonly established. Figure 8-2 shows a design that involves the same WINS servers as shown in Figure 8-1, with the addition of another four WINS servers.

When using hub-and-spoke clusters, multiple hub-and-spoke topologies are connected to each other in the form of a replication relationship between the hubs. This replication relationship allows data changed on any WINS server to be replicated to all WINS servers in both hub-and-spoke environments. You may be wondering what advantage this has over creating one giant hub and spoke. Using hub-and-spoke clusters provides the ability to reduce the overhead on the hub servers as well as increases the availability of your WINS environment.

When a WINS server is a hub, it takes on a tremendous amount of processing responsibility. This device, in addition to having to register and resolve names for NetBIOS clients, must also

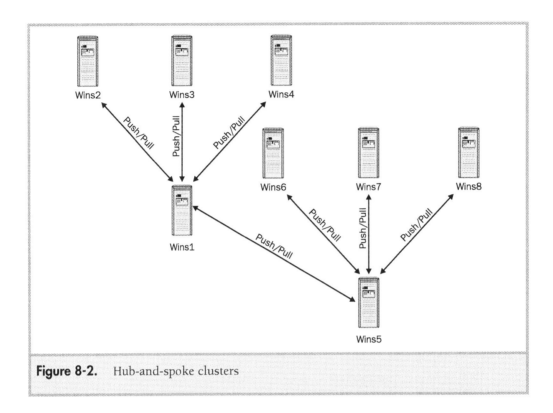

Figure 8-2. Hub-and-spoke clusters

manage all replication partnerships throughout the environment. The amount of data being replicated is small, but it is not the amount of data that causes processing overhead per se. Replication overhead is incurred by the endless replication events and update events that must be tracked and processed by the hub for each spoke. This server has to potentially push and pull data from all spoke servers, in addition to managing all of the replication partnerships.

Therefore, the hub server's database will tend to be more bloated than a spoke server's database. By reducing the number of spoke servers, you can keep the processing overhead on the hub under control. For example, if all of the servers in Figure 8-2 were to use WINS1 as a single hub, WINS1 would have to manage seven replication partners at once. When you introduce hub-and-spoke clustering, you reduce that number to four replication partners (WINS2, WINS3, WINS4, and WINS5).

Using hub-and-spoke clustering also provides fault tolerance by distributing the hub role over multiple WINS servers. Again, let's use Figure 8-2 as an example and assume that all WINS servers are spokes to WINS1. In this scenario, if WINS1 fails, then all clients throughout the organization are at risk of receiving stale data because all replication has been halted. If you take the same failure scenario using Figure 8-2, only clients accessing WINS2, WINS3, and WINS4 can fall victim to stale WINS data if WINS1 fails. Because WINS6, WINS7, and WINS8 all use WINS5 as a hub, they continue to replicate data even if WINS1 is down.

If you choose to implement a hub-and-spoke topology, use the following guidelines:

- **Limit your spokes** – Limit the number of spokes per hub to four or five. This will allow you to achieve growth not only in the area of spoke devices but also in other hub devices. Too many replication partners can become problematic.

- **Limit your hub partners** – Along the same lines of reducing the number of spokes, limit your hub partners. Consider using the approaches detailed in the "Hub-and-Spoke Hybrid" section of this chapter. Not only does using this hybrid method increase performance on the hubs, it also reduces latency.

- **Push/pull for everyone** – All partners in this design should be both push and pull partners to decrease latency.

- **Business resumption** – Consider building a contingency process that everyone in your organization could implement if they needed to bypass a failed hub. This plan should detail the process to take a predefined spoke and create the proper replication relationships on all WINS servers, to convert the spoke to a hub. This will ensure that if there is a catastrophic failure, you will be ready to service your users.

Daisy Chain

All IT professionals should be familiar with the phrase *daisy chain*. In a topology using daisy-chain replication, each WINS server has a replication partner that in turn has a replication partner, and so on and so on. This creates a large circular replication model, as shown in Figure 8-3.

When using a daisy-chain topology, an entry placed in the database of one WINS server is replicated to a WINS replication neighbor. Once the WINS replication neighbor receives the change, it passes it along to the next neighbor. This process continues until each WINS server has received the update. Let's examine replication latency by taking the same scenario found in the "Hub-and-Spoke Topology" section and applying it to a daisy-chain topology.

Once the user boots her machine for the first time and new records are placed in WINS4, in 30 minutes or less, that record is replicated to WINS3 and WINS5 because a replication relationship exists with both devices. Thirty minutes later, the record is replicated to the partner of WINS3, which is WINS2, and to the partner of WINS5, which is WINS6. After another 30 minutes, the record is replicated to WINS2's partner, WINS1, and to WINS6's partner, which is WINS7. The only WINS server that hasn't received the update yet is WINS8, which gets the record at the next update interval. By the time all WINS servers have received a copy of the user's records, 120 minutes have passed.

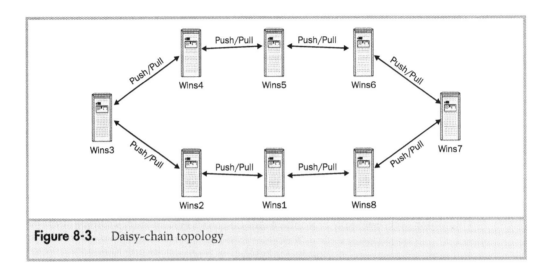

Figure 8-3. Daisy-chain topology

Compare this to using a hub-and-spoke cluster design where all WINS servers would have had the record in their databases in 90 minutes. On the other hand, if any WINS server were to fail anywhere, there is an alternate route because all WINS servers have two replication partners. This makes the daisy-chain method more available and redundant. You could argue that by the time a record is replicated to all WINS servers in a daisy-chain topology in instances of failure, you could have had the hub back up already. Don't forget that the estimated 120-minute convergence time is based on the fact that all WINS servers are functioning. If a single WINS server is broken, convergence times can as much as double.

Hybrid Topologies

As the name implies, *hybrid topologies* bring some components of the hub-and-spoke model and the daisy-chain model into a single topology model. There are endless possibilities and ways to mix and match the two foundation topologies to come up with your own design. I will share with you a couple of common hybrid models and a hybrid model that I have put together for my own use.

NOTE: Because these hybrid models don't have "official" names, I attempted to give them names that make sense. Needless to say, if you search on these names in any Microsoft documentation, you will yield no results.

Hub, Spoke, and Daisy-Chain Hybrid   This hybrid model leverages mostly the hub-and-spoke topology model. It uses a traditional hub-and-spoke model with a twist. One or more spokes may have a replication partner that is not an existing hub or an existing spoke, as shown in Figure 8-4.

There isn't much value added to this type of design at all. It brings nothing to the table except for the headache associated with having an owner's data show up in all of your WINS servers' databases, with which none but the spoke has a partnership. This design also increases latency to and from the daisy-chained partner because a record has to replicate to the spoke, to the hub, and finally, to the other spokes. It is much easier to create a replication partnership between this daisy-chained server and the hub, which will make it a true spoke. I mention this scenario because I see it a lot in different companies. I think that administrators don't realize the consequences of their actions when they implement this type of scenario.

Daisy-Chain Hub-and-Spoke Hybrid   This hybrid model involves clusters of hub-and-spoke topologies that participate in daisy-chain replication between the hubs. This method, which is shown in Figure 8-5, is the most common configuration when more than two hub-and-spoke clusters exist in an environment.

This hybrid has become the de facto way of connecting three or more hub-and-spoke clusters, even though it makes sense for no more than three hub-and-spoke clusters to be configured like this. As you can see in Figure 8-5, when connecting three clusters together, replication to all hubs is never more than one replication hop away at any time. When you add a fourth cluster, this model falls apart. Adding a fourth cluster breaks this model for two reasons: number of replication partners and latency.

When your environment grows to a state that has more than four hub-and-spoke clusters, you are in danger of overloading the hubs with too many replication partners. With this hybrid model, each hub will have a number of replication partners that is equivalent to the number of spokes plus two (one for each daisy-chain partner). This number can grow to be approximately seven replication partners and potentially more.

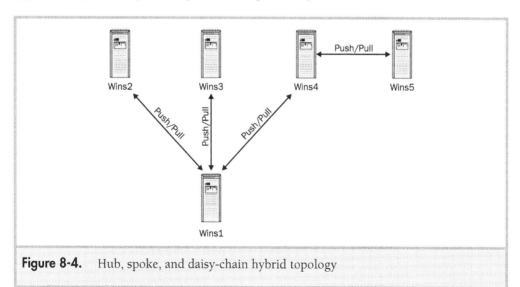

Figure 8-4.   Hub, spoke, and daisy-chain hybrid topology

Latency also increases when you have more than four hub-and-spoke clusters. This is because all replications must be sent to all hubs in the same way that replication is sent to a WINS server in a daisy-chain topology. For example, in a scenario with just four hub-and-spoke clusters, a record must be replicated to a WINS server's neighbor WINS servers at one interval and then to the other hub at the next interval. By the time all WINS servers, both

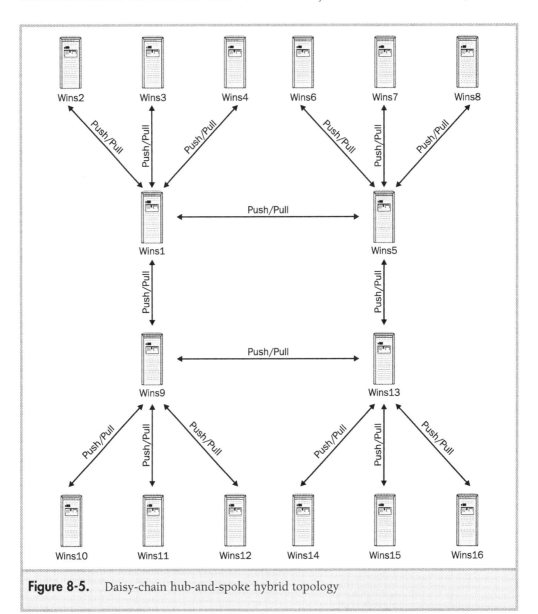

Figure 8-5. Daisy-chain hub-and-spoke hybrid topology

hubs and spokes, have received the record, 90 minutes have passed. Compare this to the numbers given in the "Hub-and-Spoke Hybrid" section that follows, which addresses the same problem but in a different way.

Hub-and-Spoke Hybrid   The hub-and-spoke hybrid is a model that I came up with to address the deficiencies of the daisy-chain hub-and-spoke hybrid model. The problem is clear: there must be a way to optimize replication traffic between many hub-and-spoke clusters. The solution is pretty easy: implement Master Of Master (MOM) logic. MOM technology has been established in the industry in many different database and directory offerings. I didn't invent MOM; I just extended the MOM model to WINS. MOM models use a hierarchical approach to resolve many issues, which creates a centralized parent-type of object in the database or directory leveraging the technology. To address the latency problems that can occur with multiple (over four) hub-and-spoke clusters, consider implementing the architecture shown in Figure 8-6.

Figure 8-6 depicts five hub-and-spoke clusters that are all configured to replicate with a single MOM hub. This hub really serves the same role that other hubs do, which is to reduce replication latency by reducing replication hop counts. Using a MOM hub will reduce the

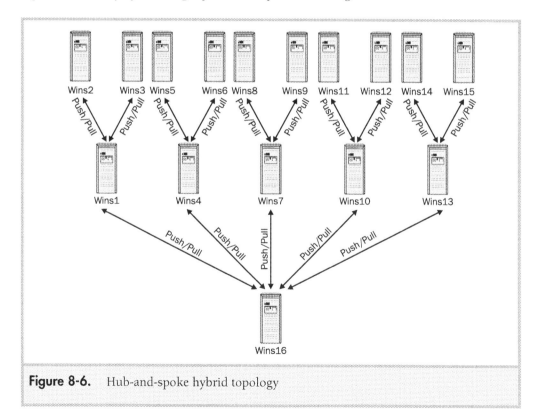

Figure 8-6.   Hub-and-spoke hybrid topology

replication times significantly. No matter how many hub-and-spoke clusters you add to your topology, no WINS server will ever be more than two hops from the MOM hub; therefore, replication latency does not increase as you add more hub-and-spoke clusters. Instead, it remains a constant four hops, which will never take more than two hours to replicate. (In our examples, replication was sent to a partner every 30 minutes.)

This design is of benefit to any organization that has a large WINS deployment. The only drawback to this hybrid is that you are once again faced with a single point of failure with the MOM hub. You can easily overcome this limitation by implementing multiple MOM hubs, which would serve the same purpose as the hub-and-spoke clusters, just on a larger scale. Figure 8-7 shows this variation of the hub-and-spoke hybrid. Notice that even with the added fault tolerance, only one extra hop is added to the total number of replication hops. This option will be very attractive as your WINS environment begins to approach the size of seven hub-and-spoke clusters.

General Replication Considerations

The following sections provide just a few suggestions to consider when designing your new WINS environment or when optimizing your current WINS environment.

Relationships   Except in certain circumstances, all of your replication partners in any replication topology should be push and pull partners. By configuring each partner as both push and pull, you help ensure that replication will occur rapidly. Pull partners request records from a partner after a certain amount of time has expired, and push partners send each replication partner notification for the need to update after so many changes have occurred; therefore, they are complementary roles. Both partners should have push and pull relationships built with each other. If these two-way relationships are not established, data will replicate in only one direction.

| TAKE COMMAND |

Netsh is a utility found in the default installation of any Windows 2000 Server product. This tool is the primary command-line administrative interface for WINS, RAS, and DHCP servers. Netsh has a number of command-line augments that you can use to create and modify WINS replication partners. To launch into the Netsh shell, type **netsh** at the command line. To enter the WINS configuration interface, type **wins** in the Netsh shell. To connect to a WINS server, type **server (IpAddress)** in the WINS interface shell.

To add a replication partner, type the following:

add partner (ServerName) (IpAddress) (Type)

where:

❖ **ServerName** – The NetBIOS name of the WINS partner to be added.

❖ **IpAddress** – The address of the WINS partner to be added.

❖ **Type** – The replication partnership type. Supported values are 0 (pull), 1 (push), and 2 (both). If no type is specified, the default value of 2 will be applied.

To delete a replication partner, type the following:

delete partner (ServerName) (IpAddress) (Type).

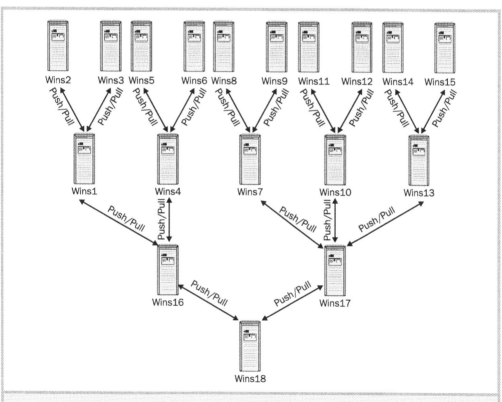

Figure 8-7. Multiple MOM hub-and-spoke hybrid topology

Replication Frequency   How much replication is too much replication? Determining at which intervals your WINS data is replicated can be difficult. You have to weigh the cost associated with the benefit. Intervals that occur too frequently can bog the WINS server down with replication traffic but provide the most dynamic environment. Intervals that occur too infrequently reduce this processing load on the WINS servers but cause the data to become stale and less usable.

There is no right or wrong answer. The parameters to use depend on your environment because all values are not created equally. For example, if a small organization configured a push every 20 version-ID changes, there would be no problem. If this same value were applied to a large organization, it would bring WINS to its knees due to all of the frequent record updates.

Your push partnership should be the value that represents your most aggressive replication interval. This value ensures a certain amount of updates to the version ID before the contents are replicated; consequently, it is an excellent means of making sure that data is replicated only when it has changed. On the other hand, you should use pull replication as a backup replication method. Because in pull replication a partner always asks for updates at a specified interval even if there are no changes to the partner's database, it is best used as a backup to push replication. Your pull value should be very high, someplace in the neighborhood of four to six hours to prevent excessive chatter. With these principles in mind, establish a baseline push and pull–replication interval and trend its progress. Trending will help you determine if a particular value is too low or too high.

TAKE COMMAND

Sure, you can configure a replication partner's push and pull intervals by using the WINS MMC, but that's no fun. Instead of using the GUI, do what UNIX administrators have been doing for years: go primal. Here are a few Netsh tools (launched from the same shell as detailed in the previous section) that enable you to set push and pull intervals from the command line.

To configure a pull partner's replication pull configuration, type the following:

set pullpartnerconfig state=(State) server=(ServerName) start=(StartValue) interval=(IntervalValue)

where:

◈   **State** – The flag to enable or disable persistent connections. Supported values are 0 (disabled) and 1 (enabled). If no value is specified, the default value of 1 is used.

◈ **ServerName –** The NetBIOS name or IP address of the pull partner.

◈ **StartValue –** The start time for pull replication to begin in seconds from the time that the command was run.

◈ **IntervalValue –** The frequency after the **StartValue** that pull replication occurs.

To configure a push partner's replication, type the following:

set pushpartnerconfig state=(State) server=(ServerName) update=(UpdateValue)

where:

◈ **UpdateValue –** The numerical value that defines how many changes to the version ID of the local database must occur before a push notification is sent

At the risk of sounding like a broken record, I want to tell you one more time to use persistent connections between all Windows 2000 WINS servers. No matter how you establish your push and pull partnerships, it will significantly reduce your rate of replication failure.

Maintaining Your WINS Environment

No matter how solid your WINS design may be, if you do not properly maintain your WINS environment, you are in for a world of pain. WINS is one of those services that you can neglect for a certain amount of time. That time may be weeks, months, or sometimes years. One day everything will be fine, and the next day, everything is broken.

WINS is so easy to set up that some administrators get the false sense that it is a touchless service. However, if you don't touch WINS, it will eventually reach out and touch you (probably with its preverbal foot in your rear end). Maintenance and continual monitoring is essential for keeping your WINS servers happy and your data available.

Documenting Your WINS Environment

Documenting every aspect of your environment is the key to maintaining a healthy WINS environment. Although documenting your WINS design seems like a no-brainer, you might be surprised how many organizations don't document their architecture. Having your IT staff members who have been around for a while fill in the new employees on the intricacies of your WINS design (a.k.a. the spoken-word approach) is not acceptable. Neither is the old trial-by-fire method where most of the WINS discovery process occurs in the wee hours of the morning while troubleshooting a problem. You need to document your environment.

Determining What Is Important

Ideally, all components that "touch" your WINS servers should be documented. A little overdocumentation never hurt anybody. I can't say the same thing about underdocumentation. If time does not permit or you are simply opposed to defining your entire environment, here is a punch list of the most important components to document.

- **Local server configuration** – This is such a broad area. Your local server configuration includes all aspects that define your servers. You should capture the operating system that is installed as well as the role that the server plays in the domain (DC vs. member server). Including information about the local operating system is very helpful if the server ever has to be rebuilt on the fly. Also include information about the hardware that is installed on the server and any relevant driver revision levels. Hardware information is important to capture because it will simplify the task of identifying critical hardware fixes that need to be deployed. Don't forget to document the network configuration of your servers, too. Ensuring that your WINS servers' addresses are well known will help you document the service area of a given WINS server. Ideally, all of your servers should be configured the same way, so documenting this information should be fairly easy.

- **Patches** – This subject is a hot button for me. Most people don't document which service pack and hotfix level their machines are at. The lack of documentation in this area makes it impossible to determine which fixes still need to be applied. Be sure to document not only the patches that are applied to your WINS servers, but also the files that each patch contains. Knowing which files have been installed by which patch can be a useful proactive tool to help you ensure that any future patches don't step on the existing patches. (This is a constant problem.) Also, if you ever have problems with your WINS servers and have to open a ticket with Microsoft, one of the first things they ask you for is a list of patches that have been applied. Once your patches are documented, consider using a third-party service pack and hotfix monitoring tool in conjunction with your list to ensure that all servers have the patches they are supposed to have.

- **Replication topology** – Without knowing how WINS should be replicating, you will have a hard time determining if there is a problem with replication. As a way to trend usage and expose potential room for performance increases, document your replication topology. Once you have documented all aspects of replication (including push, pull, and push/pull configuration of each replication partner), you can use this data to build a topology map. This topology map will become useful as you add more WINS servers or begin to participate in merger-related actives. Let's not discount the usefulness of replication documentation if there is a WINS server failure. Proper documentation allows you to quickly recreate the environment that was established before the outage, instead of having to rebuild from scratch.

 ◈ **Automated jobs** – This chapter talks a lot about scripting particular WINS maintenance jobs to run. All automated jobs should be documented as much as possible. Include information about what each script does as well as its contents. Don't forget to include information about how the job is launched as well as in which security context the job runs. You can use this information to create a build document for the particular job. Creating a build document for each job helps you maintain consistency across multiple WINS servers by ensuring that each job is built and implemented the same way on each WINS server.

 ◈ **Areas of service** – The areas that each WINS server services should be well defined. In fact, you should go as far as creating a client configuration chart that shows which servers should be primary and secondary to each client based on their locations. By making this information available to the users who statically configure their devices as well as to the DHCP administrators, you will make sure that each device in your environment is pointed to the right set of servers.

Publish Your Findings

When all is said and done, you should have an informative architecture document that allows even a new administrator to walk into your organization and access facts about your WINS environment. Because WINS information is always in demand from both users and administrators, consider publishing your documents internally. Your method of publication will vary, but it is common to place these documents on an intranet server that all internal

Create a Build Document

Creating a comprehensive build document for your WINS servers is a great idea. A build document should include detailed steps about how a particular server should be configured. While it is important to capture the steps that must be taken to install the operating system, you should also make it a point to detail any WINS configuration that should be consistent across all WINS servers in your environment. Without build documentation, it is nearly impossible to make sure that all of your WINS servers look the same. Inconsistencies in your WINS servers make administration more difficult and will increase TCO.

users can access. Using an intranet site ensures that all clients can view your documents—no matter which applications and viewers they have installed on their desktops.

You also have the option of publishing your documents in their native format by means of a network share, but this will limit who can view your documentation to those who have the correct viewer or application installed. (It's kind of hard to open a .vsd file without Visio installed.) Also, by placing your documents up on a share, you have to worry about viewer or application version mismatch, which can occur when someone accessing your document has an older version of the viewer or application than the one used to create the document. Make your life easy: go with the Web-site solution.

Performance Monitoring

Documenting your environment is a step in the right direction towards maintaining a healthy WINS environment. However, production problems are not normally caused by design issues but instead, by issues that arise after you have deployed WINS. To capture conditions in WINS preemptively, you need to establish some level of monitoring. Many different products are on the market that specialize in server and service health monitoring. Because the number of tools is too vast and this is a Windows 2000 WINS book, not a 3rd party monitoring tool book, I will focus on the Windows 2000 Performance Monitor.

Performance Monitor (PerfMon) can monitor many aspects of server health, but we are interested only in certain data that PerfMon can provide. This section details PerfMon counters that are related only to WINS. Although monitoring the basic system components is important, I am going to assume that you already know what to look for in these areas. I am also assuming that you are already familiar with PerfMon and the terminology used within PerfMon.

Useful WINS Counters

Whether you are using PerfMon to log data, chart data, or send alerts, the counters you use to detail the performance of your WINS servers will not change. The following is a list of some of the counters that you can use to trend WINS usage and performance. I have not included all of the available counters because many of those included in PerfMon have limited usefulness for WINS.

Counters found in the WINS Server performance object include the following:

❖ **Failed Queries/sec** – The total number of queries received per second, for which WINS could not find a name. A value that is excessively high in comparison to successful queries may indicate a database problem.

❖ **Group Registrations/sec** – The number of group names registered per second.

❖ **Group Renewals/sec** – The number of group names renewed per second. This can be useful to compare how often names are renewed compared to how often names are registered. This type of data is helpful in trending and sizing efforts.

❖ **Queries/sec** – The number of queries—despite their rate of successful or failed lookups—that are received in a second. By looking at this number in conjunction with processor and memory counters, you can formulate some basic capacity planning numbers.

❖ **Releases/sec** – The number of name release requests received per second. Typically, this number is significantly higher than the value found in **Successful Releases/sec**.

❖ **Successful Queries/sec** – The number of queries received in a second for which a name was found. In a healthy WINS environment, this number should be equal to 75 – 85 percent of the value shown in **Queries/sec**. Any number lower may indicate excessive replication latency or database corruption.

❖ **Successful Releases/sec** – The number of successful release requests.

❖ **Total Number of Conflicts/sec** – The total number of conflicts in all record types per second. A high value indicates a potential database problem.

❖ **Total Number of Registrations/sec** – The number of all registration requests received by the WINS server in a given second for all record types. This number does not reflect only positive or negative registrations, but reflects their sum instead. This number can be used to build a baseline of service and to trend growth.

❖ **Total Number of Renewals/sec** – The total number of renewal requests per second. Useful when compared to the **Total Number of Registrations/sec** counter to determine which percentage of traffic is new registration and which percentage is renewal related.

The following are counters found in the Process performance object when focusing on the WINS process:

❖ **% Privileged Time** – The percentage of time that the WINS process's threads executed code in privileged mode. When collected and trended over time, this number can be helpful in identifying misbehaving WINS code by showing excessive spikes in usage.

❖ **% Processor Time** – The percentage of time that threads in WINS were accessing the processor. If this number is high (over 60 percent), consider upgrading your hardware or increasing the number of WINS servers in your environment to help distribute load. Adding another processor is also helpful in lowering this number, which ideally should be no higher than 40 percent.

❖ **Handle Count** – The total number of current handles in use by the WINS process. This number should grow and shrink but never continually grow. Continual growth can mean that you have misbehaving code installed, and you should start looking for any WINS patches or fixes available from Microsoft.

❖ **IO Data Operations/sec** – The total number of I/O read and write operations issued by WINS to the file system, network subsystem, or any device. A high value can indicate that your WINS server is I/O-starved and might benefit from an I/O upgrade.

❖ **IO Read Operations/sec** – The total number of I/O reads issued to any I/O channel. When compared to the **IO Write Operations/sec**, this number can be helpful in indicating if your WINS environment is more read- or more write-intensive.

❖ **IO Write Operations/sec** – The total number of I/O writes issued to any I/O channel. When compared to the **IO Read Operations/sec**, this number can be helpful in indicating if your WINS environment is more read- or write-intensive.

❖ **Page Faults/sec** – The number of times per second that the WINS process must fetch a page from either main memory or disk if the requesting data is not found in the WINS working memory set. This number should not be excessively high unless your system is short on memory or the working set for WINS needs to be increased.

Monitoring Replication

Unless you use a .dll provided in the Microsoft Resource Kit, you will be unable to determine what is actually happening with replication. Sure, your server's Application Log gives you some information, but it is pretty weak. Events in the Application Log tend to read something like "Something happened someplace to some service. Please call your administrator."

The only way to get a complete view of what is occurring with replication and find out why it is happening is to install the WINS Replication Network Monitor Parser (Wins.Dll). Wins.Dll is included in the Windows 2000 Resource Kit and can be activated by editing the Tcpip.Ini and the Parser.Ini files. This .dll is used with Network Monitor to filter non-WINS replication events, in addition to providing some experts to evaluate replication data. Follow these steps to enable Wins.Dll.

1. Copy the Wins.Dll from the Resource Kit to the Parsers subdirectory found in the installation location of Network Monitor.

2. Open Tcpip.Ini (found in the Parsers subdirectory of the Network Monitor installation location) in a text editor such as Notepad.

3. In the **[TCP_HandoffSet]** section of the file, add **42=WINS** to the list of services. Place it in the list sequentially by using the number associated with WINS.

4. Save and close Tcpip.Ini.

5. Open Parser.Ini (found in the \Netmon directory of the Network Monitor installation location) in a text editor such as Notepad.

6. In the [**Parsers**] section of the file, add **WINS.DLL = 0: WINS** to the bottom of the list.

7. Add a new section named [**WINS**] to the end of the Parser.Ini file that contains the following data:

> Comment = "WINS Server Replication"
>
> FollowSet =
>
> HelpFile =

8. Save and close the Parser.Ini file.

After the Wins.Dll has been enabled, you can use Network Monitor to capture WINS replication data by modifying the Expression settings after a network capture has occurred. You need to open the Display Filter screen of Network Monitor and add a protocol expression that will display only the protocol named "WINS." This will filter out the data that is not important to WINS replication from the network capture.

CAUTION: Network Monitor does not consider fundamental TCP/IP conversations and negotiations to be part of WINS replication traffic. Sometimes you might need to remove or alter this filter to troubleshoot a TCP or network problem that is causing replication errors.

Common Administrative Tasks

Certain tasks will become part of your daily, weekly, or monthly WINS administration routine. You can complete all of these types of tasks by using the WINS MMC, but sometimes, being able to execute an administrative task from a command line is desirable. Microsoft has done a pretty good job of expanding their command-line support for WINS administration by adding tools to the Resource Kit. It would be nice if these WINS tools came on the Windows 2000 CD, but I am just happy to have them at all.

Upgrading Jet

When you upgrade an NT WINS server to Windows 2000, many Microsoft-provided documents indicate that only the operating system upgrade must be completed to make your NT WINS server a Windows 2000 WINS server. Unfortunately, this is not the case. As you already know, the Jet database used in Windows 2000 is different from the version used in NT. Because the operating-system upgrade is just an update to the bits, it does not address the database conversion that must be completed to upgrade your Jet database. If you follow most Microsoft documentation and just upgrade the operating system without fixing up your database, the operating-system upgrade will complete but WINS won't start.

To fix up your Jet database, you need to use the Esentutl utility, which will look familiar if you've worked with Exchange. Esentutl.Exe launches Microsoft Database Utilities version 6, which is used to complete a number of functions on all databases that are of various Jet versions. To upgrade your NT WINS database to a Windows 2000 Jet format, type the following:

net stop wins

esentutl /u (*DatabaseName.mdb*) **/d** (*PreviouseDllName.dll*) [Options]

net start wins

where:

- ❖ **DatabaseName.mdb** – The database file that you want to upgrade. In a default installation, it is Wins.Mdb.
- ❖ **PreviouseDllName.dll** – The Jet.Dll used in the old database found in the System32 directory.
- ❖ **Options** –The options you wish to specify, each of which is separated by a space following the switch. Supported values are **/d<db>** (makes a backup of the database to the file location and name specified), **/t<db>** (sets the temporary database name, which is Tempupgd.Mdb by default), **/p** (preserves the temporary database, which leaves the original database intact and uses the upgraded temp database for WINS), and **/o** (suppresses the logo).

CAUTION: Make sure your database is in a compact and consistent state before upgrading the database format. If your database has not been properly groomed before this operation, database corruption may occur. For information on how to run a compaction and consistency check, please consult the documentation for the operating system from which WINS was installed.

Compacting the WINS Database

Compacting your WINS database is the single most important administrative task that you will ever complete. WINS creates whitespace like nobody's business. It is "normal" for a WINS database to contain over 30 percent whitespace. This space is created as a result of replicated and direct changes to the database because WINS is inefficient at reclaiming unused space. Because WINS is so dynamic, records and attributes are constantly being added, removed, and changed. When changes to the database occur and data is added or moved, the space that has been freed up as a result of entry removals is not used to house the new entries. This means that the database will continue to grow unless the database is compacted regularly.

You complete Jet database compaction by using the Jetpack utility. Jetpack.Exe is a command-line driven tool that requires a lock on the database, which means that WINS must be stopped when Jetpack runs. To run Jetpack, type the following command at the command prompt:

net stop wins

jetpack <*DatabaseName.mdb*> <*TempDatabaseName.mbd*>

net start wins

The Jetpack utility works by taking data out of the specified WINS database and placing it into the temporary database. Because this copy process does not copy empty space, all of the empty database structure is not transferred to the temporary database. Once all of the data has been copied out of the WINS database and into the temporary database, the temporary database is given the same name as the WINS database and is copied over the old file. The next thing you know, your WINS database is the size of the temporary database.

Depending on how large your database is and how long it has been since your last compaction, Jetpack may take a long time to complete. Therefore, it is best to schedule it to run after hours. I recommend running Jetpack once a week to maintain database health.

CODE BLUE

Because running Jetpack requires that the WINS service be stopped on the WINS server, you need to consider how running Jetpack might affect automatic scavenging. As you may recall, scavenging runs at an interval equal to half of the renew interval established on the WINS server. By default, the renew interval on a WINS server is six days, which means that scavenging will occur every three days.

Also keep in mind that the scavenging clock is based on the uptime of your WINS service, not the WINS server. So if you stopped and restarted the WINS service the second day after it was started, a scavenge would occur three days after the restart,

> not the day after the restart. This information is important when considering a cycle to complete the Jetpack process.
>
> Be sure that you are not running Jetpack in a manner that interferes with the WINS scavenging clock; otherwise, your database will never be cleaned of old records.

Consider creating a Jetpack command file that will compile all of the tasks that need to be completed into a single file. Not only will this allow you to automate many of the command-line parameters, but creating this file will also allow you to use a scheduling product to automate its execution. Automating the execution of Jetpack is desirable for several reasons. Because Jetpack needs to be run on each WINS server in your environment and it is bad from a data-consistency and availability perspective to have all WINS servers down at the same time, execution of Jetpack should be staggered between servers. Also, because it is recommended to run Jetpack after hours, running Jetpack on all of your servers at different times proves to be an all-night task. Using a scheduled job to run Jetpack resolves these issues.

Create a command file (.cmd) to automate all tasks that you want to complete during the Jetpack process. You can either write your own file or use the following commands to create an automation file.

NOTE: The lines preceeding a command that begins with a pound (#) sign are used only for descriptive purposes. You can either leave them in the file or take them out. It does not change the behavior of the file.

#Stop the WINS service.

net stop wins

#Delete the last Jetpack-created temp file that was created in the location specified during the last Jetpack to prevent a file-already-exists error.

del Drive:\Folder\SubFolder\TempDbFileName.Mdb

#Run the Jetpack.

jetpack DatabaseName.mdb TempDbFileName.mdb

#Restart the WINS service.

net start wins

This file (or the file that you create on your own) can then be used with either the Windows 2000 Command Scheduler (also known as the AT command) or the Scheduled Tasks feature. I recommend using Scheduled Tasks, which is new to Windows 2000. Creating a scheduled task allows you to complete many functions related to scheduling and account usage that the AT command doesn't allow. Also, all scheduled tasks created are placed into a share that is easily accessible by other systems that have the right level of access. By placing the jobs on a share, it is easy to create a job in one place and copy that job to multiple servers.

The Importance of Free Disk Space

I am going to take this opportunity to point out the importance of free disk space on a WINS server. It's no big secret that any server should have plenty of free disk space, but WINS has some unique needs. WINS, as well as other services that use a Jet database, uses log files to store database changes before they are committed to the database. These log files remain on the local disk of the WINS server until a backup procedure has been completed. Because these files are never overwritten, WINS continues to create new log files to handle database transactions. This means that you can potentially have several hundred megabytes of log files in addition to your WINS database on the same server.

WINS tries to ensure that even if you are close to running out of disk space, it can create new log files by using two reserve files. These reserve files (.res) hold 10 MB of space each, and they are used for logging transactions if a new log file can't be created due to disk-space limitations. Although this is a handy algorithm, it works only until the third log file needs to be created. If your hard disk runs out of space, your WINS server will fail.

In addition to normal operations, your disk should have enough free space to accommodate Jetpack. Make sure that you have enough free space to allow Jetpack to create the temporary database.

I like to have at least 500 MB of free space on the drive/partition that is housing WINS. This leaves room for database and log growth, in addition to accommodating the needs of Jetpack.

Checking for Consistency

Checking database consistency is an important task. Over time, your local WINS database can become corrupt or can begin to contain data that isn't the same data found in the database of other WINS servers. Running a consistency check allows you to verify all records in your WINS server's local database against the database of the server that owns the records being verified. Executing a consistency check can be very disruptive because it requires a substantial amount of processing time, memory, and network bandwidth. Never run a consistency check on a WINS server during business hours or on more than one WINS server at once. Because corruption is pretty rare, especially if you are Jetpacking once a week, consistency checks should have to be run only on a semiannual basis during a scheduled maintenance window.

As you may recall, a consistency check (also called verification) can be run either manually or at a scheduled interval by using the WINS MMC. Both ways of running verification are defined in Chapter 6, so I won't go ever them again. Instead I'd like to talk about some other tools that can also spawn verification/consistency checks of your databases.

Winscl   You can use the Windows 2000 Resource Kit utility named Winscl to start a consistency check. Open a command prompt and type **winscl**, which will launch the Winscl shell. In the Winscl shell, complete the following steps:

1. Type either **1** to use TCP/IP or **0** for named pipes. I recommend using 1. Press ENTER.

2. Type in the IP address of the WINS server to send the consistency check request to. If you're running winscl from the same WINS server, you can enter in the loopback address (127.0.0.1) of the device. Press ENTER.

3. Type **CC** and press ENTER.

4. The next question you are asked is a little confusing. Type **1** if you want to verify all records no matter what their age. Type any other value if you want to verify only those records that are older than the value defined as the verification interval value. Press ENTER.

5. You can now choose to turn WINS checking on or off for overload condition. This feature will force the consistency check to determine the amount of load on the WINS server before running a consistency check. If the load on the server is too high, the operation will attempt to run again in an hour. Type **1** to enable this feature; type any other value to shut it off. Input your desired value. Press ENTER, and the consistency check will begin.

CODE BLUE

A consistency check does not record any significant events in the Event Log by default, just a single entry for the start of the process. For any level of detail greater than recording the start of either process, you must enable detailed logging for WINS. When detailed logging is enabled, each milestone in each process is recorded to the System Log. Keep in mind that both processes are chatty when detailed logging is enabled, so either bump up the size of your System Log or risk wrapping events.

Netsh   You must navigate the Netsh interface to get into the WINS configuration shell. Once in Netsh, type **wins** and press ENTER to bring you into the WINS shell. At the WINS shell, type **server** and press ENTER, which will focus you on the local WINS server's database. You can also specify addresses of WINS servers that are accessible through the network. To execute a consistency check, type **check database** and press ENTER.

Winschk   Yet another Resource Kit utility that allows you to perform a consistency check of your WINS database is Winschk. The consistency check that this tool performs is not the same check that the other tools detailed in this chapter perform. Instead, it compares the last known version ID of a replication partner only with the actual version ID of the partner. This check can help you determine if you have a replication problem that has prevented some records from replicating.

By launching Winschk.Exe, you open the Winschk shell. From the shell, you have several choices. Type **2** and press ENTER. Next, you will be asked to provide the IP address of the WINS server against which to run the verification. Enter the IP address and press ENTER. Then the tool will show you each partner, their status, and the state of the version ID. This tool is also helpful in indicating which WINS servers in your topology have been removed from the network but not from the WINS database.

Force Replication

Let's face it, sometimes waiting on WINS to decide to replicate is like watching paint dry. Sure, it is on a set schedule, but that doesn't always mean that replication will occur the exact moment that it is supposed to. This becomes problematic if you have a record that needs to be replicated to the rest of the WINS environment in short order. You could go to the WINS MMC and use the GUI to force replication, but like other tasks run from the WINS MMC, it is sometimes easier to force replication from the command line.

Forcing a Pull   You can force your WINS server to pull records from another partner by using either Winscl or Netsh. Both tools complete the required task essentially the same way.
To force a pull of records with Winscl, follow these steps:

1. Launch Winscl.Exe. Give the tool the correct options to connect to your WINS server.

2. From the winscl shell, type **pullt** and press ENTER.

3. At the address prompt, type the address of the WINS partner for which you should pull records. Keep in mind that a WINS server must have a replication partnership established with the server specified in the address line in order for replication to work.

To force a pull of records with Netsh, follow these steps:

1. Launch Netsh.exe. When in the Netsh shell, type **wins** and press ENTER.

2. From the WINS shell, type **server**. When asked for an IP address, enter the address of the machine that will pull records from a partner.

3. Type **init pull server=(IP Address of Server)** and press ENTER. Keep in mind that a WINS server must have a replication partnership established with the server specified in the address line in order for replication to work.

TIP: Both Winscl and Netsh support pulling blocks of records. Winscl achieves this by using the **PRR** option. Netsh achieves this by using the **init pull range** option.

Forcing a Push   You can use Winscl and Netsh to push records to replication partners from your WINS server too.
Follow these steps to force a push of records with Winscl:

1. Launch Winscl.Exe. Give the tool the correct options to connect to your WINS server.

2. From the Winscl shell, type **pusht** and press ENTER.

3. At the address prompt, enter the address of the WINS partner to which you should push records. Keep in mind that a WINS server must have a replication partnership established with the server specified in the address line in order for replication to work.

Follow theses steps to force a pull of records with Netsh:

1. Launch Netsh.Exe. When in the Netsh shell, type **wins** and press ENTER.

2. From the WINS shell, type **server**. When asked for an IP address, enter the address of the machine that will pull records from a partner.

3. Type **init push server=(IP Address of Server)** and press ENTER. Keep in mind that a WINS server must have a replication partnership established with the server specified in the address line in order for replication to work.

Disaster Recovery

In the pecking order of servers that are important to be backed up, WINS rates almost at the bottom of the list. Don't get me wrong: WINS is the most mission-critical service that exists in an NT/Windows 2000 environment. Forget your domain controllers, Exchange server, SQL boxes, or whatever other server or service you think are mission-critical. Without NetBIOS name resolution, you won't be able to get to any of your other servers no matter how available they are. Not too many people (especially management) realize this fact. Without WINS, the IT world breaks down.

So it isn't that WINS is not important; it's just that its replication scheme makes disaster recovery much easier. When one WINS server replicates with another WINS server, all contents of both WINS servers' databases are replicated to both WINS servers. In this sense, each WINS server is backing up all other WINS servers. This replicated backup methodology

More on Winscl, Netsh, and Winschk

These three tools are essential to keeping your WINS servers healthy. Each of them supports a vast array of commands. Some are common across all tools, while others are unique to a particular tool. In either case, there isn't enough room in this chapter to list all of the possible options, but I can point you to a few Microsoft documents that list the options of each tool.

- ❖ **Winscl** – The best place to find explanations of all supported options is in the Windows 2000 Server Resource Kit help files in a document named "WinsCl Options." All other documents, including KB articles, deal only with a single task that can be completed with this tool.

- ❖ **Netsh** – Once again, I have to point you to a help file. There is a help document named "Netshell Commands for WINS," found in the help files loaded on a default Windows 2000 Server installation.

- ❖ **Winschk** – Here comes another help file reference. Don't they document these things in any other way anymore? At any rate, check out the topic "Winschk Options" for a list of all options supported by this tool.

protects against most failures. I say *most failures* because if one of your WINS servers corrupts its database and replicates that corruption to other WINS servers, the replicated backup may become corrupt too. Corruption replicates. Depending on the level of corruption, the whole database on the partnering WINS server could also be corrupt, but this is extremely rare.

Although in all but some extremely rare circumstances, the replication backup of your WINS server will be sufficient, you must also be able to recover from database corruption. Use the following sections as guidelines on how to use replication and standard backup-based disaster-recovery procedures to restore your ailing WINS environment.

Replication-Based Disaster Recovery

If one of your WINS servers crashes and you are unable to recover the server or its database, replication-based disaster recovery is your best bet. As long as the WINS database on that server has not replicated corruption to its WINS server partners, this method will work. The process behind replication-based disaster recovery involves bringing a new WINS server up that has the same IP address as the WINS server that died.

Once this is done, a replication relationship is established with the existing WINS replication topology, and the previous WINS server's records are replicated back to the new WINS server. This all works because the new WINS server is using the same address as the old WINS server. By using the same IP address, WINS assumes that the new WINS server is the same device as the old WINS server.

NOTE: If you want to make your life easier, consider backing up the registries of your WINS servers. By restoring the registry keys detailed in the next section to a WINS server that is going to leverage replication-based disaster recovery, you will be able to maintain the local configuration of your old WINS server (replication partnerships, any blocked owners, etc).

Backup/Restore-Based Disaster Recovery

If your database has become corrupt or your WINS server did not replicate with its partners for a long time before it failed, restoring the database from a backup is your best option. Of course, this option works only if you have taken the time to define a backup strategy.

You can back up a WINS server in one of two ways. You can either use the built-in WINS Backup utility or a disk-level backup product (such as Ntbackup or Commvault's Galaxy for Windows) depending on your needs. When it comes time to choose a backup-and-restore technology for your WINS servers, you first need to consider the type of data that will be backed up and how its importance fits into your disaster recovery strategy. From a disaster-recovery perspective, you must be concerned about two components: the WINS files and the WINS registry settings.

The WINS files are located in the folder in which WINS was installed (minus the .chk file). The WINS files hold all committed and noncommitted entries in the WINS database. The WINS registry key HKLM\System\CurrentControlSet\Services\Wins and all of its subkeys need to be backed up to maintain WINS state. WINS state is all of the configuration settings specific to that WINS server, such as replication partners, TTL settings, and blocked owners. While backing up the WINS files is mandatory, backing up the registry is not. If you do not back up the WINS registry information, you will still be able to restore the WINS database, but all configuration options will be lost.

Getting back to the two methods of backing up WINS data (Wins Backup and a disk-level product), your choice of backup-and-restore technology depends on the data you want to capture. While WINS Backup is reliable for backing up the WINS files, it does not back up any WINS registry state. Also, WINS Backup is limited to placing backed-up files on local drives, so if the server failure was the result of a bad hard drive, you may lose both your WINS server and the backup database.

Disk-level backup products, on the other hand, will back up all files and all registry locations (provided the registry backup is supported, which is the norm) to any location supported by the product (magnetic media, tape, optic, etc.). The only potential problem with a disk-level backup product is that it will need to gain lock-level access on the WINS database in order to back it up. Because WINS itself has a lock on the WINS files, unless the disk-level backup product implements a file-sharing mechanism that will allow both services to lock the database, you may be forced to stop WINS just to back it up. The nice thing about WINS Backup is that all backups are completed while the WINS service is running.

What is important to you? Is it more important to have your database on the wire 100 percent of the time or to be able to recover your WINS server without reconfiguring basic options? If you use a hybrid approach, you can have the best of both worlds. Use WINS Backup to back up the WINS files to the local file system, followed by a disk-level backup that will back up the WINS files and registry settings to on-line media. This will allow you to back up the database while WINS is running and also back up registry data and store it all on media that is not the local drive of the WINS server.

WINS Log Files

When a backup occurs with WINS Backup, all log files with entries that have already been committed to the database are removed. This helps you keep disk space usage under control. This feature alone makes it attractive to use WINS Backup in some capacity.

No matter which method you choose, restoring is easy. The WINS files are just that: files. Restoring the WINS files to an alternate location and then copying them to the folder that the WINS server is configured to use for WINS files is a quick and easy process. Alternately, you can use the interface that is native to your backup tool of choice. Both methods complete the same task for the WINS files. When restoring registry state, it is best to use the interface provided by your disk-level backup software vendor.

NOTE: For further details on how to use WINS Backup to back up and restore the WINS database, please see Chapter 6.

What's One More WINS Server?

Most administrative tasks that need to be completed on or against a WINS server can be considered disruptive. Events like complex queries and data dumps can bring your WINS server to its knees. A WINS server that is spending most of its processor cycles completing administrative tasks is a WINS server that will be answering queries and registering devices very slowly. For this reason, most administrative tasks are completed after hours or in scheduled outage windows. But completing administrative tasks after hours or only during scheduled outage windows can also be disruptive. Do you want to wait for an outage window before you can get to the information you need right now? Besides, who wants to work after hours, anyways? Not me. I try to work smart, not hard.

This problem is easy to address: use an administrative-only WINS server. A device that has been configured as an administrative-only WINS server participates in the replication topology as a pull partner. Administrative-only WINS servers pull records from a single WINS partner that is also configured to push records to the administrative-only WINS server.

Configuring replication in this fashion allows your administrative-only WINS server to contain all records that exist in your WINS environment without having the ability to place records in the enterprise WINS database. This WINS server should be used exclusively by administrators for the sole purpose of completing process- or database-intensive WINS administration tasks. No devices should be pointed at or registering with this WINS server. Remember, any data that is placed in the local database of this WINS server will not be replicated because it is configured only to pull data or receive pushes.

Once you have established an administrative-only WINS server, you don't have to wait for an outage window to complete most administrative tasks. Instead, most administrative tasks can be run during normal business hours without disrupting service to your users. However, using an administration-only WINS server will not help you for certain administrative tasks that involve manipulating a particular WINS server's database, as is the case with tasks like Jetpack.

So now let me ask you this question: What is one more WINS server, anyway? It is only one more server that doesn't need to be high end or highly available. When you compare the low cost to the benefits, I think using an administrative-only WINS server provides tremendous value to any organization.

NOTE: Using an administrative-only WINS server is not something that Microsoft has suggested or even commented on; its role was created out of necessity. So if you try to find official documentation on how to configure an administrative-only WINS server, you will come up with a big goose egg.

Chapter 9

Merging WINS Environments

I t is nearly impossible to pick up the business section of any newspaper without reading about a pending merger or acquisition. Unlike the business world of yesterday, merger and acquisition (M&A) is a critical tool used by most successful organizations today. Your first priority in any merger or acquisition is to achieve interoperability between the systems of the merging organizations. Name resolution is a critical component that is essential to interoperability and the integration between systems. Before any other group or division can begin sharing information, you must address all name resolution issues—both DNS and WINS related.

WINS Integration

Configuring multiple WINS environments to work together is much more difficult than addressing the same problem in DNS. When you consider the differences between the two name resolution services, it makes sense. Unlike DNS, WINS doesn't implement either a forwarding or delegation model. This lack of functionality means that you can't configure WINS clients to ask another namespace to resolve a name if the request can't be satisfied by the native namespace. Without the ability to forward names to another namespace, you are forced to merge WINS environments together to resolve names found in both WINS namespaces. This merged database houses names of all devices that existed in both WINS environments before the merger.

Also unlike DNS, all names in WINS are in the same namespace and are unqualified. For example, two devices named ComputerA, each in different WINS databases, are in contention for the same name if their WINS databases are ever merged. Because both ComputerA device names are unqualified, there is no way for WINS to differentiate between the two ComputerA entries that exist in the WINS databases.

Without qualification of names, you are forced to ensure the uniqueness of every name in all WINS namespaces to be merged. Because there is no qualification in WINS, if the two WINS databases used in the example were to be merged, the name ComputerA would be duplicated. To resolve a duplicate name, one of the name owners would have to rename his or her device or face loss of network connectivity. Therefore, you must identify and resolve all duplicate names before merging the WINS databases.

Collecting the WINS Data

Finding any duplicate device names should be your top priority. Not only is finding duplicate device names a painful process, but identifying the owner of a particular device also always proves to be challenging. If you do not identify and resolve any potential duplicate NetBIOS names before you merge WINS, your users will be adversely affected.

The first step in identifying any duplicate NetBIOS names is extracting data from WINS. Once the data has been pulled from WINS and is placed into a format that is reusable and not proprietary, you can use it to find duplicate names.

You have to collect a data dump from both WINS environments. The data from each WINS environment will be combined and used to locate duplicate device names and their addresses. You dump data from WINS either by using the WINS Export feature or by using Winsdmp.Exe. Which tool you choose depends on which operating system is running on both the WINS server and the device that is capturing the data. Both tools pipe all entries from the WINS Jet database into a comma-separated value (.csv) or text (.txt) formatted file. You can then use these files with a database product to find duplicate NetBIOS names.

Using WINS Export

The WINS Export feature allows you to pipe data out of your WINS database and into a flat file. You access the WINS Export utility in the WINS MMC by right-clicking any WINS server and selecting Export List from the drop-down menu. This command opens a Save As dialog box, which is where you specify the location, name, and file type to house the WINS data dump.

BUG ALERT In the WINS Export Save As dialog box, you might assume that you should select the Save Only Selected Rows check box if you want to export only the results of a filter you have applied to the Active Registrations object. However, selecting this box exports an empty dump, saving only the column headings. No clear definition exists in any Microsoft document that explains the purpose of this check box.

WINS Export is a processor- and memory-intense task. If you run it during normal business hours, your users may experience delays in name resolution and in some cases, complete failure. Also, because the WINS server that the WINS Export is being run against is so busy sending data out of WINS, replication tends to suffer. When replication doesn't work properly, convergence times increase. When convergence times increase, so do the number of calls to your help desk.

Depending on the size of your WINS environment, executing WINS Export during normal business hours may not be a big deal. The smaller your WINS database is, the less impact WINS Export is likely to have. In my experience, the dump process takes about four hours for every 50 MB of WINS data in your database. (The time may vary depending on server utilization.)

TIP: Using an extra WINS server only for administrative purposes, as detailed in Chapter 8, is a great way to ensure that you can export WINS data at the exact time that you need it. This is a nice convenience because you can collect your data without having to worry about how your clients will be affected. Simply run WINS Export or Winsdmp from your administrative-only WINS server.

When you use WINS Export to export data from WINS, each entry in WINS is represented by a single row. Each row has multiple columns with the following names and data:

❖ **Record Name** – The user-defined portion of the NetBIOS name, which can be no longer than 15 characters.

❖ **Type** – The 16th character of the NetBIOS name, which defines a service on the device followed by the name of the service. Displaying the name of the service in this column is helpful to those administrators viewing the data who don't know that [20h] is the Server service.

❖ **IP Address** – The IP address of the device. As detailed in Chapter 6, this column holds only the first IP address of any device (which is a bug Microsoft is currently addressing). Due to this bug, the export of your WINS data will not display all of the addresses configured on multihomed devices, nor any group record that contains more than one IP address, such as the domain record.

❖ **State** – The details of the state the record is in relative to the registration lifecycle. Supported values are Active, Released, and Tombstoned.

❖ **Static** – The type of record that the row defines. If the value of this column is blank, then the record has been placed into the database dynamically. If the value is the word "static," then this record has been manually placed into the database.

❖ **Owner** – The IP address of the WINS server that owns the record.

❖ **Version** – The High DWORD version ID for the record. Version IDs are used by other WINS servers to track any outstanding changes to another WINS server's database. If the version IDs don't match, replication will occur.

❖ **Expiration** – The date that this record will expire.

	A	B	C	D	E	F	G	H	I
1	Record Name	Type	IP Address	State	Static	Owner	Version	Expiration	
2	-__MSBROWSE__-	[01h] Other	10.17.9.250	Active		10.17.9.250	1	########	
3	DOMAIN	[00h] Workgroup	10.17.9.250	Active		10.17.9.250	8	########	
4	DOMAIN	[1Bh] Domain Master Browser	10.17.9.250	Active		10.17.9.250	5	########	
5	DOMAIN	[1Ch] Domain Controller	10.17.9.250	Active		10.17.9.250	7	########	
6	DOMAIN	[1Eh] Normal Group Name	10.17.9.250	Active		10.17.9.250	6	########	
7	SERVER1	[00h] WorkStation	10.17.9.250	Active		10.17.9.250	4	########	
8	DUSTIN	[03h] Messenger	10.17.9.250	Active		10.17.9.250	2	########	
9	SERVER1	[20h] File Server	10.17.9.250	Active		10.17.9.250	3	########	
10									

Using Winsdmp (a.k.a. WINS Dump)

Winsdmp is an NT 4 Resource Kit utility that pipes data from the WINS database into a .csv or .txt file. Because Winsdmp is a Resource Kit utility, it is not found on the default installation of an NT 4 WINS server. This is a shame because it, as well as many other WINS related tools that are only found in the Resource Kit, is vital to keeping WINS healthy.

Unfortunately, Microsoft does not support using Winsdmp on a Windows 2000 WINS server. Like many other Microsoft-unsupported configurations, using this tool does work: Microsoft just hasn't been able to test it enough to ensure that it will not cause any problems. Winsdmp was written to take advantage of the older Jet database that shipped with NT 4 WINS and therefore hasn't been optimized or even ported over to support the new Jet database found in Windows 2000 WINS. Despite the Jet database version conflicts, the Winsdmp tool works just fine. The only caveat is that Winsdmp will not run from a Windows 2000 device. Instead, you must run it from an NT device and configure it to dump data from your Windows 2000 WINS. You can't live without Winsdmp in M&A activities.

The Winsdmp utility is a command-prompt tool launched by running Winsdmp.Exe. To dump the contents of your WINS database, use the following syntax:

winsdmp (*IPAddress or HostName of WINS Server*) > *filename.ext*

For example, if you have a WINS server with an IP address of 10.1.2.3 and you want to pipe the data out to a file called Mywins.Csv, enter:

winsdmp 10.1.2.3 >mywins.csv

You can run Winsdmp either on the actual WINS server or from a remote workstation. Once again, keep in mind that running Winsdmp on the local server only works if the WINS server is of the NT 4 variety.

Like WINS Export, Winsdmp exports data in a format that places each WINS record in its own row. Each row's values are defined by the file's columns. Unlike the WINS Export utility, when Winsdmp dumps data to a file, the file does not contain any column heading or naming information. I have given names to each column such as Column 1, Column 2, etc., for the purpose of illustration. Here are the columns that you will find in a Winsdmp-produced file:

NOTE: For readability, I have included the name of the value that each column holds in parenthesis next to the column number. This information does not appear in the Winsdmp file.

- **Column 1 (owner IP)** – The IP address of the WINS server that owns this particular record.

- **Column 2 (device name)** – The user-assigned NetBIOS name of the device or service.

- **Column 3 (type)** – The NetBIOS 16th character of the device's name.

- **Column 4 (characters)** – The sum of the total number of characters defined by the user-configured NetBIOS name and the yype name.

- **Column 5 (type of record)** – The value that defines which type of NetBIOS record this is. Supported values are 0 (Unique), 1 (Normal Group), 2 (Special Group), and 3 (Multihomed).

- **Column 6 (state)** – The value that defines where the record is in the extinction lifecycle. Supported vales are 0 (Active), 1 (Released), and 2 (Tombstoned).

- **Column 7 (high version ID)** – The high version ID used to track changes to the WINS database that have not been replicated to other WINS servers.

- **Column 8 (low version ID)** – The same purpose as the high version ID but houses different data used to determine a replication starting point.

- **Column 9 (static flag)** – The value that indicates whether the entry was manually placed into WINS or dynamically added. Supported values are 0 (Dynamic) and 1 (Static).

- **Column 10 (time stamp)** – The time when the record was placed into the database.

- **Column 11 (number of records)** – The item that defines how many records are held in this entry. In the case of group-type entries, this number may be more than one.

◆ **Columns 12 – 37 (IP addresses)** – This represents all of the IP addresses that have
been assigned to the device. WINS supports up to 25 IP addresses for one entry, each
of which is defined in its own column.

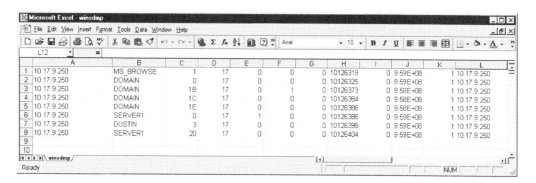

WINS Output Compatibility

So far, everything seems pretty straightforward. If you have to dump data from Windows
2000 WINS, use WINS Export. If you have to dump data from NT 4 WINS, use Winsdmp.
Both WINS Export and Winsdmp work well alone (except for the bug in WINS Export
allowing only one address to dump), but when their data has to play together, all hell
breaks loose.

In mergers, each organization typically runs different versions of WINS. In the NT 3.51
and 4 days, this wouldn't have been a big deal because the Winsdmp utilities from each
operating system formatted the dumped data the same way. However, when merging NT 4
and Windows 2000 WINS environments, the native tools for each system do not output data
in a compatible format. The problem is that each tool places data in certain columns and
uses certain values that are not compatible with the other tool.

If you take a look at a Winsdmp-produced file and a WINS Export–produced file, you
will see the following formatting differences:

◆ **Data in different places** – Any particular column's data item that is found in one
tool's output isn't in the same order in the other tool's output. For instance, take the
NetBIOS name data. NetBIOS name data appears as the second column in a Winsdmp
file but as the first column in a WINS Export file. The same can be said of ownership
information, which in Winsdmp appears in the first column but in WINS Export
appears in the sixth column. This becomes a problem in the import process because
data will need to be mapped differently depending on which tool was used to create
the output file. The only way to work around this is to use the Column Mappings

And Transformation screen in the SQL import tool to map the contents of the first column from an old WINS dump to the data already imported into the sixth column, or vice versa. (Don't worry, this will all be discussed in the next section.)

◆ **Not the same data** – Even when you do map the columns, the data contained in each field is not the same. For example, just the 16th character of the device's NetBIOS name is displayed in the appropriate column in a Winsdmp file, but both the 16th character and the friendly name of the service are defined in the comparable field found in the WINS Export file. This difference in data makes it difficult to find all duplicates because the query logic you will use looks for an exact record type (let's say the 1C record). When one entry contains a 1C record and another entry contains a (1C) Domain record, no duplicate will appear. This is because while these domains may be actual duplicates, the data in the field is formatted differently and therefore gives the false appearance of uniqueness. Even if WINS Export didn't use a friendly name, the use of parentheses around the service name makes the data in the field different from the same data that does not have parentheses. To resolve this problem, you must expand your SQL query logic with OR statements to establish the logic that will be required to view 1C and (1C) Domain as the same data.

◆ **No parity** – There is no parity between the two formats. Some values are displayed in one tool that never appear in the other. For example, Winsdmp contains both a low and high version ID, while WINS Export contains only the high version ID. Also, as I have already pointed out several times, WINS Export doesn't support more than one IP address per entry. There is no practical way to work around this. While it doesn't directly affect the detection of duplicate names, it does provide inconsistencies in your data, which is not good in the long run.

Using both tools and then bringing the data into one database is not impossible, just painful. It requires a lot of extra steps that you would not have to take if Microsoft had thought about backward compatibility when they built WINS Export. Be that as it may, you can resolve these problems by using one of two methods. You can use the SQL mapping functionality in conjunction with query logic to make use of the data from both tools, which is very painful and not cost-effective. Alternately, you can decide to use the same tool on both Windows 2000 and NT WINS, circumventing the formatting problem completely.

Using the same tool to capture data from both environments is by far the more practical approach to resolving this problem. The only real question is which tool do you use, WINS Export or Winsdmp? The answer, which might surprise you, is to use Winsdmp even though it is not supported when used with Windows 2000. I have reached this conclusion because of the great depth of data that a Winsdmp file gives you as compared to a WINS Export file. Plus, the fact that you can't see more than one IP address per entry when using

WINS Export is not only annoying, but it can prevent you from finding the owner of a particular device.

NOTE: The good news is that Microsoft has agreed to support the use of Winsdmp in both Windows 2000 and future versions of Windows. Winsdmp will be included in the Resource Kits. I am still trying to talk them into giving you the option to dump from WINS Export in a backward-compatible format.

Using SQL to Find and Resolve Duplicate Names

SQL is the product of choice (at least my choice) for mining WINS data. It is a robust solution that is capable of handling the sometimes strange data that a WINS dump can produce. Because I consider SQL 7 the preferred choice for these WINS migration tasks, I will use SQL 7 as the database provider in all of the examples given in this chapter. You can use any other database product that you are familiar with, but you need to be sure that the queries you write and the processes you define are comparable with the examples I give.

CAUTION: Do not use Access to complete this process. It has a lot of quirks that make importing data from WINS into a database table practically impossible.

Mining the Data in SQL

Once you have collected dumps for both WINS environments, you are ready to start mining the data. The WINS dumps you have harvested provide you with text output of many fields, yet only a few of the fields are interesting. You must capture this interesting data in a database for future use and analysis. Here is the information you need to find any potential duplicate NetBIOS names, as well as explanations of how the data is used.

- **Device name** – The NetBIOS name of all devices is used to identify duplicate named devices within a service type.

- **Type** – Determining which type of record is associated with a NetBIOS name is the only way of knowing what an entry is representing. By examining the type fields of both dumps, you can determine if there is true duplication between entries with the same user-defined NetBIOS name. For example, consider two entries in WINS with a NetBIOS name of Yoda; one represents a computer and the other represents a domain. Although each entry has the same NetBIOS name (Yoda), because each entry represents a different NetBIOS services type (Yoda [00] vs. Yoda [1C]), there is no true duplicate record.

 ✦ **IP address(es)** – Once you determine that you have a valid duplicate device name, the IP addresses of this device will help you track down the owner of the device that is in duplication.

 ✦ **WINS ownership information** – When looking at a list of potentially hundreds if not thousands of duplicate names, it is useful to determine which WINS environment the record belongs to. This information helps keep the records for each environment logically separated even when all of the data has been compiled together.

Importing WINS Data into SQL

After you have exported the WINS data, you must bring both of the WINS data dumps together into a single database. Once all of the data has been compiled into a single database, you can begin to identify duplicate names. You bring data from both WINS dumps into a single database by using a SQL feature called Import. An Import in SQL, as the name implies, takes data out of one location and places it into a SQL table. By importing both WINS dump files into a single table, you can refine your table and query logic inside SQL.

You import data into SQL by completing the following steps:

1. Open the SQL Import utility by selecting the SQL Import And Export Data menu item found in the program group of applications that was installed with SQL.

2. On the Welcome screen, click Next.

3. On the Choose A Data Source screen, select Text File from the Source drop-down box, which will let SQL know that you intend to pull data in from a flat file.

4. Once you select Text File, the contents of the Choose A Data Source screen will change. Enter the location to the first WINS dump file in the File Name box.

5. Click Next.

6. On the Select File Format screen, select Delimited. Accept the rest of the default options.

TIP: If you are importing a WINS Export file, then you might consider selecting First Row Has Column Names. This will save you the time of having to input the column names into the table.

7. Click Next.

8. On the Specify A Delimiter screen, ensure that the comma option is selected. You should also see a sample view of how your data will look once imported.

9. Click Next.

10. On the Choose Destination screen, ensure that the Destination drop-down box shows Microsoft OLE DB Provider For SQL Server.

11. In the Server field, type the SQL server's name that will be housing the database. If applicable, supply the appropriate credentials to perform the task.

12. In the Database field, select the database that will house your WINS merging information. If you have already created a database for this function, select it now. If you have not created a database yet, select New, which will spawn the Create Database applet.

13. In the Create Database applet, specify a database name, its size, and its log file's size. Click OK in the Create Database applet. The name of your new database will be placed in the Database field.

14. Click Next.

15. On the Select Source Tables screen, select the table that will hold this data from the drop-down menu under the Destination Table column. If you have not created a table ahead of time, SQL will create a new table for you. All you need to do is specify the name of the table in the last set of brackets in the destination table path. For example, if you wanted to create a table named table1, the information in the Destination Table column should read [**Database Name**].[**dbo**].[**table1**].

16. Click the button under the Transform column.

17. On the Column Mappings And Transformation screen, modify the following components to customize your import:

    ❖ **Source** – This is the source column from the text file. If there is a column that you don't want to import, select Ignore from the drop-down list of the associated column name. I recommend importing all values in this table, which will give you a complete snapshot of your new WINS environment. When you start querying you will begin to ignore certain fields, but it is always good to have a table with all of the data. There should be no need to modify the source settings.

    ❖ **Destination** – This is the name that will be given to the column housing the data defined in the source column. If you are pulling data from Winsdmp, you may want to rename these items to reflect something more intuitive. If you are pulling data from different WINS dump tools, this is the place where you will have to match the data fields of one format to the other.

    ❖ **Type** – This defines the kind of data that will be populating the column. In all WINS activities, "char" works best.

◈ **Nullable** – This flag determines if the value of this column can be empty or null. Ensure that all columns that you are importing have this flag set. WINS has a nasty habit of piping out empty fields when using either WINS Export or Winsdmp.

◈ **Size** – By default, this is set to 255, which is a bit overkill. You won't need any column to support more than 15 characters, so you may want to set this number lower. Decreasing this number can reduce the size of your database. If you want to set these numbers lower, pay careful attention to which column you are adjusting values for. Assigning a value that is too low will cause some data to be truncated, which is dangerous when looking for duplicates. I recommend setting the NetBIOS name column to 15, which will reduce the potential for junk characters to be displayed in WINS data.

TIP: If you are a diehard SQL administrator, you can click the Edit SQL button to manually edit the SQL commands that will be executed as a result of this screen's configuration settings. Then again, if you are a diehard SQL administrator, you probably already know what this button does.

18. Click OK to close the Column Mappings And Transformations screen.

19. Click Next on the Select Source Tables screen.

20. The Save, Schedule And Replicate Package screen allows you to create jobs and execute them either at a later time or immediately. For purposes of illustration, ensure that Run Immediately is selected and click Next.

21. On the Completing The DTS Wizard screen, confirm that what is about to be executed is what you have configured. Click Finish to begin the import.

22. Sit back and watch the pretty graphics and think to yourself "If I were doing the same thing on a UNIX box, I would just be seeing a bunch of dots move left to right in a command prompt. Evolution is cool."

23. Click OK to close the success message.

24. Repeat steps when importing the other WINS dump using the following modifications:

◈ **Step 12** – When specifying the database name, make sure you are using the same database into which you placed the data from the first import.

◈ **Step 14** – When specifying the table name, make sure you are using the same table into which you placed the data from the first import.

CAUTION: If the second WINS dump that you are intending to import was not produced by the same tool as the first, please review the earlier section named "WINS Output Compatibility" before importing the second database.

Congratulations! After completing the preceding steps, you now have all of the data from both WINS environments in a single table. This table will be used to create other tables and ultimately to find duplicate device names.

Query for Duplicate Names

From a data-mining perspective, the most difficult work is behind you. Once you have all of the data in a single table, querying for relevant data is easy. You must first determine which data is of primary concern that will be a problem if duplicated. You need this data so you can base your query logic on it.

Figuring Out What Is Important   Finding duplicates in WINS proves to be a potentially interesting task for a few reasons. You see, just the existence of a duplicate user-assigned NetBIOS name is not a true duplicate. A true duplicate occurs when not only the name is in use but also the service that the device is attempting to register is in use. For example, if a user named his or her device Yoda, which registered both a workstation (00) and server (20) record, there would not be a true duplicate if a domain named Yoda were found. Although the name Yoda is being used by two different entities, from a WINS perspective, they are three separate registrations: Yoda(00), Yoda(20), and Yoda(1C). You need to be concerned only when there are two devices named Yoda and both are trying to register the same 16th NetBIOS character record.

Hundreds of possible name/service combinations register in WINS. All of these possible combinations can make it impossible to find all duplicate names. However, if we separate the record types into different tables and then use queries to find duplicate names within the table, this task is much more manageable. If we carefully separate the types of service entries that are used to identify a host or logical entity, we can ensure uniqueness. If we ensure host and entity uniqueness, then there should be no service duplication. The easiest way to identify hosts is to search for all workstation, server, and domain records. Each record type should then be placed into its own table. Here is what each record type will tell you:

◈ **Domain (1C)** – This record is the heart and soul of all domain location efforts by WINS clients. It is used exclusively to find DCs that can service logon requests. Ensuring that the name of the domain associated with the 1C record is unique between the systems is paramount. If you have a legitimate duplicate domain on the wire, you are in for a world of hurt. There is nothing easy about renaming a domain, as discussed in the "Renaming a Domain" sidebar later in this chapter.

◈ **Workstation (00)** – This record is registered by all clients who have the ability to access a "Microsoft" network. This record is used to identify all Microsoft client operating systems that are WINS aware, which is the largest segment of the devices that will have a duplicate name. Because all devices that host the Server service must also have the Workstation service enabled, this record will provide a complete list of all devices that are on the network.

◈ **Server (20)** – As I said before, all devices registering this record will also register the Workstation service, so its appearance in this list may seem redundant. Running a query to identify Server service–enabled devices helps you determine which kind of device a particular duplicate record is representing. For example, if you found a record that was in duplication named Luke but you weren't sure if Luke was a workstation or server, you could cross-reference the device name with this list to determine if it had registered the Server service. While this is not a foolproof method, because some workstations also register the Server service, it does allow you to determine your level of impact when make renaming decisions.

By isolating these workstation, service, and domain entries, you can more easily identify any duplicates within a record type.

Divide and Conquer   Now that we have established that we are looking only for the 00, 20, and 1C records in WINS, you need to separate out the different record types. By separating the different record types, it is easy to write a SQL query that will return the names of any devices that are in duplication within a single record type. You achieve separation by exporting the data from your single table into three different tables: one for the Workstation service, one for the Server service, and one for the domain record. These tables will then be used to run queries that will produce a list of true duplicates.

To export data from one table into a new table, complete the following tasks:

1. In the SQL Enterprise Manager, right-click the table you created to hold all WINS data and select All Tasks from the menu.

2. From the All Tasks menu, select Export Data.

3. Click Next on the DTS Wizard Welcome screen.

4. On the Choose A Data Source screen, select Microsoft OLE DB Provider For SQL Server from the Source drop-down box.

5. Ensure that your local SQL server name appears in the Server field. Supply alternate credentials if necessary.

6. Confirm that in the Database field, the name of the database reflects the database that is housing your current table.

7. Click Next.

8. On the Choose Destination screen, ensure that the Destination drop-down box shows Microsoft OLE DB Provider For SQL Server.

9. In the Server field, type the SQL server's name that will be housing the new table. If applicable, supply the appropriate credentials to perform the task.

10. In the Database field, select the database that will house this new table.

11. Click Next.

12. On the Specify Table Copy Or Query screen, select the Use A Query To Specify The Data To Transfer option.

13. Click Next.

14. You should now see the Type SQL Statement screen, where you will enter the following query syntax:

> **select** [*TableName*].[*NameOf ColumnToTransfer*]
>
> **from** [*TableName*]
>
> **where** [*TableName*].[*NameOfColumnThatHoldsServiceType*]=*"X"* **OR** [*TableName*].[*NameOfColumnThatHoldsServiceType*]= *"X"*
>
> **order by** [*TableName*].[*ColumnToSortBy*]

This SQL command uses four different commands. The first is **select**, which tells the query which data to pull into the new table. You must add all columns that you want to view in the new table to the **select** command. Anything not defined in the **select** statement otherwise will not be copied to the new table. There is no limit on the number of items that can be specified with this command. The second command name is **from**, which sets the source table of the query. Next, the **where** command actually performs the query. Finally, the **order by** command sets the display sort order of the query results. The **order by** command supports multiple values that will be used in the order specified to display any results.

Here is an explanation of the variables from each command:

❖ **TableName** – The name of the table that the data is being sourced from. This is case sensitive.

❖ **NameOfColumnToTransfer** – The values specified in this parameter determine which columns will be transferred but not queried. Think of them as extra pieces of information that may prevent you from going back to the main table to find information such as a device's IP address; they have no relevance on the query structure but provide extra information about the record.

❖ **NameOfColumnThatHoldsServiceType** – The column that you have defined to hold the 16th NetBIOS character.

❖ **X** – The value to be queried on in the **NameOfColumnThatHoldsServiceType** column. It appears in the example twice because on some versions of Winsdmp, the 00 record exports as 0 and the 20 record exports as 2. Therefore, I always use an **OR** expression and specify that a successful hit is either 20 **OR** 2.

The following sample query is looking for the Server service in a table named tbl_wins_data. This query will report the WINS owner (which is in a column named Owner_IP), the device's NetBIOS name (which is in a column named NetBIOS_Name), and the NetBIOS 16th character (which is in a column named Service_Type):

> **select** [tbl_wins_data].[Owner_IP], [tbl_wins_data].[NetBios_Name], [tbl_wins_data].[Service_Type]
>
> **from** [tbl_wins_data]
>
> **where** [tbl_wins_data].[Service_Type]="20" **OR** [tbl_wins_data].[Service_Type]="2" **OR** [tbl_wins_data].[Service_Type]= "[20]WorkStation"
>
> **order by** [tbl_wins_data].[NetBios_Name]

15. Verify that you have not fat-fingered the syntax by clicking the Parse button. When a message comes back stating that the SQL command is valid, click OK to clear the message and then click Next.

16. On the Select Source Tables screen, select the table that will hold this data from the drop-down menu under the Destination Table column. Specify an intuitive table name, making sure not to use any spaces in the name.

17. Click Next.

18. On the Save Schedule And Replicate Package screen, select Run Immediately and then click Next.

19. Confirm your settings and click Finish to create the new table.

20. Complete steps 1 – 19 for the workstation, server, and domain record types.

Find Those Duplicates   Now you have all of the relevant records sitting in three different tables. All you need to do now is write a query that will display only those devices that exist within a table that have the same NetBIOS name. This query produces a list of devices that have a naming conflict. The best way to produce this list of duplicates is by creating the query in a stored procedure.

To create a stored procedure, complete the following steps:

1. In the database that is housing your tables, right-click the Stored Procedure object and select Net Stored Procedure from the shortcut menu.

2. You are now looking at a query window. Enter the following syntax:

   CREATE PROCEDURE [*ProcedureName*]

   AS

   select rtrim(ltrim(*ColumnOfNetBiosName*)) **as** *DesiredNetBiosColumnName*, *DesiredServiceTypeColumnName*,

   count (*ColumnOfNetBiosName*) **as total**

   from *TableName*

   group by *DesiredNetBiosColumnName*, *DesiredServiceTypeColumnName*

   having count (*ColumnOfNetBiosName*) **>1**

   order by *Column1*, *Column2*

where:

❖ **ProcedureName** – The name that this stored procedure will be given. An example might be Duplicate_Servers.

❖ **ColumnOfNetbiosName** – The name of the column that contains the user-defined NetBIOS name in the table that this stored procedure will be run against.

❖ **DesiredNameOfNetBiosColumnName** – The stored procedure will place the results of the query in a row-and-column formatted display. The name given here will determine which column name is given to the NetBIOS name information.

♦ **DesiredServiceTypeColumnName** – The name given here determines which name is given to the column that houses the service type in the stored procedure view.

3. Click the Check Syntax button to ensure that the command is valid.

4. Click OK.

5. Complete steps for each service type table by changing the SQL syntax in each table.

Although you have built the query, you still have not seen the results. There isn't a clean display tool built into SQL. Instead, you are forced to either view the results of your query by using Query Analyzer or export the data to a .csv or .txt file. Using Query Analyzer is a quick way to view the fruits of your labor. Open Query Analyzer (found in the program group that was created for SQL). After you have specified the SQL server to bind to, enter **exec** *NameOfStoredProcedure* in the text box. Select the name of your database from the DB drop-down box found in the upper-right corner of Query Analyzer. To view the results of your stored procedure, press F5. The lower portion of Query Analyzer will display the results of the query.

Unfortunately, the results of Query Analyzer are stored only in memory. To view the results of your query in a reusable format, you must export the results to a flat file. Then you can use programs like Excel to display the duplication data. Because stored procedures don't support a flat file export directly from the SQL MMC, you are forced to run an export from the table that contains the data. The export that you run uses basically the same syntax found in the stored procedure, with some minor modification. To export your duplicate device names to a flat file, complete the following:

1. In the SQL Enterprise Manager, right-click the table that contains the service types in which you want to find duplicates. From the shortcut menu, select All Tasks.

2. From the All Tasks menu, select Export Data.

3. Click Next on the DTS Wizard Welcome screen.

4. On the Choose A Data Source screen, select Microsoft OLE DB Provider For SQL Server from the Source drop-down box.

5. Ensure that your local SQL server name appears in the Server field. Supply alternate credentials if necessary.

6. Confirm that in the Database field, the name of the database reflects the database that is housing your current table.

7. Click Next.

8. On the Choose Destination screen, ensure that the Destination drop-down box shows Text File.

9. In the File Name field, enter the name of the file to which you want to export the data. If you plan on using Excel to view these contents, give the file a .csv extension.

10. Click Next.

11. On the Specify Table Copy Or Query screen, select the Use A Query To Specify The Data To Transfer option.

12. Click Next.

13. In the Query Statement field, enter the same SQL query that was used in your stored procedure to view the same results. Make sure that you remove the **CreateProcedure** and **AS** statements from the syntax string.

14. On the Select Destination File Format screen, unless you have a reason to change the default options, click Next.

15. On the Save, Schedule And Replicate Package screen, select Run Immediately.

16. Click Next.

17. Click Finished on the Summary screen and click OK on the confirmation screen that appears after the file has been created.

You are now ready to view this data in any product that supports .csv or .txt files.

NOTE: I do not claim to be a SQL expert in any way, shape, or form. I use SQL like I use scripting and coding: just enough to get the job done. If you want to learn about SQL from someone who is an expert, check out *Admin911:SQL Server 2000* by Brian Knight.

After creating the query logic to find all of the duplicate names within each of the tables, you need to reconcile the data. The information that you have found about duplicate domain names can be left as is. Anything that shows up as a duplicate domain name is legitimate. When analyzing duplicate names returned within the server and workstation records, keep in mind that a device will often show up in both lists. Devices that show up in both lists are just devices that are hosting multiple services, not two different sets of duplicates. Use the information from all three queries to compile a list of all duplicates between the organizations.

Resolve Those Duplicates

Now that you have a list of devices that have the same name between the two WINS environments, your next task is to find the owners of the devices that have duplicate names. Once the owners of these devices have been found, a discovery process should be initiated that will conclude when you have all the relevant data about these devices. This information should then be used to determine how difficult it would be to rename either device.

By analyzing this discovery data, you will be able to ascertain which device is the easiest to rename and which device is more difficult to rename. At the conclusion of this analysis, you should be able to determine which device gets to keep its name and which device must be renamed. The ownership discovery process is incredibly time-consuming. Make sure to leave yourself enough time to identify all objects before you merge WINS by starting the ownership discovery process as early as possible.

Finding the Owners   Finding an owner of a device is pretty easy in AD, provided that you have established an OU structure that fits some sort of logical or organizational structure (which most companies do). But until all devices are moved into AD and are represented by a computer object in the directory, determining ownership of a particular device is almost impossible. These tips may help you find that device's owner:

   ✧   **Check computer object owner** – If the device has an object in AD, which limits this tip's usefulness to NT and Windows 2000 clients, you may be able to find the owner of the device by determining who created the object in AD. The easiest way to do this it to use Active Directory Users And Computers to view the properties of the computer object. Once you have the dialog box opened, click the Security tab. On the Security tab, click the Advanced button. Finally, on the Advanced Security screen, click the Owner tab. The data in the field named Current Owner Of This Item reflects the name of the user or group that created and/or owns this object. Often, you will be able to cross-reference this name or group to an actual person in your environment. This person may not be the actual owner but will probably have some intimate knowledge about the device.

   ✧   **Check AD for hints** – Depending on your OU design, the placement of a computer account in AD can also help you identify the owner of a device. If devices are placed into OUs that follow some logical or organizational scheme, you should be able to determine who is the owner of the OU that houses the device. When you have this information, you can then turn to the owner of the OU for help.

   ✧   **Use any existing data** – It is worth a try to see if any data in your IP database (provided that you have one) can provide you with a hint or two. Most companies keep a database that contains IP addresses that have been assigned to any device that has a static address. Often, these databases also house contact or ownership information for each IP address that has been assigned. Provided that some of the devices you are looking for have static IP addresses, you might find a few owners.

◈ **Check WINS for last logged on user** – By querying WINS for all entries that have the same IP address as the device that has a duplicate name, you will sometimes be able to find the name of the last user who logged on to the device. When a user logs on to a device, his or her Messenger service is registered in WINS. When the Messenger service registers in WINS, the entry that is placed into WINS reflects the logged on user's user name. Viewing this data will provide you with an account name to cross-reference against AD or NT. When the account name is found in either NT or AD, you will be able to obtain the full name of the user. You can infer that the last logged on user either owns the device or at least knows who the owner of the device is. Now for the bad news. You can't query WINS for an IP address by using any tool that Windows 2000 provides; you can complete this task only on an NT WINS server or by using the Winscl Resource Kit utility that was detailed in Chapter 8. Also, if the user has logged on with the administrator account, the name Administrator will be registered as the Messenger service, which is worthless information.

◈ **Net send** – The net send command allows you to send a message to any device or user. As one of your last resorts, send a net send message indicating that if the owner of the device doesn't contact you, the device will fail. This will get the owner's attention pretty quickly. However, this strategy doesn't work so well if the device is a server because someone isn't normally sitting at the console all the time.

◈ **Corporate communication** – Your last-ditch effort should be to send a mass e-mail to all users or all technologists in your organization to explain what is occurring and when. This e-mail should also contain a list of devices whose ownership information is unknown, as well as the consequence of not responding to the e-mail.

Renaming   As you may have guessed, the only way to resolve a duplicate name is to rename one of the devices. This can be either rather simple or extremely difficult. You need to consider the impact of your actions when renaming devices. Always keep in mind that it is far less disruptive to rename a workstation than it is to name a server, no matter how high up the corporate food chain the owner of the workstation is. Avoid renaming servers at all costs. It is a disruptive process because not only do you have to determine who is accessing your servers, but you also need to ensure that all users have been made aware of the name change and have updated their local configuration.

Renaming a Domain

If you are one of those unlucky souls who happens to have discovered that both organizations have a domain with the same name, your choices are limited. You can either retire one of the domains, which isn't a very realistic solution, or you can rename one of the domains. Renaming a domain, which is supported only in NT, is one of the most invasive procedures that you will ever have to undertake. If you have found a duplicate domain name and one of the domains in question is a Windows 2000 domain, you have no choice but to rename the non-Windows 2000 domain. If both of the domains are Windows 2000, consider disabling NetBIOS on one of the domains to resolve this problem.

Even the most successful domain-renaming project is filled with problems. Not only does renaming an NT domain require a huge amount of work from the domain perspective, but you also need to embark on a painful discovery process. This process must determine which services, servers, or other entities are referencing an account or group by using the duplicate domain name.

To make matters worse, one of the domains must be renamed before any WINS data can be merged. Do not merge WINS until all domain duplicates have been resolved. If you have a duplicate domain name, expect to complete a lot of work in a short amount of time because its rename is the only event halting your WINS merger. For complete details on how to rename your domain and to find out about the ripple effects that renaming creates, check out Microsoft's KB article *Q178009 – Renaming a Domain: Process and Side Effects*.

Cleaning Up WINS

Before you even think about merging WINS environments, you need to clean house. Merging WINS creates a ton of replication traffic, which can be hard on your database. You want to clean your WINS data before you merge WINS environments not only to fortify your database but also to ensure that you don't send a bunch of junk entries to your new WINS partners.

The process to clean WINS is slow. At minimum, you will want to span the following tasks (with the exception of patch application) over the course of a few days. Don't wait too long, though. The cleanup process will involve breaking existing replication partnerships to weed out bad entries. Extended amounts of time without replication can create a stale and useless database.

Patches

Making sure that your WINS servers have the most recent service packs and hotfixes is essential to the overall health of your WINS environment. Let's face it, because WINS is on its way out, not a whole lot of prerelease testing went into it in Windows 2000. As a result, WINS in Windows 2000 has a lot of bugs, which you resolve by applying a combination of service packs and hotfixes. Once you have decided to use particular service pack and hotfix versions, either make sure that both WINS environments have all the same patches, or make sure that they at least have compatible patch versions.

Jetpack

After reading Chapter 8, you should already know what Jetpack is and how it works. But in case you are using this chapter as a reference and you are not reading sequentially, here's a summary. Jetpack is a tool used to compress the Jet database on which WINS is built. It provides an easy mechanism for reclaiming the whitespace in your database that is not only taking up hard drive space but also compromising the stability of your WINS data.

Once again, the syntax for Jetpack is as follows:

Jetpack *WinsDatabaseName.mdb TempWinsDatabaseName.mdb*

where:

⬧ **WinsDatabaseName.mdb** – The name of your existing WINS database.

⬧ **TempWinsDatabaseName.mdb** – The name of the temporary jet file you want to use for the compression. This also serves as a disaster-recovery file if anything should happen during the Jetpack process.

You can run Jetpack only when the WINS service has been stopped. It can be either a very quick process or a very long process depending on the size of your database, as well as the amount of time that has expired since your last Jetpack.

Each WINS server should have Jetpack run in close succession to the other WINS servers in the environment. This ensures that as you move forward swiftly, your data will be as tight as possible.

Deleting Invalid Owners and Records

Over time, WINS servers and network devices are added and removed. You would assume that for a dynamic name registration service such as WINS, adding and removing devices would not be a problem. Unfortunately, it is. Due to the WINS multimaster replicate-anywhere scheme, a phenomenon often occurs in WINS when a record (both dynamic and static) or a

WINS partner is removed from the local database but added again as a result of replication. This behavior is most problematic when it affects the deletion of a WINS server and its records from the database.

The enterprise WINS database is a collection of each WINS server's local databases. As you will recall from Chapter 6, each WINS server is known as the owner of a particular set of WINS entries. When a WINS owner is removed from the network and its entries need to be removed from the database, you have two options: use the verification process or manually delete the owner. No matter which option you choose, the result is the same. If an owner is deleted in one server's copy of the WINS database but another WINS server still has that owner in its local database, it will replicate that owner's entries back to the WINS server that has just deleted the owner and all of its records.

This problem is very annoying indeed. You can resolve it in two ways. You can try like a mental patient to quickly remove the owner from all of your WINS servers before replication occurs again, which is impossible even in a medium-sized environment, or you can make use of the Blocked Owners feature found in WINS (the artist formerly known as PersonaNonGrata).

By blocking a particular owner, you are telling WINS never to accept any replica data about a particular owner no matter who it comes from. This allows you to block an owner in strategic locations to prevent the circular replication behavior of WINS. Once an owner has been blocked, you can delete the owner from all of the WINS databases without worrying about records being replicated back.

There is no need to establish an owner block on each WINS server in your environment unless your replication topology is daisy chain. If you followed my recommendations in Chapter 8 and used a hub-and-spoke approach, only the hubs need to block owners. Because the spokes don't talk directly with one another (instead all replication has to go from its hub to another spoke), placing a block on the hub will prevent those records from being replicated to any other partner.

You should closely examine your WINS database and compare it to your existing WINS environment. All owners who appear in the database that are not valid should be deleted. Invalid owners should be removed in both WINS environments by completing the following steps:

1. Open the WINS MMC to establish a blocked owner entry for the owner to be deleted.

2. Right-click the Replication Partners object that appears under the WINS server that you want to block the owner on.

3. Select Properties from the drop-down menu.

4. Click the Advanced tab on the Replication Partners Properties screen.

5. Click Add, which will open the Add Server screen.

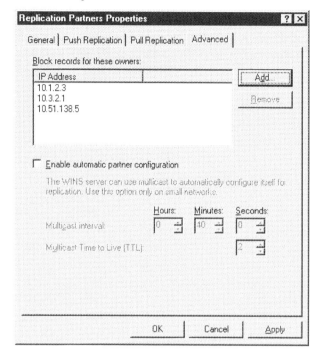

6. In the WINS Server field, add the IP address of the owner who should be blocked. Using the device name is a bad idea because after you delete the server's data, its name may become unresolvable. An unresolvable name defined in a blocking filter may allow replication to occur.

7. Click OK. Notice that the server has been added to the list of blocked owners.

8. Close the Replication Partners Properties screen.

9. Complete steps 1 – 8 on all WINS servers that serve as hubs or on all WINS servers in a daisy-chain replication topology.

10. Right-click the Active Registrations object that appears under the WINS server from which you want to delete the owner. (This should be the device on which the block was established.) Select Delete Owner.

11. On the Delete Owner screen, select the IP address of the owner who in you want to remove. Because you are going to manually remove this owner from all WINS servers in the environment, there is no need to select Replicate Deletion To Other Servers (Tombstone).

12. Click Yes on the confirmation screen and voilà—the owner has been removed.

13. Complete steps 10 – 12 on each WINS server, making sure to delete the owner from the hubs first. If you delete the owner on a spoke when it doesn't have the owner defined as a blocked owner, the owner may be replicated right back to you from the hub.

Break Push–Pull Partnerships

This may sound a little wacky, but it is legitimate. The only way that you are going to be able to successfully verify records from other owners (as you will be doing in the next section) is to temporarily stop replication. This is for the same reason discussed in the previous section: circumstance may make an older record appear as the most recent entry and may overwrite the data that you are in the process of verifying. It is also for this reason that all replication partnerships must be broken, not just selective partners.

Breaking replication partnerships isn't that big of a deal if you do it right. You must always consider time as your top priority when deleting these partnerships. If at all possible, replication should not be broken with any given partner for more than two days. After two days, you run a greater risk of records aging out and affecting clients. Consider completing the steps defined in this section, the "Consistency Check" section, and the "Scavenging" section of this chapter over the course of a weekend on all of your WINS servers. This may be a large task, but it will pay off in user uptime.

CAUTION: Before breaking your replication partnership, make sure that you have detailed your replication configuration as recommended in Chapter 8. Because you will eventually reestablish these relationships, unless you have their configuration detailed, you will find yourself building a new replication topology instead of simply replacing what existed.

Break each replication partner by completing the following steps:

1. In the WINS MMC, open the Replication Partners object under the WINS server that you want to delete the partnership with.

2. In the right pane, right-click the partner to be deleted and select Delete from the drop-down menu.

3. On the confirmation screen, click Yes.

4. Complete steps 1 – 3 on all WINS servers for all replication partners.

NOTE: Even though you have deleted the replication partnership, all records owned by this device are still present in the local database.

Consistency Check

Let's review what state our WINS environment is in right now. We have compacted each database, deleted any invalid owners and their data, and we have just isolated each WINS server by breaking its replication partnerships. It's now time to verify all records in the WINS database. Manually spawning verification will force the WINS server to verify the existence and data for all records that it does not own. WINS does this by contacting the owner of the record and comparing its copy of the record with the copy that the owner holds. Although you might think that changes to a particular record would have been picked up by replication, you would be wrong. Certain records that may have become corrupt in the local copy of the WINS database will be identified and resolved as a result of verification.

To manually run verification, complete the following steps:

1. Right-click WINS Server and select Verify Database Consistency.

2. On the warning screen, click Yes. You will see a message indicating that the request has been queued and to check the Event Log for details.

3. Check the Event Log for details.Complete the previous steps for all WINS servers.

CODE BLUE

Although both the verification and scavenging processes report that you should check the Event Viewer for the status of each task, no relevant information is ever displayed in any log. By default, when running either verification or scavenging, the System Log will report only that the job has started. There are no progress indicators or completion events recorded for either process. If you are like me, you want to know when a task that you started has finished. For any level of detail greater than recording the start of either process, you will have to enable detailed logging for WINS. Then each milestone in each process is recorded to the System Log as well as messages when the task has been completed. Keep in mind that both processes are chatty when detailed logging is enabled, so either bump up the size of your System Log or risk wrapping events.

Scavenging

Your next step is to run a manual scavenge on all WINS servers. This is necessary because your automatic scavenging clock is based on the uptime of the WINS server. It is typical during the course of these changes to reboot your servers or restart your WINS service for one reason or another, which prevents automatic scavenging from ever reaching its thresholds to run. Even if you haven't been rebooting your WINS servers, running a scavenge before reestablishing replication is a good way to reduce the size of your database.

Force a scavenge on all WINS servers by right-clicking the WINS server that you wish to run the scavenge on in the WINS MMC and selecting Scavenge from the drop-down menu. Once you have done this, you will see a message indicating that the scavenge process has started and its progress can be tracked through the Event Log (which we know is not true).

Jetpack Revisited

You have just completed some very database-intensive tasks on all of your WINS servers. Each step of the way, you have been adding and deleting records in one way or another, which creates whitespace. While we ran Jetpack the first time to not only shrink the database but also to resolve any consistency problems, this time, running Jetpack performs a straight space recovery role. You'd be amazed at the size of your database when you compare it to the size it was before you began disinfecting WINS. Sure is a lot of junk in there, huh?

Reestablish Replication

Now you are ready to reestablish all of your existing replication partnerships. Hopefully, you heeded my words of caution and as a result, you have all of the pertinent replication configuration information documented. If your replication topology is well documented, this step should be a breeze. If you didn't document your topology, all I can say is, have a good time redesigning your replication topology. Once you delete replication partners, WINS keeps their data in the database but discards any information about that replication relationship.

Once a replication partner is established, WINS will determine which changes it needs to replicate from a replica partner by using the version ID for any pull partners. Push partners will be notified of any changes so they can then request replication to bring their database up to date.

Cover Your Posterior

It is a plain and simple fact that no matter how much effort you put into finding the owners of duplicate device names, you aren't going to catch them all. Depending on how the two organizations were structured before the merger (and their use of naming standards), you may have an extremely large number of duplicates that need to be resolved. Although the recommendations that I have given to find a device's owner do work pretty well, they are not 100 percent guaranteed. The fact is, NT and Windows 2000 are lousy at letting you know what a device is and who the last user was to use a device.

It is best to assume that you will not find everyone; therefore, a certain amount of failure due to duplication is unavoidable. Knowing this, you need to keep excellent records of every step that you have taken to resolve every duplicate. You also need to make sure that everyone has been notified about the pending changes to reduce the "You never told me that" factor.

Document Everything

Document every conversation, every net send message that was taken, and each step you took to find each duplicate. Also save any e-mails you sent or received. I know it seems like a bunch of mundane and unnecessary work, but it will pay off in spades if you run into either a vocal or important owner of a duplicate device that couldn't be resolved before the integration work began.

Set a Drop-Dead Date

At some point, you will have to realize that you have done all you can possibly do to resolve duplicate device names before the integration. The rest will have to be dealt with in a reactive capacity. Finding this sweet spot is sometimes difficult. Everyone wants to prevent as much downtime as possible, but you need to keep the following in mind. Every day that goes by after you have taken the WINS dumps from the systems is another day that new duplication can occur. Because WINS dumps are only snapshots of the present database, any duplicates that occur after the point when you take the WINS dump (oh, grow up!) will not be captured. Therefore, one can argue that waiting too long in an effort to resolve as many names as possible can do as much damage as good.

When you decide that the proactive work is complete and that it is time to get merging, stick to your guns. Many people will ask you to wait longer in an effort to find the other devices. Don't show any weakness because once you say yes, it becomes more difficult to say no. WINS integration is not something that you want to build a career around.

Corporate Communication

Most companies have a mass e-mail distribution method that is targeted either at all users or just at the technical staff. Consider sending at least three different communications to groups in both of the merging organizations. Early in the process (like when you are creating a list of duplicates), craft an e-mail that is targeted to all users on both networks. This message should be basic and unassuming because its target audience may be the same group of people who are still looking for that elusive "any" key. This communication should explain in plain English what WINS does, why the merging organizations need to integrate their environments, and what it means if WINS is broken. Also include a tentative date for when the activities will begin, and identify a contact within your group who will field the questions that this communication will generate.

Your second communication should come after you have created a list of duplicate device names. This communication should remind the users about the activities that are going to take place. For some reason, users tend to have a short-term memory about technical events that may affect them. Include in this communication the names of all duplicate devices that you have identified. Also include the information on how to get in contact with the right person in your group if the ownership information of an identified duplicate is known. This communication is a fishing expedition at heart, but you just may find a few owners as a result.

The third communication should occur no further ahead of the migration than a week. If you send a final communication any sooner than that, the whole short-term memory problem rears its ugly head again. This communication should provide the exact date and time when the integration activities will begin. It should also contain the names of devices whose ownership information could not be found. Don't be afraid to put some frightening verbiage in this communication that explains what will happen if the owners of these devices don't step forward and claim ownership.

Help Desk and Support Documentation

While this whole process seems fairly clear to you and me, a number of technical staff members will be affected by this change who have no prior knowledge of the events leading to the WINS merger. You can't spend your time educating and notifying every last person in your IT division, but you should take the time to educate and notify those people who will be most affected when something breaks.

Providing documentation to help desks and local support staff is a great use of your time. These are the people—although they have nothing to do with this integration effort—who will bear the brunt of the complaints from any service disruption. You should document what you are doing and when you are doing it, and offer steps to resolve any problems if they arise. For example, when I am merging WINS environments, I always send out a document that not only talks about what is occurring but also walks the help desk and support staff through the process of renaming the NetBIOS and/or host name for each operating system. These step-by-step instructions really help out.

TIP: Include in your documentation a process to handle scenarios where a device owner calls in claiming that he or she cannot rename their device under any circumstance. In most cases, you will want your help desk and support staff to point these types of problems out to you for further analysis.

Determine Your New Replication Topology

It's almost time to pull the trigger, which means you need to sit down and figure out exactly how you are going to join the two environments.

Detailing Your Existing Environment

Hopefully, you haven't waited for a WINS merger to occur before detailing your existing WINS environment. If you followed the advice I gave you in Chapter 8 and documented all of your relevant WINS information, you should be in good shape. Only after you have a good idea of what is in place can you determine which kind of environment you want to move to.

If you haven't completed a comprehensive view of your existing WINS architecture, here is a list of items to document before you migrate the WINS environments:

- **Ownership** – Be sure you know who owns engineering and support of the WINS environment. This information will help you determine which group should take ownership of the new environment once everything has been merged. Because ownership is a political phenomenon, not a technical one, all I will say on the matter is that there should be only one owner of WINS.

- **Replication partners and relationship** – Each environment should document how its replication topology currently exists (hub and spoke vs. daisy chain vs. hybrid). Each replication partner's configuration should be detailed to include which type of relationship exists (push and pull vs. push vs. pull) and at which thresholds replication is triggered (how many version IDs and how many record changes). This information will be useful in determining the convergence time of your database. Also pay attention to how many records are replicated on average per hour during peak replication times.

- **Link speeds** – Determine how fast the links are at all locations where any replication partner exists. This information will bring to light any potential network-related replication problems. You also want to determine at which speed and configuration the networks that house each WINS environment are attached, which will help you determine the replication interval between the environments.

- **Processing load** – Trend the use of each WINS server to detect any overburdened devices, which should not be used as focal points for replication.

Sure, They Say They're Ready, But Are They?

In most mergers or acquisitions, the network goes through many changes. At first, the networks are normally connected by the use of a firewall or other filtering device. As the merger process progresses, more ports are opened up on the firewall to facilitate the connectivity that is needed for systems interoperability. This process of trusting continues until at some point, the firewall goes away. Unfortunately, WINS mergers usually occur early in the merger lifecycle, so ensuring that the network can support your WINS replication and resolution traffic across the organization's network boundaries is important.

Don't take their word for it, either. Use a port scanning piece of software to interrogate the firewalls to determine if the right ports are opened. Please let the firewall owners know that you are doing this and why. Firewall owners tend to be a little security-sensitive and will go into battle mode if they detect an unauthorized scan. Alternately, you could choose to set up replication between two test WINS servers well ahead of the integration to test replication of an empty WINS database. If it works, you know that all of the ports are opened. For a list of which ports need to be opened and why, see Chapter 8.

Determine How You Want to Integrate

You can combine two WINS environments into one in two ways. Because Microsoft did not conceive of these methods, they don't have professional-sounding names. I have taken a stab at naming these two approaches in a fashion that reflects their use while still sounding professional. I call them the Spackle approach and the Borg approach.

Spackle Approach   As the name implies, when using the Spackle approach, you are adhering two separate WINS environments together. The advantage to this approach is that it is transparent to the user community because it doesn't require that any configuration at the desktop occur. The downside to this, as you will read more about in the "Borg Approach" section, is that you are inheriting the entire existing WINS infrastructure from both organizations.

When you choose to implement the Spackle approach, you simply need to define a replication point between the two environments. The point that the two environments should be connected is up to interpretation, but there are some guidelines to use. In general, you should try to connect the environments between two existing hub points in the replication topology. Connecting environments at the hub point reduces convergence times, which makes data more quickly available to users. Also try to avoid connecting the environments at multiple points to reduce redundant links and circular replication. Connecting multiple hub-and-spoke environments in multiple locations can result in the creation of a hybrid or daisy-chain environment before you know it.

Borg Approach   Assimilation is the key to the Borg approach. Using the Borg approach involves migrating users and servers from one organization's WINS servers to the other organization's WINS servers. Although this approach is much more invasive than the Spackle approach, it is necessary in many cases.

Let's be honest. When most WINS environments that exist today were designed several years ago, the designs tended to be overly complex and the hardware tended to be too widely deployed. Back in the days when WINS was king of the hill, Microsoft recommended that for every 10,000 users, you should have a primary and backup WINS server. These numbers—while useful and valid on the hardware that was running WINS in the NT 3.51 days—were never updated. To this day, you can still find documentation that talks about these ridiculously low capacity numbers despite the kind of performance you can achieve from today's hardware. Microsoft is obviously dedicating little time to WINS in the Windows 2000 space, which is why these numbers haven't been updated.

At any rate, more often than not, most organizations' WINS environments not only have enough hardware to support the low load numbers that Microsoft recommends, but they also have enough WINS hardware deployed to power their company plus a company of the same size. In short, WINS designs always tend to be bloated. If you read Chapter 8, you know about some of the consistency and replication problems that occur when you have a WINS environment that is too large.

The advantage of the Borg approach is that instead of joining the two environments together, which will create a bigger mess, you can move all devices to a subset of approved WINS servers that make up your new, going-forward design. This reduces a lot of the maintenance, administration, and support headaches found with the Spackle approach. The disadvantage is that all devices that are currently configured to use a WINS server that will be retired will have to be reconfigured: short-term pain for long-term gain.

Using the Borg approach involves moving groups of devices from one WINS environment to the other while still retaining complete name resolution of the devices that have been moved. As each computer is moved to the new WINS environment, its records are left in the old WINS database even when it registers its records in the new WINS database. This multiregistration is allowed because each WINS environment is still separate. By allowing the name to remain in the old WINS environment, clients who have not yet migrated will still be able to resolve the migrated device's name. For this strategy to work, you must carefully plan your migration, and you must modify the WINS configuration in the old WINS environment.

Deciding which devices will be moved at what time is critical to the success of the Borg approach. The idea is to move groups of devices that need to maintain communications with one another at the same time. When a device is moved to the new WINS environment, it will be unable to resolve names of devices that exist in the old WINS environment due to the lack of replication. As a result, although users and other devices will be able to see the migrated devices from both environments, the migrated device won't be able to see any devices that are not in the new WINS environment.

NOTE: Domain controllers in the same domain should be moved at the same time; otherwise, you will be unable to manage your domain devices.

Depending on your migration timeline, you may need to adjust your TTL intervals in your old WINS environments. Because the devices that are being moved out of the WINS environment will no longer be able to update their own records, all resolution of their names is facilitated through records that they have left behind. As you know, records that are not being updated by the WINS client that owns them are subject to tombstoning and eventual scavenging, which would prevent name resolution. To prevent this, you must increase the values for your WINS server's registration interval, extinction interval, extinction timeout, and verification interval.

By increasing these TTL parameters, all entries will remain in the database longer and will therefore be resolvable long after the device has moved. Because WINS clients will learn about these new values only once they update data in WINS, make sure that any modification to these values is completed well before your devices start to move. If you do not provide ample time for the WINS clients to learn about these new settings, you may move a server whose records were not updated with the longer TTLs.

Once you have decided on the timeline for your move and have configured your TTL parameters to a level that will support your timeline, you need to start moving your devices. Continue moving them off the old WINS servers until they are unpopulated, at which time you can retire them and reclaim the hardware.

Replicate or Merger and Verify

Using the data that you have already captured about both WINS environments, decide at which point you will enable replication or begin to move devices from one environment to another. The best time to complete both tasks is after hours, especially when using the Spackle approach. Replication of WINS data is sent bit for bit over the network, so is it not only costly but also time-consuming.

Once replication has started, no event in WINS will let you know that the initial replication pass has completed. Instead, you must obtain the current version ID from the

WINS partner with which your WINS server is replicating and compare that against the highest version ID your local database has for that owner. If the numbers are the same, then replication is up to date. If the numbers are different, there is still some replication to be done. You can estimate the amount of time that replication should take if you have good trending information about your current replication times.

If you have chosen to move forward with the Borg approach, you won't be done until all devices have been pointed at other WINS servers. Because all entries will remain in the database for a long time due to their increased TTL (which can make the database appear falsely populated), your best bet for determining usage is to monitor the WINS server statistics. This will help you determine if anyone is still registering or querying your WINS server even after you think that everyone should be migrated off of it.

Build a Naming Standard

Has it occurred to you yet that this whole process would have been much easier if there were no duplicate names? Did you also notice that the obscure names used (such as the serial number of a device) were never duplicated, but devices with common names like *Server* were? Don't you think that a naming standard might help you in the future by ensuring that no devices are given easily duplicated names?

While a naming standard does you absolutely no good at the present moment from a WINS perspective, it does permit you to be more proactive about the next big WINS merger. By taking the time today to implement a logical yet unique naming standard, you will greatly reduce the chance of duplicate names during your next WINS merger.

Your naming standard should be logical but unique. Consider using something that is unique to your organization as part of the device name, such as group name or organizational affiliation. Using group and department information is also helpful in identifying an area of your organization that a device belongs to, which may be helpful if you ever need to find the owner of that device.

Part III

Appendixes

Appendix A

Registry Information

F inding a complete set of registry values for any Microsoft feature, application, or service is more difficult than snapping a picture of Bigfoot playing backgammon with the Loch Ness Monster. I don't know how some authors can write complete books on registry settings. Not only is the information documented in a million different places, but it is normally poorly detailed and often contradicts statements about the same information made in other documents.

This appendix presents the closest thing to a complete list of DNS and WINS registry hacks possible. I'm sure there are others that aren't defined or only known internally to Microsoft. I'm also sure that the trend of making new registry values available at each service pack will continue, so it is important to mention list only registry values found in a new installation of pre-SP1 Windows 2000. This appendix doesn't address any registry hacks that may increase operating-system or general network performance, both of which can greatly impact your DNS and WINS environment. For a complete list of all registry hacks known to man throughout space and time, check out *Admin911: Windows 2000 Registry* (ISBN: 0072129468), written by Kathy Ivens (Osborne/McGraw-Hill, 2000). Although this appendix isn't as exciting as Kathy's book, it's a good starting point.

Default Service Settings

Each service that is installed in Windows 2000 is represented by a subkey found in the HKLM\System\CurrentControlSet\Service registry key. Although the exact name of the key will vary, the items found in each key are fairly consistent. These consistent items affect the way that the DNS, DNS Cache, NetBT, and WINS services load. These data items, found in the HKLM\System\CurrentControlSet\Service\Dns, HKLM\System\CurrentControlSet\Service\DnsCache, HKLM\System\CurrentControlSet\Service\NetBT, and HKLM\System\CurrentControlSet\Service\Wins locations, are detailed here.

- ❖ **DependOnGroup** – A REG_MULTI_SZ item that lists any groups that this service depends on.

- ❖ **DependOnService** – A REG_MULTI_SZ item that lists the services that this service depends on.

- ❖ **Description** – A REG_SZ item that holds the description that is given to this service. This is the information that is displayed in the Services MMC.

- ❖ **DisplayName** – A REG_SZ item that houses the service name.

- ❖ **ErrorControl** – A REG_DWORD item that sets the state of Last Known Good if this service fails to load. Supported values are 0, 1, 2, and 3. A value of 0 indicates that the device will continue to boot normally without even recording an event in the Event

Log. A value of 1 will cause an error to be logged, but the system will still continue to boot normally. A value of 2, which is severe, will cause an error to log and the Last Known Good function to be set. A value of 3, which is critical, will cause the system to log an error and use Last Known Good at next boot.

NOTE: Values of 2 and 3 may also cause the operating system to take additional steps in an attempt to recover. These steps will vary from implementation to implementation.

- **ImagePath** – Either a REG_SZ or a REG_EXPAND_SZ item that points the system to the executable to be used to launch the service.

- **Start** – A REG_DWORD item that establishes where in the boot process this service will be launched. Supported values are 0 (load at boot), 1 (load at kernel initialization), 2 (loaded automatically at GUI startup), 3 (load manually), and 4 (disabled).

- **Type** – A REG_DWORD item that indicates where the service fits into the Windows 2000 architecture. Supported values are 1 (kernel driver), 2 (file system driver), 4 (adapter augments), 10 (a Win32 program), and 20 (a Win32 service that can share a process with other Win32 services).

NOTE: Because all of these items are created as a result of a service installation, they have no default values or behavior.

DNS Registry Settings

Many registry settings affect both the DNS client and the DNS server. Some of them are well known and documented, while others are so hard to find that they qualify as being downright obscure. I've attempted to compile a list from multiple sources of all registry settings that pertain to DNS. This is the most complete list of DNS registry values that I am aware of.

Some basic assumptions apply for each registry value. Unless specified otherwise, assume the following:

- Values are valid on both DNS servers and DNS clients, unless specified otherwise or unless the description makes a distinction clear.

- Modification of a value requires the DNS server and/or DNS client service to be restarted. If the value modifies a parameter that is also configurable in the DNS MMC, modification via the DNS MMC doesn't require the services to be restarted.

✦ Values that require a service restart can be modified by the Dnscmd tool, which doesn't require a service restart. However, I recommend restarting any service that has been modified via a registry change, despite Microsoft's claims.

✦ The location for any registry value location specified in the text of another registry value is in the same key location.

All references to registry values and keys are those that are present on a fresh install of Windows 2000; therefore, you may find some values on your upgraded DNS server that aren't referenced here. This is by design. All values here represent the supported values of Windows 2000 DNS. Although other values might have the same meaning and configuration result, use the Windows 2000 equivalent when possible.

HKLM\Software\Policies\Microsoft\System\DNSClient

This subkey stores entries that are created as a result of a Group Policy Object that sets values for DNS clients. The system receives these policy settings and applies changes to the registry, which are subsequently read by the DNS Client service.

NV PrimaryDnsSuffix

This REG_SZ data item serves as a temporary storage space for the value of the Primary DNS Suffix policy established in the Computer Configuration\Administrative Templates\ System\DNS Client policy object. The value of this data item is the primary DNS suffix for the client that is the target of the Group Policy. If you don't apply the policy or you disable it, the data item is removed from the registry.

The value of the policy is stored here until the system reboots, at which time the contents of **NV PrimaryDnsSuffix** is copied to the **PrimaryDnsSuffix** data item.

This data item isn't supported on domain controllers.

PrimaryDnsSuffix

This REG_SZ data item stores the primary DNS suffix value that is configured as a Group Policy (using the Computer Configuration\Administrative Templates\System\DNS Client policy in the Group Policy Editor). The value is copied from the **NV PrimaryDnsSuffix** registry item when the system is rebooted after the Group Policy has been applied.

This setting takes precedence over any user-defined primary DNS suffix setting, which is normally stored in the **Domain** data item found in HKLM\System\CurrentControlSet\Service\ Tcpip\Parameters. This item isn't supported in domain controllers.

HKLM\System\CurrentControlSet\Services\DNS\ Parameters

This subkey holds configuration parameters for the DNS service.

AddressAnswerLimit

This REG_DWORD item defines the maximum number of A records that can be inserted into a single response to a client. The item doesn't exist in the registry unless you add it to modify the default system behavior, which is to place no limit on the number of A records returned to the resolver. This is only supported on DNS servers.

Supported values for this item are 0, 5–28. A value of 0 indicates that there is no limit to the number of A records returned (the system default). Values in the range of 5–28 correspond to the maximum number of A records returned (i.e., a value of 7 places seven A records in a response).

AdminConfigured

This REG_DWORD item is used by the DNS service to determine whether your server is in an "unconfigured" state. If so, you haven't run the Configure The Server Wizard from the DNS MMC. Setting this value to 0 forces the DNS server to place a warning in the DNS MMC that indicates that the server hasn't been configured. A value of 1 indicates that this server has already been configured. Don't modify this registry setting because it could mask the real configuration state of your DNS server.

AutoCacheUpdate

This REG_DWORD value allows you to modify a feature of Windows 2000 DNS, which permits the DNS server to ask any root-level servers for an updated list of InterNic-approved root-level servers. The information is used to update the DNS server's cache. If this value doesn't exist or it does exist with a zero value, the default behavior is maintained, and auto cache update is used. If the value is anything other than zero, this feature is disabled. This item is valid only on DNS servers.

AutoConfigFileZones

This REG_DWORD item determines whether the DNS server updates all records in DNS referencing its Fully Qualified Domain Name (FQDN) when the server's FQDN is modified, in order to reflect the new name. The following values are supported:

❖ 0 – Doesn't modify existing records that contain the old FQDN of the DNS server.

❖ 1 – Updates records only in dynamic-update–supported zones.

❖ 2 – Updates records only in nondynamic update zones.

❖ 3 – Modifies all zones.

The default value for this item is 1, and the item is supported only on DNS servers.

BindSecondaries

This REG_DWORD item enables or disables the use of fast zone transfers, as explained in Chapter 2. Because fast zone transfers are supported only in BIND 4.9.4 and greater, the use of pre-4.9.4 BIND secondaries requires this feature to be disabled.

The supported values are 0 and 1: a value of 0 enables fast zone transfers; a value of 1 disables this feature. The default value is 1.

The use of fast zone transfers can also be configured on the Advanced tab of any DNS server's properties found in the DNS MMC. This registry item is valid only on DNS servers.

BootMethod

This REG_DWORD item determines the location from which the DNS server loads the server configuration and zone data. This data item is modified as a result of changes you apply in the DNS MMC (in the Server Properties\Advanced\Boot Method drop down box). The following values are supported:

❖ 0 – No startup source defined. While this value is supported, it is never used.

❖ 1 – Uses the Boot file located in the **%SystemRoot%\System32\Dns** folder. The Boot file is the non-RFC–compliant BIND configuration file used in some older BIND implementations.

❖ 2 – Starts by reading DNS configuration information from HKLM\System\CurrentControlSet\Services\DNS key.

❖ 3 – Loads configuration and zone information from both the registry and Active Directory. This option is available only if the server is hosting an AD-Integrated zone.

CasePreservation

By default, when a DNS server receives a name query, it changes the case of the characters received in the query for the host name to lowercase. In some scenarios, where queries are being forwarded from your Windows 2000 DNS server to another type of DNS server, this may cause the query to fail if the record isn't lowercase in the authoritative zone. Changing this REG_DWORD's value to 1 forces DNS to maintain the case of the host name that was received in the query. This item doesn't exist in the registry unless you add it (the default behavior applies), and it is valid only on DNS servers.

DatabaseDirectory

By default, when using a standard zone, the DNS database is located in **%SystemRoot%\ System32\Dns**. Modifying this REG_SZ item permits administrators to specify an alternate database location.

DefaultAgingState

This REG_DWORD data item sets the default scavenging state on all newly created AD-Integrated zones. If this item isn't present or its value is set to 0, new AD-Integrated zones do not use scavenging. A value of 1 indicates that scavenging is enabled.

When a new zone is created, the value of **DefaultAgingState** is copied into the **Aging** data item found in the HKLM\CurrentControlSet\Services\DNS\Zone\ZoneName key. The system uses the **Aging** value for all future scavenging processes. This data item is ignored if the **ScavengingInterval** data item hasn't been configured. This item is valid only on DNS servers.

DefaultNoRefreshInterval

This REG_DWORD data item is used to specify the default No Refresh Interval for all new AD-Integrated zones. Supported values are 1–0xFFFFFFFF, which is a hex representation of the number of hours that must expire before a record can be updated. The default value is 168 hours (one week) unless scavenging has been disabled, in which case this item is ignored. The value defined in **DefaultNoRefreshInterval** is copied to the **NoRefreshInterval** item in HKLM\CurrentControlSet\Services\DNS\Zones\ZoneName when a new AD-Integrated zone is created and it is used thereafter. This item is valid only on DNS servers.

DefaultRefreshInterval

This REG_DWORD item sets the default Refresh Interval for all newly created AD-Integrated zones. The item can be modified in the DNS MMC by configuring the Refresh Interval option in the Set Aging/Scavenging For All Zones screen of any DNS server. **DefaultRefreshInterval** supports a value range of 1–0xFF, which represents the refresh interval in hours. Each time a new AD-Integrated zone is created, the value specified in **DefaultRefreshInterval** is copied to the **RefreshInterval** data item located in HKLM\CurrentControlSet\Services\DNS\Zones\ZoneName, which is then used to specify the refresh interval thereafter. This value is valid only on DNS servers.

DisableAutoReverseZones

This REG_DWORD item causes a DNS server to create and make itself authoritative for three "default" reverse lookup zones: 0.in-addr.arpa, 127.in-addr.arpa, and 255.in-addr.arpa. Supported values are 0 (enabled) and 1 (disabled). This item is valid only on DNS servers.

EventLogLevel

This REG_DWORD data item determines the level of logging that is displayed in the DNS log in Event Viewer. The following values are supported:

- 0 – No logging
- 1 – Errors only
- 2 – Errors and warnings
- 4 – All events

This item doesn't exist unless you add it. If this value does not exist, the system behaves as if the value for this item is set to 4.

ForceSoaExpire

Modifying this REG_DWORD data item allows you to configure the value for the Start of Authority (SOA) expiration interval for all zones hosted on the DNS server. The value is the expiration interval in milliseconds. This item doesn't appear in the registry by default and is valid only on DNS servers. This item affects any existing zones and serves as the default configuration value for all zones created thereafter. Because this item overrides the expiration interval defined in the SOA, there is no default value other than that specified in the SOA.

ForceSoaMinimumTtl

Modifying this REG_DWORD data item allows you to configure the value for the SOA time to live (TTL) of all zones hosted on the DNS server. The value is the time of the TTL in milliseconds. This item doesn't appear in the registry by default and is valid only on DNS servers. This item affects any existing zones and serves as the default configuration value for all zones created thereafter. Because this item overrides the TTL interval defined in the SOA, no default value exists other than that specified in the SOA.

ForceSoaRefresh

Modifying this REG_DWORD data item allows you to configure the value for the SOA refresh interval of all zones hosted on the DNS server. The value is the refresh interval in milliseconds. This item doesn't appear in the registry by default and is valid only on DNS servers. This item affects any existing zones and serves as the default configuration value for all zones created thereafter. Because this item overrides the refresh interval defined in the SOA, there is no default value other than that specified in the SOA.

ForceSoaRetry

Modifying this REG_DWORD data item allows you to configure the value for the SOA retry interval for all zones hosted on the DNS server. The value is the retry interval in milliseconds. This item doesn't appear in the registry by default and is valid only on DNS servers. This item affects any existing zones and serves as the default configuration value for all zones created thereafter. Because this item overrides the retry interval defined in the SOA, there is no default value other than that specified in the SOA.

ForceSoaSerial

Modifying this REG_DWORD data item allows you to configure the value for the SOA serial of all zones hosted on the DNS server. The value is the serial to be used. This item doesn't appear in the registry by default and is valid only on DNS servers. This item affects any existing zones and will serve as the default configuration value for all zones created thereafter. Because this item overrides the initial serial number defined in the SOA, there is no default value other than that specified in the SOA.

ForwardDelegations

When a DNS server receives a query for a delegated subdomain, the default behavior is to send the query to the subdomain. Setting the value of this REG_DWORD item to 1 allows the DNS server to forward all queries for a name in a subdomain to other servers outside of its delegation model; a value of 0 maintains the default behavior. This registry item doesn't exist unless you add it, and the system default is the same as a value of 0.

ForwardingTimeout

This REG_DWORD data item determines how long DNS will wait for a forwarder to respond before considering the request outstanding. Once a request is outstanding, a query is sent to the next server defined in the list of forwarders. This data item—found in the registry only if forwarding has been enabled on a DNS server—supports a value range of 1–0xFFFFFFFF, which represents the number of seconds that DNS will wait for a response from a forwarder. Because forwarding is considered a type of recursive lookup and is subject to recursive-based configuration settings, this value is used only if the value of **RecursiveTimeout** is higher than the value defined in **ForwardingTimeout**. The default value for this data item is 5 seconds.

Forwarders

This REG_SZ item holds the list of servers to which queries are forwarded. Although this is normally modified on the Forwarders tab of any DNS server in the DNS MMC, you can also modify this REG_SZ data item to add or remove forwarders. Unlike most DNS entries, changes to this item don't require the DNS service to restart before it can be used.

IsSlave

This REG_DWORD item specifies whether the server is a slave. A value of 0 (the default) indicates that the server isn't a slave, and DNS will issue standard iterative queries to resolve the name. A value of 1 indicates that this server is a slave. This value can be modified in the DNS MMC (DNS ServerName | Forwarders | Do Not Use Recursion). The item is valid only on DNS servers.

ListenAddresses

DNS in Windows 2000 gives you the ability to select which IP addresses on your DNS server should respond to DNS queries. By default, all IP addresses listen and respond to DNS queries on a DNS server, but you can change this by modifying this REG_BINARY item to include all addresses that should respond to DNS queries. You can also modify this behavior on the Interfaces tab of the Properties dialog box of any DNS server. This item isn't included in the registry by default, and it's valid only on DNS servers.

LocalNetPriority

This REG_DWORD determines the order in which the DNS server returns multiple A records for the same name to DNS clients. Windows 2000 DNS supports the use of traditional round-robin load balancing as well as subnet prioritization, in which the DNS server attempts to send the host address that is closest to the resolver. A value of 0 disables the default behavior, forcing the DNS server to hand records to resolvers in the order in which they were placed into the database. A value of 1 or a non-existent value enables the default behavior, the use of net priority.

You can also modify this behavior by altering the Enable Netmask Ordering flag set in the properties of any DNS server. This item is valid only on DNS servers.

Because round-robin load balancing competes with (rather than complements) subnet prioritization distribution of A records, keep the following in mind:

If the **RoundRobin** data item has been set to 1, a **LocalNetPriority** of 0 will cause the DNS server to hand records to resolvers in a round-robin method. A value of 1 for **LocalNetPriority** permits the DNS server to attempt to send back a host address of the A record that is closest to the resolver.

LogFileMaxSize

This REG_DWORD item specifies the maximum size of Dns.log. The supported values are 0x10000–0xFFFFFFFF, which represents in hex the maximum size that this log can be. The system default is 4 MB.

When the maximum value is reached, the log overwrites the oldest entries. This item isn't found in the registry by default, and it's supported only on DNS servers.

LogFilePath

This REG_DWORD item specifies the location of the Dns.log file used to house the DNS debugging log. The default value is **%SystemRoot%\System32\Dns\Dns.log**, but it can be changed to any directory or filename.

NOTE: A bug in Windows 2000 prevents the Logging tab in the DNS MMC from accurately reporting the location of the log file. No matter which location you specify as the value of this data item, the MMC always shows the log file located in *%SystemRoot%\System32\Dns*.

LogLevel

This REG_DWORD item specifies the level of logging that's reflected in the Dns.log file. Multiple values are supported, each representing one piece or logging option. The collective result of this data item determines what is captured in the log. Supported values are as follows:

- 0x0 – No logging.
- 0x1 – Logs queries.
- 0x10 – Logs notification messages.
- 0x20 – Logs updates.
- 0xFE – Logs nonquery transactions.
- 0x100 – Logs DNS questions.
- 0x200 – Logs DNS answers.
- 0x1000 – Send packet logging.
- 0x2000 – Receive packet logging.
- 0x4000 – Performs UDP packet logging.
- 0x8000 – Performs TCP packet logging.
- 0xFFFF – Logs all packets.
- 0x10000 – Performs AD write transaction logging.
- 0x20000 – Logs AD update transactions.

> ❖ **0x1000000** – Performs full packet logging.

> ❖ **0x80000000** – Performs write-through transaction logging.

> ❖ **0x8100F331** – Logs all available logging options.

This data item is supported only on DNS servers and isn't found in the registry by default. You can modify logging options via the DNS MMC on the Logging tab of a server's Properties dialog box. Once logging has been enabled, the default value of this item is 0x0.

LooseWildcarding

Wildcarding is defined in RFC 1034 as a way to take failed queries and attempt to find the closest or best match to satisfy the query. Microsoft's implementation "does not strictly comply" with the RFC on wildcarding. Since, in my opinion, wildcarding is such a bad idea that I've never used it, I can't tell you what Microsoft is doing that the RFC doesn't define. As you may have guessed, finding documentation about where Microsoft ignores the RFC is difficult. To enable wildcarding, add this REG_DWORD item and specify a value of 1, which enables the feature. The default behavior, when the item isn't present or it is set to 0, is to disable wildcarding. This item is valid only on DNS servers.

MaxCacheTtl

This REG_DWORD item configures the TTL for entries held in the DNS server's cache. Supported values are 0, which signifies that no entries are to be cached, and any number in the range 1–0xFFFFFFFF, which represents in hex the number of seconds that is used as a TTL. Because this item doesn't exist until you create it, the default behavior is to assign a TTL of 86,400 seconds, or one day, to each cached entry. This item is supported only on DNS servers.

NameCheckFlag

This item specifies which character standards for host names are applied to DNS. Supported values for this REG_DWORD item are the following:

> ❖ **0** – ANSI characters that comply with DNS RFCs.

> ❖ **1** – ANSI characters that don't comply with RFCs.

> ❖ **2** – Multibyte UTF8 characters that don't comply with RFCs.

> ❖ **3** – All characters supported, which is definitely not RFC compliant.

You can also modify the behavior on the Name Checking box located in the Advanced tab of a DNS server's Properties dialog box. This item is valid only on DNS servers, which will behave as if the value is set to 3 if no registry entry exists.

NoCacheRanking

This REG_DWORD item allows you to turn off ranking data as defined in RFC 2181. Supported values are 0, which allows ranking data, and 1, which turns off ranking data. This item isn't found in the registry by default and is supported only on DNS servers. If this item isn't located in the registry, the server enables ranking data.

NoRecursion

This REG_DWORD data item is used to determine whether the DNS server participates in recursive resolution requests. The valid values are 0 and 1. A value of 0 indicates that if the server is asked to perform or participate in a recursive query, it will. A value of 1 dictates that the server not participate in any recursive activity. This item doesn't exist in the registry by default, but the system behaves as if the value is set to 0. This item is supported only on DNS servers.

PublishAddresses

This REG_SZ item specifies which IP addresses configured on the device are registered with DNS. The value is equivalent to the IP addresses that should be placed into DNS. By default, this entry doesn't exist in the registry and all devices register all addresses with DNS.

PublishAutonet

Automatic Private IP Addressing (APIPA) addresses aren't automatically registered in DNS by default. If you want to change this behavior, create this REG_DWORD item with a value of 1. This item also supports a value of 0, which disables this feature. This item is valid only on DNS servers that are using APIPA.

PreviousLocalHostname

This item is used to store the host name before it is changed on the host. Values from the **HostName** and **PrimaryDnsSuffix** data items are copied into the **PreviousLocalHostname** item, which is then used to hold host name data after it has been changed. This data item is REG_SZ and supports a single FQDN as the value. The item is supported only on DNS servers.

RecursionRetry

This REG_DWORD data item determines how long a DNS server will wait for a recursion response before considering the query no longer valid. Supported values are 1–0xFFFFFFFF, which represents the number of seconds that DNS will wait before issuing another lookup request. This item isn't found in the registry by default, so you must add it if you want to modify the default value of 0x3. It's supported only on DNS servers.

RecursionTimeout

This value, like **RecursionRetry**, is used to take action if a recursive query isn't answered. Unlike **RecursionRetry**, this value indicates the amount of time that can expire before the search is terminated and an error returned to the resolver. Supported values are 1–0xFFFFFFFF, and the default value is 0xF, or 15 seconds. This value must be added to the registry if any value other than the default value is to be used.

RoundRobin

When this data item is present and its REG_DWORD value is set to 1, and if **LocalNetPriority** is set to 0, then round robin is used to return records to resolvers. If **RoundRobin** is set to 1 and **LocalNetPriority** is also set to 1, subnet prioritization is enabled. If **RoundRobin** is set to 0, the load-balancing method defined by **LocalNetPriority** is used. This item doesn't exist in the registry by default and can be enabled only on DNS servers.

RpcProtocol

This REG_DWORD item defines which protocols should be used for administrative functions that use a Remote Procedure Call (RPC). Supported values are as follows:

- 0 – No protocol used and RPC is disabled for DNS.
- 0x1 – TCP/IP.
- 0x2 – Named Pipes.
- 0x4 – LPC.
- 0xFFFFFFFF – All protocols (This is the default setting.).

This item is valid only on DNS servers.

ScavengingInterval

When you select and configure the Enable Automatic Scavenging Of Stale Records setting on the Advanced tab in a server's Properties dialog box in the DNS MMC, you are modifying this **ScavengingInterval** REG_DWORD data item. This item supports values of 0 – 0xFFFFFFFF, which represents the number of hours between scavenging events. The default value is 0 but can be modified to one of the following values:

❖ **0** – Sets the scavenging interval to 0 hours, which will disable automatic scavenging.

❖ **1–0xFFFFFFFF** – Enables scavenging as well as specifies the interval between scavenging passes.

SecureResponses

This REG_DWORD item allows you to cache resolution results in the server's cache only if the results are from a server or host in the same domain as the server resolving the name. Microsoft claims that this can be useful in preventing malicious attacks by preventing rogue root servers from placing entries in your DNS server's cache. This item isn't found in the registry by default and can be enabled with a value of 1 and disabled with a value of 0.

SendOnNonDnsPort

This item determines which UDP port number to send DNS queries to. The default behavior is to use port 53, but you may need to modify this if your DNS servers are separated by devices that restrict access to certain ports, such as a router or firewall. This REG_DWORD item supports a value that is equivalent to the port number to be used, and this item isn't found in the registry by default. It serves the same purpose as the **SendPort** item and is supported only on DNS servers.

SendPort

This REG_DWORD data item configures a specific UDP port number to be used to send queries. The DNS server sends iterative queries out through port 53 unless this item is present and its value is set to a number representing the port number to be used. This item, which serves the same function as the **SendOnNonDnsPort**, doesn't appear in the registry by default and is valid only in the registry of a DNS server.

StrictFileParsing

This REG_DWORD data item configures the behavior of a DNS server when a zone transfer is received that contains data that doesn't conform to RFC naming standards. A value of 0 allows the DNS server to continue to load the data and just record any problems to the Event Log. When the value is set to 1, the DNS server will halt the loading of the bad data immediately. This item isn't in the registry by default but can be modified by enabling the Fail On Load If Bad Zone Data option of a DNS server's properties. Because DNS clients can't transfer zones, this data item is supported only on DNS servers.

UpdateOptions

This REG_DWORD item prevents certain types of records from being dynamically updated in a zone. Supported values include these:

- ❖ **0x0** – No restrictions on dynamic updates.
- ❖ **0x1** – Prevents SOA.
- ❖ **0x2** – Prevents NS.
- ❖ **0x4** – Prevents delegation NS.
- ❖ **0x8** – Prevents server A.
- ❖ **0x100** – Prevents SOA on secure updates.
- ❖ **0x200** – Prevents root NS on secure updates.
- ❖ **0x30F** – Prevents NS, SOA, and server A records on standard updates and root NS and SOA on secure updates.
- ❖ **0x400** – Prevents delegation NS on secure updates.
- ❖ **0x800** – Prevents server A on secure updates.
- ❖ **0x1000000** – Prevents DS peer records.
- ❖ **0x80000000** – Disables dynamic updates.

This item is supported only on DNS servers accepting dynamic updates. Although this item doesn't exist in the registry by default, the server will behave as if the value for this item is set to 0x30F.

WriteAuthorityNS

DNS has the ability to either return NS records only in the Authority section of referrals, per RFC 1034 and 2181, or it can return NS records in all responses. I don't know when or why you would want to provide NS data in all responses, but you can configure it by setting this REG_DWORD's value to 1. A value of 0 (the system default) indicates that this DNS server will conform to RFCs concerned with NS data in responses to resolvers. This item isn't present in the registry by default and is supported only on DNS servers.

XfrConnectTimeout

This REG_DWORD item defines the amount of time a primary name server will wait for a secondary name server to connect before breaking a connection established for a zone transfer. Supported values are 0–0FFFFFFFF, which represents the number of second to wait in hex. This item doesn't appear in the registry by default and is valid only on DNS servers hosting primary zones. The default behavior when this item isn't present in the registry is to wait on the secondary name server for 30 seconds.

HKLM\System\CurrentControlSet\Services\DNS\Zones\ <ZoneName>

This subkey, which exists for each zone, holds the settings discussed in this section on a zone-by-zone (subkey-by-subkey) basis.

Aging

If this REG_DWORD data item's value is set to 0, scavenging is disabled on the zone of the same name as this registry key's last value. If the value is set to 1, scavenging is enabled on the zone. This is normally configured by selecting the Scavenge Stale Resource Records check box in the Properties dialog box of any zone in the DNS MMC. The default value for this item depends on the occurrence of the **DefaultAgingState** data item and its value for AD-Integrated zones. If there is no occurrence of the **DefaultAgingState** data item, the default value for **Aging** is 0. If **DefaultAgingState** is configured, the Aging item's default value will be the same value as that defined in **DefaultAgingState**, as explained in the section by the same name. For Standard zones, the default value is always 0. Also, this setting will be ignored unless the **ScavengingInterval** value has also been established in the HKLM\CurrentControlSet\ Services\DNS\Parameters key.

AllowUpdate

This REG_DWORD item determines whether the zone accepts dynamic updates. Supported values are 0 (no dynamic updates), 1 (accepts dynamic updates), and 2 (accepts only secure dynamic updates). This item is valid on the name server hosting the primary zone when using Standard zones, and on all servers when using AD-Integrated zones. The default value of this data item is 0 for Standard zones and 2 for AD-Integrated zones.

DatabaseFile

This REG_SZ item specifies the name of the database file for the Standard zone, which must be in the location specified by the **DatabaseDirectory** item found in HKLM\System\ CurrentControlSet\Services\DNS\Parameters.

DsIntegrated

This REG_DWORD item determines whether the DNS zone is stored in AD or in a file. Two values are supported: 0 and 1. A value of 0 indicates that the zone is stored on the file system as a file. A value of 1 means that the zone is stored in AD. This item, although found on all DNS server types, is read only by DNS servers housing AD-Integrated zones.

MasterServers

This REG_SZ data item contains a list of primary name servers from which the secondary name server receives zone transfers. This item is valid only on DNS servers hosting a secondary zone, and its setting can also be modified by configuring the Master IP Addresses boxes in the Properties dialog box of a DNS server.

NoRefreshInterval

Setting this item establishes the earliest time that a record can be renewed in DNS once it has been registered. This REG_DWORD item supports values of 1–0xFFFFFFFF, which is a hex representation of hours that must expire before a refresh can occur. The default value for standard zones is 168 hours, while the default value for AD-Integrated zones is equivalent to the value of the **DefaultNoRefreshInterval** set in HKLM\System\ CurrentControlSet\Services\DNS\Parameters.

NotifyLevel

This REG_DWORD data item determines which secondary DNS servers will be notified when changes are committed to the zone on the primary DNS server. This data item supports values of 0, 1, and 2:

- ❖ 0 – The primary DNS server doesn't notify any secondary servers of changes to the zone.

- ❖ 1 – All DNS servers that have an NS record in the zone are notified. This is the default value for Standard zones.

- ❖ 2 – Notification is sent only to servers defined in the **NotifyServers** registry setting. This is the default setting for AD-Integrated zones.

This item may be found in the registry of secondary DNS servers but is ignored on any DNS servers besides a primary name server.

NotifyServers

This REG_SZ data item contains a list of DNS servers that host secondary zones. The data item supports the addition of multiple IP addresses, each of which represent a single secondary DNS server. This setting is valid only when found on primary DNS server.

RefreshInterval

This data item's value is manipulated when you configure the refresh interval on a DNS server via the MMC. This REG_DWORD item supports values of 1 – 0xFF, which represents in hours the amount of time a record has to be updated before it's considered stale (and becomes subject to removal). The default value depends on the type of zone. If the zone is Standard, the default value is one week. If the zone is AD-Integrated, the value is the same as that specified in the **DefaultRefreshInterval**, which is configured in HKLM\System\CurrentControlSet\Services\DNS\Parameters.

ScavengeServers

This REG_EXPAND_SZ data item contains a list of DNS servers that are permitted to perform scavenging operations on the zone. This data item doesn't appear in the registry by default, and if it's manually implemented, it will be used only if the scavenging interval has also been configured through the use of the **ScavengingInterval** data item, the DNS MMC, or the Dnscmd tool.

SecondaryServers

This REG_SZ data item holds the IP addresses of all DNS servers that are secondary for the zone. It's used to determine which servers receive a zone transfer. The information held here can also be accessed in the DNS MMC on the Zone Transfers tab of a zone's Properties dialog box. This item isn't in the registry by default, and when it is manually created, it's valid only on primary DNS servers when the value of **SecureSecondaries** is 2.

SecureSecondaries

This item controls which servers receive zone transfers from the primary zone. A value of 0 for this REG_DWORD item allows zone transfers to any DNS server that requests them. A value of 1 sends zone updates only to DNS servers that have an NS record in the zone. You can also specify specific servers that may request a zone transfer by setting this value to 2, as well as by configuring the **SecondaryServer** registry setting. When **SecureSecondaries** is set to 3, no zone transfers occur. This item doesn't exist in the registry by default, but primary servers hosting Standard zones behave as if the value were 0, while AD-Integrated zones act as if the value were 3.

Type

This item specifies whether a zone is primary or secondary. This REG_DWORD data item supports values of 1 and 2. Primary zones have a value of 1 and secondary zones have a value of 2. The value is modified when the zone type is modified through the Zone Type setting found in the Zone Properties sheet of any zone in the DNS MMC.

HKLM\System\CurrentControlSet\Services\Dnscache\ Parameters

This subkey, which controls the parameters for the DNS cache, contains the data items discussed in the following sections.

AdapterTimeoutCacheTime

This item determines how long the DNS client will wait after a network interface card (NIC) is considered down before it attempts to send another DNS query through it. Supported values for this REG_DWORD item are 0–0xFFFFFFFF, which represents in hex the number of seconds to wait until trying the adapter again. This item is valid only on multihomed DNS clients and has a default value of 300 seconds (5 minutes).

CacheHashTableBucketSize

This REG_DWORD item establishes the maximum number of columns of cached data that can be held in the client-side cache. The default value for this item is 10.

CacheHashTableSize

This REG_DWORD item that establishes the maximum number of rows of cached data that the client-side cache can hold. The default value is 211.

MaxCacheEntryTtlLimit

This REG_DWORD value defines the TTL for cached entries for all resource records except SOA. This entry is used only if its value is greater than the TTL given to the client for the record by the DNS server. Supported values are 0–0xFFFFFFFF, which represents the TTL in seconds that must expire before an entry is purged. This item is supported by both DNS clients and servers, and it supercedes the **MaxCacheTtl** value found in the HKLM\System\ CurrentControlSet\Services\DNS registry key on DNS servers.

MaxSOACacheEntryTtlLimit

This item sets the maximum amount of time that an SOA can remain in cache. This REG_DWORD value will supercede the TTL given to the SOA from the DNS server only if it's greater than the value given by the DNS server. Supported values are 0–0xFFFFFFFF, which represents the SOA TTL in seconds.

NegativeCacheTime

This REG_DWORD value defines the TTL for cached negative responses for all resource records except the SOA. Supported values are 0 – 0xFFFFFFFF, which represents the TTL in seconds that must expire before an entry is purged. This item is supported by both DNS clients and servers.

NegativeSOACacheTime

This item sets the maximum amount of time that a negative response for an SOA can remain in cache. Supported values for this REG_DWORD item are 0–0xFFFFFFFF, which represents the SOA TTL in seconds.

NetFailureCacheTime

If a network failure is detected by Windows 2000 Professional, DNS queries are suspended until the value of this REG_DWORD item has expired. Supported values are 0–0xFFFFFFFF, which is a hex representation of the total number of seconds to wait. The default value is 0x1E, or 30 seconds.

TransportBindName

This REG_SZ data item was used in the production stage of the product but somehow managed to make it into the final version for no good reason. This item should never be modified from its set value of "\device\".

HKLM\System\CurrentControlSet\Services\Netlogon\ Parameters

This subkey contains DNS information used by Netlogon. The subkey holds the values discussed in the following sections.

DnsRefreshInterval

This REG_DWORD data item determines how often Netlogon renews or reregisters the device's names with DNS. By default, the Netlogon service reregisters its names 5 minutes after the first successful registration. After that, it reregisters its names at an interval equal to double the amount of time that expired between the last reregistration process. When that amount of time reaches the value defined here, Netlogon only reregisters at the interval defined by this value. Supported values are 0, which disables reregistration of DNS names, or any other hex value between 0x1 and 0x418937. The default value is 0xE10, or 3600 seconds. Modifying this value doesn't require a reboot.

DnsTtl

This REG_DWORD item configures how long DNS clients will cache entries placed into DNS by the Netlogon service. Supported values are 1–0x7FFFFFFF, which is a hex representation of the TTL in seconds. The value 0 is also a supported value that prevents these types of entries from being cached. This item isn't found in the registry by default, but all DNS clients will behave as if the value is set to 0x258, or 600 seconds. Modifying this item doesn't require the service to be restarted.

RegisterDnsARecords

By default, a domain controller will register its A records in DNS. This behavior can be changed by adding this REG_DWORD item to the registry. Supported values are 0, which disables registration of A records for a domain controller, and 1, which enables A record registration. This item is valid only on domain controllers and will also prevent A records from registering for the Global Catalog service, if it is hosted. Modifying this item doesn't require the service to be restarted.

UseDynamicDns

UseDynamicDns is a REG_DWORD data item that configures the Netlogon service to support dynamic updates of host names related only to Netlogon. Supported values are 0 and 1. A value of 0 indicates that the device shouldn't attempt dynamic registration and updates. A value of 1 indicates that the device should attempt dynamic registration and updates, which is the default behavior for all domain controllers. This value is valid only on domain controllers and isn't present by default. Modifying this item doesn't require the service to be restarted.

HKLM\System\CurrentControlSet\Services\RasMan\PPP\ControlProtocols\BuiltIn

This subkey contains configuration information for Routing and Remote Access (RRAS), including the DNS- and WINS-related values discussed in the following sections.

RegisterRoutersWithNameServers

When this REG_DWORD item is configured with a value of 1, a device with RRAS installed will register itself with the remote network's DNS and WINS servers. If the value is 0, no registration occurs. This item isn't added to the registry by default, but if it's manually added, it will be enumerated and used the next time the router dials the remote network. All RRAS devices behave as if this value is set to 0 when this data item isn't present.

RequestNameServerAddresses

This REG_DWORD item configures a client using IPCP to request the DNS and WINS servers from the RAS server. A value of 0 prevents the client from asking for DNS and WINS server information. A value of 1 enables the client to ask for addresses from RAS, which is the default behavior when this item isn't present in the registry. This value is valid on all Windows 2000 clients but must be created, and it is used only when accessing RAS services. The value is read during session negotiation.

HKLM\System\CurrentControlSet\Services\ RemoteAccess\Parameters\Ip

This subkey holds RAS parameters. One of the data items pertains to DNS.

DNSNNameServer

This REG_MULTI_SZ item specifies the DNS servers the RRAS client uses. By default, the system assigns the RAS server's DNS server to the client. This registry item doesn't exist unless you add it to the RRAS server to change the automatic assignment.

HKLM\System\CurrentControlSet\Services\Tcpip\ Parameters

This subkey holds configuration data that applies to the Transmission Control Protocol/Internet Protocol (TCP/IP) service. The data items covered in the sections that follow are those related to DNS.

AllowUnqualifiedQuery

This REG_DWORD data item specifies whether the DNS service allows unqualified queries. A value of 0 (the default) doesn't permit unqualified queries to be sent to a DNS server. A value of 1 allows unqualified queries to be sent to DNS for resolution. This item is supported on all versions and roles in Windows 2000 and doesn't require the service to be restarted if modified.

DatabasePath

This REG_EXPAND_SZ item defines the location of the HOSTS, LMHOSTS, NETWORKS, and PROTOCOLS files. The default location is **%SystemRoot%\System32\Drivers\Etc**, but you can change the location of all the files.

DisableDynamicUpdate

This REG_DWORD item enables or disables all dynamic updates on all adapters in the system. A value of 0 enables dynamic updates. A value of 1 disables dynamic updates. This item isn't in the registry unless you add it, but the system default is to enable dynamic update registration.

DisableReplaceAddressesInConflicts

This REG_DWORD item specifies how the client behaves when it detects a duplicate name in DNS upon registration. By default, a client will replace the existing DNS record with its own information unless the zone is secured. Setting the value of this item to 1 causes the client to halt the registration process if a duplicate name is detected. A value of 0 permits the client to overwrite the existing entry. This data item isn't in the registry unless you add it. The default system behavior is the same as a value of 0. Modifying this item doesn't require the service to be restarted.

 NOTE: For more information on securing dynamic updates, please see Chapters 2, 3, and 4.

DisableReverseAddressRegistrations

This REG_DWORD data item determines whether the DNS client dynamically registers pointer resource records (PTRs) with DNS. Although this item doesn't exist in the registry unless you add it, the default behavior of the client is to attempt to register PTRs. Giving this data item a value of 1 prevents the client from registering PTR. A value of 0 permits registration. Modifying this item doesn't require the service to be restarted.

DNSQueryTimeouts

This REG_MULTI_SZ item determines how long a DNS client waits for each DNS query. Once this timeout expires, the client will issue another query to the DNS server using the next value listed. The value is a list of five time limits in seconds, and must be followed by a 0. This item doesn't exist unless you add it, but the device will behave as if the value is set to 1, 2, 2, 4, 8, and then 0. Modifying the value doesn't require the service to be restarted.

Domain

This REG_SZ data item stores the primary DNS suffix that is configured in the system properties. Information is written to **Domain** from the **NV Domain** data item after the system has been rebooted. This value is overridden if the data item **PrimaryDnsSuffix** is present, located in the HKLM\Software\Policies\Microsoft\System\DNSClient key. Modifying this item doesn't require the service to be restarted.

DefaultRegistrationTTL

This REG_DWORD data item configures the default TTL to DNS in the header of any outgoing dynamic updates. TTLs specified in a packet header define how long a packet can be outstanding on the network until it is considered invalid. Supported values are 0 – 0xFFFFFFFF, which represents the TTL in seconds. Unless you add this data item, the default TCP/IP TTL is used for all packet headers, which is 0x4B0, or 20 minutes.

Hostname

This REG_SZ value represents the host name of the device.

NameServer

This REG_SZ item contains a list of DNS servers configured for this adapter to use for host name resolution.

NV Domain

This REG_SZ item holds changes made to the primary DNS suffix setting located in the system properties. Settings established in the system properties are written to **NV Domain** immediately. Once the system is rebooted, values here are copied to **Domain**, which is then used until any configuration changes occur again. Modifying this item doesn't require the service to be restarted.

SearchList

This REG_SZ data item holds a list of DNS domain suffixes that should be appended to an unqualified name query. This information can also be configured in the Advanced DNS properties of the TCP/IP protocol bound to the NIC. Modifying this item doesn't require the service to be restarted.

UpdateSecurityLevel

This REG_DWORD data item establishes the level, if any, of secure updates to DNS supported by the registration process on the client. This item doesn't exist in the registry by default, but it supports the following values:

- 0 – Sends secure dynamic updates only if nonsecure updates are refused by DNS. This is the default behavior if this data item isn't present.
- 16 – Sends only nonsecure updates.
- 256 – Sends only secure updates.

The system default is the same as a value of 0.

UseDomainNameDevolution

Devolution is the process of removing the leftmost domain label of the DNS suffix on a query that couldn't be resolved, in the hope of making the query more general and easier to resolve. For example, if a query failed to find resource devicea.sub1.sub2.domain.com, devolution would remove the leftmost portion of the DNS suffix, sub1, and submit a query for devicea.sub2.domain.com. This item isn't found in the registry by default, but DNS clients behave as if this REG_DWORD item exists and is set to 1, which enables devolution. This item also supports a value of 0, which disables devolution. You can also change the state of devolution by clearing the Append Parent Suffixes Of The Primary DNS Suffix check box found on the DNS tab of TCP/IP's Properties dialog box. Modifying this item doesn't require the service to be restarted.

HKLM\System\CurrentControlSet\Services\Tcpip\ Parameters\Interfaces\<InterfaceName>

This subkey holds configuration data specific to its TCP/IP communications interface. A subkey exists for each interface name.

DhcpDomain

This REG_SZ item specifies the domain name associated with the interface that is configured by DHCP. If both this item and the **Domain** item are present, **Domain** takes precedence.

DhcpNameServer

This REG_SZ item stores a list of IP addresses of DNS servers that have been provided to the interface by DHCP. If both this item and the **NameServer** item are present, **NameServer** takes precedence.

DisableDynamicUpdate

This REG_DWORD data item specifies whether DNS dynamic update registration is enabled or disabled for this interface. A value of 0 enables dynamic updates. A value of 1 disables dynamic updates. This data item isn't present in the registry by default, but the system behaves as if the value were set to 0. Because dynamic updates must be either disabled or enabled on both the system and interface level, this item is interdependent on the HKLM\ System\CurrentControlSet\Servivices\Tcpip\Parameters\DisableDynamicUpdate data item.

Domain

This REG_SZ item specifies the domain name associated with the interface that is configured by the user via the GUI. If both this item and the **DhcpDomain** item are present, this takes precedence.

EnableAdapterDomainNameRegistration

This REG_DWORD item specifies whether the NIC registers its configured domain name with DNS dynamically. A value of 0 disables dynamic updates. A value of 1 enables dynamic updates. This item doesn't exist in the registry unless you add it. The default system behavior is the same as a value of 0.

NameServer

This REG_SZ item stores a list of IP addresses of the DNS servers manually configured on the interface. This is what is modified when you add or remove DNS servers from the TCP/IP configuration of your NIC in the GUI. If this item and the **DhcpNameServer** item are present, this value takes precedence. Modifying this item doesn't require the service to be restarted.

NetBIOS and WINS Registry Settings

In this section, I'll go over the registry settings that affect the configuration and behavior of NetBIOS and WINS in your Windows 2000 system.

HKLM\System\CurrentControlSet\Services\Netbt\ Parameters

The configuration settings for NetBT are related to and also affect TCP/IP. The sections that follow cover some of the NetBIOS/WINS settings found in this subkey.

BcastNameQueryCount

By default, a NetBIOS client broadcasts name queries three times before determining that the name isn't found or isn't valid on the local segment. You can change this behavior by modifying this REG_DWORD item to a hex number between 1 and 0xFFFF, which represents the number of tries before a failure is issued. Modifying this item doesn't require the service to be restarted.

BcastQueryTimeout

This REG_DWORD item dictates how long the client will wait after issuing a broadcast name query before broadcasting another query. Supported values are 100–0xFFFFFFFF, which represents the number of milliseconds defining the interval. The default value is 750 milliseconds. Modifying this item doesn't require the service to be restarted.

BroadcastAddress

You can add this REG_DWORD item to the registry to force a NetBIOS client to use a defined address for all broadcast packets. Supported values are 0–0xFFFFFFFF, which represents in hex the address to be used for all broadcast transmissions. Modifying this item doesn't require the service to be restarted.

CacheTimeout

This REG_DWORD item determines how long nonstatic entries remain in the NetBIOS cache before being considered stale (and ultimately being removed). You can change the default value of 600,000 milliseconds (10 minutes) by modifying the value of this item to a hex number between 60000 and 0xFFFFFFFF. Modifying this item doesn't require the service to be restarted.

DhcpNodeType

This REG_SZ item stores the NetBIOS node type provided to the client from a DHCP server. If the **NodeType** item exists in the registry with a valid value, it supercedes any value defined here.

DhcpScopeId

This REG_DWORD item stores the NetBIOS scope name given to the WINS client by the DHCP server. If both this item and the **ScopeId** item exist, **ScopeId** takes precedence.

EnableDns

This REG_DWORD item specifies that NetBIOS name requests are to be sent to DNS if they aren't resolvable via other NetBIOS methods. Supported values are 0, which prevents DNS queries for NetBIOS names, and 1, which allows DNS queries. The default value is 0.

EnableLmhosts

This REG_DWORD item enables the LMHOSTS file to be parsed for NetBIOS names. Supported values are 0 and 1. A value of 0 allows NetBT to ignore the LMHOSTS file. A value of 1 causes NetBT to parse the LMHOSTS file. The default value for WINS clients is 1. Modifying this item doesn't require the service to be restarted.

EnableProxy

This REG_DWORD item determines whether the device acts as a WINS Proxy. Supported values are 0, which disables the WINS Proxy service, and 1, which enables the WINS Proxy. The default value on all WINS clients is 0.

EnableProxyRegCheck

This REG_DWORD data item specifies whether a WINS Proxy sends negative responses to broadcast clients that attempt to register a name that is already in use (or are in the cache of the WINS Proxy but with another address). Supported values are 0, which disables this feature, and 1, which enables this feature. The default value is 0. Use of this item is supported only on devices configured as WINS Proxies. Modifying this item doesn't require the service to be restarted.

InitialRefreshT.O.

This REG_DWORD item specifies the TTL that NetBIOS will use for all registered names before a TTL is sent back to the client as part of the successful registration packet from the WINS server. Supported values are 960000–0xFFFFFFF, specifying the TTL in milliseconds. This item doesn't exist in the registry by default, so until it is created and the value is modified, the NetBIOS client behaves as if the value were 960,000 milliseconds (16 minutes).

LmhostsTimeout

This REG_DWORD item specifies the timeout for NetBIOS queries that have been handed to either the LMHOSTS file or DNS for resolution. If a response isn't received within the specified time, an error is issued to the requestor. Supported values are 100–0xFFFFFFFF, and the measurement is milliseconds. This item isn't in the registry unless you add it. The system default behavior is 6 seconds.

MaxDgramBuffering

This REG_DWORD item specifies the maximum amount of memory NetBIOS will reserve to keep track of packets that are outstanding on the network. After this number is exceeded, no other packets are sent until space is available. Supported values are 0–0xFFFFFFFF, which represents the kilobytes of committed memory. This item doesn't appear in the registry by default, and the system default is 0x20000 (128 KB).

NameServerPort

This REG_DWORD value defines the UDP port that the client uses to send WINS traffic. The value can be in the range of 0–0xFFFF, which represents the port number in hex. The default value is 0x89 (UDP port 89).

NameSrvQueryCount

This REG_DWORD item determines how many times a query is sent to a single WINS server without receiving a response. The default value is 3, and you can modify the value within the range of 0–0xFFF.

NameSrvQueryTimeout

This REG_DWORD item defines in hex the interval between name queries to the same name server for the same name. The default value is 1500 milliseconds, but it can be changed to any value between 100 and 0xFFFFFFFF.

NbProvider

This REG_SZ item defines which network provider is used for RPC communications related to WINS. By default, the value is tcp, which defines TCP/IP as the provider. The only supported value for this item is tcp.

WARNING: The NbProvider registry item should never be modified.

NodeType

This REG_DWORD item specifies the type of NetBIOS Node for which this client is configured. The following values are supported:

 ◈ 1 – B-Node.

 ◈ 2 – P-Node.

 ◈ 4 – M-Node.

 ◈ 8 – H-Node.

This registry entry doesn't appear by default. In normal situations, the node type is determined by your WINS configuration. If you have at least one WINS server configured, the default node type is H. If you have no WINS servers configured, your node type is B. If both this item and the **DhcpNodeType** item appear, this item overrides the value defined in **DhcpNodeType**.

RandomAdapter

This REG_DWORD item determines which IP address is returned in a query response client when more than one IP address exists on the WINS server. By default, NetBT randomly selects an address to package in the response to the client. You can change that behavior by setting this value to 0, which causes the WINS server to return only the IP address of the NIC that received the query. A value of 1 allows NetBT to randomly select an address. This item doesn't exist in the registry unless you add it. This item is valid only on multihomed WINS servers.

RefreshOpCode

This REG_DWORD item defines which NetBIOS opcode is used in name refresh packets. Supported values are 8 and 9 (representing the opcode), and the system default for any WINS client is 8. This item doesn't exist in the registry unless you add it.

SessionKeepAlive

This REG_DWORD item determines the interval between NetBIOS session keepalive messages. The default value is 3,600,000 milliseconds (1 hour), but you can enter any value between 60,000 and 0xFFFFFFFF. Modifying this item doesn't require the service to be restarted.

SingleResponse

By default, in response to a request from a WINS client, a multihomed WINS server returns all IP addresses bound to the NIC that is responding to the name query. By setting this REG_DWORD item's value to 1, a multihomed WINS server will return only one IP address to the client in a query response. The default behavior is to act as if this value is 0. This item doesn't exist in the registry unless you add it.

Size/Small/Medium/Large

This goofily named REG_DWORD entry allows you to modify the size of the NetBIOS cache. Supported values are these:

- ❖ **1** – Small: 16 kb (This is the default value.)
- ❖ **2** – Medium: 128 kb
- ❖ **3** – Large: 256 kb

WinsDownTimeout

This REG_DWORD item defines how long the NetBIOS client waits before trying to contact WINS again after a WINS failure. Supported values in hex are a range of 1000–0xFFFFFFFF. The value is for milliseconds. This item doesn't appear in the registry unless you add it, and the system default is 15 seconds.

HKLM\System\CurrentControlSet\Netbt\Parameters\ Interfaces\Tcpip_ <ID of Adapter>

This registry subkey exists for each adapter in the device. The following sections cover the data items in these subkeys that relate to NetBIOS configuration on an individual adapter basis.

DhcpNameServer

This REG_SZ item stores the IP address of the primary WINS server that is given to the client by DHCP. If this item and the **NameServerList** item are present, this item is ignored.

NameServerList

This REG_MULTI_SZ item contains the IP address of the WINS servers that have been configured on the WINS client. If this item and the **DhcpNameServer** item are both present on a system, this item will supercede any value defined in **DhcpNameServer**.

NetbiosOptions

This REG_DWORD item sets the enabled and disabled state of NetBIOS on a particular adapter. Supported values are 1, which enables NetBIOS, and 2, which disables NetBIOS. The default value for this item is 1.

ScopeId

This REG_SZ item defines the NetBIOS scope name for the NetBIOS client. The value is a character string that represents the name of the NetBIOS scope. The default value is null.

HKLM\System\CurrentControlSet\Services\ RemoteAccess\Parameters\Ip

This subkey holds RAS parameters, and the data items that pertain to WINS are covered in the following sections.

WINSNameServer

This REG_SZ item holds the IP address of the primary WINS server that is provided to RAS clients when they log on to the RAS server. This item doesn't exist in the registry unless you add it. The system default is to provide RAS clients with the same WINS servers that the RAS server is configured to use.

WINSNameServerBackup

This REG_SZ item holds the IP address of the secondary WINS server that is provided to RAS clients when they log on to the RAS server. This item doesn't exist in the registry unless you add it. The system default is to provide RAS clients with the same secondary WINS servers that the RAS server is configured to use.

HKLM\System\CurrentControlSet\Services\WINS\ Parameters

This subkey holds general configuration data for WINS.

BackupDirPath

This REG_SZ item houses the path to the directory that WINS uses to back up its database. Because backup isn't established by default, there is no default value for this item.

BurstHandling

This REG_DWORD item specifies whether the WINS server is enabled for burst handling. A value of 0 disables burst handling. A value of 1 enables burst handling. This entry is valid only on WINS servers and has a default value of 0. Modifying this item doesn't require a restart of the service for the change to take effect.

DataFiles

This REG_SZ item holds the path that is used by the **DoStaticDataInit** item to load the static database on the WINS server. This item doesn't appear by default, so if you want this functionality, you'll need to add it.

DbFileNm

This REG_EXPAND_SZ item stores the path to the WINS database file. The default value is **%SystemRoot%\System32\Wins\Wins.mdb**.

DoBackupOnTerm

Setting this REG_DWORD data item to 1 forces the WINS service to back up the WINS database every time the service gracefully stops. The default value, 0, indicates that the service doesn't initiate a backup upon service stop.

DoStaticDataInit

This REG_DWORD specifies whether the WINS server initializes the WINS static database defined in the HKLM\System\CurrentControlSet\Services\WINS\Parameters or the **DataFiles** item in HKLM\System\CurrentControlSet\Services\WINS\Parameters. A value of 0, which is the default, specifies that WINS shouldn't initialize the database. A value of 1 specifies that the WINS server should initialize the database.

InitTimePause

This REG_DWORD item allows you to have your WINS server start in a paused state until the first replication event has completed. In a paused state, WINS won't accept any WINS traffic other than that related to replication. Supported values are 0, which indicates that WINS will start normally, and 1, which starts WINS in a paused state. The default value for this item is 0. If you want to change the value to 1, you must perform either of the following tasks:

❖ Set the value of **InitTimeReplication** (located in both the HKLM\System\CurrentControlSet\Services\WINS\Parameters\Pull and HKLM\System\CurrentControlSet\Services\WINS\Parameters\Pull keys) to force the WINS server to attempt to replicate upon startup.

❖ Remove all values from **InitTimeReplication**, which has the same effect as a value of 1.

LogDetailedEvents

This REG_DWORD item specifies the logging level of the WINS service to the Event Log. A value of 0 specifies only the logging of errors. A value of 1 specifies the logging of errors, warnings, and informational messages. The default value is 1. This can also be configured by selecting the Log Detailed Events to the Windows Event Log check box in the advanced properties of the WINS server.

LogFilePath

This REG_EXPAND_SZ item specifies the location of the WINS log files used to track changes to the WINS database. The default value is **%SystemRoot%\System32\Wins**.

LoggingOn

This REG_DWORD item specifies whether all changes to the WINS database are recorded in a log file that can be used for disaster recovery purposes. By default, the value of this item is 1, which allows changes to be written to the Jet.log file. You can also configure this item to use a value of 0, which will prevent the changes from being recorded in a log file.

McastIntvl

This REG_DWORD data item configures the interval between multicast announcements sent by the WINS server. The default value for this item is 2400 seconds. Supported values are the following:

- **0x960–0xFFFFFFFE** – A hex interval of seconds between multicast messages.
- **0xFFFFFFFF** – WINS won't send any multicast messages.

McastTtl

This REG_DWORD item defines the maximum number of hops that a WINS multicast packet can transverse. Supported values are 1–32 hops. This behavior can also be modified through the advanced properties of the Replication Partners object in the WINS MMC. The default value is 2 when multicast support is enabled.

MigrateOn

By default, in Windows 2000, if a dynamic registration request is received for a name that is already in use by a static entry, the name is overwritten by the dynamic registration. This behavior is configured through the use of this REG_DWORD item that supports values of 0 and 1. A value of 0, which is the default, permits dynamic registration to overwrite static entries. A value of 1 defends static records and will reject any dynamic registrations for the name in use by the static record. You can also configure this behavior by setting the Overwrite Unique Static Mappings At This Server (Migrate On) option in the properties of the Replication Partners object.

NoOfWorkThreads

Worker threads are used to reserve and complete single tasks for a service or an application. By default, the number of worker threads is equal to the number of the processors in the WINS server. This can be modified by adding this REG_DWORD item to the registry and assigning it a value between 1 and 40. Changes to this value take effect immediately and don't require a WINS service restart.

PersonaNonGrata

This REG_MULTI_SZ item contains a list of WINS servers whose records should be excluded from the local replica copy of the WINS database. Modifying this entry has the same effect as defining a server in the Block Records for These Owners screen. Any change to this value is reflected on the WINS server immediately.

PriorityClassHigh

This handy REG_DWORD item allows you to set the scheduling priority of the WINS server service to either Normal or High, which can be useful if you're running a multirole WINS device. This item supports the following values:

- ❖ 0 – WINS will run with a Normal priority, which will make it subject to be bumped by a process or service that has a priority of High, causing WINS to wait for processor face time.

- ❖ 1 – WINS runs in a High priority, which can cause other processes or services with a lower priority to be bumped.

Randomize1cList

This REG_DWORD item allows your WINS server to randomly send the IP addresses listed in the domain record (1CH) to clients resolving a domain name. This serves as a quasi-load-balancing solution for domain controllers. A value of 0, or a nonpresent value, disables this feature. A value of 1 enables it. By default, this item doesn't appear in the registry, and the default behavior of the WINS server is not to use randomization.

RefreshInterval

This REG_DWORD item specifies how often a client must refresh its registered device names in WINS. Supported values are the range of 0x960–0x7FFFFFFF, which represents the total number of seconds after a record is marked extinct that it is removed from the database. The default value is 0x7E900, or six days, and it can be modified either through the registry or through the Renew Interval field in the WINS MMC. Although WINS clients use this value, it's valid only on WINS servers.

RplOnlyWCnfPnrs

Setting this REG_DWORD item to 1 configures the WINS server to replicate contents with partners that have been defined only on the local WINS server. A value of 0 allows any WINS server to replicate contents to and from the WINS server.

TombstoneInterval

This REG_DWORD item sets the interval at which entries that have a state of released are changed to an extinct state. Supported values are 0x960–0x7FFFFFFF, which represents the number of seconds that must expire before the record's state changes. The default value is 0x54600, or four days. You can also adjust this value by using the Extinction Interval field in the WINS MMC. Because the WINS MMC has some math-related logic built into it that warns you if you adjust any value that will affect or nullify another WINS client update value, I recommend using the MMC to change this value.

TombstoneTimeout

This REG_DWORD item houses the same value entered in the Extinction TimeOut field in the WINS MMC. Because the WINS MMC has some math-related logic built into it that will warn you if you adjust any value that will affect or nullify another value, I recommend using it to change this value. Supported values are 0x960–0x7FFFFFFF, which represents the total number of seconds after a record is marked extinct that it's removed from the database. The default value is 0x7E900, or six days.

UseRplPnrs

During a verification of entries in WINS, a WINS server, by default, attempts to contact the owner of the record that needs to be verified to determine whether the record is still valid. You can set the behavior in the WINS MMC via either the Owner Servers or the Randomly Selected Partners options of a WINS server's Database Verification screen. Or you can add this REG_DWORD data item to the registry. Supported values are the following:

❖   0 – WINS contacts only the owner of the stale record.

❖   1 – WINS contacts a replication partner to verify that the record is still valid. This option provides the greatest performance but can cause inaccurate data. If you're concerned about consistency, use value 0.

UseSelfFndPnrs

This REG_DWORD item specifies whether the WINS server detects or ignores multicasts from another WINS server. A value of 0 (the default) means that multicast support in WINS is turned off. A value of 1 means the WINS server detects multicasts from other WINS servers. This behavior can also be modified through the advanced properties of the Replication Partners object in the WINS MMC.

VerifyInterval

This REG_DWORD item specifies how long a record belonging to another WINS server can fail to be updated on the local WINS server before the record's owner to verify that the record is still valid. This behavior can be modified through the Verification Interval field in the WINS MMC or by changing the value of this item to any hex number between 0x1FA400 and 0x7FFFFFFF. The value represents the number of seconds before verification occurs. The default value is 0x1FA400, or 24 days. Because the WINS MMC has some math-related logic built into it that will warn you if you adjust any value that will affect or nullify another value, I recommend using it to change this value.

NOTE: If the value is not equal to at least three times the amount of the **TombstoneInterval** item, then it is ignored and the value of **TombstoneInterval** is tripled and used instead.

VersCounterStartVal_HighWord

This REG_DWORD item stores a hex number that identifies the high DWORD value of the most recent version ID used in the WINS database.

VersCounterStartVal_LowWord

This REG_DWORD item stores a hex number that identifies the low DWORD value of the most recent version ID used in the WINS database.

HKLM\CurrentControlSet\Services\WINS\Parameters\ ConsistencyCheck

This subkey is optional, and you can add it to the registry to specify that WINS should perform periodic database consistency checks.

MaxRecsAtATime

This REG_DWORD value sets how many records are sent to either the owner or replication partner in a given verification interval. This value is valid only if verification has been established on the WINS servers. Supported values begin at 1000, and there's no limit. The default value, 30,000, sends 30,000 records per verification cycle. This item doesn't appear in the registry by default, so if you want any value other than 30,000, you must add it. This item is also supported only on WINS servers.

SpTime

This REG_SZ item stores a time format value, which indicates at what time of the day the WINS consistency check (i.e., verification) occurs after the WINS service has been started. Any subsequent consistency checks will be spawned by the value located in the **TimeInterval** data item. The default value when consistency checking has been enabled is 2:00 A.M.

TimeInterval

This REG_DWORD item, which doesn't exist in the registry by default, determines how often WINS performs a consistency check after the value in the **SpTime** has expired. The value in hex is the number of seconds between consistency checks. Valid values are 0x5460 –0xFFFFFFFF, and the default value is 0x15180, or 86,400 seconds (one day).

HKLM\System\CurrentControlSet\Services\WINS\ Partners\Pull

This subkey holds entries that determine when and how replicas are pulled from another WINS server.

CommRetryCount

WINS servers attempt to replicate contents from a pull partner three times before issuing an error. The number of retries can be changed by either modifying the Number Of Retries box in the Replication Partners object's properties, or by modifying this REG_DWORD value. Supported values are 0–999.

InitTimeReplication

This REG_DWORD value determines when the WINS server will initiate pull replication from partners. A value of 0 configures the WINS server to pull contents as often as the value for the **TimeInterval** item located in HKLM\System\CurrentControlSet\Services\ WINS\Pull*IP Address of Pull Partner>*. A value of 1 tells the WINS server to replicate when the WINS service begins or when there is a change to the replication partner.

HKLM\System\CurrentControlSet\Services\WINS\ Partners\Pull\<IP Address of Pull Partner>

The Pull subkey contains a subkey for each pull partner, using the IP address of each partner.

MemberPrecedence

This REG_DWORD item determines whether the addresses in an Internet group from a WINS partner are assigned a high or low precedence in the domain group record. Modifying this value to 0 assigns this partner a lower priority, while changing the value to 1 assigns the partner a higher priority. This item serves as a quasi-load-balancing and costing mechanism for WINS clients by making a particular WINS server seem closer or farther from the client.

SpTime

This REG_SZ item specifies the time at which the WINS service should initiate its first pull replication with a partner after the WINS service has been started. Thereafter, pull replication occurs as defined in the value of the **TimeInterval** data item. The format for the value of this item is hh:mm:ss.

TimeInterval

This REG_DWORD item sets the pull replication schedule with the partner. Supported values are as follows:

- 0–Database isn't replicated.
- 0x258–0xFFFFFFFF – Interval in seconds between pull replication.

The default value for this item is 0xt08, or 30 minutes.

HKLM\System\CurrentControlSet\Services\WINS\ Partners\Push

The Push subkey contains data items that specify when and how the WINS server sends update notification messages to its push partners.

InitTimeReplication

This REG_DWORD value determines when the WINS server will push update partners by sending an update notification. A value of 0 prevents the WINS server from sending updates to push partners. A value of 1 enables the sending of updates.

PropNetUpdNtf

This REG_DWORD item determines whether the WINS server propagates push notifications received from other push partners to its pull partners. A value of 0 indicates that push notification isn't forwarded to pull partners. A value of 1 sends push notification messages to pull partners. Changing this value doesn't require WINS to be restarted.

RplonAddressChg

This REG_DWORD item determines whether the WINS server sends an update notification to a push replication partner when only the address of a mapping changes. A value of 0 (the default) indicates that notification won't be sent when an address changes, but rather when the version ID for the record changes. A value of 1 specifies that the server will send updates to push partners when the address of an entry changes. This can also be set via the When Address Changes check box in the Properties dialog box of the Replication Partners object in the WINS MMC.

HKLM\System\CurrentControlSet\Services\WINS\ Partners\Push\<IP Address of Push Partner>

A subkey exists for each push partner, using the IP address as the subkey name.

NetBIOSName

This REG_SZ item contains the NetBIOS name of the WINS server that has been defined as a push partner.

OnlyDynRecs

This REG_DWORD item lets you specify which types of records are pushed to other servers for replication. Your choices are to either receive both static and dynamic registrations, or to receive only the dynamic registrations. A value of 0 sends both static and dynamic records to partners and is the default behavior of WINS. A value of 1 replicates only dynamic records.

UpdateCount

This REG_DWORD item determines the number of changes to the version ID that must occur before a push notification is sent to the partner. Supported values are any hex number in the range of 0x14–0x8FFFFF. This item holds an invalid value until you configure your push partners.

Appendix B

Useful DNS RFCs

In the past, I've found it difficult to find a complete listing of all DNS-related RFCs. That may be the greatest understatement of all time. Finding all RFCs that concern any particular technology is painful because no RFC or standard exists on how to index and/or name RFCs. Currently, all RFCs are indexed by their title or number. This means that to effectively search through the indexes, you need to search on not only every possible acronym that could be used (DNS, DDNS, etc.), but also the actual name (Domain Name System, Dynamic Domain Name System, etc.), in addition to any relevant components that are a part of the technology (IXFR, serial number arithmetic, host names, etc.). Maybe I should write an RFC on RFC indexing. Hmmm.

RFCs are essential for understanding the technology at hand, and they're also useful when you're evaluating different solutions that are proposed by software vendors. It is always good to know where a technology or product is headed in the future when you're designing in the present.

This appendix contains a list of all RFCs that pertain to DNS, as of the writing of this book. I've taken the RFCs that I used for the book and augmented them with the other existing RFCs about DNS to compile this list. Just this list alone is worth the cost of admission.

Before we move on to the RFCs, it's important to know the types of RFC statuses to help you figure out where a particular technology is in its life cycle.

- ❖ **Standard Protocol** – Technology outlined here contains the Internet Engineering Steering Group (IESG) stamp of approval. If the technology in the RFC will be implemented, it must be implemented exactly as dictated in the RFC. Standard Protocols also are assigned a Standard Number by combining a prefix of *STD* and four numeric characters that are incremented after assignment (STD0001, STD0002, etc.). This number is a cross-reference to a Standards Document.

- ❖ **Draft Standard Protocol** – This is a protocol that might already be in implementation but has yet to receive approval from IESG. A status of Draft indicates that the IESG is currently considering a Standard status for the RFC.

- ❖ **Proposed Standard Protocol** – This standard outlines technology that is in implementation but will most likely be modified before it is given a Draft or Standard status.

- ❖ **Experimental Protocol** – The technology detailed here is not for general use and can cause problems or instabilities if used.

- ❖ **Informational Protocol** –Used to publish proprietary specifications to the Internet community for information purposes only. An Informational Protocol might be assigned an Informational Number by combining a prefix of *FYI* and four numeric characters that are incremented after assignment (FYI0001, FYI0002, etc.). This number cross-references an Informational Document.

❖ **Historical Protocol** – An older, preexisting document that might be useful is given this state. No new RFCs are published as historical.

❖ **Unknown** – This status is given to RFCs that don't conform to one of the previous statuses. Although this isn't explicitly stated anywhere, the Unknown status seems to be given to older RFCs before the forum was standardized.

❖ **Best Current Practice** – This status is used to provide approved best practices for implementation of the technology. Best Current Practice Protocols may be assigned an Informational Number by combining a prefix of *BCP* and four numeric characters that are incremented after assignment (BCP0001, BCP0002, etc.). This number cross-references a Best Current Practice Document.

An RFC can also have one of five different state designations. The following list provides information about those State designations:

❖ **Required Protocol** – This technology is a requirement for every IP system.

❖ **Recommended Protocol** – Information contained in this document is highly recommended for implementation, but it won't cause any great harm if it's not implemented.

❖ **Elective Protocol** – This technology completely optional.

❖ **Limited Use Protocol** – This technology should be implemented only on a narrow base of systems that require the technology.

❖ **Not Recommended Protocol** – This protocol should be removed from your system if implemented in the past. This state also indicates that this RFC shouldn't be implemented on any new systems.

You can obtain a complete list of all RFCs at http://www.ietf.org/rfc. Be warned, it can get ugly because thousands and thousands of RFCs exist. Finding what you need can be difficult.

The list in this appendix contains the RFC number, title, a summary, status, and publication date, as well as any information about any RFCs that makes another RFC obsolete.

❖ 805 *Computer Mail Meeting Notes:* Summarizes a meeting in early 1982 where the decision was made to move the existing mailbox format from *user@hostname* to *user@host.domain*. Status – Unknown; Publication Date – 1982.

❖ 811 *Hostnames Server:* Defines the host name server as a centralized service for host-name lookup. Status – Unknown; Publication Date – 1982; Obsoleted by RFC 953.

❖ 819 *The Domain Name Convention for Internet User Applications:* First RFC to talk about Internet namespaces becoming hieratical in nature and, as a result, proposes host name format and lookup to change from *name@host* to *name@domain.name*. Status – Unknown; Publication Date – 1982.

❖ 881 *The Domain Names Plan and Schedule:* Expands further on the change to a hieratical domain namespace and its effect on the Internet community. Status – Unknown; Publication Date – 1983; Updated by RFC 897.

❖ 882 *Domain Names: Concepts and Facilities:* Serves as an introduction to DNS and DNS concepts. Status – Unknown; Publication Date – 1983; Obsoleted by RFC 1034 and 1035; Updated RFC 973.

❖ 883 *Domain Names: Implementation Specification:* Provides a comprehensive view of DNS and DNS protocols. Status – Unknown; Publication Date – 1983; Obsoleted by RFC 1034 and 1035; Updated by RFC 973.

❖ 897 *Domain Name System Implementation Schedule:* Outlines the timeline for implementation of DNS throughout the Internet community. Status – Unknown; Publication Date – 1984; Updates RFC 881; Updated by RFC 921.

❖ 920 *Domain Requirements:* Details the process to implement a new domain on the Internet. Status – Unknown; Publication Date – 1984.

❖ 921 *Domain Name System Implementation Schedule:* Outlines the updated timeline for implementation of DNS throughout the Internet community. Status – Unknown; Publication Date – 1984; Updates RFC 897.

❖ 953 *Hostname Server:* Further defines the centrally provided Hostname server, but includes more detail on protocol and communication. Status – Historic; Publication Date – 1985; Obsoletes RFC 811.

❖ 973 *Domain System Changes and Observations:* Memo discussing updates to RFC 882 and 883, experiences of early adopters and stated problem areas. Status – Unknown; Publication Date – 1986; Obsoleted by RFC 1034 and 1035; Updates RFC 882 and 883.

❖ 974 *Mail Routing and the Domain Systems:* Explains how mail is routed between multiple domain names. Introduces concept and use of MX records. Status – Standard (STD0014); Publication Date – 1986.

❖ 1032 *Domain Administrators Guide:* Describes the registration process for new domains with the NIC and provides guidelines for implementation and administration in conjunction with RFC 920. Status – Unknown; Publication Date – 1987.

❖ 1033 *Domain Administrators Operations Guide:* Provides operations guidelines for DNS and domains. Knowledge of DNS is assumed. Status – Unknown; Publication Date – 1987.

❖ 1034 *Domain Names - Concepts and Facilities:* Serves as an introduction to DNS and DNS concepts. Status – Standard (STD0013); Publication Date – 1987; Obsoletes RFC 882, 883, and 973; Updated by RFC 1101, 1183, 1348, 1876, 1982, 2065, 2181, 2308, and 2535.

❖ 1035 *Domain Names - Implementation and Specification:* Provides a comprehensive view of DNS and DNS protocols. Status – Standard (STD0013); Publication Date – 1987; Obsoletes RFC 882, 883, and 973; Updated by RFC 1101, 1183, 1348, 1876, 1982, 1995, 1996, 2065, 2136, 2137, 2181, 2308, 2535, and 2845.

❖ 1101 *DNS Encoding of Network Names and Other Types:* Updates definition set for network names and their addition to DNS. Status – Unknown; Publication Date – 1989; Updates RFC 1034 and 1035.

❖ 1122 *Requirements for Internet Hosts - Communication Layers:* Supplements existing primary protocol standards as they relate to host configuration. It is meant to define the link, IP, and transport layers and be used in conjunction with RFC 1123. Status – Standard (STD003); Publication Date – 1989.

❖ 1123 *Requirements for Internet Hosts - Application and Support:* Compliments RFC 1122 by specifying the upper layers of the protocol stacks as it relates to the host configuration. Status – Standard (STD0003); Publication Date – 1989; Updates RFC 822; Updated by RFC 2181.

❖ 1178 *Choosing a Name for Your Computer:* Provides guidelines for device naming to conform to other DNS/host-related RFCs. Status – Informational (FYI0005); Publication Date – 1990.

❖ 1183 *New DNS RR Definitions:* Suggests the use of four new RRs in DNS and details their implementation. The four types are AFS Database Location (AFSDB), Responsible Person (RP), X25, and ISDN. Status – Experimental; Publication Date – 1990; Updates RFC 1034 and 1035.

◆ 1348 *DNS NSAP RRs:* Defines the format and use of the NSAP and NSAP-PTR RR. Status – Experimental; Publication Date – 1992; Obsoleted by RFC 1637; Updates RFC 1034 and 1035; Updated by RFC 163.

◆ 1383 *An Experiment in DNS Based IP Routing:* Specifies a potential solution to conventional network routing by the use of MX routing methods. Very interesting. Status – Experimental; Publication Date – 1992.

◆ 1386 *The US Domain:* Details the implementation and methodology used for the root-level US domain. Status – Informational; Publication Date – 1992; Obsoleted by 1480.

◆ 1401 *Correspondence Between the IAB and DISA on the use of DNS:* Contains three letters exchanged between the Internet Activities Board and the Defense Information System Agency about the use of DNS and the phasing out of Hosts.Txt. Status – Informational; Publication Date – 1993.

◆ 1464 *Using the Domain Name System to Store Arbitrary String Attributes:* Uses TXT record types to store arbitrary information in DNS. Status – Experimental; Publication Date – 1993.

◆ 1480 *The US Domain:* Provides an update regarding the U.S. domain implementation. Status – Informational; Publication Date – 1993; Obsoletes RFC 1386.

◆ 1535 *A Security Problem and Proposed Correction with Widely Deployed DNS Software:* Provides information about a security hole in the client resolver of many DNS implementations at the time of this RFC publication, along with a proposed solution. Status – Informational; Publication Date – 1993.

◆ 1536 *Common DNS Implementation Errors and Suggested Fixes:* Discusses some commonly seen design flaws and their potential fixes. Status – Informational; Publication Date – 1993.

◆ 1537 *Common DNS Data File Configuration Errors:* Discusses some commonly seen flaws in data contained in the DNS database. Also includes recommendations for resolution. Status – Informational; Publication Date – 1993; Obsoleted by RFC 1912.

◆ 1591 *Domain Name System Structure and Delegation:* Explains all aspects of Internet entities as they relate to DNS. Status – Informational; Publication Date – 1994.

❖ 1611 *DNS Server MIB Extensions:* Defines the use of Management Information Bases (MIBs) on DNS servers to be used in a Simple Network Management Protocol (SNMP) architecture for monitoring purposes. Status – Proposed Standard; Publication Date – 1994.

❖ 1612 *DNS Resolver MIB Extensions:* Defines the use of MIBs on DNS Resolver to be used in an SNMP architecture for monitoring purposes. Status – Proposed Standard; Publication Date – 1994.

❖ 1637 *DNS NSAP Resource Records:* Defines the format and use of the NSAP and NSAP-PTR RR. Status – Experimental; Publication Date – 1994; Obsoletes RFC 1348; Obsoleted by RFC 1706; Updates 1348.

❖ 1664 *Using the Internet DNS to Distribute RFC1327 Mail Address Mapping Tables:* Provides information on using DNS to store mapping information needed by e-mail gateways and other services that need to map domain names into X.400 names, or vice versa. Status – Experimental; Publication Date – 1994; Obsoleted by RFC 2163.

❖ 1706 *DNS NSAP Resource Records:* Updates the use of NSAP RR in DNS. Status – Informational; Publication Date – 1994; Obsoletes RFC 1637.

❖ 1712 *DNS Encoding of Geographical Location:* Defines the use of a GPOS RR that can define the geographical location of an object within the DNS database. Details all aspects of its implementation. Status – Experimental; Publication Date – 1994.

❖ 1713 *Tools for DNS debugging:* This document shows the use of some common but outdated DNS tools. Status – Informational (FYI0027); Publication Date – 1994.

❖ 1794 *DNS Support for Load Balancing:* Discusses in broad terms ways of implementing load balancing for hosts whose records are in DNS. Status – Informational; Publication Date – 1995.

❖ 1811 *U.S. Government Internet Domain Names:* Provides registration policies for the root-level .gov domain. Status – Informational; Publication Date – 1995; Obsoleted by RFC 1816.

❖ 1816 *U.S. Government Internet Domain Names:* Provides registration policies for the root-level .gov domain. Status – Informational; Publication Date – 1995; Obsoleted by RFC 2146.

❖ 1876 *A Means for Expressing Location Information in the Domain Name System:* Another attempt to associate location information with objects in the DNS database. This time the use of an RR named LOC is defined. Status – Experimental; Publication Date – 1996; Updates RFC 1034 and 1035.

❖ 1884 *IP Version 6 Addressing Architecture:* Mostly addresses IP v6 issues but also talks about DNS issues related to its implementation. Status – Historic; Publication Date – 1995; Obsoleted by RFC 2373.

❖ 1886 *DNS Extensions to Support IP Version 6:* Talks more specifically about DNS's support for IP v6. Status – Proposed Standard; Publication Date – 1995.

❖ 1912 *Common DNS Operational and Configuration Errors:* Discusses some commonly seen design flaws and their potential fixes. Status – Informational; Publication Date – 1996; Obsoletes RFC 1537.

❖ 1956 *Registration in the MIL Domain:* Describes the policy for registering a subdomain in the root-level .mil domain. Status – Informational; Publication Date – 1996.

❖ 1982 *Serial Number Arithmetic:* Defines the way serial numbers are generated for DNS-related functions. Status – Proposed Standard; Publication Date – 1996; Updates RFC 1034 and 1035.

❖ 1995 *Incremental Zone Transfer in DNS:* Defines the what, where, when, and how of IXFR zone transfers. Status – Proposed Standard; Publication Date – 1996; Updates RFC 1035.

❖ 1996 *A Mechanism for Prompt Notification of Zone Changes (DNS NOTIFY):* Details the DNS UPDATE communications that occur to notify secondary servers of changes on the primary server. Status – Proposed Standard; Publication Date – 1996; Updates RFC 1035.

❖ 2010 *Operational Criteria for Root Name Servers:* Specifies requirements of root name servers including hardware, software, network connectivity, etc. Status – Informational; Publication Date – 1996; Obsoleted by RFC 2870.

❖ 2052 *A DNS RR for Specifying the Location Services (DNS SRV):* Provides the initial definition of SRV records, which enables lookup of services provided by a host. Status – Experimental; Publication Date – 1996; Obsoleted by RFC 2782.

❖ 2053 *The AM (Armenia) Domain:* Provides an abstract of the .am root-level domain. Status – Informational; Publication Date – 1996.

✦ 2065 *Domain Name System Security Extensions:* Describes extension to support digital signatures, certificates, and other cryptographic methods to security-aware clients. Status – Proposed Standard; Publication Date – 1997; Obsoleted by RFC 2535; Updates RFC 1034 and 1035.

✦ 2136 *Dynamic Updates in the Domain Name System (DNS UPDATE):* The RFC that defines the process and functions that make up DDNS. Status – Proposed Standard; Publication Date – 1997; Updates RFC 1035.

✦ 2137 *Secure Domain Name System Dynamic Update:* Addresses the lack of security in RFC 2136. Calls for the securing of updates through the use of digital signatures. Status – Proposed Standard; Publication Date – 1997; Updates RFC 1035.

✦ 2142 *Mailbox Names for Common Services, Notes and Functions:* Promotes the use of Internet mailboxes for every function of an organization. Status – Proposed Standard; Publication Date – 1997.

✦ 2146 *U.S. Government Internet Domain Names:* Provides further clarification to RFC 1816. Status – Informational; Publication Date – 1997; Obsoletes RFC 1816.

✦ 2163 *Using the Internet DNS to Distribute MIXER Conformant Global Address Mapping (MCGAM):* Provides information on using DNS to store mapping information needed by e-mail gateways and other services that need to map domain names into X.400 names, or vice versa. Status – Proposed Standard; Publication Date – 1998; Obsoletes RFC 1664.

✦ 2168 *Resolution of Uniform Resource Identifiers using the Domain Name System:* Defines a new RR type called Naming Authority Pointer (NAPTR), which is used to map Uniform Resource Identifiers (URI) to domain names. Status – Experimental; Publication Date – 1997; Updated by RFC 2915.

✦ 2181 *Clarification to the DNS Specification:* Fills in some gaps in the original DNS specifications. Status – Proposed Standard; Publication Date – 1997; Updates RFC 1034, 1035, and 1123; Updated by RFC 2535.

✦ 2182 *Selection and Operation of Secondary DNS Servers:* Discusses issues related to design and implementation of secondary name servers. Topics include placement, load balancing, etc. Status – Best Current Practice (BCP0016); Publication Date – 1997.

✦ 2219 *Use of DNS Aliases for Network Services:* Talks about the different methods to alias devices and services. Formally defines CNAME. Status – Best Current Practice (BCP0017); Publication Date – 1997.

- ❖ 2230 *Key Exchange Delegation Record for the DNS:* Defines a KX RR for IPSec to be used when one host is willing to act as a Key Exchanger for another host. Status – Informational; Publication Date – 1997.

- ❖ 2240 *A Legal Basis for Domain Name Allocation:* Deals with the problem of multiple entities attempting to use the same domain names to define their space on the Internet. Intended to propose a consensus to deal with issues like cyber-squatters. Status – Informational; Publication Date – 1997; Obsoleted by 2352.

- ❖ 2247 *Using Domains in LDAP/X.500 Distinguished Names:* Ties in LDAP names with DNS name registration. Useful for those who are going to implement Active Directory. Status – Proposed Standard; Publication Date – 1998.

- ❖ 2307 *An Approach for Using LDAP as a Network Information Service:* Discusses mapping entries related to TCP/IP and UNIX systems into X.500, which is accessible via LDAP, rather than using DNS. Status – Experimental; Publication Date – 1998.

- ❖ 2308 *Negative Caching of DNS Queries (DNS NCACHE):* Extends negative caching in RFC 1034 to allow for a name server to hand NCACHE responses to clients. Status – Proposed Standard; Publication Date – 1998; Updates RFC 1034 and 1035.

- ❖ 2317 *Classless IN-ADDR.ARPA delegation:* Describes how to create IN-ADDR.ARPA mappings for non-octet boundary subnets. Status – Best Current Practice (BCP0020); Publication Date – 1998.

- ❖ 2345 *Domain Names and Company Name Retrieval:* Defines a mapping service based on the tool WHOIS for company-name-to-URL resolution. Status – Experimental; Publication Date – 1998.

- ❖ 2352 *A Convention for Using Legal Names as Domain Names:* Addresses the potential solution to cyber-squatters by using a company's legal name as its domain name. Status – Informational; Publication Date – 1998; Obsoletes RFC 2240.

- ❖ 2373 *IP Version 6 Addressing Architecture:* Mostly addresses IP v6 issues but does talk about DNS issues related to its implementation. Status – Proposed Standard; Publication Date – 1998; Obsoletes RFC 1884.

- ❖ 2377 *Naming Plan for Internet Directory-Enabled Applications:* Another attempt to use X.500 and LDAP instead of DNS. Status – Informational; Publication Date – 1998.

❖ 2517 *Building Directories from DNS: Experiences from WWWSeeker:* Details lessons learned during the WWWSeeker implementation of a directory service. Status – Informational; Publication Date – 1999.

❖ 2535 *Domain Name System Security Extensions:* Describes extension to support digital signatures, certificates, and other cryptographic methods to security-aware clients. Status – Proposed Standard; Publication Date – 1999; Updates RFC 1034, 1035, and 2181; Updated by 2931.

❖ 2536 *DSA KEYs and SIGs in the Domain Name System (DNS):* Proposes the use of U.S. government Digital Signature Algorithm keys and signatures in DNS by using two new RRs: KEY and SIG. Status – Proposed Standard; – Publication Date – 1999.

❖ 2537 *RSA/MD5 KEYs and SIGs in the Domain Name System (DNS):* Discusses storage of RSA and MD5 keys and signatures in DNS by using KEY and SIG RRs. Status – Proposed Standard; Publication Date – 1999.

❖ 2538 *Storing Certificates in the Domain Name System (DNS):* Defines the use of a CERT RR to store information about certificates in DNS. Status – Proposed Standard; Publication Date – 1999.

❖ 2539 *Storage of Diffie-Hellman Keys in the Domain Name System (DNS):* Defines the use of the KEY RR to store information about Diffie-Hellman keys in DNS. Status – Proposed Standard; Publication Date – 1999.

❖ 2540 *Detached Domain Name System (DNS):* Outlines proposal for offline and archival storage of DNS information. Status – Experimental; Publication Date – 1999.

❖ 2541 *DNS Security Operational Considerations:* Provides instructions for administrators of secure DNS environments leveraging KEY and SIG RRs. Status – Informational; Publication Date – 1999.

❖ 2606 *Reserved Top Level DNS Names:* Details new and existing root-level domains. Status – Best Current Practice (BCP0032); Publication Date – 1999.

❖ 2671 *Extension Mechanisms for DNS(EDNSO):* Describes potential backwards-compatible mechanism in DNS's protocols. Status – Proposed Standard; Publication Date – 1999.

❖ 2672 *Non-Terminal DNS Name Redirection:* Implements a new RR called DNAME. DNAME maps a portion of one namespace to a separate namespace.

This is much like a CNAME for domains. Status – Proposed Standard; Publication Date – 1999.

❖ 2673 *Binary Labels in the Domain Name System:* Defines a bit-string label that represents a sequence of single-bit labels and enables records to be stored at any bit boundary in a binary-named section of the name tree. Status – Proposed Standard; Publication Date – 1999.

❖ 2694 *DNS Extensions to Network Address Translators:* Defines application-level implementation of methods to alter DNS payloads when used in conjunction with NAT. Status – Informational; Publication Date – 1999.

❖ 2782 *A DNS RR for Specifying the Location of Services (DNS SRV):* Updates the use of SRV RRs that are used to locate hosted services. The interesting aspect of this RFC is that it uses the Microsoft implementation of SRV entries, which use an underscore (_) in front of the Service and Protocol portion of the record. There's nothing wrong with this, but it's a new addition to the existing SRV RFC, which may stifle some of the claims that the use of an underscore isn't RFC compliant. Status – Proposed Standard; Publication Date – 2000; Obsoletes RFC 2052.

❖ 2826 *IAM Technical Comment in the Unique DNS Root:* States the technical reasoning behind the use of a single parent level root of the period (.) and reasoning behind not changing it. Status – Informational; Publication Date – 2000.

❖ 2845 *Secret Key Transaction Authentication for DNS (TSIG):* Offers a method for secure transactions by leveraging shared secrets and hashing. Status – Proposed Standard; Publication Date – 2000; Updates RFC 1035.

❖ 2870 *Root Name Server Operational Requirements:* Provides operations guidelines and procedures for the root-level name servers. Status – Best Current Practice (BCP0040); Publication Date – 2000; Obsoletes RFC 2010.

❖ 2874 *DNS Extensions to Support IPv6 Address Aggregation and Renumbering:* Defines changes in DNS to support IP v6, which includes changes in traditional zone definitions. Status – Proposed Standard; Publication Date – 2000.

❖ 2915 *The Naming Authority Pointer (NAPTR) DNS Resource Record:* Further defines the use of NAPTR. Also suggested that NAPTR be used to support a broader range of RRs. Status – Proposed Standard; Publication Date – 2000; Updates RFC 2168.

❖ 2916 *E.164 Numbers and DNS:* Addresses the use of DNS to store E.164 numbers by using a new zone name of e164.arpa to store a new RR type of NAPTR. Status – Proposed Standard; Publication Date – 2000.

❖ 2929 *Domain Name System (DNS) IANA Considerations:* Talks about what considerations and criteria the Internet Assigned Number Authority (IANA) applies across DNS queries, headers, and optionally, query/response opcode. Status – Proposed Status, Best Current Practice (BCP0042); Publication Date – 2000.

❖ 2930 *Secret Key Establishment for DNS (TKEY RR):* Introduces the use of a TKEY RR used to establish shared secret keys between resolvers and servers. Status – Proposed Standard; Publication Date – 2000.

❖ **2931** *DNS Request and Transaction Signatures:* Introduces an RR named SIG(0) leveraging public keys. Based on an actual implementation, flaws were found in RFC 2535 and this RFC was created to address them. Status – Proposed Standard; Publication Date – 2000; Updates RFC 2535.

Index

Symbols

(pound sign)
 before commands, 286
 before extensions, 241
. (period) in namespaces, 8, 18
03h record, using with NetBIOs 16th
 characters, 189
10.100.2.20, connecting clients to, 31-32
16th character in NetBIOS, 188-190
1CH, 1BH, and 1EH domain records, 261

A

A record returns, changing defaults to optimize
 DNS resolution, 119-120
A resource record type, 20, 45
AAAA resource record type, 21, 45
ACL (Access Control Lists)
 and attribute classes, 57-58
 modifying for dnsNode objects, 60
 role in implementing AD-Integrated
  zone security, 141-142
Active Directory Installation Wizard,
 launching, 42-43

Active Registrations object for WINS servers,
 194-195
AD (Active Directory) group limitations, 143
AD data, backing up, 177-178
AD directory structure, exposing to processes,
 169
AD DIT files, configuring placement of,
 150-151
AD domains, renaming, 131
AD files, configuring with Ntdsutil
 command-line driven shell, 151-152
AD-Integrate option, relevance to
 interoperability, 144
AD-Integrated primary zones, 11, 51, 132
 adding new DNS servers to, 63
 benefits of, 51-53
 creating, 62-63
 and dnsNode objects, 56
 and dnsZone objects, 55-56, 57-59
 domain and zone relationships of, 60-61
 ensuring zone availability in, 136-137
 implementing security for, 141-142
 performing disaster recovery for,
  176-179

◆ B

❖ Q

❖ R

❖ S

INTERNATIONAL CONTACT INFORMATION

AUSTRALIA
McGraw-Hill Book Company Australia Pty. Ltd.
TEL +61-2-9417-9899
FAX +61-2-9417-5687
http://www.mcgraw-hill.com.au
books-it_sydney@mcgraw-hill.com

CANADA
McGraw-Hill Ryerson Ltd.
TEL +905-430-5000
FAX +905-430-5020
http://www.mcgrawhill.ca

GREECE, MIDDLE EAST, NORTHERN AFRICA
McGraw-Hill Hellas
TEL +30-1-656-0990-3-4
FAX +30-1-654-5525

MEXICO (Also serving Latin America)
McGraw-Hill Interamericana Editores S.A. de C.V.
TEL +525-117-1583
FAX +525-117-1589
http://www.mcgraw-hill.com.mx
fernando_castellanos@mcgraw-hill.com

SINGAPORE (Serving Asia)
McGraw-Hill Book Company
TEL +65-863-1580
FAX +65-862-3354
http://www.mcgraw-hill.com.sg
mghasia@mcgraw-hill.com

SOUTH AFRICA
McGraw-Hill South Africa
TEL +27-11-622-7512
FAX +27-11-622-9045
robyn_swanepoel@mcgraw-hill.com

UNITED KINGDOM & EUROPE (Excluding Southern Europe)
McGraw-Hill Education Europe
TEL +44-1-628-502500
FAX +44-1-628-770224
http://www.mcgraw-hill.co.uk
computing_neurope@mcgraw-hill.com

ALL OTHER INQUIRIES Contact:
Osborne/McGraw-Hill
TEL +1-510-549-6600
FAX +1-510-883-7600
http://www.osborne.com
omg_international@mcgraw-hill.com

www.ingramcontent.com/pod-product-compliance
Lightning Source LLC
Chambersburg PA
CBHW080143060326
40689CB00018B/3835